THE RETURN OF JESUS

WHAT EVERY CHRISTIAN SHOULD KNOW

ROB PHILLIPS

high
street
press·

CONTENTS

SECTION IV: RECEIVE ME

ACKNOWLEDGMENTS

The author and staff of High Street Press wish to thank the following people for their contributions to this book:

Executive editor: Dr. John Yeats
Senior editor: Gary Ledbetter
Cover design and graphics: Katie Shull
Layout: Tony Boes & Rob Phillips
Production management: Gary Ledbetter
Electronic production: Tony Boes & Rob Phillips
Scripture verification: Christie Dowell
Proofreading: Nancy Phillips & Jill Campbell

High Street Press is the publishing imprint of the Missouri Baptist Convention (MBC) and exists because of the generous support of Missouri Baptists through the Cooperative Program. To learn more about the MBC and the way 1,750 affiliated churches cooperate voluntarily for the sake of the gospel, go to mobaptist.org. To learn more about High Street Press, visit us online at highstreet.press.

FOREWORD

As we compare the dynamic of the first-century church with the twenty-first century church, it may well be that the greatest chasm between the two is the way we respond to our Lord's many promises to "come again." His promised second coming has become a forgotten subject in most of our more sophisticated Sunday gatherings. We have raised a generation of young people in our churches who know little about this coming great and climactic event.

Yet, it was his promise to come again that was constantly on the minds and lips of early believers. The New Testament writers referred to the second coming of Christ more than any other single subject, prominently mentioning it with over 300 references.

There was a word that constantly escaped the lips of these first-century believers: *Maranatha.* It literally means, "The Lord is coming." They greeted each other with this word. They comforted one another with this word. This is the word they shouted across the cursing crowds to their friends dying on crosses for their faith or burning at the stakes of martyrdom. They arose every single morning and pillowed their heads every single night living with expectation, looking for and eagerly anticipating their soon-coming King.

In a day when talk of prophecies of the last days draws raised eyebrows, rolled eyes, and verbal yawns, the volume you hold in your hand has never been more needed in the church of the Lord Jesus Christ. This is an urgent call to begin to live with the same expectation that those who "turned their world upside down" manifested every day. We lament today's lack of evangelistic passion and fervor in our churches, and this very issue is one of the missing elements. When we lose our expectation of hope in the future, we have no power in the present.

Rob Phillips has given the church a much-needed gift in this book. Unlike many volumes from the past, he does not seek to connect every current event with some obscure verse of Scripture to prove his point. He simply lets the words of Scripture speak for themselves as he covers every possible aspect of our "blessed hope, his glorious appearing."

The last of the over 8,000 promises recorded in the Bible comes from the lips of our Lord in Revelation 22:20, "Surely, I am coming quickly." He thought it important enough to leave us with this final word of hope. And the last recorded prayer in all the Bible follows. John responded in the same verse, "Even so, come, Lord Jesus." I am convinced that you will finish this volume and join the apostle by whispering that same petition, "Even so, come, Lord Jesus."

O. S. Hawkins

O. S. Hawkins is president emeritus of GuideStone Financial Resources of the Southern Baptist Convention. He is a former pastor of First Baptist Church, Dallas, Texas, and bestselling author of the "Code" series of devotionals, including *The Joshua Code* and *The Bible Code*. Visit him at www.oshawkins.com.

INTRODUCTION

Prepare to be disappointed. This book features no apocalyptic timelines, no unveiling of the antichrist, no previews of Armageddon, and no reading of Scripture through the lens of today's headlines.

Even so, scriptural end-times prophecies *are* divinely inspired and therefore vital if we're to understand our future inheritance as adopted children of God. And the order of events surrounding Christ's return is of great interest to all followers of Jesus. After all, we look forward to his glorious appearance. There are many worthy resources that explore pre-, post-, and amillennial views of the end times. We've included an overview of various scenarios in Appendix I. Proponents of each position tend to be godly men and women who love Jesus and eagerly anticipate his return.

But the devil is in the details of the second coming. Literally. The evil one commands a scorched-earth policy as his domain shrinks and his days as a roaming lion draw short. As such, he mocks when Christians argue over the minutiae of Christ's return. He sneers when self-proclaimed prophets "reveal" details about the second coming to which even Jesus wasn't privy on earth. And he laughs fiendishly when Christians split churches and quarrel over elaborate timetables of the end of days.

These theological fights keep Christians distracted so we fail to prepare properly for Christ's *parousia*, or glorious appearing. We become inwardly focused and thus disregard Christ's command to engage in kingdom business until he returns (Luke 19:13).

It's not that the order of events lacks value. It's that the order is, in some respects, unclear to us. For reasons beyond our grasp, it seems the Lord has deliberately left some details fuzzy. Maybe that's to dissuade us from creating eschatology check lists and doomsday countdown calendars. Maybe it's so we don't become like the Millerites of the 19th century, or the many cultists who've come after them, declaring the precise day of Christ's return and disposing of all earthly goods while gazing expectantly into the heavens – only to be devastated when Jesus doesn't show.

To state it plainly, eschatology is a third-tier doctrine. That is, it's not a non-negotiable belief such as the Trinity or justification by faith. Neither is it a second-tier doctrine like baptism in the Holy Spirit, or the mode and meaning of water baptism, which distinguish the body of Christ along denominational lines. Rather, eschatology is a third-tier doctrine in that members of the same congregation may engage in lively debate about the topic without accusing one another of heresy or refusing to eat the other's coleslaw at a church picnic.

We often devote so much attention to the chronological details of the second coming that we forget how much Christians share in common about this future event. That's what this study seeks to address. Specifically, we focus on the truths about Jesus' return that are stated plainly in Scripture, and on which nearly all Christians agree. That way, we're better prepared for his return – unified in our anticipation of it and better equipped to share the good news that the returning Jesus came the first time to secure salvation for us.

In Section I, we look at the certainty of Christ's return, with an emphasis on Jesus' promise to return, the testimony of New Testament eyewitnesses, and Old Testament prophecies that require a two-stage messianic ministry – led first by a Suffering Servant, then completed in the conquering King.

In Section II, we examine the nature of Christ's return. He's coming personally, powerfully, victoriously, and suddenly.

In Section III, we view the reasons for his return. We see that Jesus is coming back to establish his kingdom in fullness; to resurrect and judge all people; to glorify the saints and sentence unbelievers; to cast Satan and demons into hell; and to create new heavens and a new earth.

Finally, in Section IV, we look at the preparation for Jesus' return. We see that Christ is coming for his bride, the church; that his return is imminent; and that we are to be ready for his *parousia* at all times. Unbelievers are warned to repent while there's still time to do so.

Each chapter ends with a summary of key points, along with questions for personal or group study.

It is our desire that this resource encourages Christians with the biblically clear and commonly held truths of Christ's return; that it strengthens our faith as we grasp God's revelation about his Son's glorious appearing; that it exhorts us to godly living; and that it spurs unbelievers to repent of their sins and trust in Jesus as Savior while there is still time.

SECTION I: TRUST ME

THE CERTAINTY OF JESUS' RETURN

Although it's been nearly two thousand years since Jesus ascended into heaven, and two testifying angels assured the apostles of his return, we should not lose heart that his *parousia* is delayed. If we trust in Jesus for salvation, we should wait confidently for his return to glorify us, purge the cosmos of sin and its stain, and create new heavens and a new earth.

After all, Jesus promises, "I will come again" (John 14:3). Further, the eyewitnesses of Jesus' death, burial, and resurrection eagerly anticipate his return in their writings. Finally, Old Testament writers foresee a messianic age that only Jesus can fulfill.

_____ A _____

It is not for Jesus' first-century followers to know the Father's timetable. Neither is it for us.

_____ Ω _____

1

"I WILL COME AGAIN"

JESUS PROMISES TO RETURN

On March 11, 1942, U.S. General Douglas MacArthur escaped the island fortress of Corregidor under orders from President Franklin Roosevelt. After a harrowing thirty-five-hour boat ride through rough seas laced with Japanese mines, MacArthur flew in a B-17 Flying Fortress to Australia to begin planning the liberation of his beloved Philippines.

The agony of leaving troops under his command trapped in the islands prompted him to issue the now-famous statement to the press, "I shall return." It was a mantra he repeated often in public appearances over the next two and a half years, promising neither to forget nor abandon American soldiers and the people of the Philippines.

Commanding limited forces, MacArthur launched a major offensive in New Guinea, winning a string of victories. Then, gaining support from the U.S. Joint Chiefs and Admiral Chester Nimitz's Pacific Fleet, MacArthur turned his attention to an invasion of the Philippines. On October 20, 1944, a few hours after his troops landed, MacArthur waded ashore on the island of Leyte. In a radio announcement later that day, the general declared, "People of the Philippines, I have returned!"

It would take months to recapture Corregidor, and even longer to take Manila. By the time the Philippines were fully liberated, only one-third of the men MacArthur had been forced to leave behind survived to see his return. "I'm a little late," he told them, "but we finally came."[1]

MacArthur was awarded the Congressional Medal of Honor for his valiant defense of the Philippines. He is remembered not only for his bold promise to return, but for his steely determination to make good on it. In a very real sense, MacArthur helped set things right in the Pacific Theater. And on September 2, 1945, aboard the U.S.S. Missouri in Tokyo Bay, MacArthur received the Japanese surrender on behalf of the U.S. and its allies.

MacArthur's promise to return, and his fulfillment of that promise, serve as pinnacles in a storied military career featuring many peaks and valleys. They also cast a long shadow backwards in history to an intimate dinner in a borrowed upper room. In the hours leading up to his passion, Jesus gathers with his apostles and prepares them for his departure – first to the cross and then, after his resurrection, into heaven. But he makes a bold prediction: "I will come again" (John 14:3).

It's a promise his disciples struggle to understand in the context of a Passover meal, and a promise for which Jesus' followers are still waiting fulfillment. Yet, in a divine resolve that eclipses the tenacity of great leaders like General MacArthur, Jesus sets the stage for a return in which he recaptures the world, vanquishes his foes, and sets everything right.

In this regard, MacArthur's life is a dim analogy of a future conquest, when the Lion of Judah splits the skies and sets his feet on the Mount of Olives.

ONE MISSION, TWO CAMPAIGNS

As we begin to explore the return of Jesus, we may ask whether Jesus has any thoughts about coming back to earth. If so, what are they? How and when – and to whom – does he express these ideas?

It's clear that Jesus understands his mission to earth. This mission consists of two major campaigns. Jesus comes the first time as the Suffering Servant (Isa. 42:1-9; 49:1-13; 50:4-11; 52:13 – 53:12). In his own words, he comes to lay down his life for his sheep (John 10:11, 15); to give his life as a ransom for many (Matt. 20:28; Mark 10:45); to seek and to save the lost (Matt. 18:11 HCSB; Luke 19:10); to die and rise again (Mark 9:31).

Through his miraculous conception in a virgin's womb, the eternal Son of God adds sinless humanity to his deity. He lives a sinless life while running the gauntlet of temptation (Heb. 4:15), and he offers up that perfect life on the cross to satisfy the justice of God. He bears God's wrath so we may enjoy God's mercy. He bears our guilt so we may experience God's forgiveness. He bears our shame so we may have a place of honor at the marriage supper of the Lamb. He is despised and rejected so we may be adopted sons and daughters of God.

As our great high priest, Jesus offers his own blood once for all time to appease the wrath of God. And through the sacrifice of his perfect humanity, he tears down the veil that has separated sinful people from holy God ever since the Fall (Heb. 10:19-22).

In short, Jesus' first campaign to earth is a rescue mission to save us from God, from Satan, and from ourselves. It is the ultimate home invasion – a dramatic intrusion into Satan's domain. Jesus has bound the strong man and now plunders the strong man's goods – people once held captive who are set free, escaping the kingdom of darkness and entering the secure kingdom of God (see Matt. 12:22-32).

This first campaign in Christ's rescue mission is completed in Jesus' death, burial, and resurrection. Jesus shouts victoriously from the cross, "It is finished" (John 19:30) – a declaration that no doubt carries great significance for the Roman soldiers and Jewish religious leaders waiting eagerly for his death. To the Romans, "It is finished" is the cry of their commander, overseeing the battlefield, when it becomes clear the opponent is vanquished. To the Jewish leaders, it is the cry of the high priest on the Day of Atonement after emerging victoriously from the holy of holies, God having accepted the blood sacrifice that covered the people's sins for another year.

Surely, "It is finished" is Jesus' declaration that his suffering for humanity's sin has accomplished its purpose. Three days later, he emerges from a borrowed tomb, sealing the fates of Satan and evil spirits.

After his resurrection, Jesus appears to many people over a period of forty days, including more than five hundred people at one time (1 Cor. 15:6). But before ascending into heaven to resume his place at the Father's right hand, Jesus tells his followers a second campaign is required in the battle to restore the fallen cosmos.

Many of the Old Testament's messianic prophecies describe a conquering king, a lion from the tribe of Judah, a military and political genius who sits on David's throne and rules the world in righteousness. So, it shouldn't surprise us that many Jewish religious leaders reject Jesus as Messiah. He refuses to be installed as Israel's king, shows little interest in deposing Caesar, and seems more concerned about a kingdom "not of this world" than the oppressive Roman Empire that keeps Jesus' countrymen in poverty and despair (John 18:36).

After his resurrection, Jesus' disciples still wrestle with the unfinished business of Jesus the Suffering Servant becoming Jesus the King. We pick up the story in the first chapter of Acts:

While he [Jesus] was with them, he commanded them not to leave Jerusalem, but to wait for the Father's promise. "Which," he said, "you have heard me speak about; for John baptized with water, but you will be baptized with the Holy Spirit in a few days."

So when they had come together, they asked him, "Lord, are you restoring the kingdom to Israel at this time?"

He said to them, "It is not for you to know times or periods that the Father has set by his own authority. But you will receive power when the Holy Spirit has come on you, and you will be my witnesses in Jerusalem, in all Judea and Samaria, and to the ends of the earth" (Acts 1:4-8).

The disciples are trying to wrap their heads around all that has transpired in recent days. They are beginning to understand the once-incomprehensible reality of Jesus' death, burial, and resurrection as foretold in the Hebrew Scriptures. They are still euphoric over Jesus' finished work, which has defeated Satan, sin, and death. But the unresolved question still hangs densely in the air: What about the restored kingdom of Israel? What about Messiah on his throne? What about the bloody Romans? Come on, Jesus. Please, don't leave us in the dark. We get the Suffering Servant part of the ancient prophecies. But where is the conquering king?

Jesus' answer is instructive. It is not for Jesus' first-century followers to know the Father's timetable. Neither is it for us. God has revealed much about the who, what, where, why, and how of the last days, but not the *when*. Even Jesus, exposing the limits of his human nature, once confessed he didn't know the day and hour of his own return (Matt. 24:36).

However, as we await Christ's return, we have the benefits of another Counselor – the Holy Spirit, who empowers us to attest to the finished work of Jesus and to announce his imminent return. The promised Spirit comes in power on the Day of Pentecost, enabling every follower of Jesus to testify to his finished work on the cross.

Since that day, the Spirit takes up permanent residence in the heart of every believer. The ancient tabernacle, and then the temple, are no longer needed as venues where God meets humans. The *Shekinah* glory of God no longer is confined to the holy of holies, accessible only once a year and only by the high priest. Now, because of the completed work of Jesus as our great high priest, the *Shekinah* glory resides in the spirits of every believer. As Paul makes clear, believers' bodies are God's new temples (1 Cor. 3:16; 6:19).

In Acts 1, not long before Jesus' ascension, he prepares the disciples for his temporary absence. And it may be a lengthy delay before his return, if his parables of the kingdom are any indication. Even so, Jesus has joyfully endured the cross (Heb. 12:2). He has successfully completed the first campaign in his rescue mission to earth. He has voluntarily laid down his life and taken it up again. He has offered us a marriage covenant. And he is heading back to his Father's house to prepare a bridal chamber for us. The timing of his return is unknown, as is the coming of the groom in a Galilean wedding. But the certainty of his return is not in doubt: "I will come again …."

TWO STATEMENTS IN JOHN'S GOSPEL

Let's look at two of Jesus' statements regarding his return as recorded in the Gospel of John. Then, we'll explore other passages in which Jesus expresses the certainty of his second coming.

John 14:1-6

"Don't let your heart be troubled. Believe in God; believe also in me.

"In my Father's house are many rooms. If it were not so, would I have told you that I am going to prepare a place for you? If I go away and prepare a place for you, I will come again and take you to myself, so that where I am you may be also. You know the way to where I am going."

"Lord," Thomas said, "we don't know where you're going. How can we know the way?"

Jesus told him, "I am the way, the truth, and the life. No one comes to the Father except through me."

In this section of John's Gospel, Jesus prepares his disciples for his betrayal, arrest, and crucifixion. They don't understand who the betrayer is or where Jesus is going. Jesus tells them, "Where I am going, you cannot come" (John 13:33).

Peter asks, "Lord, where are you going?"

Jesus replies, "Where I am going you cannot follow me now, but you will follow later" (13:36).

Peter insists, "Why can't I follow you now? I will lay down my life for you."

Jesus then predicts Peter's thrice-denial of his Lord (13:37-38).

Sensing the rising angst in the upper room, Jesus offers assurance: "Don't let your heart be troubled. Believe in God; believe also in me" (14:1).

Jesus then explains that his pending departure is for their good. In fact, a little later, he assures his followers it's to their advantage that he goes away. That's so he may send the Holy Spirit as the agent of the triune God's work of redemption throughout the church age (John 16:7).

While Jesus is away in heaven, he's busy preparing a place for his followers. This harkens back to Jesus' parable of the ten virgins (Matt. 25:1-13), a parable from a Jewish wedding custom in which a young man, espoused to his future bride, returns to his father's home – often for a year or so – to prepare a special wedding chamber for his bride-to-be.

Jesus is telling Peter, and us, that while he is away, he is making things ready for his glorious return when, like a bridegroom, his presence lights up the streets and his coming is shouted from the rooftops. He personally returns to fetch his bride – the church – and take her to his Father's house.

John 21:20-23

So Peter turned around and saw the disciple Jesus loved following them, the one who had leaned back against Jesus at the supper and asked, "Lord, who is the one that's going to betray you?" When Peter saw him, he said to Jesus, "Lord, what about him?"

"If I want him to remain until I come," Jesus answered, "what is that to you? As for you, follow me."

So this rumor spread to the brothers and sisters that this disciple would not die. Yet Jesus did not tell him that he would not die, but, "If I want him to remain until I come, what is that to you?"

John corrects a false rumor in this passage. Some apparently think John is going to remain alive on earth until Jesus returns. But, as John writes, Jesus did not tell Peter that John would escape death, but that it's no concern of Peter's. For the disciples' part, it's more important to follow Jesus than to be concerned about the timing of Christ's return or the longevity of another person's ministry.

The key point is that Jesus prepares his followers for his temporary absence and future return. He has not revealed the day and hour – nor does Jesus know, for this matter is in his Father's hands (Matt. 24:36). But until Christ returns, his followers are to "Engage in business until I come back" (Luke 19:13).

SON OF MAN

Many of Jesus' teachings on the second coming revolve around his favorite self-designation: Son of Man. In fact, Jesus uses the title *Son of Man* roughly eighty times in the Gospels to refer to himself. While Jesus prefers to use this title rather than *Son of God* or *Messiah* to identify himself, it shouldn't be assumed he has any doubts about his identity or wishes to be coy with his followers. His use of *Son of Man* is purposeful.

Jesus clearly reveals his deity at strategic times. For example, he applies the divine name *I AM* to himself (John 8:58). He claims equality with the Father (John 10:30). He receives worship (John 20:28). He forgives sins (Mark 2:1-12). He teaches with divine authority (Mark 1:21-22). He affirms in advance what the apostles write concerning his deity (John 1:1-3, 14; cf. Phil. 2:5-11; Col. 1:15-16; 2:9; Heb. 1:1-4). And he displays the attributes unique to God (Matt. 28:18-20; John 1:1; 5:22; 16:30; Heb. 1:8; 13:8).

The term *Son of Man* accomplishes two primary goals. First, it illustrates that Jesus shares humanity with us. In Philippians 2:5-8, Paul spells out the humble manner in which the eternal Son of God adds sinless humanity to his deity. But a second goal is of equal importance. In calling himself *Son of Man*, especially in front of Israel's religious elite, he reveals himself as the divine being of Daniel 7:13-14:

> I continued watching in the night visions, and suddenly one like a *son of man* was coming with the clouds of heaven. He approached the Ancient of Days and was escorted before him. He was given dominion and glory and a kingdom, so that those of every people, nation, and

language should serve him. His dominion is an everlasting dominion that will not pass away, and his kingdom is one that will not be destroyed [emphasis added].

Jesus is especially careful to identify himself as the Son of Man so his listeners understand he is the one Daniel sees, the one who receives an eternal kingdom. Nowhere is this stated more plainly than in the house of Caiaphas on the night of Jesus' arrest. The high priest tells Jesus, "I charge you under oath by the living God: Tell us if you are the Messiah, the Son of God."

"You have said it," Jesus replies. "But I tell you, in the future you will see the Son of Man seated at the right hand of Power and coming on the clouds of heaven."

Caiaphas goes ballistic. He tears his robes and seethes, "He has blasphemed! Why do we still need witnesses? See, now you've heard the blasphemy" (Matt. 26:63-65).

The religious leaders, in concert with the Romans, carry out what God has already ordained: the death of the Son of Man for our sins. Rather than a humiliating defeat, the cross and the grave are milestones on the pathway to victory over Satan, sin, and death. Because of this, we may rest assured that when the Son of Man returns, he will fulfill Daniel's vision of the Son of Man, receiving an eternal kingdom and ruling over it.

In many other Scriptures, Jesus employs *Son of Man* language to depict his return. Consider the following samples (emphases added):

Matthew 16:27 – "For the *Son of Man* is going to come with his angels in the glory of his Father, and then he will reward each according to what he has done" (cf. Luke 9:26).

Matthew 24:27 – "For as the lightning comes from the east and flashes as far as the west, so will be the coming of the *Son of Man*."

Matthew 24:29-31 – "Immediately after the distress of those days, the sun will be darkened, and the moon will not shed its light; the stars will fall from the sky, and the powers of the heavens will be shaken. Then the sign of the *Son of Man* will appear in the sky, and then all the peoples of the earth will mourn; and they will see the *Son of Man* coming on the clouds of heaven with power and great glory. He will send out his angels with a loud trumpet, and they will gather his elect from the four winds, from one end of the sky to the other."

Matthew 24:37 – "As the days of Noah were, so the coming of the *Son of Man* will be."

Matthew 25:31-32 – "When the *Son of Man* comes in his glory, and all the angels with him, then he will sit on his glorious throne. All the nations will be gathered before him, and he will separate them one from another, just as a shepherd separates the sheep from the goats."

Mark 8:38 – "For whoever is ashamed of me and my words in this adulterous and sinful generation, the *Son of Man* will also be ashamed of him when he comes in the glory of his Father with the holy angels."

Mark 14:62 – "I am [Messiah, Son of the Blessed One]," said Jesus, "and you will see the *Son of Man* seated at the right hand of Power and coming with the clouds of heaven."

Luke 12:40 – "You also be ready, because the *Son of Man* is coming at an hour you do not expect."

Luke 18:8 – "I tell you that he will swiftly grant them justice. Nevertheless, when the *Son of Man* comes, will he find faith on earth?"

Luke 21:27 – "Then they will see the *Son of Man* coming in a cloud with power and great glory."

Luke 21:34-36 – "Be on your guard, so that your minds are not dulled from carousing, drunkenness, and worries of life, or that day will come on you unexpectedly like a trap. For it will come on all who live on the face of the whole earth. But be alert at all times, praying that you may have strength to escape all these things that are going to take place and to stand before the *Son of Man*."

John 5:25-29 – "Truly I tell you, an hour is coming, and is now here, when the dead will hear the voice of the Son of God, and those who hear will live. For just as the Father has life in himself, so also he has granted to the Son to have life in himself. And he has granted him the right to pass judgment, because he is the *Son of Man*. Do not be amazed at this, because a time is coming when all who are in the graves will hear his voice and come out — those who have done good things, to the resurrection of life, but those who have done wicked things, to the resurrection of condemnation."

Note some common threads in these passages related to the Son of Man's return:

- Jesus is coming in the glory of his Father – *glory* being a term often identified with deity in Scripture (e.g., Exod. 16:10; 40:34-35; Lev. 9:23).
- He's coming with/on the clouds of heaven, a further reference to his deity. Clouds often are associated with theophanies, or manifestations of God (e.g., Exod. 24:15-18). Jesus ascends into heaven in a cloud, and is promised to return in a similar manner (Acts 1:9-11). Meanwhile, believers are surrounded by a heavenly cloud of witnesses to the divine work of God – great heroes of the faith (Heb. 12:1).
- He's coming with the holy angels. Among other duties, such as delivering divine messages, angels carry the spirits of believers to rest in the afterlife (Luke 16:22), and they execute God's judgments (Gen. 19:13).
- He's coming visibly and publicly; every eye will see him (Rev. 1:7; cf. Zech. 12:10). This is no mere theophany, in which the invisible God temporarily breaks into the

physical realm; it is the incarnate Christ coming back in his physical, glorified body.

- He's coming in divine authority. The Father has placed all authority in the hands of his Son (Matt. 28:18).
- He's coming suddenly. Paul writes that our resurrection and glorification at the sounding of the trumpet are "in a moment, in the twinkling of an eye" (1 Cor. 15:52).
- He's coming unexpectedly. Several of Jesus' parables of the kingdom of heaven focus on his surprising return and the need for our readiness (e.g., Matt. 24:36-44).
- He's coming in judgment, which the Father has placed in his hands (John 5:22).

There can be no doubt that Jesus, the Son of Man, has promised to return one day and fulfill the yet-unfulfilled prophecies pertaining to the kingdom he has received from the Ancient of Days.

JOHN'S TESTIMONY FROM PATMOS

In the visions John receives while exiled on the Isle of Patmos, he often records the words of Jesus foretelling his return. John may have recorded these visions as early as the A.D. 60s or as late as the A.D. 90s. In any case, Jesus assures his followers – and warns his opponents – that his return is certain.

> **Revelation 1:8** – "I am the Alpha and the Omega," says the Lord God, "the one who is, who was, and who is to come, the Almighty."

God the Father most likely makes this statement, although some English translations ascribe them to Jesus. It seems best to understand this verse as the Father putting his divine signature on the prophecy of the second coming in verse 7: "Look, he is coming with the clouds, and every eye will see him, even those who pierced him. And all the tribes of the earth will mourn over him."

Jesus repeats the Father's self-description as "the Alpha and the

Omega" and applies it to himself in Revelation 22:13. Further, Jesus refers to himself as "Lord" in the Gospels (e.g., Matt. 12:8; John 13:13-14), and eyewitnesses of Jesus ascribe to him the same title (e.g., John 20:28; Acts 2:36). Jesus and the New Testament writers also affirm the deity of Christ, which includes his transcendence and omnipotence. Thus, both the Father and the Son may rightly lay claim to being "the one who is, who was, and who is to come, the Almighty."

While this verse is not an explicit promise of Jesus' return, it places the Father's stamp of approval on Old Testament prophecies of the second coming. And it ties together the redemptive work of the triune Godhead to be completed when Jesus returns.

> **Revelation 2:16** – "So repent! Otherwise, I will come to you quickly and fight against them with the sword of my mouth."

While a majority of believers at Pergamum are faithful followers of Jesus, some have embraced false teachings. Specifically, these involve two heresies. The first relates to Balaam, a corrupt Old Testament prophet-for-hire who plotted to use Moabite women to seduce the Israelites into idolatry and immorality. The second involves the first-century Nicolaitans, who abuse the biblical teaching on Christian liberty and teach that Christians may engage in pagan orgies.

Jesus calls the entire church to repent – not only those who have fallen into idolatry and immorality, but those faithful members who neglect to enact church discipline. Jesus' statement, "I will come to you quickly," is not an explicit prophecy of his second coming. However, his coming in judgment on this church foreshadows his coming in judgment on the whole world (cf. 1 Pet. 4:17; Rev. 19:11-21).

> **Revelation 3:11** – "I am coming soon. Hold on to what you have, so that no one takes your crown."

Jesus commends the faithful church at Philadelphia. Further, he promises to deal harshly with those from "the synagogue of Satan" –

ethnic Jews persecuting the poor and outnumbered followers of Jesus in that city.

Christ's promise to come soon (or quickly) seems to point more to his second coming than to temporal judgment on the enemies of the church. His charge to "hold on ... so that no one takes your crown" looks toward the judgment seat of Christ, when Jesus rewards his faithful servants (Rom. 14:10; 1 Cor. 3:11-15; 4:5; 2 Cor. 5:10).

The word "crown" is *stephanos* in the Greek. It depicts a laurel wreath presented to victorious athletes and soldiers. Believers cannot lose their salvation, for we are eternally secure in Christ. But we may lose rewards God has prepared for us, and we may find ourselves ashamed at his coming (1 Cor. 3:15; 1 John 2:28).

> **Revelation 16:15** – "Look, I am coming like a thief. Blessed is the one who is alert and remains clothed so that he may not go around naked and people see his shame."

The imagery of Jesus coming like a thief appears several times in the New Testament. In the Olivet Discourse, Jesus warns his followers to be alert, like a homeowner on guard against a thief, because they do not know the day of Christ's return (Matt. 24:42-44). Paul reminds the Thessalonians that "the day of the Lord will come just like a thief in the night" (1 Thess. 5:2), a truth Peter affirms (2 Pet. 3:10). And Jesus warns the church at Sardis, "If you are not alert, I will come like a thief, and you have no idea at what hour I will come upon you" (Rev. 3:3).

Regarding the events of the last days, Jesus' command to stay faithful assures us of the certainty of his return, even though the timing has not been revealed to us. Kendell Easley writes, "*I come like a thief* notes the imminency of the day of the Lord: nothing keeps this from happening, just as nothing keeps a thief from breaking into a house at night. Thieves come unexpectedly, on a schedule they determine."[2]

However, we should bear in mind that Jesus' return as a thief is not to steal but to take back what is rightfully his. The admonition to be alert and remain clothed may be a reference to guards or homeowners who are tempted to sleep naked in the summer heat. But when a home's perimeter is breached, the persons responsible for protecting the property may find themselves ashamed, chasing a thief in their birthday suits. Similarly, followers of Jesus should conduct ourselves in a manner that brings praise rather than rebuke whenever our Lord returns.

> **Revelation 22:7** – "Look, I am coming soon! Blessed is the one who keeps the words of the prophecy of this book."

Three times in the epilogue of Revelation, Jesus declares, "I am coming soon" (Rev. 22:7, 12, 20). This accentuates the urgency of Christ's return and affirms his previous promises in the Gospels and the Book of Revelation. His repeated statement also validates what John has seen and heard on Patmos, and what the apostles have written in their eyewitness accounts and epistles.

Jesus attaches a blessing to the promise of his imminent return: "Blessed is the one who keeps the words of the prophecy of this book." This is the sixth of seven blessing statements, or beatitudes, in Revelation.[3] While we wait expectantly for the Lord's return, our lives should reflect the truth of Scripture. When we conduct ourselves in this way, we find ourselves happy.

We may not fully understand the details surrounding the Day of the Lord, but the New Testament writers make several truths plain: (1) Jesus is returning one day – physically, visibly, in power and great glory; (2) we do not know the day or the hour of his return; (3) we should live in view of his imminent return; (4) when he comes, all people will know it; (5) Jesus is judging all people personally, rewarding believers according to their faithfulness and punishing unbelievers in varying degrees according to their evil deeds; (6) he creates new heavens and a new earth, setting everything right; and (7) the glory of eternity with Christ causes the "previous things" of this world to fade away (Rev. 21:4).

Eternity may seem far off to us. Yet if we keep the prophecies of

Revelation in front of us, we learn to live more comfortably in the tension between the *already* and *not-yet*.

> **Revelation 22:12-13** – "Look, I am coming soon, and my reward is with me to repay each person according to his work. I am the Alpha and the Omega, the first and the last, the beginning and the end."

Again, Jesus warns of his imminent return. This time, however, he reminds us that the Alpha and the Omega is coming in judgment "to repay each person according to his work." This echoes Jesus' words to his disciples in Matthew 16:27: "For the Son of Man is going to come with his angels in the glory of his Father, and then he will reward each according to what he has done."

This does not even begin to suggest that forgiveness of sins and eternal life are earned through good behavior. As Jesus and the New Testament writers make abundantly clear, salvation is by the grace of God alone through faith in Jesus alone (e.g., John 5:24; Rom. 4:4-5; 6:23; Eph. 2:8-9; Tit. 3:5-7). To advocate a works-based path to eternal life is to trample the blood of the crucified, buried, and risen Lord. So then, why does Jesus say his reward is with him to "repay" each person?

The word translated "repay" is *misthos* in the Greek and appears twenty-nine times in the New Testament, most often as "reward," but also as "wages," "payment," or "profit." The Greek noun means "pay for service" and can be used to describe compensation for good or bad service. It appears Jesus has in mind the final judgment of believers before the judgment seat of Christ and of unbelievers before the great white throne. The focus in each of these final judgments is not *where* a person spends eternity, but *how*.

There are degrees of punishment in hell just as there are varying rewards in heaven. Eternity in hell is not the same for the mass murderer and the law-abiding citizen, but it is outer darkness nonetheless.

It is a common expression at funerals that the deceased have gone on to their eternal reward. Meant to comfort mourners that their loved ones are "in a better place," the statement glosses over the deeper truth that indeed all people ultimately are repaid for their lives on earth. The reward may be our Savior's greeting, "Come, you who are blessed by my Father; inherit the kingdom prepared for you from the foundation of the world" (Matt. 25:34). Or, the reward may be the words of the one seated on the great white throne: "Depart from me, you who are cursed, into the eternal fire prepared for the devil and his angels!" (Matt. 25:41).

Ultimately, everyone gets the eternal destiny they choose, based on their acceptance or rejection of Christ. In addition, everyone spends eternity as close to, or as far away from, their creator as they desire based on how they have lived out their response to Christ. Jesus reminds us in the Book of Revelation that when he returns, he sets all things right. This should prompt all people to search their hearts and take stock of their lives.

> **Revelation 22:20** – He who testifies about these things says, "Yes, I am coming soon."

Jesus offers one final assurance of his personal return. He testifies to the truth of what John has witnessed and written in the Book of Revelation. He affirms what the angels we encounter in Revelation have declared. And he places a divine exclamation point at the end of it all with the promise, "Yes, I am coming soon."

John can only reply with affirmation, "Amen! Come, Lord Jesus!" (v. 20).

In closing this chapter, we should note the repeated emphasis on the word "soon" in Revelation 22. It appears four times (vv. 6, 7, 12, 20). The Greek *tachys* may mean shortly, quickly, without delay, suddenly, by surprise, or readily. We explore the meaning of *tachys* in greater detail in Chapter 15.

Meanwhile, as followers of Jesus, we should not entertain thoughts that Jesus is being coy with us, or vague, or even disingenuous with respect to the nearness of his return. It appears that Jesus is not telling us the prophecies of Revelation are to be fulfilled within a few months or years. Rather, they happen certainly and quickly when the Day of the Lord comes.

Joseph Seiss shares this insight:

> The impending Advent is the theme which pervades [Revelation] from its commencement to its close. And just in proportion as he who is awake to the great truth of the Saviour's speedy coming, and is engaged in waiting and preparing himself accordingly, is a better man, and in a safer condition, and really more happy, than the half-christian and the lukewarm; in that same proportion is he who reads, hears and keeps the words of this prophecy blessed beyond all other people. This book, at least its subject-matter, thus becomes to him an instrument of security and attainment to save him from surprise when his Lord cometh, and from the tribulations which shall try the indifferent; as well as a passport to admit him to the marriage supper of the Lamb, and to the highest awards of eternity.[4]

HE TOLD US SO

Jesus is certain of his return, and he tells us so. Having completed the first campaign in God's two-part mission to redeem fallen humans and restore the cosmos to sinless perfection, Jesus returns temporarily to heaven, where he's seated at the Father's right hand. There, he serves as our mediator and intercessor. And from his place in heaven, he rules over a kingdom that is largely invisible today but is going to be revealed in blazing glory for everyone to see.

Today, Jesus is in heaven preparing a bridal chamber for us. He also intercedes for us at the Father's right hand. He advocates for us, serves as our great high priest who is always – not just once a year – in the presence of the Almighty. He has left his kingdom in our hands, having empowered us with the Holy Spirit. One day, he is returning to fulfill all things: to sit on the throne of David; to resurrect and judge all people; to cast Satan, demons, and all unbelievers into the lake of fire; and to create new heavens and a new earth.

His delay in coming may give scoffers an opportunity to impugn the Son of Man, but what they refuse to see is that his delay is for their benefit. It's an opportunity to repent and trust the risen Savior and returning King (2 Pet. 3:3-9). Jesus most certainly is returning. He has given us his word, and we may take comfort in that assurance.

REVIEW

Key takeaways from this chapter

1. Jesus' mission to earth consists of two major campaigns: he comes the first time as the Suffering Servant; he returns one day as the conquering King. The combined effect of Jesus' first and second comings is to defeat Satan, sin, and death, to redeem sinful humans, and to restore the cosmos to its pristine perfection.

2. God has revealed much about the who, what, where, why, and how of the last days, but not the *when*. Even Jesus, exposing the limits of his human nature, once confessed he didn't know the day and hour of his own return (Matt. 24:36).

3. While the timing of Jesus' return is unknown, its certainty is not in doubt: "I will come again …." (John 14:3).

4. Jesus calls himself *Son of Man* about eighty times in the Gospels. This self-designation accomplishes two primary goals. First, it illustrates that Jesus shares humanity with us (Phil. 2:5-8). Second, it reveals Jesus as the divine being of Daniel 7:13-14, who receives an eternal kingdom from the Ancient of Days.

5. In the visions John receives while exiled on Patmos, he often records the words of Jesus foretelling his return. In these statements, Jesus assures his followers – and warns his opponents – that his return is certain.

6. Jesus says he is returning "soon" four times in Revelation 22. The Greek *tachys* may mean quickly, suddenly, or by surprise. It appears that Jesus is not telling us the prophecies of Revelation are to be fulfilled within a few months or years. Rather, they happen certainly and quickly when the Day of the Lord comes.

DISCUSS

Questions for personal or group study

1. What are the two major campaigns in Jesus' mission to earth? What are the distinguishing elements of each campaign? And what is the unified purpose?

2. Why does Jesus so often refer to himself as *Son of Man*? What's the significance of that title with respect to his return?

3. Why do you think Jesus' disciples have such a hard time accepting his teaching about going to the Father and returning to earth one day?

4. How can we be certain of Jesus' return, even though it's been two thousand years since he promised to come "soon"?

5. What does Jesus tell his followers to do while he is temporarily away?

* * *

"WE EAGERLY WAIT FOR A SAVIOR"

THE EYEWITNESSES OF JESUS ANTICIPATE HIS RETURN

*H*ow could "the worst" of sinners, suffering confinement in Rome, write a letter to a distant church, expressing gratitude and joy? Paul's letter to the Philippians is a remarkable epistle that proclaims the joys of knowing Christ, the rewards of persevering in the faith, and the secret of contentment.

Paul writes to thank the Philippians for their financial support. He assures them that their messenger, Epaphroditus, who delivered the church's gift to Paul, has recovered from a grave illness. And he desires to maintain his close relationship with fellow believers from whom he has been isolated. While Paul cannot assure the Philippians of his release from prison, or promise them relief from their own sufferings for the cause of Christ, he writes jubilantly with the full assurance of Christ's return and believers' future glory.

"Our citizenship is in heaven," Paul writes, "and we eagerly wait for a Savior from there, the Lord Jesus Christ" (Phil. 3:20). Paul does not take his Roman citizenship lightly. In fact, he leverages his citizenship to appeal to Caesar, whose government keeps him in chains (Acts 25:10-11). But he knows there is a more enduring citizenship, one in which the king already has heard Paul's appeal, acquitted him, and prepared a place for him at the royal banquet table. One day, that very king returns to sit on the throne of David and set things right. Until that time, nothing separates Paul from the love of God. Even in death, Paul passes immediately into God's presence to await the king's return in glory.

Paul and other eyewitnesses write often of Christ's return. They proclaim its certainty, await its glory, warn of its vengeance, and urge followers of Jesus to live in the light of its impending reality. In this chapter, we survey passages in which the eyewitnesses of Jesus, including angels, testify to the certainty of Christ's return.

This is a lengthy chapter, but the biblical content explored in the following pages makes it clear the New Testament writers are confident in the return of the king.

Let's begin with Paul.

THE TESTIMONY OF PAUL

Paul faces uncertainty in his pursuit of obedience to Christ. As he boldly takes the gospel message to the Gentiles, he is imprisoned, beaten, stoned and left for dead, shipwrecked, heckled, mocked, opposed by Jewish zealots and pagan idolators alike, worried for the spiritual health of the churches he has planted, and forced to defend his apostleship against the rising tide of false teachers who have infiltrated the Christian community.

Paul may not know what tomorrow brings, but he's steadfast in his faith in Christ and his certainty of the Savior's return. Time and again, throughout his itinerant mission work and in his epistles, Paul maintains his confidence in Christ, who is returning one day to set things right.

The Book of Acts

In Acts 17, Paul finds himself in Athens, having fled jealous Jews and angry mobs in Thessalonica and Berea. Distressed at the city's rampant idolatry, Paul engages Jews in the synagogue, as well as

Epicurean and Stoic philosophers, all the while proclaiming the crucified and risen Jesus.

At last, Athenian thinkers and leaders direct Paul to the Areopagus, a small hill covered in stone seats northwest of the city. There, he's invited to present his "new" and "strange" teaching. Paul seizes the opportunity. He acknowledges his listeners' devotion to religious pursuits. He observes the many idols that adorn the city, including a curious altar on which are inscribed the words, "To an Unknown God."

Paul then sharpens his focus:

> Therefore, what you worship in ignorance, this I proclaim to you. The God who made the world and everything in it – he is the Lord of heaven and earth – does not live in shrines made by hands. Neither is he served by human hands, as though he needed anything, since he himself gives everyone life and breath and all things (Acts 17:23-25).

The one true God has made every person and set the boundaries of their lives. Unlike the gods that gold, silver, and stone represent, the Lord desires a personal relationship with each person and has provided sufficient evidence of his existence and majesty. In further contrast to pagan gods, God is holy. And while he is gracious and merciful, he "now commands all people everywhere to repent" (Acts 17:30).

Paul's voice strains with urgency. A day of reckoning is coming. God has "set a day when he is going to judge the world in righteousness by the man he has appointed. He has provided proof of this to everyone by raising him from the dead" (v. 31). The Greek view of time is that it simply continues. Paul counters this belief with the truth of an approaching climactic moment when the resurrected Christ returns in judgment.

Paul's emphasis on resurrection – particularly the resurrection of Jesus, the God-Man and judge of all things – brings his message to a close. Some ridicule him – likely, the Epicureans, who believe the soul and body die together. Others, like the Stoics, believe the soul lives on after death, but they can't conceive of a reconstituted corpse. Still others maintain an intellectual interest in Paul's words and invite him to speak again.

It seems Paul's message largely falls flat. But that would miss Luke's point. The writer makes it clear that "some people joined him and believed" (Acts 17:34). This includes Dionysius the Areopagite, one of perhaps a hundred of the most notable leaders in the community. It also includes Damaris, who may have been a philosopher, or more likely a student of one.[1]

1 Corinthians

Three times in Paul's first letter to the Corinthians, he reminds his readers of Christ's imminent return.

> **1 Corinthians 1:6-8** – In this way, the testimony about Christ was confirmed among you, so that you do not lack any spiritual gift as you eagerly wait for the revelation of our Lord Jesus Christ. He will also strengthen you to the end, so that you will be blameless in the day of our Lord Jesus Christ.

In his greeting to the Corinthians, Paul acknowledges their giftedness, particularly in "all speech and knowledge" (1 Cor. 1:5). These gifts seem particularly important to the Corinthians in light of their culture. The nearby Isthmian Games feature not only athletic events, but speech contests; knowledge is associated with philosophical wisdom. Of course, Paul emphasizes the spiritual gifts related to speech and knowledge, which he addresses in more detail later.

While 1 Corinthians features a fair amount of rebuke, Paul sets the stage with encouraging words. He also urges his readers to exercise their spiritual gifts with the end in mind – the revelation of the Lord Jesus. The one who grants spiritual gifts also empowers believers to exercise them. The goal is to build upon the foundation Christ has laid (1 Cor. 3:11). This is rewarded at the judgment seat of Christ (2 Cor. 5:10). However, there is the possibility of lost rewards

– and even shame at the return of Christ (1 Cor. 3:12-15; cf. 1 John 2:28).

> **1 Corinthians 4:5** – So don't judge anything prematurely, before the Lord comes, who will both bring to light what is hidden in darkness and reveal the intentions of the hearts. And then praise will come to each one from God.

Paul has cautioned the Corinthians not to make celebrities of human leaders, whether they be philosophers or "managers of the mysteries of God" (1 Cor. 4:1). Paul and Apollos are the Lord's servants. They strive to be faithful. And they are not subject to the Corinthians' fleshly judgments. Only God truly knows the human heart. Christians must evaluate their leaders in light of final judgment.

So, Paul points his readers to the day Christ returns and reveals the secrets known only to him. Jesus and other Jewish teachers speak of God shining light on secret thoughts at the day of judgment (Matt. 12:36-37; cf. 1 Chron. 28:9; Isa. 29:15; Jer. 17:10). Therefore, it's important for followers of Jesus not to seek the praise of people, but to desire what God honors on judgment day.

> **1 Corinthians 11:26** – For as often as you eat this bread and drink the cup, you proclaim the Lord's death until he comes.

Paul offers stern correction for the manner in which many Corinthian believers have abused the Lord's Supper (1 Cor. 11:17-34). He even points out that sinning against the body and blood of the Lord has resulted in the divine chastisements of illness and death.

In the middle of his rebuke, Paul returns his readers to the first Lord's Supper, in which Jesus takes the unleavened bread and wine of the Passover and establishes a new covenant meal. The bread symbolizes Jesus' body, broken for his people. The cup symbolizes his perfect blood shed for our sins. A proper observance should unify Christ's followers, humble them, and cause them to live in the light of his imminent return.

Followers of Jesus celebrate the Lord's Supper as a memorial of his sacrificial and substitutionary death on the cross. But the cross and the tomb are not the end. The resurrected Jesus has ascended into heaven and today sits at the Father's right hand. One day, he returns in power and glory to set things right. When we eat the communion bread and drink the cup, we are to look both backward and forward in time.

Philippians

Paul points to the return of Jesus three times in his letter to the Philippians. Twice, he refers to "the day of Christ" or "the day of Christ Jesus." In the third reference, Paul shares the hope of our future resurrection when our Savior returns from heaven.

> **Philippians 1:6** – I am sure of this, that he who started a good work in you will carry it on to completion until the day of Christ Jesus.

Paul adapts Old Testament references about "the day of the Lord" to his first-century audience. In so doing, he affirms the deity of Jesus, calling his return "the day of Christ Jesus."

The apostle expresses his confidence that the Philippians are going to persevere to the end. He bases this on what he has experienced so far: they have been partners in the gospel from the beginning (Phil. 1:5), and they are partners in Paul's imprisonment, and in the defense and confirmation of the gospel (v. 7).

> **Philippians 1:9-10** – And I pray this: that your love will keep on growing in knowledge and every kind of discernment, so that you may approve the things that are superior and may be pure and blameless in the day of Christ ….

Building on his great affection for the Philippians in verse 8, Paul now shares his desire for their love to keep growing, evidenced in

knowledge and godly discernment that result in purity and blameless-
ness when Jesus returns.

Philippians 3:20-21 – Our citizenship is in heaven, and we eagerly
wait for a Savior from there, the Lord Jesus Christ. He will transform
the body of our humble condition into the likeness of his glorious
body, by the power that enables him to subject everything to himself.

Paul rallies the Philippians with the remarkable truth that their
citizenship transcends Philippi, and even the Roman Empire. They
are but pilgrims on earth. Their names are written in heaven (Luke
10:20). Christ is preparing a place for them there (John 14:1-3). As a
result, the Philippians may look beyond the hardships of this life and
eagerly anticipate the day when Christ returns.

As the firstfruits of those raised from the dead (1 Cor. 15:20), the
resurrected Jesus is our personal guarantee of glorification – the
completed work of redemption in which we are given immortal
bodies like Christ's resurrected body. What great hope for those
struggling through this life. We should always look up, for Jesus
assures us that our redemption draws near (Luke 21:28).

Colossians

Colossians 3:4 – When Christ, who is your life, appears, then you also
will appear with him in glory.

Christians in Colossae are attracted to mystical elements in
Judaism, or to Greek philosophy that permeates first-century thought.
As a result, they are prone to embracing "self-made religion, false
humility, and severe treatment of the body" (Col. 2:23).

Paul reminds them these practices are of no value in curbing self-
indulgence. Rather, true Christian living is grounded in Christ, and
specifically in his sinless life, death, burial, and resurrection – historical realities as opposed to mystical ideals.

Rather than seeking Jewish visions of God's throne, or Greek visions of the ultimate deity, who is separate from the world of matter, Christians are to focus on our identity in Christ. We have died with him, been raised with him, and now live with him in his exalted position at the right hand of God (Col. 2:20; 3:1-3).

What the mystics and philosophers can only imagine gives way to the revealed truth of the resurrected and ascended Christ, who is returning one day to finish the work of redemption in us. Christ is our very life – right now. And when he returns, we appear with him in glory. This is similar to John's declaration that we will see Jesus as he is and be like him (1 John 3:2).

1 Thessalonians

While preaching Jesus as Messiah in Thessalonica, Paul is accused of proclaiming a king other than Caesar (Acts 17:7). Now, the young church in that city suffers persecution. But Paul cheers them on with the promise of a future hope that includes Christians who already have died. The apostle addresses Christ's return in no fewer than seven places.

> **1 Thessalonians 1:9-10** – for they themselves [believers in Macedonia, Achaia, and elsewhere] report what kind of reception we had from you: how you turned to God from idols to serve the living and true God and to wait for his Son from heaven, whom he raised from the dead — Jesus, who rescues us from the coming wrath.

False religions in Thessalonica include the Egyptian cults of Serapis and Isis, the cult of Cabiri from the Aegean island of Samothrace, the worship of Greek gods like Dionysus, and the veneration of the Roman emperor. Statues of these deities are everywhere.[2]

Paul commends Christians in that city for turning from these idols to the one true God, and for fixing their gazes on the future return of the resurrected and ascended Christ. Christ's victory over the grave ensures their future resurrection and glorification.

Further, when Christ returns, he delivers his followers from "the coming wrath." The Old Testament often speaks of God's wrath in terms of his judgments in history. But the New Testament writers extend this to the outpouring of God's wrath in the day of the Lord, when Christ returns to punish the wicked (Rom. 2:5; cf. Isa. 13:9, 13; 26:21; 30:27; Zeph. 1:18).

> **1 Thessalonians 2:19-20** – For who is our hope or joy or crown of boasting in the presence of our Lord Jesus at his coming? Is it not you? Indeed you are our glory and joy!

In the preceding verses, Paul expresses his desire to see the Thessalonians again. His departure was not one of his choosing, and he truly misses them. But Satan has hindered previous efforts to return, perhaps through Jewish opposition (1 Thess. 2:14-16) or obstacles laid by city magistrates (Acts 17:8-9).

In any case, Paul knows he will see his brothers and sisters at the return of Christ. This thought gives him great joy. While the second coming results in resurrection and judgment for believers, including "crowns" for faithful Christian service, Paul considers the Thessalonians' present-day perseverance and future glorification as his own reward.

> **1 Thessalonians 3:13** – May he make your hearts blameless in holiness before our God and Father at the coming of our Lord Jesus with all his saints. Amen.

Paul offers a prayer for the church in 1 Thessalonians 3:11-13. First, he desires to be reunited with the Thessalonians, asking God the Father and the Lord Jesus to "direct our way to you" (v. 11). Next, he petitions the Lord for an overflow of love among the Thessalonians – a love that spills out and embraces everyone (v. 12).

Finally, Paul asks for hearts that are "blameless in holiness," prepared for the return of Jesus with all his saints. In his teachings, Jesus urges his followers to be alert, waiting expectantly for his return. John warns us not to drop our guards, lest we be ashamed at Christ's coming (1 John 2:28). Here, Paul asks the Lord to ensure the faithfulness of the Thessalonians as they live in the light of his return.

The phrase "with all his saints" likely is a reference to believers returning with Christ. But the Greek *hagios* ("saints") also may mean angels. Scripture is clear that Jesus is returning with his "holy ones," which appears to include both saints and angels (Dan. 7:9-27; Zech. 14:5; Matt. 13:39-41, 49-50; 16:27; 24:30-31; 25:31; Mark 8:38; 1 Cor. 6:2-3; 2 Thess. 1:7-10; Rev. 2:26; 3:21).

> **1 Thessalonians 4:13-18** – We do not want you to be uninformed, brothers and sisters, concerning those who are asleep, so that you will not grieve like the rest, who have no hope. For if we believe that Jesus died and rose again, in the same way, through Jesus, God will bring with him those who have fallen asleep. For we say this to you by a word from the Lord: We who are still alive at the Lord's coming will certainly not precede those who have fallen asleep. For the Lord himself will descend from heaven with a shout, with the archangel's voice, and with the trumpet of God, and the dead in Christ will rise first. Then we who are still alive, who are left, will be caught up together with them in the clouds to meet the Lord in the air, and so we will always be with the Lord. Therefore encourage one another with these words.

Paul seeks to comfort his persecuted readers with a message of hope in Christ's return, their future resurrection, and their reunion with those who already have passed through the vale of death. He draws from the teachings of Jesus – "a word from the Lord" – to offer divine assurances of a glorious life beyond the grave. This stands in sharp contrast to Gentile beliefs in a shadowy afterlife in the underworld, as well as to elaborate Jewish grief rituals.

There is much in these verses to stir joy in our hearts. First, Paul ties our future resurrection to the historic reality of Christ's victory over the grave; he is "the firstfruits of those who have fallen asleep" (1 Cor. 15:20), thus he ensures that a full harvest of saints is brought in.

Second, Christ doesn't return alone; he brings with him "those who have fallen asleep" – a common euphemism for physical death, and thus a reference to Christians who are "away from the body and at home with the Lord" (2 Cor. 5:8).

Third, the Lord descends from heaven, where he currently sits at the Father's right hand as our mediator and intercessor (Luke 22:69; Rom. 8:34; Col. 3:1; Heb. 12:2).

Fourth, the archangel's voice and the trumpet of God herald Christ's coming. Michael, the chief archangel in Jewish literature, is considered Israel's guardian angel and figures prominently in the final battle between good and evil.[3] This series of events necessarily involves New Testament believers, who are part of true Israel. Meanwhile, trumpets are used to gather an assembly or to call armies to battle. Both may be in view here. Christ calls his church to meet him in the air, and then he leads the charge against their mutual enemies on earth (Rev. 19:11-16).

Fifth, deceased Christians are the first to rise from the dead. Their spirits already are with Christ in heaven, awaiting future resurrection (2 Cor. 5:1-10). Their bodies come out of the graves, glorified like the body of Jesus, and are reunited with their spirits.

Sixth, Christians on earth undergo an instantaneous transformation in which they, too, receive glorified bodies, but without experiencing physical death. They are "caught up" – from the Greek *harpazo*, which means to seize, carry off by force, or to claim for one's self. Certainly, Christ dramatically snatches believers out of the world and declares us his own. The Latin translation of *harpazo* is *rapio*, which lends itself to the popular term "rapture," describing the future resurrection of Christians.

Seventh, glorified saints meet the Lord "in the air." Christ descends from the third heaven (the throne of God), passes through the stellar heaven, and breaks into the atmosphere. There, the King of kings meets the Christian emissaries who have come out to welcome him. In a first-century setting, ambassadors would leave their city to meet an approaching dignitary and escort him into their town. This very imagery of Christians welcoming their King to earth is sure to provoke hostility from those who worship Caesar as lord.

The "clouds" to which Paul refers harken back to Old Testament imagery of the coming day of God's judgment (e.g. Ezek. 30:3; 32:7; Joel 2:2), as well as the coming of the Son of Man (Dan. 7:13). Jesus applies this language to his return (Matt. 24:30; 26:64; Rev. 1:7).

Finally, followers of Jesus should encourage themselves that they will always be with the Lord. Jesus offers the same promise in John 14:3: "If I go away and prepare a place for you, I will come again and take you to myself, so that where I am you may be also." Jesus assures us that our everlasting life is pinned to his eternal life: "In a little while the world will no longer see me, but you will see me. Because I live, you will live too" (John 14:19).

In these few verses, the apostle packs a treasure trove of teaching with respect to the return of Jesus. No matter what the Thessalonians are experiencing, they should rest in God's promise to reunite them – and all believers – with Christ at his glorious appearing.

> **1 Thessalonians 5:2** – For you yourselves know very well that the day of the Lord will come just like a thief in the night.

Paul's readers understand "the day of the Lord" as the time of God's final judgment at the end of the age. The Old Testament speaks of a sudden and unexpected end (Ezek. 30:3; Joel 3:14; Obad. 15), yet one preceded by signs. Paul does not deny that signs accompany Jesus' second coming, only that these signs do not provide sufficient warning to pinpoint the day and hour (see Matt. 24:36).

Paul picks up the teachings of Jesus, who confirms the suddenness of his return in Matthew 24:42-44: "Therefore be alert, since you don't know what day your Lord is coming. But know this: If the homeowner had known what time the thief was coming, he would have stayed alert and not let his house be broken into. This is why you are also to be ready, because the Son of Man is coming at an hour you do not expect."

1 Thessalonians 5:23 – Now may the God of peace himself sanctify you completely. And may your whole spirit, soul, and body be kept sound and blameless at the coming of our Lord Jesus Christ.

Paul closes this epistle with instructions for treating one another in a Christlike manner (1 Thess. 5:12-15), conducting proper worship (vv. 16-22), and living in the light of Christ's return (vv. 23-28). This includes a "wish prayer" that God would sanctify the Thessalonians – make them more like Jesus – and thus prepare their whole being (spirit, soul, and body) for the day Jesus returns (v. 23).

2 Thessalonians

2 Thessalonians 2:1-3 – Now concerning the coming of our Lord Jesus Christ and our being gathered to him: We ask you, brothers and sisters, not to be easily upset or troubled, either by a prophecy or by a message or by a letter supposedly from us, alleging that the day of the Lord has come. Don't let anyone deceive you in any way. For that day will not come unless the apostasy comes first and the man of lawlessness is revealed, the man doomed to destruction.

The second coming of Jesus is an overarching theme of 2 Thessalonians. An "apostasy," or rebellion, must precede Christ's return, according to Paul, along with the appearance of the "man of lawlessness." When Jesus comes, however, he will defeat this evil world ruler (2 Thess. 2:8), bring justice to oppressed Christians, and deliver wrath to their persecutors and to unbelievers in general (2 Thess. 1:5-10; 2:9-15).

Apparently, some Thessalonians think they are *in* the day of the Lord, or that it has come and gone, leaving them in anxiety, despair, or even slothfulness (2 Thess. 3:6-13). Perhaps this is due to a false prophecy, a misguided message, or even a counterfeit letter being circulated among church members. In any case, Paul seeks to assure his readers that Christ's coming remains in the future.

Paul urges the Thessalonians to be discerning. And he reminds them of two significant signs that must precede the glorious appearing of Jesus: unparalleled apostasy and the antichrist. Commentators have interpreted "the apostasy" in a number of ways, from a worldwide rebellion against God to the snatching away of the church from the world. In like manner, "the man of lawlessness" is understood in a variety of ways, from first-century Roman emperors to any number of subsequent world rulers.

Since Jesus has yet to return, we should follow Paul's exhortation not to be deceived. Rather, we should live godly lives in faithful anticipation that Christ will fulfill his promise to come again and set things right.

> **2 Thessalonians 2:8** – and then the lawless one will be revealed. The Lord Jesus will destroy him with the breath of his mouth and will bring him to nothing at the appearance of his coming.

This chapter's first twelve verses have a lot to say about "the lawless one." He will be revealed. He is doomed to destruction. He opposes and exalts himself above every so-called god or object of worship. He sits in God's temple, proclaiming that he himself is God. He is currently restrained in some way that Paul does not make clear. His coming is based on Satan's working – false miracles, signs and wonders, and wicked deceptions. He leads a multitude of those who believe his lies as a result of strong delusion sent by God.

If Paul's readers understand "the lawless one" to be a figure in their time – perhaps a Roman emperor such as Claudius, or Nero, who would follow Claudius – he would only serve as a type of the ultimate antichrist yet to come. John reminds us that "even now many antichrists have come" (1 John 2:18).

As much as we struggle to understand who "the lawless one" is, we share with the Thessalonians Paul's assurance that Jesus will utterly destroy him with "the breath of his mouth and will bring him to nothing" at the time of Christ's return. The breath with which Jesus spoke the world into existence and made man a living soul (Gen. 2:7; John 1:1-3; Col. 1:16), the breath that conferred the Holy Spirit on his followers (John 20:22), and the breath by which he gave us Scripture (2 Tim. 3:16), is the same breath that proceeds like a sword from Jesus' mouth to destroy the wicked at his glorious appearing (Rev. 19:15).

The details may be shrouded in mystery for now, but we may hold to the firm promise that God's timing is perfect and his plan to conquer evil is flawless.

1 Timothy

1 Timothy 6:13-16 – In the presence of God, who gives life to all, and of Christ Jesus, who gave a good confession before Pontius Pilate, I charge you to keep this command without fault or failure until the appearing of our Lord Jesus Christ. God will bring this about in his own time. He is the blessed and only Sovereign, the King of kings, and the Lord of lords, who alone is immortal and who lives in unapproachable light, whom no one has seen or can see, to him be honor and eternal power. Amen.

Paul draws a contrast between Timothy and the false teachers who "imagine that godliness is a way to material gain" (1 Tim. 6:5). As a "man of God" – unlike the false teachers, who are not men of God – the young pastor is to flee from false doctrine and pursue "righteousness, godliness, faith, love, endurance, and gentleness" (v. 11). Further, Timothy is to persevere in faithfulness until "the appearing of our Lord Jesus Christ," which God will bring about "in his own time" (vv. 14-15).

While Timothy faces opposition in Ephesus, Paul urges him to labor on with an eye toward standing one day before God, who will reward Timothy for his good stewardship. The false teachers may harass Timothy, but they are no match for "the blessed and only Sovereign, the King of kings, and the Lord of lords, who alone is immortal and who lives in unapproachable light" (vv. 15-16).

In writing about God, Paul uses names and descriptive terms that elsewhere in the New Testament describe Jesus, demonstrating both the deity of Christ and the close relationship between the members of the Trinity. For example, John sees the returning Christ as "King of Kings and Lord of Lords" (Rev. 19:16). In testifying to the saving work of Christ, Paul worships Jesus as "the King eternal, immortal, invisible, the only God" (1 Tim. 1:17).

The timing of Christ's return is in the Father's hands (Matt. 24:36), but all judgment has been given to the Son (John 5:22), who possesses all authority and is the fullness of deity in human flesh (Matt. 28:18; John 1:1; Col. 2:9).

2 Timothy

2 Timothy 4:1 – I solemnly charge you before God and Christ Jesus, who is going to judge the living and the dead, and because of his appearing and his kingdom ....

While imprisoned in Rome, Paul writes a second letter to Timothy. Prominent themes include persecution from outside the church and false teaching from within. So, Paul instructs the young pastor to focus on the Scriptures and teach sound doctrine.

With the words, "I solemnly charge you before God and Christ Jesus," the apostle places Timothy under an oath to "Preach the word; be ready in season and out of season; correct, rebuke and encourage with great patience and teaching" (1 Tim. 4:2). One day, Christ is going to judge his servants, whether they are alive at the Savior's return or resurrected from the dead.

All judgment has been granted to Jesus (John 5:22), as well as all authority in heaven and on earth (Matt. 28:18). This final judgment comes at the "appearing" of Christ (see 1 Tim. 6:14; 2 Tim. 4:8; Tit. 2:13) and the commencement of his earthly rule from the throne of David, when the kingdom of the world becomes "the kingdom of our Lord and of his Christ, and he will reign forever and ever" (Rev. 11:15).

So, Timothy is to soldier on, enduring the resistance of unbelievers while looking forward with great hope toward the return of Christ.

2 Timothy 4:8 – There is reserved for me the crown of righteousness, which the Lord, the righteous Judge, will give me on that day, and not only to me, but to all those who have loved his appearing.

Paul is nearing the end of his life. He tells Timothy, "I am already being poured out as a drink offering, and the time for my departure is close" (2 Tim. 4:6). But he has remained faithful despite tremendous persecution and opposition. Having finished his race, Paul looks forward to receiving "the crown of righteousness," a heavenly laurel wreath that acknowledges his perseverance.

But the crown isn't just for Paul. It's for Timothy and others who serve Christ with an eye toward Jesus' return in glory in the presence of his holy angels. Jesus is "the righteous Judge" who reveals himself and executes final judgment at his return.

Titus

Titus 2:13 – while we wait for the blessed hope, the appearing of the glory of our great God and Savior, Jesus Christ.

The second chapter of Titus is an encouragement to embrace sound teaching and godly living. Paul urges older men and women to set good examples, and younger men and women to follow them. This is so God's word won't be slandered.

Titus is to make himself an example to others so that opponents of the gospel fail to find "anything bad to say" about him or his church family (Tit. 2:8). Meanwhile, slaves are to exhibit utter faithfulness so "they may adorn the teaching of God our Savior in everything" (v. 10).

As followers of Jesus live in a "sensible, righteous, and godly way in the present age," we are to wait expectantly for "the blessed hope, the appearing of the glory of our great God and Savior, Jesus Christ" (vv. 12-13).

In Judaism, the ultimate revelation, or "appearing," of God would signal the end of the present evil age and mark the dawn of a new era. Many Jews called God "the great God" and saw him as a "savior." Paul applies both titles to Jesus, "our great God and Savior" (v. 13). Some commentators try to separate "great God" and "Savior," so as not to ascribe deity to Jesus. But as theologian Craig Keener notes, "According to the most likely reading of the grammar here, Paul applies this divine title to Jesus."[4]

Just as the Word of God became flesh and dwelt among us (John 1:14), the incarnate Word appears in glory in the last days to usher in his eternal kingdom.

THE TESTIMONY OF THE WRITER OF HEBREWS

The writer of Hebrews implores Jewish Christians to stay faithful, despite mounting pressure to return to Judaism. The same Jesus who died once for our sins will appear a second time to complete the work of salvation he began in all Christians. Meanwhile, we are to keep the Christian community intact, meet regularly, and remind ourselves that "in a very little while, the Coming One will come and not delay" (Heb. 10:37).

> **Hebrews 9:27-28** – And just as it is appointed for people to die once — and after this, judgment — so also Christ, having been offered once to bear the sins of many, will appear a second time, not to bear sin, but to bring salvation to those who are waiting for him.

Some Greeks held to Plato's belief in reincarnation. And some Jewish traditions allowed for temporary punishment in *gehenna* after death to expiate one's remaining sins.[5] But the writer of Hebrews affirms the majority first-century Jewish view, and the consensus New Testament teaching, that death ends a person's opportunity for reconciliation with God. Today is the day to set things right with our creator and judge (Heb. 4:5-7). As Jared Ingle writes, "We are profoundly limited by *Today*. It is our only opportunity to engage God."[6]

Equally important, Christ has provided reconciliation through his death, burial, and resurrection. His work to "bear the sins of many" is drawn from Isaiah 53:12. Now seated at the Father's right hand in heaven, the exalted Jesus will appear "a second time" – in his glorious future return – to finish his work of salvation in us. He is raising us from the dead and giving us glorified bodies, rewarding us for faithful service, and forever banishing death and *hades* to the lake of fire (Rev. 20:14).

Our role as followers of Jesus is to serve him faithfully in view of his imminent return. As Jesus tells his disciples in the parable of the ten minas, "Engage in business until I come back" (Luke 19:11-27, especially v. 13).

> **Hebrews 10:24-25** – And let us consider one another in order to provoke love and good works, not neglecting to gather together, as some are in the habit of doing, but encouraging each other, and all the more as you see the day approaching.

Religious associations in the Greco-Roman world were key to a sense of community. Jewish people in the first century gathered weekly at their synagogues. Christians seemed to have gathered at least weekly with an emphasis on Sunday (Acts 20:7).

But persecution may have discouraged some Christians from attending worship, even in relatively private house churches. So, the writer of Hebrews urges them not to neglect vital engagement in Christian community, especially as they see "the day approaching" – that is, the day of Jesus' return and judgment.

> **Hebrews 10:37** – For yet in a very little while, the Coming One will come and not delay.

The writer of Hebrews expresses confidence that his readers, having already endured much, will not shrink back and abandon the faith (Heb. 10:32-39). He cheers them on to faithfulness. Drawing from Habakkuk and Isaiah, he seeks to bolster their trust in the return of "the Coming One" (cf. Isa. 26:20; Hab. 2:3-4).

Habakkuk speaks of a *revelation* that is coming: "For the vision is yet for the appointed time …. Though it delays, wait for it, since it will certainly come and not be late" (Hab. 2:3). The prophet is referring to the looming judgment of Judah and the punishment of Babylon. The writer of Hebrews changes the focus to a *person*. Since Jesus is the God-Man, as well as God's last word to man (Heb. 1:1), the adaptation fits perfectly to the return of Christ.

Just as God delays his judgment of Judah and his vengeance on Babylon, he holds the return of Christ in reserve for a future day. Peter tells us this delay is an exercise of God's patience. Even so, the "day of the Lord" comes certainly and swiftly, punishing the wicked, purging the world of sin, and resulting in new heavens and a new earth (2 Pet. 3:1-13).

As Donald Guthrie notes of Hebrews 10:37, "Here the thought is of the certainty of God's intervention, which was particularly significant for the church in a time of persecution. The assurance that *the coming one* would not tarry shows that any delay should be regarded as temporary."[7]

THE TESTIMONY OF JAMES

In a single reference to the second coming, James urges his readers to be patient as they wait for Christ's return.

> **James 5:7-8** – Therefore, brothers and sisters, be patient until the Lord's coming. See how the farmer waits for the precious fruit of the earth and is patient with it until it receives the early and the late rains. You also must be patient. Strengthen your hearts, because the Lord's coming is near.

James addresses Jewish Christians caught up in the social tensions of first-century Judea that ultimately lead to the war of A.D. 66-70 and result in the destruction of the temple, the massacre of more than a million Jews, and the scattering of Jewish survivors. These are tumultuous times throughout the Roman Empire. James' wise counsel applies to first-century Christians in similar circumstances elsewhere, as well as to followers of Jesus today.

James tackles a number of issues in his letter: the pride of the rich, persecution by the rich, and the temptation of Christians to retaliate with violence, to name a few. Into this maelstrom, the leader of the Jerusalem church calls for wisdom, faith, and patient endurance. James assures his readers their oppressors will be punished (Jas. 5:1-6). At the same time, the oppressed must wait on God rather than take matters into their own hands.

The analogy of the farmer is a well-placed encouragement to be patient. Just as the sower waits for the early and late rains to nourish the soil, resulting in bumper crops, Christians must wait on the Lord's perfect timing to bring them vindication. This may not occur in their lifetimes, but it certainly comes to pass when Christ returns to set things right.

"Strengthen your hearts," James writes, "because the coming of the Lord is near." The imminent return of Jesus should always serve as a moderating factor in our thoughts, words, and behaviors.

THE TESTIMONY OF PETER

Peter employs many terms to describe the return of Jesus, as we see in a sermon in Solomon's Colonnade in the Book of Acts, and in his epistles. He describes the second coming as "the time of restoration of all things;" "the last time;" "the revelation of Jesus Christ;" "the end of all things;" the revelation of "his glory;" the appearing of the "Chief Shepherd;" and "the day of the Lord."

Acts

Acts 3:19-21 – Therefore repent and turn back, so that your sins may be wiped out, that seasons of refreshing may come from the presence of the Lord, and that he may send Jesus, who has been appointed for you as the Messiah. Heaven must receive him until the time of the restoration of all things, which God spoke about through his holy prophets from the beginning.

The Lord has just used Peter to heal a lame man on the steps of the temple – a miracle that attracts a crowd and gives Peter an opportunity to preach about the Jesus in whose name the miracle occurred. Peter calls his listeners to repent and trust in their Messiah, resulting in the forgiveness of sins, the presence of the indwelling Holy Spirit, and the joyful anticipation of Messiah's return.

Having suffered for our sins, the Jesus whom Peter declares is now in heaven at the Father's right hand, an exalted position from which he rules with all authority and even heals lame men on earth. However, "the time of the restoration of all things" is on the horizon.

The world is not as God created it, nor as he intends it to be. The whole creation groans beneath the weight of sin (Rom. 8:22), waiting for the return of Jesus, the creator and redeemer, to set things right. God has revealed all this through the Old Testament prophets (see Chapter 3), and Peter encourages his listeners to see how the Suffering Servant is also the soon-returning King.

1 Peter

1 Peter 1:3-5 – Blessed be the God and Father of our Lord Jesus Christ. Because of his great mercy he has given us new birth into a living hope through the resurrection of Jesus Christ from the dead and into an inheritance that is imperishable, undefiled, and unfading, kept in heaven for you. You are being guarded by God's power through faith for a salvation that is ready to be revealed in the last time.

Peter offers us a view of the golden chain of redemption – God's work of salvation that extends from eternity past (in foreknowledge, election, and predestination), through time (in calling, regeneration, justification, and sanctification), and out into eternity future (in glorification). Paul writes about this in Romans 8:29-30: "For those he foreknew he also predestined to be conformed to the image of his Son

... those he predestined, he also called; and those he called, he also justified; and those he justified, he also glorified."

Because of Jesus, we're made spiritually alive through the "new birth," or regeneration. We are granted a "living hope" since the resurrection of Jesus ensures our future resurrection (1 Cor. 15:20-23). And we possess an inheritance – future glorification and eternity with Jesus as his coheirs – that is kept safe in heaven for us. What's more, God keeps us secure as he sustains our faith until the end.

> **1 Peter 1:13** – Therefore, with your minds ready for action, be sober-minded and set your hope completely on the grace to be brought to you at the revelation of Jesus Christ.

The KJV renders it, "gird up the loins of your mind ...." In ancient times, men wore long robes, which they gathered and tucked into their belts for greater freedom of movement. Peter may be reminding his Jewish readers of the Passover, in which the people were to be ready to leave Egypt as soon as the meal was completed and the angel of death finished his work. In a similar way, followers of Jesus, redeemed by the ultimate Passover Lamb, should be ready at all times to follow God's call.

Just as Israelites in Egypt looked forward to entering the Promised Land, Christians are to set our hope on living forever in the new heavens and earth, which are delivered "at the revelation of Jesus Christ" – that is, at his return.

> **1 Peter 4:7** – The end of all things is near; therefore, be alert and sober-minded for prayer.

Peter is not necessarily expecting Jesus to return in a few days or weeks. Rather, he's reminding us that all the major events in God's plan of salvation – including Christ's death, burial, and resurrection, and the coming of the Spirit on the Day of Pentecost – have already occurred. Therefore, Christ's return could happen at any time.

The end of all things is near in Peter's day, as it is in ours. The delay in Christ's return is an expression of God's mercy (see 2 Pet. 3:8-9). Our appropriate response is not to stand idly, gazing into the heavens, but to live self-controlled and sober-minded lives of faithfulness.

> **1 Peter 4:13** – Instead, rejoice as you share in the sufferings of Christ, so that you may also rejoice with great joy when his glory is revealed.

Peter cheers his readers on as they suffer persecution for their faith in Jesus. Christians always have endured oppression – including martyrdom – and they always will until Jesus returns. The apostle reminds us that it is a badge of honor to share in the sufferings of Christ. Other New Testament writers express similar sentiments (e.g., Phil. 3:10; Heb. 11:35-38; Jas. 1:2).

At the same time, Christian persecution is not merely to be endured; it is something we should experience with a view toward vindication. One day, the Suffering Servant returns as King of kings and Lord of lords. He comes in glory and sits on his royal throne (Matt. 25:31). He resurrects and glorifies the saints (1 John 3:2). And he punishes those who treated his followers with contempt (2 Thess. 1:5-10). All of this occurs "when his glory is revealed."

> **1 Peter 5:4** – And when the chief Shepherd appears, you will receive the unfading crown of glory.

Peter closes out his first epistle with an exhortation to elders, with whom he identifies as "a fellow elder" (1 Pet. 5:1). He encourages them to "Shepherd God's flock among you, not overseeing out of compulsion but willingly, as God would have you; not out of greed for money but eagerly; not lording it over those entrusted to you, but being examples to the flock" (vv. 2-3).

As faithful under-shepherds, elders may look forward to the return of Jesus, when the "chief Shepherd" rewards them with the "unfading crown of glory." This is one of at least five crowns mentioned in the New Testament.[8] Sometimes, it's called *the pastor's crown*. The crown of glory is reserved in heaven for those who faithfully teach God's word and shepherd the congregation God has called them to oversee.

2 Peter

2 Peter 3:10 – But the day of the Lord will come like a thief; on that day the heavens will pass away with a loud noise, the elements will burn and be dissolved, and the earth and the works on it will be disclosed.

The apostle warns against "scoffers" who point to the delay in Christ's return as proof that our Lord isn't coming at all (2 Pet. 3:3-4). Peter reminds them of the flood that destroyed the world long ago; the very waters God used to create the earth were stored up for its destruction in the days of Noah (vv. 5-6). In a similar manner, the Lord keeps a storehouse of fire by which he will purge the world of sin, thus creating new heavens and a new earth (vv. 7, 12-13).

The "day of the Lord will come like a thief," Peter warns. Christ's return may seem far away, and Christians may even be tempted to let down their guards. But Jesus *is* returning – and his coming will be sudden and unexpected by many.

Noah preached for perhaps 120 years without any converts (see Gen. 6:3). In a similar way, Christians are to prepare for the return of Jesus – and to proclaim it in spite of growing skepticism.

Even Jesus recalls that Noah's contemporaries ignored the message that would have saved them. And he warns us against making the same mistake: "Just as it was in the days of Noah, so it will be in the days of the Son of Man: People went on eating, drinking, marrying and being given in marriage until the day Noah boarded the ark, and the flood came and destroyed them all" (Luke 17:26-27).

THE TESTIMONY OF JOHN

In John's first epistle, he urges Christians to remain faithful to Jesus so that "when he appears" we are not ashamed. Further, we see Jesus as he is and become like him in glorification. In two passages in Revelation, John sees Jesus "coming with the clouds," riding a white horse, with a sharp sword protruding from his mouth and a robe dipped in blood – all symbols of his coming in judgment.

1 John

> **1 John 2:28** – So now, little children, remain in him so that when he appears we may have confidence and not be ashamed before him at his coming.

Addressing his readers affectionately as "little children," John urges them to *remain* in Jesus. That is, they are to continue holding to sound teaching about Jesus, resisting false prophets like the Docetics, who deny Jesus has come "in the flesh" (1 John 4:2).

True followers of Jesus have "eternal life," which he himself promised (1 John 2:25; cf. John 4:14). In addition, we have "the anointing" from Jesus (1 John 2:27). This may be the Holy Spirit, which Jesus has sent (John 14:26; 15:26; 16:7), or it could be the word of God, the message of the gospel. In either case, the Lord has provided all we need to remain faithful, so that "when he appears we may have confidence and not be ashamed at his coming."

This clearly is a reference to the return of Jesus – a day that faithful Christians eagerly anticipate, and a day in which unfaithful Christians may find themselves ashamed as they lose rewards God intended them to have (1 Cor. 3:15). Worse, those who completely reject the truth of God's self-revelation in creation, conscience, the canon of Scripture, and Christ find themselves cast into the lake of fire (Rev. 20:15).

As Colin Kruse notes, "The author's point ... is that if people remain in Christ (following the teaching they heard from the beginning and which the anointing, the Holy Spirit, continues to teach them), then, when Jesus Christ appears and judges his people, they may be confident and unashamed before him."[9]

> 1 John 3:2 – Dear friends, we are God's children now, and what we will be has not yet been revealed. We know that when he appears, we will be like him because we will see him as he is.

John stakes his apostolic authority, at least in part, on the fact that he is an eyewitness of Christ. He opens his letter declaring "what we have heard, what we have seen with our eyes, what we have observed and have touched with our hands, concerning the word of life" (1 John 1:1). But now his focus is on the future. Followers of Jesus may rest assured that we are adopted children of God. That means one day we receive the promised inheritance of glorification – being fully conformed to the image of Christ.

In our present earthly state, we can't fully comprehend the benefits of sharing in Christ's immortality; God has not revealed the details of these promises. But John, who saw the resurrected and glorified Christ, tells us to look up. When Jesus "appears" – that is, when he returns – we experience the great exchange about which Paul wrote to the Corinthians: corruption for incorruption; dishonor for glory; weakness for power; the natural for the spiritual (1 Cor. 15:42-44).

We will see Jesus as he is – the glorified God-Man – and be like him. Not that we attain deity, for that is the exclusive nature of the triune God. Rather, we are restored to the sinless perfection of Eden. Body, soul, and spirit are rescued from the power and presence of sin, and we enjoy face-to-face harmony with our creator. We no longer see Jesus in the days of his earthly ministry, nor with the eyes of faith, but in his heavenly glory. The very sight of the returning Christ is enough to make us pure like him.

Revelation

> **Revelation 1:7-8** – Look, he is coming with the clouds, and every eye will see him, even those who pierced him. And all the tribes of the earth will mourn over him. So it is to be. Amen. "I am the Alpha and the Omega," says the Lord God, "the one who is, who was, and who is to come, the Almighty.

John blends Daniel 7:13 (coming with the clouds) with Zechariah 12:10 (those who pierced him) to depict the appearing of the Son of Man in glory. In predicting his own return, Jesus combines these same two phrases from Daniel and Zechariah: "Then the sign of the Son of Man will appear in the sky, and then all the peoples of the earth will mourn; and they will see the Son of Man coming on the clouds of heaven with power and great glory" (Matt. 24:30).

Clouds in the Old Testament often are connected with divine activity: as a display of God's physical presence (Exod. 13:21; Num. 11:25); as a means of concealing God's holiness so people would not see him and die (Exod. 33:20; Isa. 6:5); and as a means of divine transportation (Isa. 19:1). The Messiah's connection with the clouds of heaven is seen many times in the New Testament (e.g., Mark 13:26; Acts 1:9; 1 Thess. 4:17).

Clouds play a secondary role to the returning King of kings and Lord of lords and serve to magnify his presence. Believers are not instructed to look for the clouds of heaven, but to wait expectantly for the one coming with the clouds.

When Jesus appears, "every eye will see him, even those who pierced him." Further, "all the tribes of the earth will mourn over him." While the primary focus seems to be on the Jewish people who rejected Jesus and crucified him, we should consider a broader application. As David Stern writes, the phrase "those who pierced them" is not limited to Jews, nor does it mean only the Jews and Gentiles historically responsible for Jesus' death. "Rather, it includes all who have not acknowledged his atoning sacrificial death, who by their sins participated in and continue to participate in piercing him."[10]

God the Father then declares, "I am the Alpha and the Omega …
the one who is, who was, and who is to come, the Almighty" (Rev. 1:8).
This is similar to the words of Jesus in Revelation 22:13: "I am the
Alpha and the Omega, the first and the last, the beginning and the
end." In these identifying bookends to Revelation, the Father and Jesus
demonstrate they are distinct persons who share deity, eternality,
creativity, and sovereignty.

Like the Father, Jesus is sovereign over all things, knows all things,
and directs human history to its climax in his personal return, by
which he sets all things right. What a comfort to John's first-century
readers – who suffer greatly for their faith – to know the Almighty is
with them through their persecutions, and promises to reward them
for their perseverance. These same promises hold true today for
believers under increasing pressure to abandon their faith.

> **Revelation 19:11-16** – Then I saw heaven opened, and there was a
> white horse. Its rider is called Faithful and True, and with justice he
> judges and makes war. His eyes were like a fiery flame, and many
> crowns were on his head. He had a name written that no one knows
> except himself. He wore a robe dipped in blood, and his name is called
> the Word of God. The armies that were in heaven followed him on
> white horses, wearing pure white linen. A sharp sword came from his
> mouth, so that he might strike the nations with it. He will rule them
> with an iron rod. He will also trample the winepress of the fierce
> anger of God, the Almighty. And he has a name written on his robe
> and on his thigh: King of Kings and Lord of Lords.

There is little disagreement among scholars that the rider in this
passage is Jesus. The majority view is that John sees the return of
Christ, in which he judges the earth and sets things right.[11]

The white horse is a sign of Jesus coming in triumph. On Palm
Sunday, Jesus rides a donkey into Jerusalem, fulfilling Old Testament
prophecy (Matt. 21:1-10; John 12:12-16; cf. Zech. 9:9). Historically,
for a king to enter a city on a donkey signifies peace rather than
conquest.[12] But now, Jesus returns as King of kings. It was customary

for a triumphant Roman general to parade on the Via Sacra, a main thoroughfare of Rome, followed by evidences of his victory in loot and captives. "The white horse is thus a symbol of Christ's triumph over the forces of wickedness in the world."[13] John is describing Jesus' coming as the Jews expected him the first time – a powerful military leader.

Briefly, let's survey twelve ways John describes this rider on the white horse.

1. *He is called "Faithful and True" (v. 11).* These titles – "Faithful" and "True" – stand in contrast to the rider in Revelation 6:2, who later speaks "boasts and blasphemies" and who blasphemes God's "name and his dwelling" (Rev. 13:5-6). As Matthew Henry notes, "He is faithful and true to his covenant and promise, he is righteous in all his judicial and military proceedings, he has a penetrating insight into all the strengths and stratagems of his enemies, he has a large and extensive dominion, many crowns, for he is King of kings, and Lord of lords."[14]

2. *He judges and makes war with justice (v. 11).* The Son of God is neither weak nor aloof. His holiness demands justice, and his sovereignty demands warfare against the ungodly who seek to usurp his throne.

3. *His eyes are like a fiery flame (v. 12).* This describes Jesus' piercing holiness and his searching judgment that sees all. In John's earlier vision of the risen Lord, he sees "one like the Son of Man" with "eyes like a fiery flame" (Rev. 1:13-14). And in the opening lines of the letter to the church at Thyatira, Jesus describes himself as "the one whose eyes are like a fiery flame" (Rev. 2:18).

4. *Many crowns are on his head (v. 12).* Monarchs who claim authority over more than one country often wear more than a single crown. Thus, here we see a beautiful portrayal of Christ's universal dominion.

5. *He has a name written that no one knows except himself (v. 12).* This reminds us that the Lord has not revealed everything about himself and his plan. Yet he keeps his promises. He is working through human

history to bring his people to repentance so they may enjoy unending fellowship with him.

6. *He wears a robe dipped in blood (v. 13)*. The blood on Jesus' robe could be his redemptive blood shed on the cross or the blood of his enemies. Possibly, it's both. The passage may refer to his sacrificial death, by which the multitudes in heaven have made their robes white (Rev. 7:14). It also may look forward to his treading the winepress of God's wrath (Rev. 19:15).

7. *His name is the Word of God (v. 13)*. The Word of God indicates Jesus' deity joined to his humanity (see John 1:1-14). Just as our words reveal our thoughts and intentions to others, so the Father reveals himself to us through his Son, the incarnate Word. Warren Wiersbe writes, "A word is made up of letters, and Jesus Christ is 'Alpha and Omega' (Rev. 21:6; 22:13). He is the 'divine alphabet' of God's revelation to us."[15]

8. *The armies in heaven follow him on white horses, wearing pure white linen (v. 14)*. Note that John sees more than one army, indicating that both angels and saints accompany Jesus. The white robes signify both the righteousness of Christ and the believers' good deeds (Rev. 6:11; 7:13-14; 19:8; cf. Phil. 3:9).

9. *A sharp sword comes from his mouth, so that he might strike the nations with it (v. 15)*. This is figurative language describing the powerful spoken word of our Savior. The word translated "sword" is *rhomphaia* and is used of an unusually long sword, or even a spear, indicating a piercing action. John may be referring to Isaiah 11:4, in which a future Davidic king will "strike the land with a scepter from his mouth, and he will kill the wicked with a command from his lips."

10. *He rules them with an iron rod (v. 15)*. In Revelation 2:27, John quotes a messianic prophecy from Psalm 2:9: "and he will rule them with an iron scepter; he will shatter them like pottery." And Revelation 12:5 tells us the woman's Son – that is, Israel's Son – is going to "rule all nations with an iron rod." This symbolizes Christ's justice as he rules the earth.

11. *He tramples the winepress of the fierce anger of God, the Almighty (v. 15)*.

This reference is rooted deeply in Old Testament imagery (Isa. 63:2-3; Jer. 51:33; Joel 3:13). We also see the imagery in Revelation 14:14-20, where Christ, or an angel, harvests the earth's wicked. The color of crushed grapes vividly depicts the blood shed when Christ comes in power to take vengeance on those who reject him and revile his people.

12. *He has a name written on his robe and on his thigh: King of Kings and Lord of Lords (v. 16).* This is Christ's exalted and victorious name. In Revelation 17:13-14, this name is meant to contrast that of the beast, who receives power and authority from the kings of the earth – to no avail: "the Lamb will conquer them because he is Lord of lords and King of kings."

THE TESTIMONY OF JUDE

Brother of James and half-brother of Jesus, Jude sends a brief letter to believers combatting false teachers who live immorally and teach arrogantly. Jude's quotation from 1 Enoch – a pseudepigraphal book attributed to the great-grandfather of Noah – may be an effort to use a source the false teachers highly prized against them.

> **Jude 14-15** – It was about these that Enoch, in the seventh generation from Adam, prophesied: "Look! The Lord comes with tens of thousands of his holy ones to execute judgment on all and to convict all the ungodly concerning all the ungodly acts that they have done in an ungodly way, and concerning all the harsh things ungodly sinners have said against him."

Jude's quotation is similar but not identical to 1 Enoch 1:9. Perhaps this is because Jude cites a portion of the book the Spirit confirms as genuine. Certainly, this passage is consistent with Old Testament references to the day of the Lord.[16] The point here is that Jude does not simply snatch a convenient text from a non-canonical book in order to build his case. Rather, in quoting from 1 Enoch, he affirms the Old Testament texts from which the book is drawn.

Who does Enoch have in mind when he prophesies that the Lord is coming with "tens of thousands of his holy ones"? Most likely, Enoch is thinking of angels, since they serve as agents of judgment at the return of Christ. In addition, the coming of Christ is patterned after Yahweh's appearance on Sinai, where he came with "ten thousand holy ones" (Deut. 33:2). But we should not discount the promise of God that the saints also accompany Jesus in his glorious appearing, and reign with him.[17]

Jude writes that Enoch's prophecy, made centuries earlier, applies to the judgment of false teachers throughout the ages, including first-century apostates. The Holy Spirit has enabled Enoch to look through the telescoping lens of time, compressing the span over which false prophets and false teachers deceive people. Ultimately, they stand before the returning Christ and are held accountable for the wreckage their destructive ministries have wrought.

Jude is clear that these false teachers are not backslidden believers who have drifted from their biblical moorings. In quoting Enoch, he establishes that they are unregenerate. He quotes the word "ungodly" several times. Their deeds are ungodly. They have acted in ungodly ways. And they have spoken harsh words against the Lord, revealing themselves as ungodly sinners. With every deceitful word, every selfish deed, and every demonstration of spiritual arrogance, they store up divine wrath for the day of judgment.

THE TESTIMONY OF ANGELS

Angels proclaim the return of Jesus in at least two New Testament passages. In the first, "two men in white clothes" tell the apostles Christ's return is to be a mirror image of his ascension, which they have just witnessed. In the second, an angel flies high overhead, announcing to the earth's inhabitants that God's hour of judgment has come.

Acts 1:10-11 – While he was going, they were gazing into heaven, and suddenly two men in white clothes stood by them. They said, "Men of Galilee, why do you stand looking up into heaven? This same Jesus, who has been taken from you into heaven, will come in the same way that you have seen him going into heaven."

Jesus has instructed his apostles to remain in Jerusalem until they receive the Father's promise of the Holy Spirit. Thus empowered, they are to be Christ's witnesses in Jerusalem, in all Judea and Samaria, and to the ends of the earth. Then, Jesus ascends into heaven with a cloud taking him out of their sight (Acts 1:4-9).

In the apostles' minds, this may harken back to the ascension of Elijah in 2 Kings 2. After the prophet's dramatic exit in a whirlwind, accompanied by blazing horses and a chariot of fire, Elisha receives a double portion of Elijah's spirit to carry on the prophetic ministry.

In a similar manner, the ascending Jesus passes the torch to his apostles. The coming Holy Spirit will enable them to perform "even greater works" than the works of Jesus – that is, greater in number and geographical reach – as they carry on the gospel ministry in the wake of Christ's return to his Father (John 14:12-14).

So now, with Jesus ascending to the Father's right hand in heaven, the "two men in white clothes" – clearly angelic beings – urge the eyewitnesses to take on the mantle of their apostolic calling. Equally important, the angels remind the apostles that Christ's absence from the earth is temporary. The Lord *is* returning one day. This "same Jesus" – the resurrected and glorified God-Man – is coming back to set things right. Further, he is coming back in the "same way" – personally, physically, visibly, with the clouds of heaven.

Followers of Jesus are not to stand idly, gazing into the heavens and watching for his return. We are to be busy, engaging in the gospel ministry he has entrusted to us.

Revelation 14:6-7 – Then I saw another angel flying high overhead, with the eternal gospel to announce to the inhabitants of the earth — to every nation, tribe, language, and people. He spoke with a loud voice: "Fear God and give him glory, because the hour of his judgment has come. Worship the one who made heaven and earth, the sea and the springs of water."

Three angels appear in succession in Revelation 14:6-12.[18] They proclaim the vindication of God's people and the judgment of the wicked. Our primary interest is in the first angel, who flies high overhead and announces "the eternal gospel" to the earth's inhabitants.

The eternal gospel is the *euangelion*, the "good news" of Jesus Christ: his eternal existence, incarnation, sinless life, sacrificial death, resurrection, and ascension; his position today in heaven at the Father's right hand; his imminent return in glory; and his gracious offer of eternal life through faith in him. The gospel is eternal in that it is in the mind of the Father from the beginning. Further, Jesus is the Lamb of God slain from the foundation of the world (Rev. 13:8). And the eternal Spirit bears testimony of the risen Savior, drawing unbelievers to faith in Christ (Heb. 9:14; cf. John 16:8-11).

The eternal gospel first touches human life at the moment of Adam's fall. The promise of a coming seed is made as God clothes Adam and Eve in the animal skins of the inaugural atoning sacrifice. The gospel continues through God's gracious sparing of Noah and his family in the days of the deluge; his promises to Abraham of land, a people, and blessings to all through Abraham's offspring; his deliverance of the Israelites from bondage in Egypt; the types and shadows of the sacrificial system; the throne upon which King David sits, promising a coming redeemer; and the miraculous conception of the eternal Son of God in the womb of a teenage girl.

Salvation always has been the good news. It always comes at God's initiative and Christ's expense; it always has been offered in grace and received by faith. Every drop of sacrificial blood, from the Garden of Eden to Golgotha, points to the redeemer whose sinless life is poured out for our sins. No longer do sinful people take a spotless lamb and spill its blood, trusting in faith that the death of the innocent substitute has temporarily covered their sins. Now, they look in faith upon the Lamb of God, whose blood once and for all takes away their sin.

The fact that the angel proclaims the eternal gospel to every nation, tribe, language, and people means God graciously excludes no one who receives his Son in faith. It also means the objects of his judgment have no excuse for rejecting their creator. Grace and judgment are two sides of the same coin. God's holiness demands death to the sinner, while his love compels him to offer his own Son to pay the penalty on our behalf. Those who receive the gospel are the objects of his special grace, while those who reject it have willfully passed through the portals of hell and locked the door behind them.

REVIEW

Key takeaways from this chapter

1. Paul and other eyewitnesses write and speak often of Christ's imminent return. They proclaim its certainty, await its glory, warn of its vengeance, and urge followers of Jesus to live in the light of its impending reality.

2. Paul addresses the second coming of Jesus in numerous sermons and epistles. From a message to skeptical listeners on Mars Hill, to warnings against false teachers, to glorious details about the nature of our resurrected bodies, Paul speaks and writes with confidence about the coming day when God is going to "judge the world in righteousness by the man [Jesus] he has appointed" (Acts 17:31).

3. The writer of Hebrews implores Jewish Christians to stay faithful, despite mounting pressure to return to Judaism. The same Jesus who died once for our sins will appear a second time to complete the work of salvation he began in all Christians.

4. In a single reference to the second coming, James urges his readers to be patient in anticipation of Christ's certain return: "Strengthen your hearts, because the Lord's coming is near" (Jas. 5:8).

5. Peter employs many terms to describe the return of Jesus. The second coming is "the time of restoration of all things;" "the last time;" "the revelation of Jesus Christ;" "the end of all things;" the revelation of "his glory;" the appearing of the "Chief Shepherd;" and "the day of the Lord."

6. In his first letter, John urges Christians to remain faithful to Jesus so that "when he appears" we are not ashamed. In two passages in Revelation, John sees Jesus "coming with the clouds," riding a white horse, with a sharp sword protruding from his

mouth, and a robe dipped in blood – all symbols of his coming in judgment.

7. Jude sends a brief letter to believers combatting false teachers who live immorally and teach arrogantly. He even quotes from 1 Enoch, a pseudepigraphal book the false teachers may have prized, to remind them the Lord is coming to execute judgment on the ungodly.

8. Even angels get into the act of declaring the return of Jesus. Two angels tell the apostles that the ascended Jesus will return one day in the same way – personally, physically, visibly, with the clouds of heaven. And in Revelation, an angel preaches "the eternal gospel" to the inhabitants of earth, warning them to fear God "because the hour of his judgment has come" (Rev. 14:7).

DISCUSS

Questions for personal or group study

1. List several terms New Testament writers use to describe the return of Jesus. How do phrases such as "the end of all things" and "the appearing of the Chief Shepherd" combine to give us a well-rounded view of all that occurs at the second coming?

2. Read Acts 17:31. Why do you think Paul tells his listeners on Mars Hill that the resurrection of Jesus is "proof" of a coming day of judgment?

3. Several New Testament authors urge their readers to remain faithful as they endure persecution or strong social pressure (see 1 Thess. 1:9-10; 5:2; Heb. 10:37; Jas. 5:8; 1 Pet. 4:7). The writers promise swift and certain vindication, yet two thousand years later, the Lord has yet to return. What are some reasons for the delay?

4. Consider the following New Testament passages and note the many ways God helps us persevere until he returns:

- 1 Cor. 1:6-8
- Phil. 1:6
- 1 Thess. 3:13

- 1 Thess. 5:23
- 2 Tim. 4:8
- 1 Pet. 1:3-5
- 1 John 3:2

5. In the following Scriptures, note what Christians are instructed to do in order to be ready for the return of Jesus:

- 1 Cor. 4:5
- 1 Cor. 11:26
- Phil. 3:20-21
- 2 Thess. 2:1-3
- Tit. 2:13
- Heb. 10:24-25
- Jas. 5:7-8
- 1 Pet. 1:13
- 1 Pet. 4:7, 13
- 1 John 2:28

* * *

"HE WILL JUDGE THE NATIONS"

OLD TESTAMENT WRITERS FORESEE A MESSIANIC AGE ONLY JESUS CAN FULFILL

The second coming of Jesus is implied in hundreds of Old Testament prophecies that center on future judgment of the world and a coming kingdom of righteousness. Jesus and the New Testament writers elevate these ancient prophecies and apply them to the unfinished, but guaranteed, future work of the Savior.

One challenge of messianic prophecies is their compressed view of the future. We see predictions of a Suffering Servant who is despised, rejected, and sacrificed for our sins (Isa. 53), along with visions of a Davidic king who comes in power, judging the world and setting things right (Ps. 110). Are the Suffering Servant and Davidic king separate individuals, or are they one person conducting two major campaigns to redeem a sinful and fallen world?

The answer, of course, is the latter. The New Testament perspective clearly is the two-stage nature of Christ's redemptive work. Consider 1 Peter 1:10-12:

> Concerning this salvation, the prophets, who prophesied about the grace that would come to you, searched and carefully investigated. They inquired into what time or what circumstances the Spirit of Christ within them was indicating when he testified in advance to the

sufferings of Christ and the glories that would follow. It was revealed
to them that they were not serving themselves but you. These things
have now been announced to you through those who preached the
gospel to you by the Holy Spirit sent from heaven — angels long to
catch a glimpse of these things.

Here, Peter combines Jesus' first and second comings into a single
narrative. The same Jesus who experienced the "sufferings of Christ"
would also see "the glories" to follow. No doubt, these "glories"
include the resurrection and ascension of Jesus, as well as his promise,
fulfilled on the Day of Pentecost, to send the Holy Spirit. But they also
include the return of Jesus, a dramatic future event Peter writes about
elsewhere (2 Pet. 3:10-13). The prophets to whom the Lord revealed
the future may not have fully understood a two-stage messianic
mission. But Peter assures us these marvelous prophecies are fulfilled
in one person: Jesus of Nazareth.

We should ponder a few additional insights into Peter's words
before moving on.

First, Peter says the prophets "searched and carefully investigated"
(1 Pet. 1:10). That is, they examined their own prophecies, as well as
the writings of the prophets before them. They also may have engaged
in conversations with the Lord, as Daniel did, seeking to understand
the future events revealed to them. In short, they expressed a fervent
desire to understand more fully the events that would unfold long
after their deaths.

Likely, the prophets' primary interest was discerning *when* their
predictions would be fulfilled. Perhaps they even hoped to see fulfillment in their day. However, these predictions are for a later time, as
Peter points out. The prophets simply didn't know the time of fulfillment, but Peter's readers are seeing the predictions come to pass. As
we see throughout the New Testament, Christ's suffering and glory
are common elements of gospel preaching (Acts 2:14-36; 3:11-26;
13:16-39).

Jesus makes it clear that his followers possess a unique opportunity: "Blessed are your eyes because they do see, and your ears because

they do hear. For truly I tell you, many prophets and righteous people longed to see the things you see but didn't see them, to hear the things you hear but didn't hear them" (Matt. 13:16-17).

After his resurrection, Jesus gently chides his two companions on the road to Emmaus:

> "How foolish you are, and how slow to believe all that the prophets have spoken! Wasn't it necessary for the Messiah to suffer these things and enter into his glory?" Then beginning with Moses and all the Prophets, he interpreted for them the things concerning himself in all the Scriptures (Luke 24:25-27).

Later, Paul testifies to King Agrippa:

> To this very day, I have had help from God, and I stand and testify to both small and great, saying nothing other than what the prophets and Moses said would take place — that the Messiah would suffer, and that, as the first to rise from the dead, he would proclaim light to our people and to the Gentiles (Acts 26:22-23).

While the Old Testament prophets "searched and carefully investigated," the eyewitnesses of Jesus actually see these prophecies fulfilled. The works of the Savior are more than fanciful stories; they are grounded in historical truth. The Gospel writer Luke confirms this, making it clear that he "carefully investigated everything from the very first" (Luke 1:3).

Second, the "Spirit of Christ" is the Holy Spirit. In harmony with the Father and the Son, the Spirit creates all things (Gen. 1:2; cf. Gen. 1:1; John 1:3; Col. 1:16). Further, throughout the Old Testament, the Spirit speaks, empowers, guides, and reveals the future. This same Spirit – the third person of the triune Godhead – is the one Jesus sends on the Day of Pentecost. Peter illustrates the collaborative work of the Trinity in salvation past, present, and future (see 1 Pet. 1:1-12). The same Spirit who inspired the prophets now speaks authoritatively through the gospel message.

Third, messianic prophecies were meant for later generations, specifically the first-century eyewitnesses and subsequent followers of Jesus. While these prophecies had great value to ancient Israelites, assuring them of God's promises to reverse the effects of the Fall through a second Adam, their fulfillment would come long after the deaths of the Old Testament prophets who received these revelations. Peter encourages his readers to marvel at the great privilege they have of seeing these prophecies fulfilled in their lifetimes.

Fourth, the same Holy Spirit who revealed future events to Old Testament prophets now confirms their fulfillment through the preaching of the gospel. Peter, an eyewitness of the resurrected Christ and a member of the Lord's inner circle of apostles, bears testimony to this.

Finally, the work of Christ continues to fascinate holy angels. Peter writes that "angels long to catch a glimpse of these things" (1 Pet. 1:12). The word "long" (Gr. *epithymeo*) is used in the New Testament to speak of very strong desires, both good and evil. Here, of course, the word refers to the good desires of holy angels. The verb is in the present tense and thus cannot be restricted to a former longing – that is, before Christ came. Rather, Peter reveals that angels continue to observe the unfolding redemption of Christ and desire to see more.

Wayne Grudem writes, "The longing must therefore include a holy curiosity to watch and delight in the glories of Christ's kingdom as they find ever fuller realization in the lives of individual Christians throughout the history of the church."[1]

The phrase "catch a glimpse" comes from the Greek *parakypto*. It means to peep into a situation from the vantage point of an outsider, usually one who himself or herself is not observed. Marvin Vincent notes that it is a "very graphic word, meaning to stoop sideways. Here it portrays one stooping and stretching the neck to gaze on some wonderful sight."[2]

The same Greek word occurs in James 1:25, describing one who looks into the perfect law of liberty as into a mirror. In Luke 24:12 and John 20:5 and 11, the term refers to Peter, John, and Mary stooping and looking into Christ's empty tomb. Perhaps the Holy Spirit revived this memory of the Resurrection in Peter's mind to inspire him to use this particular Greek term. The angels long for fresh insights into God's work of salvation, which they may only observe, not experience.

In summary, 1 Peter 1:10-12 shows us how Peter sees Old Testament messianic prophecies fulfilled in the life and work of Jesus of Nazareth – and how that fulfillment requires a first and second visit of Christ to earth.

LUKE'S VANTAGE POINT

Another example of New Testament passages revealing the two-stage nature of Messiah's redemptive work is Luke 4:16-20:

> He [Jesus] came to Nazareth, where he had been brought up. As usual, he entered the synagogue on the Sabbath day and stood up to read. The scroll of the prophet Isaiah was given to him, and unrolling the scroll, he found the place where it was written:
>
> The Spirit of the Lord is on me, because he has anointed me to preach good news to the poor. He has sent me to proclaim release to the captives and recovery of sight to the blind, to set free the oppressed, to proclaim the year of the Lord's favor.
>
> He then rolled up the scroll, gave it back to the attendant and sat down. And the eyes of everyone in the synagogue were fixed on him. He began by saying to them, "Today as you listen, this Scripture has been fulfilled."

Jesus chooses Isaiah 58:6 and 61:1-2 to emphasize his messianic consciousness as he begins his earthly ministry. He applies selected portions of these verses to himself, declaring their fulfillment in his life and work. Leon Morris explains, "Jesus saw himself as coming with good news for the world's troubled people. The acceptable year of the Lord does not, of course, represent any calendar year, but is a way of referring to the era of salvation."[3]

Perhaps most significant is that Jesus stops his quotation of Isaiah 61:2 in mid-sentence and then lays down the scroll. That's because the rest of that verse refers, not to Jesus' present ministry, but to his future coming: "… and the day of our God's vengeance."

Jesus tells his audience, "Today as you listen, this Scripture has been fulfilled" (Luke 4:20). The word "today" is key. Jesus' contemporaries are confident God's kingdom is coming *someday*. But Jesus tells them *today* is that day. There is a future day of God's vengeance, but that is not the present focus of Messiah's ministry. He has come to seek and to save the lost, and to call many to salvation.

The response to Jesus is telling. It begins with curiosity: "They were all speaking well of him and were amazed by the gracious words that came from his mouth; yet they said, 'Isn't this Joseph's son?'" (Luke 4:22). They are amazed at Jesus' words and astonished that someone from their own town, the apparent son of a carpenter, could speak with such eloquence. But they didn't take it to heart. His pedigree gives them pause. Jesus perceives their thoughts and responds with a three-fold rebuke.

First, he cites a proverb that reveals their desire for him to prove he is Messiah: "No doubt you will quote this proverb to me: 'Doctor, heal yourself. What we've heard that took place in Capernaum, do here in your hometown also'" (Luke 4:23). But Jesus is not about to meet their demands for further evidence. They have witnessed plenty. It's time to believe.

Second, Jesus says, "Truly I tell you, no prophet is accepted in his hometown" (Luke 4:24). He understands how the Israelites have a long history of rejecting the prophets God sends them. So, he leverages a common saying to predict his future rejection at the hands of religious leaders.

Third, Jesus recalls the history of Israel in the period of Elijah and Elisha:

> But I say to you, there were certainly many widows in Israel in Elijah's days, when the sky was shut up for three years and six months while a great famine came over all the land. Yet Elijah was not sent to any of

them except a widow at Zarephath in Sidon. And in the prophet Elisha's time, there were many in Israel who had leprosy, and yet not one of them was cleansed except Naaman the Syrian (Luke 4:25-27).

The days of Elijah and Elisha mark a low point in Israel's history, prompting God to move his works of mercy outside the nation into Gentile regions.

That does it. The crowd seethes with anger. The prospect of Messiah's blessings falling on the Gentiles, bypassing the Israelites, sticks in their craws. They drive Jesus to the edge of Nazareth and intend to hurl him off the cliff on which the town was built. Luke records, "But he passed right through the crowd and went on his way" (Luke 4:30).

This is not the only time the Israelites respond viscerally to Jesus' words. Some try to install him as king (John 6:15), while others seek to upend him as a Sabbath breaker (Luke 6:1-11). But a more common response is disappointment in Jesus, who seems uninterested in fulfilling the messianic prophecies of a political and military leader that rescues them from Roman oppression.

Clearly, many people are not ready to receive the Suffering Servant. They want the conquering king. Jesus, of course, is both. But by rejecting one, the people also reject the other and thus set the stage for future judgment: "the day of our God's vengeance" (Isa. 61:2).

Darrell Bock notes, "The price of rejecting God's message is severe: mercy moves on to other locales. It is quite risky to walk away from God's offer of deliverance. This exchange reveals the basic challenge of Jesus' ministry: the choice he presents carries high stakes."[4]

Now, let's look now at a sampling of Old Testament passages that point to Messiah's second coming.

SECOND COMING IN THE LAW

The first Old Testament reference to the second coming is found in Deuteronomy:

> When all these things happen to you — the blessings and curses I have set before you — and you come to your senses while you are in all the nations where the LORD your God has driven you, and you and your children return to the LORD your God and obey him with all your heart and all your soul by doing everything I am commanding you today, then he will restore your fortunes, have compassion on you, and gather you again from all the peoples where the LORD your God has scattered you (Deut. 30:1-3).

An alternative rendering of "restore your fortunes" is "bring you back from captivity." Surely, after Assyria's conquest of Israel in 722 B.C. and Babylon's conquest of Judah in 586 B.C., God brings back a remnant of Jews to their homeland. And the reestablishment of the State of Israel in 1948 ends a long Jewish drought after the Romans destroy the temple in A.D. 70. But Moses has an even longer view of God's work of redemption. The regathering of Israelites to their ancient land, and their physical and spiritual restoration, are ultimate acts of God in the last days.

As in Deuteronomy 30, the Old Testament "seldom pictures the Second Coming *per se*, but often dwells on the circumstances of the Second Coming, such as the … regathering of Israel to the land, and the results of the Second Coming – the judgment of the nations, deliverance of Israel, and a kingdom of righteousness and peace on earth."[5]

We see these future promises in the writings of Old Testament prophets.

For example:

Regathering of Israel to the land. Jeremiah records the words of the Lord:

> "... look, the days are coming" — this is the LORD's declaration —
> "when I will restore the fortunes of my people Israel and Judah," says
> the LORD. "I will restore them to the land I gave to their ancestors
> and they will possess it" (Jer. 30:3).

The prophet Amos writes:

> I will restore the fortunes of my people Israel. They will rebuild and
> occupy ruined cities, plant vineyards and drink their wine, make
> gardens and eat their produce. I will plant them on their land, and
> they will never again be uprooted from the land I have given them.
> The LORD your God has spoken (Amos 9:14-15).

While these and other prophecies carry a near-term promise of fulfillment – a return to the land after exile – their ultimate realization awaits the Messiah and his rule from the throne of David.

Judgment of the nations. Isaiah sees a glorious future for Judah and Jerusalem:

> He will settle disputes among the nations and provide arbitration for
> many peoples. They will beat their swords into plows and their spears
> into pruning knives. Nation will not take up the sword against nation,
> and they will never again train for war (Isa. 2:4).

All of this happens "in the last days" (Isa. 2:2). Many Old Testament prophets look ahead to the days when the Lord judges the nations that have abused God's chosen people. This may happen when one nation conquers Israel's enemies, such as the Persians displacing the Babylonians, but ultimately there is a future day when:

... the mountain of the LORD's house will be established at the top of the mountains and will be raised above the hills. All nations will stream to it, and many peoples will come and say, "Come, let's go up to the mountain of the LORD, to the house of the God of Jacob" (Isa. 2:2-3).

Deliverance of Israel. Jeremiah catches a glimpse of better days for his nation:

"Look, the days are coming" — this is the LORD's declaration — "when I will sow the house of Israel and the house of Judah with the seed of people and the seed of animals. Just as I watched over them to uproot and to tear them down, to demolish and to destroy, and to cause disaster, so will I watch over them to build and to plant them" — this is the LORD's declaration. "In those days, it will never again be said, 'The fathers have eaten sour grapes, and the children's teeth are set on edge'" (Jer. 31:27-29).

A kingdom of righteousness and peace on earth. Isaiah sees a coming day when Messiah ("a shoot ... from the stump of Jesse" – Isa. 11:1) establishes his Davidic kingdom of universal righteousness and peace:

The Spirit of the LORD will rest on him — a Spirit of wisdom and understanding, a Spirit of counsel and strength, a Spirit of knowledge and of the fear of the LORD. His delight will be in the fear of the LORD. He will not judge by what he sees with his eyes, he will not execute justice by what he hears with his ears, but he will judge the poor righteously and execute justice for the oppressed of the land. He will strike the land with a scepter from his mouth, and he will kill the wicked with a command from his lips. Righteousness will be a belt around his hips; faithfulness will be a belt around his waist. The wolf will dwell with the lamb, and the leopard will lie down with the goat. The calf, the young lion, and the fattened calf will be together, and a child will lead them. The cow and the bear will graze, their young ones will lie down together, and the lion will eat straw like cattle. An infant will play beside the cobra's pit, and a toddler will put his hand into a snake's den. They will not harm or destroy each other on my entire holy mountain, for the land will be as full of the knowledge of the LORD as the sea is filled with water (Isa. 11:2-9).

These and other Old Testament prophecies expand on Moses' words to the Israelites in Deuteronomy 30. Together, they form a mosaic that casts a beautiful image of Messiah's work of redemption and restoration.

SECOND COMING IN THE PSALMS

Often, the second coming of Christ is linked with the moral struggle between God and his creatures. Psalm 2 is a good example. The psalmist describes the world's rejection of God's sovereignty, and then declares God's purpose:

> "I have installed my king on Zion, my holy mountain." I will declare the LORD's decree. He said to me, "You are my Son; today I have become your Father. Ask of me, and I will make the nations your inheritance and the ends of the earth your possession. You will break them with an iron scepter; you will shatter them like pottery" (Ps. 2:6-9).

God fully intends to respond to the nations' rebellion against him. The Lord installs his Son as king of the earth. As a consequence, the kings of the earth are exhorted:

> So now, kings, be wise; receive instruction, you judges of the earth. Serve the LORD with reverential awe and rejoice with trembling. Pay homage to the Son or he will be angry and you will perish in your rebellion, for his anger may ignite at any moment. All who take refuge in him are happy (Ps. 2:10-12).

We should also consider Psalm 24, in which the writer declares that the earth and all that is in it belong to the Lord. After revealing that only those with clean hands and pure hearts may ascend the Lord's holy mountain, God exhorts the very gates of Jerusalem to open for his Son, the "King of glory":

> Lift up your heads, you gates! Rise up, ancient doors! Then the King of glory will come in. Who is this King of glory? The LORD, strong and mighty, the LORD, mighty in battle. Lift up your heads, you gates! Rise up, ancient doors!

> Then the King of glory will come in. Who is he, this King of glory? The LORD of Armies, he is the King of glory (Ps. 24:7-10).

Another prophecy of the second coming is Psalm 72, likely a coronation prayer used when one Davidic king dies and another comes to power. But it's more than that. It looks forward to the ultimate Davidic king – Messiah – and his reign on earth. Messiah's dominion is "from sea to sea" (v. 8). Kings and nations serve him (v. 11).

The promised benefits of the king's rule are not fulfilled in Solomon's day – at least not in the manner described in this psalm. Rather, we are to look for a future king who completes the Davidic line and sets everything right.

Psalm 72 ends with this prayer: "Blessed be the LORD God, the God of Israel, who alone does wonders. Blessed be his glorious name forever; the whole earth is filled with his glory" (vv. 18-19).

Psalm 96 declares, "The LORD reigns" (v. 10), and the psalmist concludes that the Lord is coming to judge the earth. "He will judge the world with righteousness and the peoples with his faithfulness" (v. 13).

Finally in this section, we should take special note of Psalm 110, the most-quoted psalm in the New Testament.[6] It features the declaration of the LORD (Yahweh) to David's Lord (the Messiah). Jesus applies this psalm to himself (Matt. 22:42-45). And eyewitnesses of

Jesus quote from the psalm to point their readers to him as its fulfillment (e.g., Acts 2:34-35; 1 Cor. 15:25, 27; Heb. 1:13; 10:13).

The first four verses record Yahweh's declaration of his Son as king and priest. The last three verses appear to be David's response to this oracle, with a depiction of Messiah as a warrior. Taking a New Testament perspective, we should see that the present position of Christ seated at the Father's right hand is temporary, for the day is coming when the LORD (Yahweh) sends forth David's Lord (Messiah) from Zion to execute judgment on the nations.

This is a fascinating psalm. Space permits just a few observations, beginning with verse 1: "Sit at my right hand until I make your enemies your footstool." This declaration comes into clear focus only when we get to the New Testament. It shows Messiah is:

Greater than David: In his sermon on the Day of Pentecost, Peter reminds his listeners, "it was not David who ascended into the heavens" (Acts. 2:34). And the writer of Hebrews notes, "Now to which of the angels has he [Yahweh] ever said: 'Sit at my right hand until I make your enemies your footstool'?" (Heb. 1:13).

Exalted by God though rejected by people: "The God of our ancestors raised up Jesus, whom you had murdered by hanging him on a tree. God exalted this man to his right hand as ruler and Savior ...." (Acts. 5:30-31).

Reigning today as Savior and intercessor: "Christ Jesus is the one who died, but even more, has been raised; he also is at the right hand of God and intercedes for us" (Rom. 8:34).

Seated as affirmation of his finished work: "Every priest stands day after day ministering and offering the same sacrifices time after time, which can never take away sins. But this man, after offering one sacrifice for sins forever, sat down at the right hand of God" (Heb. 10:11-12).

Waiting for the ultimate victory when his enemies surrender: "He is now waiting until his enemies are made his footstool" (Heb. 10:13; cf. 1 Cor. 15:25).

Coming as divine warrior to set things right (Rev. 19:11-21). This judgment is severe, complete, and certain. Even kings are unable to escape. The Messiah – his eyes aflame, his robe dipped in blood, and a sword proceeding from his mouth – not only destroys his enemies, he finishes the work he began as the Suffering Servant. He glorifies the saints, judges his enemies, and restores the sinful and fallen world to its pre-Fall perfection.

Psalm 110 celebrates the exaltation of Christ to the throne of an endless kingdom and a perpetual priesthood (Zech. 6:13). This involves "the subjugation of His enemies and the multiplication of His subjects, and rendered infallibly certain by the word and oath of Almighty God."[7]

Roger Ellsworth notes:

What a unique and delectable position David enjoyed! God had promised that the Messiah would physically descend from him. So the Messiah would be his son. But that same Messiah would be far more than a mere man. He would at one and the same time be God and man. The God-man! God in human flesh! So David's son would also be his Lord![8]

SECOND COMING IN THE PROPHETS

As in the law and in the psalms, the prophets foresee the coming reign of the Lord. Isaiah embraces both the Suffering Servant and the conquering king. Regarding the king's mission, Isaiah prophesies:

For a child will be born for us, a son will be given to us, and the government will be on his shoulders. He will be named Wonderful

Counselor, Mighty God, Eternal Father, Prince of Peace. The dominion will be vast, and its prosperity will never end. He will reign on the throne of David and over his kingdom, to establish and sustain it with justice and righteousness from now on and forever. The zeal of the LORD of Armies will accomplish this (Isa. 9:6-7).

In Isaiah 11, the prophet depicts Messiah's rule on earth as one of complete righteousness, justice, tranquility, and a universal knowledge of the Lord. And near the end of his book, Isaiah prays for the coming of the Lord: "If only you would tear the heavens open and come down, so that mountains would quake at your presence" (Isa. 64:1). Isaiah's prophecy concludes in chapters 65-66 with a description of Messiah's reign on earth, including his judgments and the restoration of the created order.

In a similar manner, Jeremiah anticipates the Lord's coming:

"Look, the days are coming" — this is the LORD's declaration — "when I will raise up a Righteous Branch for David. He will reign wisely as king and administer justice and righteousness in the land. In his days Judah will be saved, and Israel will dwell securely. This is the name he will be called: The LORD Is Our Righteousness" (Jer. 23:5-6).

Other passages in Jeremiah describe the deliverance of Israel and the ultimate triumph of God during the reign of Messiah. For example, chapters 30-31 look beyond the return of Judah from Babylonian captivity to a time when God restores the fortunes of Israel, and even raises up David to be king over his people again.

Daniel's vision of the Son of Man approaching the Ancient of Days reveals Messiah's dominion over the earth and his everlasting kingdom:

I continued watching in the night visions, and suddenly one like a son of man was coming with the clouds of heaven. He approached the Ancient of Days and was escorted before him. He was given dominion and glory and a kingdom, so that those of every people, nation, and language should serve him. His dominion is an everlasting dominion that will not pass away, and his kingdom is one that will not be destroyed (Dan. 7:13-14).

Jesus' reference to this passage – and to himself as "Son of Man" – seals the high priest's charge of blasphemy and results in a call for Jesus' death (Matt. 26:63-66).

The book of Joel describes the Day of the Lord through dramatic imagery such as locust swarms and fierce battles, enabling readers to grasp the magnitude of that coming day.

Joel's prophecy is unique in that there is no specific mention of Israel's sins, nor is there a specific time frame of which the prophet speaks. Yet the future events promise to bring terrible consequences. One day, God wipes out all evil and starts over again. The messianic king brings salvation to those who trust in him. Even more, the Holy Spirit comes in dramatic fashion, enabling ordinary men and women to experience visions, divine dreams, and the filling of God's Spirit (Joel 2:28-32).

Of course, that's exactly what happens on the Day of Pentecost, as Peter confirms (Acts 2:16-21). The coming of Christ has inaugurated the last days – an age marked by the finished work of the Suffering Servant, and ending with the return of the conquering king. That day, as Peter warns, draws ever nearer.

Finally, Zechariah describes a future day when the Lord comes to fight for his people:

> Then the LORD will go out to fight against those nations as he fights on a day of battle. On that day his feet will stand on the Mount of Olives, which faces Jerusalem on the east. The Mount of Olives will be split in half from east to west, forming a huge valley, so that half the mountain will move to the north and half to the south. You will flee by my mountain valley, for the valley of the mountains will extend to Azal. You will flee as you fled from the earthquake in the days of King Uzziah of Judah. Then the LORD my God will come and all the holy ones with him (Zech. 14:3-5).

The prophet goes on to reveal that "the LORD will become King over the whole earth — the LORD alone, and his name alone" (Zech. 14:9).

SUMMARY

The Old Testament offers hundreds of glimpses of Messiah's future reign on earth. At the same time, Moses, the psalmists, and the prophets tell us this coming Lion of Judah must first appear as the Lamb of God who takes away the sin of the world (John 1:29).

The breathtaking story unfolds as the eternal Son of God takes on flesh in a virgin's womb, lives a sinless life, is despised, rejected, beaten, and killed in gruesome fashion. The Son of Man then rises from the dead. He returns in victory to his Father in heaven, where he now awaits a glorious return to sit on the throne of David and rule the world in righteousness.

These Old Testament pictures are but types and shadows of their fulfillment in Jesus of Nazareth. They enable us to see through a glass darkly. But when Jesus is born in Bethlehem, the image of a singular figure who is both Suffering Servant and conquering king begins coming into sharper focus.

In stunning fashion, Jesus fulfills every Old Testament prophecy of Messiah's birthplace, manner of birth, sinless life, teaching style (parables), miracles, suffering, rejection, death, and resurrection. While the ancient prophecies of a conquering king have yet to be realized, their fulfillment is no less certain than the historic work of the Suffering Servant.

Jesus is coming again. You can take it to the bank. The Old Testament writers foresee a messianic age only Jesus can fulfill.

REVIEW

Key takeaways from this chapter

1. The Old Testament predicts both a Suffering Servant (Isa. 53) and a conquering king (Ps. 110). Jesus and the New Testament writers

help us see these two prophetic figures as the same person: the Messiah, whose redemptive work is carried out in two stages.

2. In his first epistle, Peter combines Jesus' first and second comings into a single narrative. The same Jesus who experienced the "sufferings of Christ" would also see "the glories" to follow (1 Pet. 1:10-12).

3. Jesus tells listeners in his hometown of Nazareth he is the fulfillment of Isaiah's messianic prophecy to "proclaim the year of the Lord's favor." But he stops short of declaring "the day of our God's vengeance," for that is a future work requiring his return (Luke 4:16-20; cf. Isa. 58:6; 61:1-2).

4. Old Testament prophecies of Messiah's return, beginning with Deuteronomy 30, seldom mention a second coming *per se*, but reveal promises of conditions on earth when the Day of the Lord comes: the regathering of Israel to the land; judgment of the nations; and a kingdom of righteousness and peace on earth.

5. Many psalms point to the coming Messiah and give us glimpses of his death, burial, and resurrection. But the psalm most often quoted in the New Testament is Psalm 110, which features the declaration of the LORD (Yahweh) to David's Lord (the Messiah) to sit at the LORD's right hand. Jesus applies this psalm to himself (Matt. 22:42-45). And eyewitnesses of Jesus quote from the psalm to point their readers to him as its fulfillment (e.g., Acts 2:34-35; 1 Cor. 15:25, 27; Heb. 1:13; 10:13).

6. Prophets such as Isaiah embrace both the Suffering Servant and conquering king. While Messiah is despised and rejected, bearing our sins (Isa. 53), "He will reign on the throne of David and over his kingdom, to establish and sustain it with justice and righteousness from now on and forever" (Isa. 9:7).

7. The first coming of Christ has inaugurated the last days – an age marked by the finished work of the Suffering Servant and ending with the return of the conquering king.

DISCUSS

Questions for personal or group study

1. How may we reconcile messianic prophecies of a Suffering Servant (Isa. 53) with visions of a Davidic king who comes in power (Ps. 110)?

2. Read Luke 4:16-20 and 1 Peter 1:10-12. How do these passages reveal the two-stage nature of Messiah's redemptive work – that is, his first and second comings?

3. Where do we find the first Old Testament reference to the second coming? Why isn't Moses more explicit in his description of a two-stage messianic mission?

4. What are some common themes running through the writings of Old Testament prophets concerning the last days? Hint: one theme is the regathering of Israel to the land.

5. Psalm 110 is the most-quoted psalm in the New Testament. Read Matthew 22:42-45 and explain how Jesus applies this prophecy to himself. Then, consider how eyewitnesses of Jesus quote from this psalm to point their readers to him as its fulfillment (Acts. 2:34-35; 1 Cor. 15:25; Heb. 1:13; 10:13).

* * *

SECTION II: BEHOLD ME

THE NATURE OF JESUS' RETURN

As the apostles stand on the Mount of Olives, gazing into the sky at their ascending Lord, two angels remind them this is not a final farewell: "This same Jesus, who has been taken from you into heaven, will come in the same way that you have seen him going into heaven" (Acts 1:11).

If "this same Jesus" is returning one day, what is that return like? This section deals with the nature of Christ's return. The New Testament teaches that Jesus is returning personally ("this same Jesus"), powerfully ("coming on the clouds"), victoriously (as "King of Kings and Lord of Lords"), and suddenly ("like a thief").

_____ A _____

While the incarnate Christ
suffers death, he emerges from
the tomb in glorified
immortality. As such, Jesus'
humanity does not and will
not suffer the ravages of time.

_____ Ω _____

"THIS SAME JESUS"

JESUS IS RETURNING PERSONALLY

*I*t's hard to imagine the apostles' thoughts as they gaze upward, watching Jesus ascend from the Mount of Olives and then vanish from view. Jesus had come unassumingly, born to a teenage mother in a Middle Eastern village. He lived his life humbly, refusing to be crowned king on numerous occasions, hiding his identity as Messiah until just the right moment, and then surrendering his life on a Roman cross.

Jesus' resurrection three days later proved his messianic claims and sealed his identity as Lord and Christ (Acts 2:36). He culled dozens of disciples until there were only twelve close followers – one of them a betrayer, as Jesus well knew. And he sought to prepare them for just this moment, when he returned to the Father and passed the gospel torch to his newly commissioned apostles.

But now he's gone, his glorified body rising into the air, enveloped in a heavenly cloud, to assume his place at the Father's right hand. The apostles still have questions, doubts, and apprehensions. They aren't ready to be left alone. And that's how it must have felt – left alone – with Jesus bidding them farewell.

They know it isn't quite like that. Jesus had assured them he would always be with them – even until the end of the age (Matt. 28:20). And he promised to send the Holy Spirit – another counselor, another comforter, another advocate just like him. But would they really see him again? If so, how soon? And how would they carry on an earthbound ministry with Jesus in heaven?

They don't have to wonder long. Luke records:

> … he was taken up as they were watching, and a cloud took him out of their sight. While he was going, they were gazing into heaven, and suddenly two men in white clothes stood by them. They said, "Men of Galilee, why do you stand looking up into heaven? This same Jesus, who has been taken from you into heaven, will come in the same way that you have seen him going into heaven" (Acts 1:9-11).

The two men in white clothes are angels. They urge the eyewitnesses to take on the mantle of their apostolic calling. Equally important, the angels remind the apostles that Christ's absence from the earth is temporary. The Lord *is* returning one day, even if the day and hour are hidden from them. This same Jesus – the resurrected and glorified God-Man – is coming back to set things right. Further, he's coming back in the same way: personally, physically, visibly, powerfully, and to the same location.

Followers of Jesus are not to stand idly, gazing into the heavens and watching for his return. We're to be busy, engaging in the gospel ministry he has entrusted to us. So, let's look at what it means for Jesus to return *personally* one day. More to the point, let's see what the angels mean when they say "this same Jesus" will return "in the same way."

THIS SAME JESUS

First, we need to guard against a woodenly literal understanding of the angels' words to the apostles. We are not to expect the return of Jesus to be like a video replay in reverse, with the Lord wearing the same clothes, touching the same spot on the Mount of Olives, and appearing privately to the eleven apostles. Quite the contrary.

While Jesus ascends in the common clothing of his day, he returns in a robe dipped in blood (Rev. 19:13). While he ascends carrying no weapons, he returns with a sword proceeding from his mouth – the same divine word by which he created all things (Rev. 19:15; cf. Gen. 1-2; Ps. 33:6, 9; John 1:1-3; Heb. 11:3). While he ascends alone, he returns in the company of holy angels and redeemed people (Luke 9:26; cf. 1 Thess. 4:14ff; 2 Thess. 1:7). While he ascends in the presence of a few eyewitnesses, he returns so that every eye sees him (Rev. 1:7; cf. Zech. 12:10). And while he ascends without great fanfare, he returns like lightning, which flashes across the sky (Luke 17:23-24).

So then, who is "this same Jesus" the apostles see ascending into heaven and vanishing from their gaze? At the very least, the angels make it clear that the Jesus they've come to love is true to his word. He's returning to earth one day to sit on the throne of David. He's coming back *himself* – not sending an agent or an angelic substitute. Jesus' promise to return is going to be fulfilled, even though the day and hour have not been revealed (Matt. 24:36; John 14:1-3).

But why do the angels say "this same Jesus" is coming back? Why emphasize the *sameness* of the Savior? It may be a reminder to the apostles, and to us, who Jesus really is and what he accomplished throughout his earthly ministry. In addition, it may be a call to be alert for counterfeit Christs.

Jesus is the same person both before and after the Incarnation. As the writer of Hebrews notes, Christ is the same "yesterday, today, and forever" (Heb. 13:8). The difference is that before the Incarnation, Jesus had but one nature (divine). In the Incarnation, he adds a human nature, one that exists together with his divine nature. While the incarnate Christ suffers death, he emerges from the tomb in glorified immortality. As such, Jesus' humanity will not suffer the ravages of time.

There are several key attributes that make Jesus unique and ensure that he – *this same Jesus* – must return to fulfill his promises.

First, Jesus is the eternal Son of God, the second person of the Trinity.

Jesus of Nazareth is a real person whose earthly life is grounded in history. At the same time, he is unique in that his conception in

Mary's virgin womb is not the beginning of his existence. The Bible reveals Jesus as the eternal Son of God whose deity and personhood extend from eternity past to eternity future. In becoming a man, Jesus adds sinless humanity to his deity, yet he does not become a different person.

While there's much in the Old Testament that hints at Messiah's eternal existence,[1] we see more clearly in the New Testament that Jesus is an eternal, divine person:

- He is the Word who creates all things (John 1:1-3).
- He exists before Abraham as the eternal I AM (John 8:58).
- He shares the glory of the Father before the world exists (John 17:5).
- He becomes flesh – that is, he adds sinless humanity to his deity (John 1:14).
- He is equal with God the Father (John 10:30; Phil. 2:6).
- He is the radiance of God's glory and the exact expression of God's nature (Heb. 1:3).
- He is the First and the Last, the Living One (Rev. 1:17-18).

Further, Jesus exists as a divine person distinct from the Father and the Spirit, yet in intimate fellowship with them. John depicts Jesus as living from all eternity in "the bosom of the Father" (John 1:18 NASB 1995), an ancient metaphor for love and intimacy. Later in John's Gospel, Jesus describes the Spirit as living to "glorify" Jesus (John 16:14). At the same time, the Son glorifies the Father (John 17:4) and the Father glorifies the Son (John 17:5).

We should note the many times Jesus claims equality with God. In John 10:30, Jesus states, "I and the Father are one." His frequent reference to God as Father – especially by the intimate term *Abba*, or Papa – rankles the religious leaders. John writes, "This is why the Jews began trying all the more to kill him … he was even calling God his own Father, making himself equal to God" (John 5:18).

In his high priestly prayer, Jesus anticipates once again sharing the glory he had with the Father before the world existed (John 17:5).

This is a telling claim, for the Old Testament makes it clear that God does not share his glory with anyone (Isa. 42:8; 48:11).

There is much more we could explore about the Trinity.[2] But for now, let's provide a simple definition. The word *Trinity* comes from the Latin *trinitas*, meaning "threeness." So, *Trinity* is a term used to describe the one true and living God, who exists as three distinct-yet-inseparable, co-equal, co-eternal persons – Father, Son, and Holy Spirit.

As *The Baptist Faith & Message* explains, "The eternal triune God reveals Himself to us as Father, Son, and Holy Spirit, with distinct personal attributes, but without division of nature, essence, or being."[3]

There is no doubt *this same Jesus* is the eternal Son of God, the second person of the Trinity.

Second, Jesus is the God-Man, fully divine and fully human.

Jesus is one person possessing two distinct natures: a completely divine nature and a completely human nature. Thus, we call Jesus of Nazareth the God-Man.

Through his divine nature, Jesus is God the Son, the second person of the Trinity, who shares the one divine essence fully and equally with the Father and the Holy Spirit. For example, when Jesus declares, "I and the Father are one," he means one in essence, not just purpose. The unbelieving Jews who hear these words get the meaning, for they seek to stone him for blasphemy (John 10:30-33).

Through his human nature, Jesus possesses and exhibits all the essential attributes of a human being. He gets tired, hungry, and thirsty. He feels pain, experiences abandonment, and dies.

Jesus, as one person, retains all the attributes of both natures. For example, through his divine nature, he is omniscient, while simultaneously and voluntarily, through his human nature, he experiences a temporary lack of knowledge on some matters (e.g., Matt. 24:36).

The union of Jesus' two natures is a true union. In other words, it is not simply the indwelling of the divine presence in a human being, as is the case with Christians whom the Holy Spirit indwells. Rather, in Jesus, the divine and the human come together in one person.

The two natures form a perfect, complementary union. The human nature of Jesus is never without the divine nature, nor the divine without the human. To deny the deity of Christ at any point in eternity is to undermine his eternal existence as the sovereign creator. To deny the full humanity of Jesus at any point after his miraculous conception in a virgin's womb is to refuse his necessary sacrifice on our behalf as the Word who became flesh (John 1:14).

Jesus' two natures – divine and human – are distinct and inseparably united in one person. The two natures retain their own attributes or qualities and thus are not mixed together. The human nature is not deified – that is, Jesus' humanity does not become divine – and the divine nature does not suffer human limitations.[4]

Our efforts to defend the deity of Jesus, however, require us to grapple with the unique challenges his humanity presents. Critics of the orthodox view of Jesus as the God-Man may ask: If Jesus is God, why doesn't he know the day or hour of his return (Mark 13:32)? Why does Jesus get tired, thirsty, and hungry (Mark 11:12; John 4:6; 19:28)? Why does he insist that the Father is greater than he is (John 14:28)? And, if Jesus truly is divine, how is it possible for God to die (John 19:30)?

These are challenging questions. If the Incarnation means that Jesus is completely divine and completely human at the same time, never surrendering one nature to the other, how might we explain the apparent absence of divine attributes at certain times in our Savior's life?

Theologian Bruce Ware provides marvelous insight into the two natures of Christ in *The Man Christ Jesus*. He begins with an exposition of Philippians 2:5-8, which expresses the self-emptying of the eternal Son as he takes on human nature.

First, Ware notes that Paul expresses no doubts about the deity of Christ. The phrase "though he was in the form of God" (Phil. 2:6 ESV) employs the Greek word *morphe*, which refers to the inner nature or substance of something, not its external or outward shape. Therefore, Paul's point is clear: Jesus, being in the "form" of God, exists in very nature as God, with the inner divine substance that is God's alone.

Second, when Paul writes that Christ "did not count equality with God a thing to be grasped" (Phil. 2:6 ESV), he cannot mean that Christ gave up equality with God or that he ceased to be fully God. Rather, Jesus did not cling to his privileged position at the Father's right hand, or to the rights and prerogatives that go along with full equality with the Father. Instead, he fulfilled his mission as the servant of all.

Third, Jesus "emptied himself, by taking the form of a servant" (Phil. 2:7 ESV). The Greek word rendered "emptied himself" is *ekenosen.* It means Christ "poured out himself." In other words, all of Christ, as eternal God, is poured into human skin. As Jesus becomes man, he loses nothing of his divine nature.

Fourth, Jesus "humbled himself by becoming obedient to the point of death, even death on a cross" (Phil. 2:8 ESV). Ware notes, "This is the obedience that accepts suffering, rejection, ridicule, and agony. Surely the Son, in eternity past, never had to embrace this kind of obedience in his relation to the Father.... To obey to the point of death requires the ability to die, and for this, Jesus had to be human."[5]

So, when we come to passages that tell us Jesus doesn't know something, or gets hungry or thirsty, or dies, we may understand that Jesus neither surrenders his deity nor abandons his claims of divinity. Rather, "He had to be like His brothers in every way, so that He could become a merciful and faithful high priest in service to God, to make propitiation for the sins of the people" (Heb. 2:17 HCSB).

There is no doubt that *this same Jesus* is the God-Man, fully divine and fully human.

Third, Jesus is the Son of Man, the unique divine being in Daniel 7 who receives a kingdom from the Ancient of Days.

Jesus calls himself *Son of Man* some eighty times in the Gospels – a term that embraces the Messiah's humanity while illuminating his deity. Consider Daniel 7:9, 13-14:

As I kept watching, thrones were set in place, and the Ancient of Days took his seat. His clothing was white like snow, and the hair of his head like whitest wool. His throne was flaming fire; its wheels were blazing fire.... I continued watching in the night visions, and suddenly one like a

son of man was coming with the clouds of heaven. He approached the
Ancient of Days and was escorted before him. He was given dominion,
and glory, and a kingdom; so that those of every people, nation, and
language should serve him. His dominion is an everlasting dominion that
will not pass away, and his kingdom is one that will not be destroyed.

While some interpret "one like a son of man" as an angel (perhaps
Michael), and others see him as a personification of the people of God
(Israel), Jesus connects himself with this passage.

In Mark 14, Caiaphas, the high priest, asks Jesus, "Are you the
Messiah, the Son of the Blessed One?"

Jesus replies, "I am … and you will see the *Son of Man* seated at the
right hand of Power and coming with the clouds of heaven"
(Mark 14:61-62, emphasis added).

The high priest tears his robes and says, "Why do we still need
witnesses? You have heard the blasphemy" (vv. 63-64). This affirms
Caiaphas' understanding of the "son of man" in Daniel 7:13 as a divine
person.

We should note that the expression "son of man" occurs frequently
in the Old Testament as a synonym for "man." A son of man is by
nature man himself. It is a Semitic idiom signifying "human being," as
virtually all of the 107 occurrences in the Old Testament bear out.[6]

However, in Daniel 7, and in a more subtle way in Psalm 8, the
term *Son of Man* goes further. When applied to Jesus, the designation
Son of Man means he is human as we are, a son of Adam, and that he is
the coming Messiah, who has been given authority by the Most High
and reigns over his kingdom through his weakness, seen most clearly
at the cross.[7]

As Daniel notes in his vision, one "like a son of man" conquers the
evil world system (Dan. 7:9-13), obtains authority to rule over God's
kingdom (vv. 13-14), and exercises that authority universally, sharing
his rule with the people of God (vv. 15-28). As Fred Zaspel notes,
"What is striking here is that God's kingdom is given to 'one like a son
of man' – God's kingdom in the hands of a man!"[8]

We may identify several broad associations with Jesus' self-designation as "Son of Man."

First, Jesus claims universal authority even during his earthly ministry. For example, he affirms that "the Son of Man is Lord of the Sabbath" (Matt. 12:8). He has the authority on earth to forgive sins (Matt. 9:6). And he has all authority in heaven and on earth (Matt. 28:18).

Second, Jesus uses the title "Son of Man" in connection with his rejection, suffering, death, and resurrection. For example, Jesus tells his followers the Son of Man must suffer many things, be rejected by the elders, chief priests, and scribes, be killed, and then after three days rise again (Matt. 16:21; Mark 8:31; 9:31; Luke 9:44). Yet it is through his earthly ministry of suffering, death, and resurrection that Jesus defeats Satan, sin, and death and achieves his exalted role as kingly mediator (Matt. 28:18; Acts 2:36; Phil. 2:9.) This is why we may rightly see Jesus reigning from the cross. In his seeming defeat, he rescues us by taking our place, and he brings us into God's kingdom (Col. 1:13; Rev. 5:9-10).

Third, the Son of Man realizes his kingship in stages. His kingdom is both now and not-yet. He is born a king, the promised Son of David (Matt. 2:2). He exercises his kingship throughout his earthly ministry (Matt. 12:28). He firmly establishes his kingship through his suffering, death, and resurrection (John 12:31-32). He rules today as our mediator and intercessor in heaven (Acts 2:36; Eph. 1:20-21). Even so, his kingdom is yet to be realized in fullness.

Which brings us to a fourth association between Jesus and the designation "Son of Man": his return in glory. Jesus tells us the Son of Man is returning to sit on his glorious throne (Matt. 19:28). He is coming on the clouds with power and great glory (Matt. 24:29-31). He is coming with his angels (Matt. 25:31). And he is returning victoriously on a white horse to reign forever (Rev. 19:11-16).

It's important to note that Jesus' self-understanding is steeped in Old Testament depictions of Yahweh. For example, Jesus claims that God's angels are his angels (Matt. 13:41; Luke 12:8-9) and that God's kingdom is his kingdom (Matt. 19:23-24; John 18:36). He also makes it clear that all judgment is his (John 5:22).

Further, Jesus applies several Old Testament references of divinity to himself. When the children gathered in the temple shout, "Hosanna to the Son of David," prompting the chief priests and scribes to react in rage, Jesus responds by applying Psalm 8:2 to himself: "Yes, have you never read: You have prepared praise from the mouths of infants and nursing babies?" (Matt. 21:16).

At another time, Jesus identifies the tenant farmers in the parable of the vineyard owner with the chief priests and scribes of his day, pointing them to Psalm 118:22 and Isaiah 8:14-15: "But he looked at them and said, 'Then what is the meaning of this Scripture: The stone that the builders rejected has become the cornerstone? Everyone who falls on that stone will be broken to pieces, but on whomever it falls, it will shatter him'" (Luke 20:17-18). The application of the parable is clear: Jesus is the Son who is killed, prompting divine retribution.

Jesus identifies John the Baptist as the fulfillment of God's promise to send Elijah before the Day of the Lord. In so doing, Jesus declares himself Yahweh, who comes in judgment (Mal. 3:1; 4:5-6; Matt. 11:10-15). And the judgment scene Jesus describes in the parable of the sheep and goats harkens back to several Old Testament passages foretelling a day of Yahweh's judgment (Matt. 25:31-46; cf. Dan. 7:9-10; Joel 3:1-16; Zech. 14:4ff).

It's clear that Jesus and the New Testament writers see threads of Old Testament messianic prophecies in a fresh light, revealing a rich tapestry of the Messiah's eternal existence, omnipotence, and sovereignty.

What's more, we may discover the preincarnate Christ in a most curious Old Testament figure known as the angel of the LORD. This divine messenger appears dozens of times across the pages of the Hebrew Scriptures. He not only speaks for God; he speaks *as* God. He appears as a man, a voice from heaven, a flame within a thorn bush, and a divine presence in a pillar of cloud and fire – all of which come to us as *Christophanies*, or appearances of the preincarnate Christ.[9]

There is no doubt *this same Jesus* is the Son of Man, the divine being in Daniel 7 who receives a kingdom from the Ancient of Days.

Fourth, Jesus is the Messiah, or Christ – the anointed one.

Eyewitnesses lavish the pages of the Greek New Testament with depictions of Jesus as the *Christ*, which means "anointed one," as does its Aramaic/Hebrew synonym "Messiah." Curiously, however, this title is not consistently applied to Jesus until after his ascension. Even more striking is the realization that Jesus largely avoids applying the terms "Messiah" or "Christ" to himself. Why?

As T. D. Alexander notes, the designation "Messiah" had acquired misleading connotations among Jews by the first century. So, he writes, "Jesus re-educated his followers so that they would have a more accurate appreciation of how the concept of Anointed/Christ/Messiah should be understood in light of Old Testament teaching."[10]

There is great expectation of a coming Messiah in the first century. Yet Jesus' contemporaries are looking for a king who exercises political and military clout in order to drive the Romans from Israel. Certainly, Jesus is born a king (Matt. 2:1-6). One day, he will sit on the throne of David and exercise his authority as King of kings and Lord of lords. But before reigning as king, he must come as the Suffering Servant. And this is the reality his followers struggle to grasp. Jesus must teach them that political boundaries and great armies cannot define his kingdom. Rather, his kingdom welcomes redeemed sinners from every nation and ethnicity.

The English word "Messiah" is derived from the Greek *messias*, which appears only twice in the New Testament (John 1:41; 4:25), where it's used to transliterate the Aramaic word *mesiha* or the Hebrew *masiah*.[11] To assist his Greek-speaking readers, John explains the meaning of *messias* by translating it as *christos*, the Greek term for "one who has been anointed."

Since it would have been meaningless to non-Aramaic speakers, the word *messias* is rarely used in the Greek New Testament. Rather, *christos* appears nearly 530 times, mostly in direct reference to Jesus of Nazareth. In fact, the English terms "Jesus Christ" and "Christ Jesus" occur a combined 127 times in the New Testament, signifying that Jesus is the anointed one of God.[12]

While the title "Messiah" or "Christ" is rarely applied to Jesus during his earthly ministry, all four Gospel writers confidently affirm that Jesus is the anointed one. Consider what John writes:

> Jesus performed many other signs in the presence of his disciples that are not written in this book. But these are written so that you may believe that Jesus is the Messiah, the Son of God, and that by believing you may have life in his name (John 20:30-31).

We see this in the Synoptic Gospels (Matthew, Mark, and Luke) as well, perhaps most notably in Peter's declaration that Jesus is "the Messiah, the Son of the living God" (Matt. 16:16; cf. Mark 8:29; Luke 9:20). This expresses the Old Testament expectation that God one day will send a king, linked to the Davidic dynasty, to fulfill his redemptive purposes on earth. This idea of Jesus as king is prominent in the events that surround his execution, from Pilate's interrogation (Matt. 27:11; Mark 15:2, 9, 12; Luke 23:3; John 18:33, 39), to the soldiers' mocking (Matt. 27:29; John 19:2-3), to the sign placed above Jesus on the cross (Matt. 27:37; Mark 15:26; Luke 23:38; John 19:19, 21).

The idea of Jesus as the anointed king is linked to his identification as the Son of God. The Father speaks of Jesus as his Son at Jesus' baptism and transfiguration (Mark 1:9-11; 9:2-8). Further, Jesus frequently speaks of God as his Father, especially in John's Gospel.

Even so, Jesus avoids the widespread application of "Messiah" or "Christ" to himself, preferring "Son of Man" to illustrate his role as the God-Man who comes to rule through his humiliation, suffering, death, and resurrection. The best explanation for this, according to Alexander, is the broad expectation that Messiah would revive the fortunes of the Jewish people as a nation, bringing them freedom from the yoke of Roman occupation.

For example, in the Psalms of Solomon, a text composed around 50 B.C., reflecting the views of the Pharisees, the Messiah would violently cast out the foreign nations occupying Jerusalem; judge all the nations of the earth and cause these nations to serve him; reign over Israel in wisdom and righteousness, which involves removing all foreigners from the land and purging the land of unrighteous Israelites; eliminate all oppression; and gather to himself a holy people.[13]

So, it's hardly surprising that when Peter confesses Jesus as the Messiah, he is flabbergasted that Jesus follows up with predictions of his own suffering and death (Matt. 16:21). "Oh no, Lord!" Peter declares. "This will never happen to you!" (v. 22). Jesus responds powerfully to Peter's rebuke: "Get behind me, Satan!" (v. 23).

Even John the Baptist expresses doubts about Jesus. After touting him as one sent by God to punish the wicked (Matt. 3:10-12), John is imprisoned and seemingly forgotten. He sends a message to Jesus through his disciples, asking, "Are you the one who is to come, or should we expect someone else?" (Matt. 11:2-3). Jesus responds by pointing to his miracles as affirmation of his messianic authenticity (vv. 4-6).

After his betrayal and arrest, Jesus tells Pilate, "My kingdom is not of this world" (John 18:36). Jesus does not come to establish his kingdom through political or military means, but by giving his life as an atoning sacrifice for the sin of the world. When he enters Jerusalem triumphantly on Palm Sunday, he rides a donkey – a symbol of peace – not a warrior's steed (Matt. 21:1-11; Mark 11:1-10; Luke 19:29-38; John 12:12-15).

In short, Jesus re-educates his followers as to the identity and role of the Messiah. Yes, he is the conquering king who sits on the throne of David, judges all people, and rules the world. But first, he must come humbly, as the Suffering Servant of Isaiah 53, to give his life as a ransom for us. That's why he resists being made king, and why he rarely acknowledges his messianic title.

Even in his parables, Jesus makes it clear that the kingdom of God comes in stages, with the Messiah's suffering, death, and resurrection first, followed at an unknown future date by the glorious return of the king (Matt. 13:1-52; 20:1-16; 21:28-46; 22:1-14; 24:32-51; 25:1-46).

On the Day of Pentecost, the same Peter who rebuked Jesus for

revealing his plans to suffer and die now acknowledges the enthronement of the Messiah at the right hand of God:

> For it was not David who ascended into the heavens, but he himself
> says:
>> The Lord declared to my Lord,
>> "Sit at my right hand until I make your enemies your footstool."
> Therefore let all the house of Israel know with certainty that God
> has made this Jesus, whom you crucified, both Lord and Messiah (Acts
> 2:34-36).

As the ascended Messiah, Jesus eventually brings the whole earth
under his authority, welcoming a new age of universal harmony in
fulfillment of Old Testament expectations (Acts 3:19-21).

There is no doubt *this same Jesus* is the Messiah, or Christ, the
anointed one of God. Having finished the work of redemption, he sits
at the Father's right hand, awaiting the day of his glorious return.

Fifth, Jesus is the resurrected Savior.

When Jesus returns, there is no doubt as to his identity. This is
crucial for us to remember, for the Savior warns us that false messiahs
will arise and deceive many; they'll even perform great signs and
wonders (Matt. 24:5, 24). But when Jesus comes back, he bears proof
he is the resurrected and glorified Christ. His physical body, shim-
mering with divine glory, also bears the marks of his crucifixion
(Luke 24:39-40; John 20:20, 27; Rev. 5:6).

The finished work of Jesus doesn't end with his death on a Friday
afternoon. There must be a Sunday morning. More to the point, the
gospel message is incomplete without Jesus' physical resurrection.

We should note that the phrase "physical resurrection" is something of an oxymoron, for only the body may rightly be brought back
to life. The immaterial parts of human beings – their souls/spirits –
are not extinguished in physical death.

Further, the Greek *anastasis*, which appears forty-two times in
forty New Testament verses and nearly always is translated "resurrection," describes the restoration of physical life. In Jesus' encounters

with the Sadducees (Matt. 22:23-32), Peter's sermon on the Day of Pentecost (Acts 2:14-36), Paul's address on Mars Hill (Acts 17:16-34), as well as Paul's exhortation to the Corinthians (1 Cor. 15), and in every other New Testament defense of the resurrection, the physical body is in view.

In fact, spiritual resurrection is a biblical impossibility. Unbelievers are indeed spiritually dead. That is, while physically alive and conscious, those who have rejected Christ are cut off from the indwelling presence of God. They are dead in their trespasses and sins (Eph. 2:1), alienated from God and hostile toward him (Col. 1:21), and in bondage to the evil one (2 Tim. 2:26).

As a remedy to spiritual death, however, they do not need a spiritual resurrection. Rather, the Holy Spirit must *regenerate* unbelievers, making their dead human spirits alive, and enabling them to come to faith in Christ, who grants them everlasting life (John 3:3-8; 6:37-40; 10:28). Scripture is clear that followers of Jesus are regenerated, or born again, as a result of Christ's death and resurrection, confirmed through "the living and enduring word of God" (1 Pet. 1:18-23).

But for regeneration and the other benefits of salvation to be available at all, Jesus must die physically and rise from the dead. He tells his followers, "The hour has come for the Son of Man to be glorified. Truly I tell you, unless a grain of wheat falls to the ground and dies, it remains by itself. But if it dies, it produces much fruit" (John 12:23-24).

Paul uses the same analogy to address questions the Corinthians pose about the resurrection (1 Cor. 15:35-38). The resurrected body is different in form from the buried corpse. Comparing the human body to grain, Paul argues that the seed and stalk are one and the same. But the stalk – like the resurrected body of Jesus – is the glorified version.

As Eugene Carpenter and Philip Comfort note:

> This illustration shows that Jesus' resurrected body was altogether different from the one that was buried. In death, He had been sown in corruption, dishonor, and weakness; but in resurrection, He came forth perfect, in glory and power. The natural body that Jesus

possessed as a man became a spiritual body. And at the same time Christ became a "life-giving spirit."[14]

Leading up to his crucifixion, Jesus stakes his identity as the Son of Man on his future resurrection. When the scribes and Pharisees demand a sign, he replies, "An evil and adulterous generation demands a sign, but no sign will be given to it except the sign of the prophet Jonah. For as Jonah was in the belly of the huge fish three days and three nights, so the Son of Man will be in the heart of the earth three days and three nights" (Matt. 12:39-41).

After Jesus cleanses the temple, some Jews demand, "What sign will you show us for doing these things?"

Jesus answers, "Destroy this temple, and I will raise it up in three days."

The Jews marvel: "This temple took forty-six years to build, and will you raise it up in three days?"

But John tells us that Jesus is speaking "about the temple of his body. So when he was raised from the dead, his disciples remembered that he had said this, and they believed the Scripture and the statement Jesus had made" (John 2:18-22).

After his resurrection, Jesus goes out of his way to affirm he is alive in the flesh – a glorified Son of Man. He appears multiple times to his disciples, and to more than five hundred people on one occasion (1 Cor. 15:5-8). He invites Thomas to touch the scars of his crucifixion and thus believe (John 20:24-29). He eats a piece of broiled fish in the presence of his disciples, dispelling their fear that he is a ghost (Luke 24:36-43).

Ascending into heaven, Jesus returns to the Father's right hand, still bearing the marks of his finished work at Calvary. John is granted a vision of heaven and sees "one like a slaughtered lamb standing in the midst of the throne" (Rev. 5:6). Later, John describes Jesus as "the Lamb who was slaughtered" (Rev. 13:8).

When Jesus returns, he continues to bear the marks of his crucifixion, clearly distinguishing himself from all imposters. John tells us, "Look, he is coming with the clouds, and every eye will see him, even those who pierced him" (Rev. 1:7; cf. Zech. 12:10). As Christ descends to earth, he wears a robe dipped in blood, which may be his own blood shed for our redemption (Rev. 19:13).

All of this is to dispel any doubt that the returning Jesus is *this same Jesus* – the crucified and resurrected Savior who has come to put an end to death once and for all.

THE SAME WAY

Now that we've explored several defining attributes of *this same Jesus*, let's consider what the angels may have meant when they told the apostles Jesus is returning *the same way* they witnessed his departure.

First, Jesus himself is coming.

When Jesus returns, he's not sending a prophet, apostle, angel, cherub, hologram, selfie, MailChimp marketing blast, or any other substitute. He's coming *himself*. Further, Jesus isn't appearing as a theophany – a flame in a desert thorn bush, a pillar of cloud and fire, a rider on a blazing chariot-throne, or a voice in a whirlwind. He's coming as the same resurrected Son of Man who ascended physically into heaven in the presence of his apostles (Acts 1:9). The return of Jesus always is portrayed in personal terms. Jesus tells his disciples, "I will come again and take you to myself, so that where I am you may be also" (John 14:3).

Note just a few places where Jesus assures us *he* is coming. In the Olivet Discourse, Jesus tells his disciples, "be alert, since you don't know what day *your Lord* is coming ... the *Son of Man* is coming at an hour you do not expect" (Matt. 24:42, 44, emphasis added). Later, as he begins the parable of the sheep and goats, Jesus says, "When the Son of Man comes ...." (Matt. 25:31). Several times in the Book of Revelation, Jesus points to his personal return: "I am coming soon" (3:11); "Look, I am coming soon!" (22:7, 12); "Yes, I am coming soon" (22:20).

The New Testament authors clearly understand this. Their writings reflect the universal expectation of Jesus' personal return. For example, Paul tells us we observe the Lord's Supper as a memorial of

Christ's death "until he comes" (1 Cor. 11:26). Our citizenship is in heaven, from which our Savior, the Lord Jesus Christ, is coming (Phil. 3:20). And, as followers of Jesus, we wait eagerly for "the appearing of the glory of our great God and Savior, Jesus Christ" (Tit. 2:13).

The writer of Hebrews tells us Christ "will appear a second time ... to bring salvation to those who are waiting for him" (Heb. 9:28). And Peter exhorts the elders to look forward to the day "the chief Shepherd appears" (1 Pet. 5:4).

Even the angels who promise the return of Jesus after his ascension are careful to tell the apostles, "This same Jesus, who has been taken from you into heaven, will come ...." (Acts 1:10-11). Jesus himself is returning – not a proxy.

The unfinished business of our salvation requires the personal return of Jesus. The Messiah must:

- Sit on the throne of David (Luke 1:32-33)
- Rule the nations with an iron scepter (Rev. 2:26-27; cf. Ps. 2:9)
- Resurrect and judge all people (John 5:22, 29)
- Abolish all competing kingdoms and authorities (1 Cor. 15:24-27)
- Reward the faithful and damn the rebellious (John 5:28-29)
- Separate the sheep and goats (Matt. 25:31-46)
- Banish Satan, evil spirits, and wicked people to the lake of fire (Matt. 25:41; Rev. 20:10-15)
- Put away death and the intermediate state (Rev. 20:14)
- And create new heavens and a new earth (2 Pet. 3:10-13; Rev. 21-22)

Just as God sent his Son to be the Savior of the world, so Jesus is the one who has been granted all authority (Matt. 28:19), all judgment (John 5:22), and all glory (John 17:22).

There is no doubt that for Jesus to return "in the same way" he left means Jesus himself is coming.

Second, Jesus is coming physically.

As we noted earlier in this chapter, Jesus pins his messianic claims on his physical resurrection. He foretells his resurrection as the one sign given to the unbelieving generation that witnesses the Incarnation (Matt. 12:39-41; cf. John 2:18-22). And after he rises from the dead, Jesus and the apostles make it clear he is glorified flesh and bone, not an apparition (Luke 24:36-43; John 20:24-29; 1 Cor. 15:5-8).

The apostles gaze into the sky as Jesus ascends into heaven (Acts 1:9), perhaps in part because they wonder how a physical body can enter the unseen realm. Nevertheless, Jesus has told them he is returning to his Father (John 16:5, 10), and he's promised to come back to earth one day (see Chapter 1). All of this involves a physical body.

Remember that the Incarnation is an act of the eternal Son of God adding sinless humanity to his deity. Once conceived in Mary's virgin womb, Jesus forever becomes the only person in history with two full and indivisible natures: divine and human. So, for Jesus to be our Savior, he must be fully human as well as fully divine. And in his death, burial, resurrection, ascension, and return, he must retain his humanity, which requires a physical body.

Paul understands Jesus' physical resurrection in light of the feast of firstfruits. Just as the first cut of the spring barley harvest is dedicated to the Lord as an act of faith that the full crop will come in, so Jesus' physical resurrection is his pledge that all Christians one day will be raised from the dead and fully conformed to his likeness (1 Cor. 15:20-23).

So, for Jesus to return "in the same way" he left means Jesus is coming physically.

Third, Jesus is coming visibly.

It's clear the apostles witness Christ's ascension with their own eyes. Luke tells us Jesus is taken up as they are "watching." A cloud takes Jesus "out of their sight." As Jesus departs, they are "gazing into heaven." Two angels question the apostles, asking why they stand "looking up into heaven." And the angels assure them that Jesus will return "in the same way that you have seen him going into heaven" (Acts 1:9-11).

All of this reveals that Jesus' ascension is an observable event to which multiple eyewitnesses attest. Further, the angels say Jesus' future return is going to be a similar spectacle.

Jesus tells us as much. In the Olivet Discourse (Matt. 24-25), he describes his return this way: "For as lightning that comes from the east is visible even in the west, so will be the coming of the Son of Man" (Matt. 24:27 NIV). He goes on to tell them, "Then the sign of the Son of Man will appear in the sky, and then all the peoples of the earth will mourn; and they will see the Son of Man coming on the clouds of heaven with power and great glory" (Matt. 24:30; cf. Luke 21:27).

Not long after these words to his apostles, Jesus stands before the high priest, Caiaphas, who demands to know if Jesus is the Messiah, the Son of God. Jesus replies, "You have said it.... But I tell you, in the future you will see the Son of Man seated at the right hand of Power and coming on the clouds of heaven" (Matt. 26:64; cf. Mark 14:62).

Picking up on Zechariah 12:10, John tells us, "Look, he is coming with the clouds, and *every eye will see him*, even those who pierced him" (Rev. 1:7, emphasis added). Later in the Apocalypse, John depicts the returning Christ riding a white horse – the vehicle of a conquering king as opposed to the peaceful beast of burden Jesus rides into Jerusalem on Palm Sunday (Rev. 19:11; cf. Zech. 9:9; Matt. 21:1-5; John 12:14-15).

Further, Jesus wears a robe dipped in blood, which may be his own blood shed for our redemption (Rev. 19:13). Although John includes figurative language in his account of Jesus' return – eyes like a fiery flame, and a sharp sword protruding from his mouth – there is no doubt John believes and teaches the visible return of Jesus to earth.

If Jesus ascends visibly into heaven, as the eyewitnesses attest, and if he's coming back "in the same way" he left, his return must be observable with the human eye.

Fourth, Jesus is coming powerfully – on the clouds of heaven.

First-century Jewish readers of Luke's account of the ascension would take special note that "a cloud" escorts Jesus into heaven (Acts 1:9). In the Old Testament, storms and clouds often accompany *theophanies*, or appearances of Yahweh. For example, the Lord's presence in the pillar of cloud and fire leads the Israelites across the desert (Exod. 13:17-22). Lightning, smoke, and fire accompany the Lord on Mount Sinai (Exod. 19:16-18). And God is depicted elsewhere as a consuming fire (Deut. 4:24; Heb. 12:28-29).

Psalm 97 combines theophanies that reveal thick darkness, clouds, fire, lightning, a trembling earth, and glory, which all people see:

Clouds and total darkness surround him; righteousness and justice are the foundation of his throne. Fire goes before him and burns up his foes on every side. His lightning lights up the world; the earth sees and trembles. The mountains melt like wax at the presence of the LORD – at the presence of the Lord of the whole earth. The heavens proclaim his righteousness; all the peoples see his glory (vv. 2-6).

In another psalm, notice how David depicts the Lord, who rescued the king from all his enemies:

Then the earth shook and quaked; the foundations of the mountains trembled; they shook because he burned with anger. Smoke rose from his nostrils, and consuming fire came from his mouth; coals were set ablaze by it. He bent the heavens and came down, total darkness beneath his feet. He rode on a cherub and flew, soaring on the wings of the wind. He made darkness his hiding place, dark storm clouds his canopy around him. From the radiance of his presence, his clouds swept onward with hail and blazing coals. The LORD thundered from heaven; the Most High made his voice heard. He shot his arrows and scattered them; he hurled lightning bolts and routed them. The depths of the sea became visible, the foundations of the world were exposed, at your rebuke, LORD, at the blast of the breath of your nostrils (Ps. 18:7-15).

But perhaps the single Old Testament passage that most intimately connects clouds and the presence of Yahweh is Daniel 7, as "one like a son of man" comes with "the clouds of heaven" and is escorted before the Ancient of Days.

Daniel records:

> He [son of man] was given dominion, and glory, and a kingdom; so that those of every people, nation, and language should serve him. His dominion is an everlasting dominion that will not pass away, and his kingdom is one that will not be destroyed (v. 14).

It appears that Daniel's vision is a view forward to final judgment, which makes the approach of "one like a son of man" all the more timely. In fact, Daniel 7:13 is the most-often quoted portion of Daniel in the New Testament.

As we noted earlier in this chapter, Jesus prefers "Son of Man" more than any other self-descriptive title. It seems the term "Son of Man" accomplishes two primary goals. First, it illustrates that Jesus shares humanity with us. In Philippians 2:5-8, Paul spells out the humble manner in which the eternal Son of God adds sinless humanity to his deity. But a second goal is of equal importance. In calling himself "Son of Man," especially in front of the Jewish religious leaders, he reveals himself as the divine being of Daniel 7.

This is clear in Mark 14 as Jesus stands before the Sanhedrin. After hearing multiple false testimonies against Jesus, the high priest Caiaphas puts it bluntly: "Are you the Messiah, the Son of the Blessed One?" (Mark 14:61).

"I am," Jesus replies, "and you will see the Son of Man seated at the right hand of Power and coming with the clouds of heaven" (v. 62).

The high priest immediately tears his robes and says, "Why do we still need witnesses? You have heard the blasphemy. What is your decision?" The members of the Sanhedrin condemn Jesus as deserving death (vv. 63-64).

There is much going on here. Caiaphas probably does not consider Jesus' claim to be the Messiah blasphemy. First-century Jews did not necessarily expect a Messiah who was God incarnate. However, the high priest does see Jesus' reference to the Son of Man in Daniel 7 as blasphemy. Once Caiaphas hears what he believes is blasphemy, as well as a direct threat to the high priest, he acknowledges the capital offense by tearing his robes.

While Jesus' reference to the Son of Man coming with the clouds of heaven may preview his second coming, it also serves as a solemn warning to the Sanhedrin that God's hammer of justice is about to fall on Israel – a prophecy fulfilled in A.D. 70 with the Roman conquest of Jerusalem and destruction of the temple.

Returning to Daniel 7, we see the Ancient of Days giving the one like a son of man "dominion, and glory, and a kingdom" (v. 13-14). People of every nation and language are to serve him as he rules over an everlasting kingdom that neither passes away nor may be destroyed.

Notice several clear truths in this verse. First, the Ancient of Days presents the gift of a universal kingdom to the Son of Man, just as the psalmist describes in his glimpse of a future coronation (Ps. 2:6-9).

Second, the Son of Man is to rule the kingdom, not simply receive it.

Third, people of every tongue and nation serve their king, a reality John foresees in his view of heaven (Rev. 5:9).

Fourth, the Son of Man's supreme rule lasts forever; it's as invincible as the resurrected Christ, who promises his followers that as long as he lives, they live as well (John 14:19).

Finally, while not stated here, we see the intimacy between the Ancient of Days and the Son of Man. It's an intimacy revealed again on the Mount of Transfiguration, as a cloud appears and overshadows Jesus and his disciples. A voice comes from the cloud, saying, "This is my Son, the Chosen One; listen to him!" (Luke 9:34-35). We learn later that when Christ receives the kingdom, he offers it back to his Father. Paul writes:

Then comes the end, when he [Christ] hands over the kingdom to God the Father, when he abolishes all rule and all authority and power. For he must reign until he puts all his enemies under his feet. The last enemy to be abolished is death (1 Cor. 15:24-26).

If heavenly clouds accompany Jesus in his transfiguration and ascension, and if he's coming back "in the same way" he left, his return must include the dramatic appearance of divine clouds. We should not expect the puffy white cumulus version, however. Rather, when Jesus returns, he rides the same dark, lightning-filled clouds that paved the way for Yahweh's cherubim-propelled chariot-throne across the heavens in Old Testament times (see Ezek. 1:1-28). See Chapter 5 for more on Christ's return on the clouds.

Fifth, Jesus is coming back to the Mount of Olives.

The Mount of Olives is a ridge flanking the east side of Jerusalem, separated from the city walls by the Kidron Valley. The mountain bears historic and prophetic significance. When King David's son Absolom seizes control of Jerusalem, David and his followers take an eastern route of escape:

> David was climbing the slope of the Mount of Olives, weeping as he ascended. His head was covered, and he was walking barefoot. All of the people with him covered their heads and went up, weeping as they ascended (2 Sam. 15:30).

Years later, King Solomon builds a high place for Chemosh, the god of Moab, and for Milcom, the idol of the Ammonites, on "the hill across from Jerusalem" (1 Kings 11:7). In one of Ezekiel's visions, he sees the glory of the Lord depart from Jerusalem and come to rest on "the mountain east of the city" (Ezek. 11:23).

Jesus visits the Mount of Olives many times during his earthly ministry, even spending the night there on occasion (Luke 21:37; 22:39). His visits to Bethany, where Mary, Martha, and Lazarus live, take him from Jerusalem, across the Kidron Valley, and over the Mount of Olives.

During the week of his passion, Jesus visits the Mount of Olives at least three times. The first visit sets in motion his triumphal entry into Jerusalem. His disciples fetch a donkey from the area of Bethany and Bethphage, from which Jesus rides into the city on Palm Sunday amidst thunderous acclaim. Just before his descent into Jerusalem, Jesus weeps over the city and pronounces judgment against it "because you did not recognize the time when God visited you" (Luke 19:44; cf. vv. 28-43).

Jesus' second visit to the Mount of Olives is to deliver the Olivet Discourse, in which he instructs his disciples about the impending destruction of Jerusalem, a future time of tribulation, and his second coming (Matt. 24-25; Mark 13:1-37; Luke 21:5-36). The message features several parables that encourage vigilance for followers of Jesus as they await his return.

The third visit of Jesus to the Mount of Olives during the week of his passion comes on the night he's betrayed. After observing the Passover in Jerusalem with his disciples, Jesus leads them to the Garden of Gethsemane on the western slope of the Mount of Olives. Here, Jesus agonizes in prayer while the disciples sleep, only to be awakened by the warning voice of Jesus as Judas Iscariot and a mob approach to take the Savior by force.

After Jesus' resurrection, he stands once more on the Mount of Olives with his followers. Luke tells us, "Then he led them out to the vicinity of Bethany, and lifting up his hands he blessed them. And while he was blessing them, he left them and was carried up into heaven" (Luke 24:50-51).

Immediately following Jesus' ascension, two angels tell the disciples that Jesus is returning in the same way they saw him leave, implying he's also returning to the same place (Acts 1:11). In a prophecy related to the last days, Zechariah declares:

> Then the Lord will go out to fight against those nations as he fights on a day of battle. On that day his feet will stand on the Mount of Olives, which faces Jerusalem on the east. The Mount of Olives will be split in half from east to west, forming a huge valley, so that half the mountain will move to the north and half to the south (Zech. 14:3-4).

As one commentary puts it, "The very location where David wept in defeat and where Jesus was betrayed and rejected will be the place where Jesus returns in triumph over all His enemies."[15]

We should note the view of some Bible commentators who argue that while Jesus stands on the Mount of Olives after his glorious return, he doesn't necessarily stand there *first*. That is, when we consider the many Old Testament passages that address the Day of the Lord, the return of Messiah follows the same basic path of the Exodus.

It begins with Messiah coming to Egypt – where many Jews have fled to escape tribulation – and continues across the Red Sea, to Sinai, and across the desert through Edom, before the Lord advances triumphantly into Jerusalem. There, he stands victoriously on the Mount of Olives, as Zechariah prophesies and as the angels in Acts 1 attest.

This may seem like a novel hypothesis, but it is well-grounded in the Hebrew Scriptures and does not contradict New Testament prophecies of Christ's return to the Mount of Olives.[16]

OPPOSITE ERRORS

Commenting on Luke's account of the ascension in Acts 1, John Stott writes that the apostles are guilty of two opposite errors: "The first is the error of the politicist, who dreams of establishing Utopia on earth. The second is the error of the pietist, who dreams only of heavenly bliss. The first vision is too earthy, and the second too heavenly."[17]

The apostles falsely dream of political power in the restored kingdom of Israel. Next, they allow themselves to become preoccupied with the heaven-bound Jesus, thus neglecting the Great Commission.

"This same Jesus" returns in the same way the apostles see him ascend. While we await Jesus' second coming, we should be neither politicists nor pietists, but pilgrims who engage in a journey of faith, knowing the kingdom of God comes one day in fullness, and the intersection of heaven and earth – Eden – is finally restored.

REVIEW

Key takeaways from this chapter

1. Jesus is the same person before and after the Incarnation. The difference is that before the Incarnation, Jesus had but one nature (divine). In the Incarnation, he adds a human nature, one that exists together with the original divine nature. While the incarnate Christ suffers death, he emerges from the tomb in glorified immortality. As such, Jesus' humanity does not and will not suffer the ravages of time.

2. Several key attributes of Jesus make him unique and ensure that he – "this same Jesus" – must return to fulfill his promises. These include:

(a) Jesus is the eternal Son of God, the second person of the triune Godhead;

(b) Jesus is the God-Man, fully divine and fully human;

(c) Jesus is the Son of Man, the unique divine being in Daniel 7 who receives a kingdom from the Ancient of Days;

(d) Jesus is the Messiah, or Christ – the anointed one; and

(e) Jesus is the resurrected Savior.

3. The angels at Jesus' ascension make it clear he is returning in *the same way* the disciples witnessed his departure into heaven. This means:

(a) Jesus *himself* is coming – he's not sending a substitute;

(b) he's coming physically;

(c) he's coming visibly;

(d) he's coming powerfully – on the clouds of heaven; and

(e) he's coming back to the Mount of Olives.

4. Like the apostles in Acts 1, followers of Jesus today are not to stand idly, gazing into the heavens and watching for his return. Rather, we are to be busy, engaging in the gospel ministry he has entrusted to us. At the same time, we may serve Jesus knowing that "this same Jesus" is returning one day "in the same way" (Acts 1:11).

DISCUSS

Questions for personal or group study
1. Read Acts 1:1-11. What do you think is going through the apostles' minds as they watch Jesus ascend into heaven? And how do the words of the two "men in white clothes" bring the apostles' mission into proper focus?
2. Why is it important to understand that the same Jesus who ascends into heaven is returning one day? Why would the angels stress "this same Jesus"?
3. What are the key attributes of Jesus that make him unique and ensure that he – not someone else – is returning one day to fulfill his promises?
4. List five characteristics of Jesus' return that assure us he's coming back in *the same way* he ascended into heaven.
5. Thinking about how the apostles serve Jesus after witnessing his ascension, how should we live in light of Jesus' imminent return?

* * *

"COMING ON THE CLOUDS"

JESUS IS RETURNING POWERFULLY

*I*n Chapter 4, we previewed Jesus' return on the clouds of heaven as a key feature in the Savior's promise to fulfill all things. He is returning *himself* – not sending a proxy. He's also coming physically and visibly. And he's returning to the Mount of Olives. But what does Jesus mean when he says, "and they will see the Son of Man coming on the clouds of heaven with *power* and great glory" (Matt. 24:30, emphasis added)?

The Greek word most often translated "power" in the New Testament is *dynamis*. It's the word Jesus uses here. *Dynamis* appears 119 times and essentially means "power," but it also may denote acts of power, such as miracles, or, on occasion, a person's ability. Our English word "dynamite" is a derivative. Yet dynamite's power to destroy is quite different from God's power to create, heal, judge, and restore.

God is the source of all power. Three *omni* attributes of God describe him as all-powerful (omnipotent), all-knowing (omniscient), and everywhere present (omnipresent). As John Frame notes:

Omnipotence means that God is in total control of himself and his creation. Omniscience means that he is the ultimate criterion of truth and falsity, so that his ideas are always true. Omnipresence means that since God's power and knowledge extend to all parts of his creation, he himself is present everywhere. Together they define God's lordship, and they yield a rich understanding of creation, providence, and salvation.[1]

Everything the Lord creates has power to some degree, but only *his* power is immutable, or unchanging. Animals have a conscious power to varying degrees – an ability to hunt, graze, defend themselves, and organize into groups. Nature has an unconscious power as seen in the wind and waves, and in processes like erosion and germination. Rulers have God-given power (Rom. 13:1). And creatures in the unseen realm, like angels, demons, and Satan, have power as well. But only God is omnipotent, which Paul describes as "the immeasurable greatness of his power" (Eph. 1:19).

Interestingly, *Power* is a name for God. When faced with a blunt question from Caiaphas, the high priest, as to whether Jesus is the Messiah, the Son of God, Jesus responds, "You have said it. But I tell you, in the future you will see the Son of Man seated at the right hand of Power and coming on the clouds of heaven" (Matt. 26:64).

While God's power is witnessed indirectly in creation, it is fully manifested in Jesus, the eternal second person of the triune Godhead (Col. 2:9). Jesus claimed to possess all *authority* in heaven and on earth. The Greek term used here is *exousia*, which may be translated "power," "authority," or "might." In any case, Jesus has the same divine power of the Father and the Spirit.

If God's power is most clearly manifested to us in Jesus, how does this play out in the Savior's life? And how does it help us understand the power of his return?

Let's pursue several observations about the power of Jesus in light of the New Testament.

First, Jesus is the power of God.

Through the Incarnation, God becomes flesh. The eternal Son of God adds sinless humanity to his deity via the miracle of the virgin birth (John 1:14). In this way, Jesus not only is fully divine and fully human, he also manifests the power of God in human flesh. Gerhard Kittel explains that "there is the closest possible [connection] between the power which is given to Christ and the power of God. The power of Christ is the power of God…. Jesus as the Christ is the unique Bearer of divine power."[2]

Jesus rightly tells Philip that because the disciple has seen him, Philip has seen the Father (John 14:9). After Jesus heals a disabled man, many Jews seek to kill him – not just because he heals on the Sabbath, but because he calls God his Father, making himself equal with God (John 5:18). After Jesus once again asserts his equality with the Father, the Jews try to stone him for blasphemy (John 10:30-33). Ultimately, the religious leaders cite blasphemy as the reason for putting Jesus to death (Matt. 26:65-66).

Several New Testament passages illustrate the many ways in which Jesus manifests the power of God.

Matthew 22:23-33

A group of Sadducees approaches Jesus with a "gotcha" question. The Sadducees deny the resurrection, so their goal is to catch Jesus in a contradiction about life beyond the grave:

> "Teacher, Moses said, if a man dies, having no children, his brother is to marry his wife and raise up offspring for his brother. Now there were seven brothers among us. The first got married and died. Having no offspring, he left his wife to his brother. The same thing happened to the second also, and the third, and so on to all seven. Last of all, the woman died. In the resurrection, then, whose wife will she be of the seven? For they all had married her" (Matt. 22:24-28).

The Sadducees think they have an ironclad argument. Jesus must either refute the law of Moses – it makes no sense for a woman to have seven husbands for eternity – or he must deny the afterlife. But note Jesus' four-part response.

First, he challenges the Sadducees' assumption that belief in resurrection means we're committed to trusting that all earthly institutions, such as marriage, are retained in the afterlife. None of the Hebrew Scriptures teaches this, nor does Jesus believe it. Here's the way Jesus puts it: "You are mistaken, because you don't know the Scriptures or *the power of God*. For in the resurrection they neither marry nor are given in marriage but are like angels in heaven" (vv. 29-30, emphasis added). Here, the power of God is tied to his authority to raise the dead – a power Jesus demonstrates numerous times, including the power he has to lay down his own life and take it up again (John 10:18).

Second, Jesus compares the resurrected state of men and women to that of angels (Matt. 22:30). Sadducees not only deny the resurrection; they also deny the existence of angels. Jesus is not saying deceased human beings become angels, but that the physical realm does not account for all reality.

Third, Jesus cites a text from the Sadducees' own esteemed Scriptures: Exodus 3:6. The Sadducees embrace the Torah – the first five books of the Old Testament – but not the rest of the Hebrew Scriptures. Jesus could have cited Job 19:25-27 or Daniel 12:2 to argue in favor of the resurrection. But instead, he quotes from the Torah.

Here's what Jesus says: "Now concerning the resurrection of the dead, haven't you read what was spoken to you by God: I am the God of Abraham and the God of Isaac and the God of Jacob? He is not the God of the dead, but of the living" (Matt. 22:32).

Fourth, Jesus emphasizes the verb tense. God *is* the God of Abraham, Isaac, and Jacob. Not *was*, as in the patriarchs' earthly lives. Rather, *is*, because these humans, who have passed through the portal of physical death, continue to live.

Jesus' words concerning the power of God don't seem to convince the Sadducees. But listeners with more open minds are "astonished at his teaching" (Matt. 22:33).

1 Corinthians 1:24-25

Yet to those who are called, both Jews and Greeks, Christ is *the power of God* and the wisdom of God, because God's foolishness is wiser than human wisdom, and God's weakness is stronger than human strength [emphasis added].

In verses 18-25, Paul contrasts God's power and wisdom with human weakness and foolishness. While the proclamation of the gospel is foolishness to those who are perishing, it is "the power of God to us who are being saved" (v. 18). The Jews ask for signs, and the Greeks seek wisdom, but the preaching of Christ crucified proves a stumbling block to the Jews and foolishness to the Gentiles (vv. 22-23).

To the Jews, a crucified Messiah is a *skandalon* (Greek) – a stumbling block, a death trap. It's an unredeemable offense, since those hanged on a tree bear the curse of God (Deut. 21:23). The dilemma is no easier to bear for Gentiles, who seek wisdom and see a crucified king as utter folly.

Yet, God, in his divine wisdom, is pleased to save those who believe through the foolishness of what is preached (1 Cor. 1:21). God chooses to save people by the power of the cross. His power – to create, sustain, condemn, and redeem – resides fully in his Son, who is the power and wisdom of God incarnate.

As Leon Morris explains, "Those *called* know that the crucified Christ means power. Before the call they were defeated by sin; now there is a new power at work in them, *the power of God.*"[3]

Hebrews 1:2-3

The writer of Hebrews emphasizes the "powerful word" of Jesus to express the Son's role as creator and sustainer of everything:

In these last days, he has spoken to us by his Son. God has appointed him heir of all things and made the universe through him. The Son is the radiance of God's glory and the exact expression of his nature, sustaining all things by his powerful word. After making purification for sins, he sat down at the right hand of the Majesty on high (Heb. 1:2-3).

Note several truths about Christ's deity in these verses. First, God made the universe through Jesus. That is, Jesus is the creator. When the writer of Hebrews says "through him," he does not mean Jesus is a secondary cause of creation; rather, Jesus is the agent through whom the triune God made everything. This verse corresponds with the testimony of John, who writes, "All things were created through him [the Word, or Jesus], and apart from him not one thing was created that has been created" (John 1:3; see also Col. 1:16).

Next, the writer tells us that the universe (*aionas*) was made through Jesus. This word means more than *kosmos*, or the material world. It may be rendered "ages," and it means Jesus is responsible for the existence of time, space, energy, matter – even the unseen spiritual realm.

Then, in Hebrews 1:3, we're told that Jesus is the "radiance of God's glory." That is, Jesus is the visible manifestation of the invisible God. The author uses the Greek word *apaugasma*, a sending forth of the light. Just as no one may gaze for long into the noonday sun without suffering visual impairment, or even blindness, no mortal human being may see the unveiled glory of God and live. Yet, like the light and warmth of the sun's rays, Jesus is deity clothed in human skin. He is "the light of the world. Anyone who follows me will never walk in the darkness but will have the light of life" (John 8:12).

The author of Hebrews goes on to describe Jesus as "the exact expression" of God's nature. The Greek word rendered "expression" is *charakter*, used to describe the impression made by a stamp or a die on steel. So, Jesus is the precise imprint of deity in human form, the perfect, personal emblem of divinity. This reminds us of Paul's words in Colossians 1:15: "He is the image (*eikon*) of the invisible God."

Finally, the writer assures us that Jesus is "sustaining all things by his powerful word." This is in the present tense. The same creator who called everything into existence now holds everything together in divine sovereignty. The appointed heir of all things keeps all things in place through his omnipotence, omniscience, and omnipresence.

Still other passages address the power of God manifested in Jesus. For example, the writer of Hebrews explains that Jesus is not a priest based on physical descent – he's from the tribe of Judah, not Levi – "but based on the power of an indestructible life ... a priest forever according to the order of Melchizedek" (Heb. 7:16-17).

Revelation 5:11-13

The Book of Revelation unveils heavenly scenes in which God and the Lamb are ascribed all power:

Then I looked and heard the voice of many angels around the throne, and also of the living creatures and of the elders. Their number was countless thousands, plus thousands of thousands. They said with a loud voice,
>Worthy is the Lamb who was slaughtered
>to receive power and riches
>and wisdom and strength
>and honor and glory and blessing!

I heard every creature in heaven, on earth, under the earth, on the sea, and everything in them say,
>Blessing and honor and glory and power
>be to the one seated on the throne,
>and to the Lamb, forever and ever (Rev. 5:11-13)!

Revelation 7:9-12

After this I looked, and there was a vast multitude from every nation, tribe, people, and language, which no one could number, standing before the throne and before the Lamb. They were clothed in white robes with palm branches in their hands. And they cried out in a loud voice:

> Salvation belongs to our God,
> who is seated on the throne,
> and to the Lamb!

All the angels stood around the throne, and along with the elders and the four living creatures they fell facedown before the throne and worshiped God, saying,

> Amen! Blessing and glory and wisdom
> and thanksgiving and honor
> and power and strength
> be to our God forever and ever. Amen.

Truly, Jesus is the power of God manifested in the flesh. His powerful return is an expression of his omnipotence.

A second observation about the power of Jesus is that he manifests omnipotence in his miracles.

Jesus makes it clear that all authority in heaven and on earth has been given to him (Matt. 28:18). He demonstrates this power in miraculous deeds, from raising the dead to forgiving sins. At the same time, the Lord commissions his disciples to perform signs and wonders that strike awe in people's hearts and declare that the king of God's kingdom walks among them.

Consider a few examples.

Matthew 11:20-23

Jesus denounces the towns where most of his miracles are performed. Why? Because the people do not repent. It's clear that the signs and wonders Jesus performs are not for entertainment purposes. The Lord is not a traveling minstrel who offers dinner and a show. He's not engaged in the bread-and-circus distractions of the Caesars. He's an itinerant prophet, priest, and king. His miracles powerfully illustrate his deity and foreshadow the days when the kingdom of God comes in fullness, and when the effects of sin – sickness, pain, death, and grief – are eradicated. Even so, many do not believe, as Jesus laments:

> Woe to you, Chorazin! Woe to you, Bethsaida! For if the miracles that were done in you had been done in Tyre and Sidon, they would have repented in sackcloth and ashes long ago. But I tell you, it will be more tolerable for Tyre and Sidon on the day of judgment than for you. And you, Capernaum, will you be exalted to heaven? No, you will go down to Hades. For if the miracles that were done in you had been done in Sodom, it would have remained until today. But I tell you, it will be more tolerable for the land of Sodom on the day of judgment than for you (Matt. 11:21-23).

Two chapters later, we learn that Jesus performs only a limited number of miracles in his hometown of Nazareth because of their unbelief (Matt. 13:58).

Mark 5:25-34

While some reject Jesus, despite signs and wonders attesting to his divine power, many flock to him in childlike trust. One example is a woman who has suffered from bleeding for twelve years. She has endured much under many doctors. After exhausting her savings, she is no closer to relief. In fact, Mark tells us she has gotten worse.

But she hears about Jesus and doggedly pursues him in a crowd, thinking, "If I just touch his clothes, I'll be made well" (v. 28). Instantly, her bleeding stops, and she knows she's been healed.

At that moment, Jesus realizes "power" has gone out from him. "Who touched my clothes?" he asks (v. 30).

The disciples only see the crowd, pressing on Jesus from all sides. But Jesus is focused on the woman who touched him in faith. Reluctantly, "with fear and trembling," she steps forward, falling down before Jesus, and confessing the "whole truth" (v. 33).

"Daughter," says Jesus, "your faith has saved you. Go in peace and be healed from your affliction" (v. 34).

This woman was more than ill; she was ceremonially unclean for twelve years. The power of Jesus makes her healthy and enables her to resume worship in the temple.

In a similar way, Jesus touches a leper and makes him well. He instructs the man to show himself to the priest and to follow the commands of Moses regarding leprosy "as a testimony to them" (Luke 5:12-14; cf. Lev. 13-14). Priests alone could legally readmit former lepers into the community.

No doubt, the man's testimony would draw attention to the divine power of Jesus. It also would communicate to the priests that Jesus has high regard for the Law of Moses. He has not come to abolish the law or the prophets, but to fulfill them (Matt. 5:17).

Luke 5:17-26

The Synoptic Gospel writers all record the story of Jesus healing a paralyzed man (cf. Matt. 9:1-8; Mark 2:1-12). But only Luke stresses that "the Lord's power to heal was in him" (Luke 5:17).

Jesus reveals divine power in a number of ways in this episode. He is able to "see their faith" – that is, the faith of the paralyzed man and the kind people who relentlessly pursued Jesus, even to the point of wrecking a roof.

The Lord also forgives the paralytic man's sins, something that prompts the scribes and Pharisees who witness the event to question: "Who is this man who speaks blasphemies? Who can forgive sins but God alone?" (v. 21).

Next, Jesus is able to read the religious leaders' thoughts (v. 22). And he challenges them with a powerful demonstration of his deity. While no human being can visibly witness the forgiveness of sins – a judicial act that occurs in heaven – people can watch the Son of Man make a paralyzed man well. And that's exactly what Jesus does, commanding the paralytic, "Get up, take your stretcher, and go home" (v. 24).

Immediately, the man arises, picks up the mat on which he's been carried, and heads out the door, glorifying God. Luke notes, "Then everyone was astounded, and they were giving glory to God. And they were filled with awe and said, 'We have seen incredible things today'" (v. 26).

Indeed. The power of Jesus *is* incredible. But it's not indiscriminate. Jesus shares that power with those he commissions to spread the good news of the kingdom.

First, he grants divine authority to the apostles: "Summoning the Twelve, he gave them power and authority over all the demons and to heal diseases. Then he sent them to proclaim the kingdom of God and to heal the sick" (Luke 9:1-2).

Later, he appoints seventy-two followers[4] to go ahead of him into the towns and villages he's about to visit. He tells them to heal the sick and announce that the kingdom of God is near (Luke 10:1-12). When the disciples return, they joyously proclaim, "Even the demons submit to us in your name" (Luke 10:17).

Jesus reminds them, "I have given you the authority to trample on snakes and scorpions" – a reference to evil spirits – "and over all the power of the enemy; nothing at all will harm you. However, do not rejoice that the spirits submit to you, but rejoice that your names are written in heaven" (Luke 5:19-20).

Finally, on the day of Pentecost, Peter makes it clear that Jesus' omnipotence is demonstrated in his miracles: "This Jesus of Nazareth was a man attested to you by God with miracles, wonders, and signs that God did among you through him, just as you yourselves know" (Acts 2:22).

Gerhard Kittel points out that while Jesus is not the only one in his day to work miracles, the miracles of Jesus may be distinguished in three ways. First, the miracles of Jesus have no connection with magic. Second, the miracles are evoked by the powerful word of Jesus; that is, they are "part of the invading dominion of God which Jesus brings with His own person in proclamation and act." Third, the miracles of Jesus presuppose the faith of the one who performs them and also of the one on whom they are performed. "They are thus accomplished in a wholly personal relationship."[5]

A third observation about the power of Jesus is that he declares his power as Messiah through the resurrection.

The religious leaders marvel at Jesus. He teaches with divine authority. He performs miracles that demonstrate his divine power and foreshadow life in the kingdom of God. He gathers a host of loyal followers who defy Jewish convention – tax collectors, revolutionaries, prostitutes, the poor. And he calls God his Father – he even claims equality with him – implying his own deity.

But he's not shaping up to be the Messiah the Jewish people expect. He shuns efforts to install him as king. He shows little interest in the political machinations of the day. He tells a Roman governor his (Jesus') kingdom is not of this world. And he prepares his disciples, not for his enthronement, but for his death. No wonder Caiaphas, the high priest, says with some exasperation, "I charge you under oath by the living God: Tell us if you are the Messiah, the Son of God" (Matt. 26:63).

Often, it seems, the religious leaders want some proof – some sign – that Jesus is the Son of God. In fact, in Matthew's Gospel, we see scribes and Pharisees approach the Lord with this very request: "Teacher, we want to see a sign from you" (Matt. 12:38).

Jesus responds, "An evil and adulterous generation demands a sign, but no sign will be given to it except the sign of the prophet Jonah. For as Jonah was in the belly of the huge fish three days and three nights, so the Son of Man will be in the heart of the earth three days and three nights" (vv. 39-40).

On another occasion, when Jesus cleanses the temple, the Jews confront him, demanding, "What sign will you show us for doing these things?" (John 2:18).

Jesus replies, "Destroy this temple, and I will raise it up in three days" (v. 19).

The Jews think Jesus is speaking of the temple he has just cleansed, a massive and breathtaking edifice that has been under construction for forty-six years. But they misunderstand. As John makes clear, "he was speaking about the temple of his body. So when he was raised from the dead, his disciples remembered that he had said this, and they believed the Scripture and the statement Jesus had made" (vv. 21-22).

While Jesus fulfills many messianic prophecies – his virgin birth, birthplace, miracles, and so on – he directs his listeners to one unmistakable sign: his resurrection. This means, of course, he must die first. Over and over again, Jesus urges his listeners to understand that before Messiah comes as a conquering king, he must fulfill the role of Suffering Servant (cf. Isa. 53).

Consider just a few examples of how Jesus prepares his disciples for his destiny with death, which must precede his victory over sin and the grave:

Matthew 16:21 – From then on Jesus began to point out to his disciples that it was necessary for him to go to Jerusalem and suffer many things from the elders, chief priests, and scribes, be killed, and be raised the third day.

John 10:11, 17-18 – "I am the good shepherd. The good shepherd lays down his life for the sheep…. This is why the Father loves me, because I lay down my life so I may take it up again. No one takes it from me, but I lay it down on my own. I have the right to lay it down, and I have the right to take it up again. I have received this command from the Father."

John 12:24, 32-33 – "Truly I tell you, unless a grain of wheat falls to the ground and dies, it remains by itself. But if it dies, it produces much fruit…. As for me, if I am lifted up from the earth I will draw all people to myself." He said this to indicate what kind of death he was about to die.

Indeed, Jesus *does* die – a violent, cruel, and humiliating death on a Roman cross. The Suffering Servant is despised, rejected, struck down by God, afflicted, pierced because of our rebellion, and crushed because of our iniquities (see Isa. 53). And yet, this is not the end of a messianic impostor, the just punishment of a Jewish blasphemer, or the execution of a rebel against imperial Rome. This is the foreordained death of the Son of God, as Peter declares on the day of Pentecost:

> This Jesus of Nazareth was a man attested to you by God with miracles, wonders, and signs that God did among you through him, just as you yourselves know. Though he was delivered up according to God's determined plan and foreknowledge, you used lawless people to nail him to a cross and kill him. God raised him up, ending the pains of death, because it was not possible for him to be held by death (Acts 2:22-24).

As Paul later writes, "He [the Father] made the one who did not know sin to be sin for us, so that in him we might become the righteousness of God" (2 Cor. 5:21).

The gospel message does not end with the death of Jesus, but it necessarily embraces it. As the eternal Lamb of God who comes into this world to die, Jesus also rises physically from the dead to conquer Satan, sin, and death for us. Paul tells us Jesus is declared with power to be the Son of God through his resurrection (Rom. 1:4). And he summarizes the gospel in his first letter to the Corinthians: "For I passed on to you as most important what I also received: that Christ died for our sins according to the Scriptures, that he was buried, that he was raised on the third day according to the Scriptures" (1 Cor. 15:3-4).

In a very real sense, Christ's resurrection is our resurrection as well. That is, our future resurrection is pinned to Jesus as "the firstfruits of those who have fallen asleep" (1 Cor. 15:20). In the Israelite feast of firstfruits, the people offer the first and best of their barley crops to Yahweh, acknowledging him as Lord of the harvest, and trusting him to ensure that the full harvest is brought in.

Jesus is raised from the dead on the same day the Jews celebrate the feast of firstfruits – the Sunday morning after Passover. Paul makes the connection for us. Jesus is the first to rise from the dead in a glorified body, thus ensuring that his followers are raised physically from the dead one day, sharing the immortality of our risen Lord.

Put simply, our future resurrection is tied inextricably to the resurrection of Jesus. As long as he lives, we live (John 14:19). "God raised up the Lord and will also raise us up by his power" (1 Cor. 6:14). Truly, Jesus declares his power as Messiah through the resurrection.

A fourth observation about the power of Jesus: Jesus ministers in the power of the Holy Spirit, the co-equal, co-eternal third person of the Trinity.

The Holy Spirit serves as the agent of Jesus' conception in the virgin womb of Mary (Matt. 1:18, 20). The Spirit also descends at the baptism of Jesus, initiating the Messiah's earthly ministry (Matt. 3:16). Immediately, the Spirit leads Jesus into the wilderness, where the Son of God faces intense temptation at the hands of Satan (Matt. 4:1-11). All of this illustrates the intimate work of the Spirit in the Incarnation – the divine act of God becoming flesh in the person of Jesus of Nazareth.

But we should not suppose Jesus and the Spirit meet for the first time on earth. As co-equal, co-eternal members of the Trinity, Jesus and the Holy Spirit have always existed in a loving, giving, intimate relationship that precedes their collaborative work with the Father to create the universe and then rescue fallen people from sin and death. If the triune God *is* love (1 John 4:16), not merely a deity who creates objects of love, that means the Father, Son, and Holy Spirit have always loved one another and have always shared intimate fellowship.

This is an important truth that should not be discounted. The Spirit's work in Jesus enables the incarnate Son of God to speak truth, raise the dead, cast out demons, and forgive sins. The ministry of Jesus is collaborative, leaning heavily on the Father and the Spirit. Luke testifies that Jesus ministers "in the power of the Spirit" (Luke 4:14).

Let's consider one example from Matthew 12, in which Jesus heals a demon-possessed man who is blind and mute. The crowds are astounded and ask, "Could this be the Son of David?" (Matt. 12:23).

When the Pharisees hear this, they react differently, saying, "This man drives out demons only by Beelzebul, the ruler of the demons" (v. 24).

Jesus knows their thoughts and replies, "Every kingdom divided against itself is headed for destruction, and no city or house divided against itself will stand. If Satan drives out Satan, he is divided against himself. How then will his kingdom stand?" (vv. 25-26).

Note several key truths in this passage. First, Jesus exposes the absurdity of the Pharisees' argument. Satan and the demons who rally to the evil one's cause are united in their hatred of God and God's people. For Satan to cast out demons would undermine his vile crusade against the Lord and threaten his own empire.

Next, Jesus reveals the Pharisees' envy: "And if I drive out demons by Beelzebul, by whom do your sons drive them out? For this reason they will be your judges" (v. 27). Jesus directs the Pharisees' attention to the Jewish exorcists who, with great difficulty, sometimes succeed in casting out evil spirits. Do the Pharisees believe Satan is behind these deliverance ministries? Of course not.

Finally, Jesus makes it clear the Spirit empowers him to deliver demon-possessed people from the grip of the evil one: "If I drive out demons by the Spirit of God, then the kingdom of God has come upon you" (v. 28). It is none other than the same Holy Spirit, who worked with the Father and Jesus to create the universe (Gen. 1:1-2), and who served as the agent of the Incarnation, who now empowers the Son of God to cast out demons.

And there's more. Jesus' miracles, performed in the power of the Holy Spirit, make it clear the kingdom of God has arrived, as Jesus immediately illustrates in a parable: "How can someone enter a strong man's house and steal his possessions unless he first ties up the strong man? Then he can plunder his house" (v. 29).

Satan rules over a vast kingdom in opposition to God. Jesus acknowledges this elsewhere, calling Satan "the ruler of this world" (John 12:31). But now, Messiah has come in the power of the Holy Spirit, sent by the Father, to invade Satan's kingdom and plunder his goods.

As Jesus lays down his life on the cross and takes it up again three days later, he conquers the evil one. As a result, day by day, Jesus rescues those captured by the evil one and makes them citizens of God's kingdom, joint heirs with Jesus, and adopted sons and daughters of the Father. Jesus' miracle of exorcism is proof of his role as redeemer, not a sinister cohort of Satan.

It gets worse for the Pharisees:

> Anyone who is not with me is against me, and anyone who does not gather with me scatters. Therefore, I tell you, people will be forgiven every sin and blasphemy, but the blasphemy against the Spirit will not be forgiven. Whoever speaks a word against the Son of Man, it will be forgiven him; but whoever speaks against the Holy Spirit, it will not be forgiven him, either in this age or in the one to come (Matt. 12:30-32).

By attributing the miraculous power of Jesus to Beelzebul, the Pharisees have committed an unpardonable sin. They make it clear they are not true children of the Father, having rejected him (see John 8:30-47). Further, they clearly cast off Jesus as the Son of God by attributing his miracles to Satan. But now, they utterly blaspheme the third person of the Godhead. Once you've rejected the Father, Son, and Holy Spirit, where else may you turn? The unpardonable sin, in this context, is directed at the religious leaders of Jesus' day. Their hearts are so hard that Jesus later asks rhetorically how they can escape the fires of hell (Matt. 23:33).

We might note that this same Holy Spirit raises Jesus from the dead (Rom. 8:11). This is interesting because the Scriptures tell us the Father also raises Jesus (Gal. 1:1), and Jesus raises himself (John 2:18-19; 10:18). Again, we see the collaborative work of the Trinity in creation and redemption.

A fifth observation about the power of Jesus: Jesus promises to send the Holy Spirit, who empowers Christians to share the gospel message.

Christians are the objects of God's redemptive love. Jesus promises his followers the Holy Spirit, whom he calls "the Counselor" (John

14:26). The Father sends the Spirit in the name of Jesus, and the Spirit in turn empowers the disciples to remember and apply all that Jesus has taught them.

Further, the "Spirit of truth" testifies about Jesus and enables the disciples to bear witness as well (John 15:26-27). The testifying ministry of Christ's followers is carried out in the power of the Holy Spirit, as Jesus promised: "But you will receive *power* when the Holy Spirit has come on you, and you will be my witnesses in Jerusalem, in all Judea and Samaria, and to the ends of the earth" (Acts 1:8, emphasis added).

Consider several additional New Testament passages.

Luke 24:48-49

Just before his ascension, Jesus appears to his disciples and opens their minds to understand the Hebrew Scriptures that foretell his death, burial, and resurrection. "You are witnesses of these things," Jesus says. "And look, I am sending you what my Father promised. As for you, stay in the city until you are *empowered* from on high [emphasis added]."

Acts 3:11-26

After healing a lame man at a temple gate (Acts 3:1-10), Peter proclaims to the gathering crowd that neither he nor John have the power or godliness to perform such miracles. Rather, the crucified, buried, and risen Jesus is "the source of life" (v. 15). Peter declares, "By faith in his name, his name has made this man strong, whom you see and know. So the faith that comes through Jesus has given him this perfect health in front of all of you" (v. 16).

The next day, Peter and John present the same testimony of Christ's power to the Jewish leaders, who had taken the two apostles into custody for their proclamation of the resurrected Christ (Acts 4:5-12). Later, Luke writes, "With great *power* the apostles were giving testimony to the resurrection of the Lord Jesus, and great grace was on all of them" (Acts 4:33, emphasis added).

Acts 6:8

Luke describes Stephen as a man "full of grace and *power*," who performs "great wonders and signs among the people [emphasis added]." This same Spirit-given power emboldens Stephen to proclaim the resurrected Christ to a hostile Jewish audience that, in turn, makes a deacon the first recorded martyr in the New Testament.

Acts 8:4-25

A sorcerer named Simon is called "the Great Power of God" (Acts 8:10). He amazes the people so that they pay careful attention to him. But when Simon sees Philip casting out demons and healing the sick in the name of Jesus, whom he proclaims as Messiah, Simon follows Philip everywhere. The sorcerer no doubt sees the true power that resides in Philip.

Then, when Peter and John arrive, laying hands on Samaritan believers so they receive the Holy Spirit, Simon offers them money, saying, "Give me this power also so that anyone I lay hands on may receive the Holy Spirit" (v. 19).

Peter strongly rebukes Simon. "May your silver be destroyed with you," Peter says, "because you thought you could obtain the gift of God with money!" (v. 20).

True power resides in the apostles, and those closely associated with the apostles. That power is not of human origin, nor may it be bought and sold. Rather, it is for the purpose of proclaiming Jesus as Messiah and declaring his finished work on the cross.

Acts 19:11-20

Paul is in Ephesus, and God is performing extraordinary miracles of healing and exorcism through him. This captures the attention of itinerant exorcists, including seven sons of Sceva, a Jewish high priest. They try casting evil spirits out of demonized people, saying, "I command you by the Jesus that Paul preaches!" (Acts 19:13).

In a most painful rebuke, a spirit replies, "I know Jesus, and I recognize Paul – but who are you?" (v. 15). Then, the demonized man jumps on the exorcists and overpowers them all. The sons of Sceva flee the house "naked and wounded" (v. 16).

Word travels quickly through Ephesus, and Luke notes that Jews and Greeks alike "became afraid, and the name of the Lord Jesus was held in high esteem" (v. 17).

We see a pattern emerging in the demonstrations of God's power in the Book of Acts. The Holy Spirit empowers Jesus' followers to perform signs and wonders for the purpose of declaring the crucified and resurrected Jesus as Messiah. This power clearly is beyond anything sorcerers and exorcists may conjure.

Further, this divine power may neither be purchased nor pilfered. Its value is in the declaration that the resurrected and glorified Jesus has conquered Satan, sin, and death, has brought the kingdom of God to us, and now offers people everywhere forgiveness of sins as a gift to be received by faith alone.

A sixth observation about the power of Jesus is that his kingdom comes in power.

At the beginning of Mark 9, Jesus makes a curious statement. He tells his disciples, "Truly I tell you, there are some standing here who will not taste death until they see the kingdom of God come in power" (Mark 9:1).

What does Jesus mean? Who are the "some" who will not taste death? What is the kingdom of God? How and when does the kingdom come in power?

It's important to note the context in which Jesus makes this statement. Peter has just declared Jesus the Messiah, a confession Jesus affirms (Matt. 16:16-20; cf. Mark 8:27-30). The apostle then sticks his foot firmly in his mouth by rebuking Jesus for talking about the necessity of Messiah's pending death, burial, and resurrection. Jesus responds by calling Peter "Satan" (Mark 8:31-33). Finally,

Jesus calls on his disciples to deny themselves and follow him, expecting persecution as they await the Savior's glorious return (Mark 8:34-38).

That's when Jesus talks about the kingdom of God coming in power. We may be tempted to see this as a reference to the second coming, which no doubt is a powerful manifestation of the kingdom. However, even by the end of the first century, Jesus' listeners have long since gone to their graves without having witnessed this prophesied event. So, in what way are some of the disciples to be eyewitnesses of the kingdom's appearance in power?

Commentators offer a number of explanations. Since Jesus' statement is recorded right before the Transfiguration – the most dazzling manifestation of the kingdom in power and glory prior to Christ's resurrection – it's possible that Jesus is signaling this event. The Transfiguration occurs six days later, and only "some" of the disciples – namely, Peter, James, and John – are invited to witness it (Mark 9:2-10). This seems to be a biblically faithful understanding of Jesus' words.

However, there are other possible interpretations. Some scholars believe this prophecy refers to the resurrection, which demonstrates the manifestation of Jesus and his kingdom in power even more forcefully than the Transfiguration. Certainly, the disciples are alive to witness this historic event.

Another view is that this prophecy is fulfilled on the Day of Pentecost, when the Spirit of God descends in a visible manifestation of divine power, filling the disciples and enabling them to proclaim the good news of the kingdom to Jews gathered in Jerusalem for the feast. Again, many disciples who hear Jesus' prophecy are there to attest to God's power.

And then, it's possible Jesus is talking about the destruction of Jerusalem and the temple in A.D. 70. R. C. Sproul notes:

> When these terrible events occurred in AD 70, the Christian church was finally understood as an entity distinct from Judaism. It was no longer considered a subset or a sect within Judaism. The triumph of

the Messiah's church was made visible and manifest in power with the judgment of God on the Jews.[6]

Whichever view one takes of Jesus' prophecy of the kingdom coming in power, it's important to understand that the kingdom of God spans time and eternity. To be sure, it includes the glorious return of Jesus, but it's not limited to that future event.

We examine the kingdom of God in more detail in Chapter 8. Meanwhile, it's important to keep in mind this simple definition: *the kingdom is God's reign, his authority to rule over all.*

The following truths may help us understand the kingdom in more practical terms.

First, the kingdom is God's conquest, through Jesus Christ, of his enemies: sin, Satan, and death.

Second, the kingdom comes in stages. Jewish prophets foretell the kingdom as an everlasting, mighty, and righteous reign involving the nation of Israel and its coming king, the Messiah. The kingdom comes humbly through the virgin birth of the Son of God and exists today as a mystery in the hearts of all believers. In the second coming, the kingdom at last appears in power and glory. After Christ's millennial reign on earth, he delivers the kingdom to the Father, having finally put away sin (it no longer is a reality with which to be dealt), Satan (he is cast into hell to be tormented night and day forever), and death (there is no longer physical or spiritual death).

Third, the Bible describes this threefold fact: (a) some passages refer to the kingdom as God's reign, rule, or authority; (b) some passages refer to the kingdom as the realm into which we may now enter to experience the blessings of his reign; and (c) some passages refer to the kingdom as a future realm that comes only with the return of Jesus. All three are true.

Fourth, as all kingdoms must have a king, Jesus is king of the kingdom of God. As King of kings and Lord of lords, Jesus is the eternal Son to whom, one day, "every knee will bow ... and every tongue will confess" (Phil. 2:10-11).

Fifth, people enter the kingdom – the sphere of God's rule – and become its citizens by faith in Jesus Christ.

It's also important to understand that many of Jesus' parables deal with the "mystery," or secret, of the kingdom of heaven (Matt. 13:11). The Greek word for "mystery" is *mysteria* and means what we can only know by divine revelation. This has particular value in helping us understand the kingdom of God in the present age. The Jews were looking for a political and military kingdom based on their understanding of the Hebrew Scriptures. At the same time, they missed the prophecies in Isaiah 53 and elsewhere about the Suffering Servant and thereby rejected Jesus as Messiah.

And so, the kingdom of God is here in the person of Jesus. But the mystery of the kingdom is that it must first come without fanfare in the Lamb of God who, through his death, burial, and resurrection, takes away the sin of the world. The kingdom is coming in power and great glory one day when Jesus returns as the Lion of Judah (Rev. 19:11-16; cf. 5:5).

Christ's kingdom comes in power because divine power resides in the king. This kingdom is a present reality and a future promise. It exists now and not yet. It is foreshadowed in Old Testament kings like David and in ancient kingdoms like Israel, yet the kingdom breaks through most powerfully in the Incarnation and displays its final glory when King Jesus sits on the throne and rules over new heavens and a new earth.

A seventh observation about the power of Jesus is that he returns in power.

Let's briefly survey two relevant New Testament passages.

Matthew 24:29-31

Immediately after the distress of those days, the sun will be darkened, and the moon will not shed its light; the stars will fall from the sky, and the *powers* of the heavens will be shaken. Then the sign of the Son of Man will appear in the sky, and then all the peoples of the earth will

mourn; and they will see the Son of Man coming on the clouds of
heaven with *power* and great glory [emphasis added].

In this portion of the Olivet Discourse, Jesus refers to two *powers*:
the powers of the heavens, and Jesus' own return with power. Jesus
doesn't define what he means by "the powers of the heavens,"
although he ties them to dramatic changes in the celestial order. Just
as the sun is darkened, the moon retains rather than reflects its light,
and stars fall from the sky, "the powers of the heavens" are shaken.

There are several possible ways to understand this statement in a
biblically faithful way. First, Jesus could be referring to angelic beings,
who sometimes in Scripture are spoken of in celestial terms (e.g., Job
38:7; Rev. 12:4). Whether these angels are holy or rebellious, all are
subject to God. And when the Son of Man returns, his sovereign
power outshines theirs and dramatically affects them.

Second, Jesus could be prophesying cataclysmic changes in the
celestial heavens. The darkening of the sun, the inability of the moon
to reflect the sun's diminished rays, and the chaotic paths of the very
stars by which sailors navigate and people mark their calendars, all
foreshadow the blazing brilliance by which the Son of Man returns.

It's quite possible that supernatural manipulations of celestial
bodies accompany Messiah's return. These signs in the heavens are
such that everyone on earth sees them and understands that an
unprecedented cosmic event is unfolding. As Stuart Weber notes, "If
only one of these signs were given, it might be explained away as an
eclipse or a meteor shower. But all of them together can be caused
only by the hand of God."[7]

Third, Jesus may be pointing to the overthrow of demonic powers
often associated in paganism with the sun, moon, and stars. Ancient
peoples, like the Egyptians, Assyrians, and Babylonians, commonly
worshiped the sun. Even the Israelites were lured into such pagan
practices, despite God's clear distinction between the creator and the
created order. The sun, moon, and stars were made to serve the needs
of people and were never intended to be objects of worship (Deut.
4:19; 17:2-5). Just as Jesus foresaw the fall of Satan from heaven

(Luke 10:18), he would return one day to put all rebellious angels in their place.

Finally, Jesus may be employing apocalyptic Old Testament language to describe his return. In this sense, we are not to take his words literally; rather, we are to understand them symbolically. Much of Jesus' statement echoes such Old Testament texts as Isaiah 13:9-10, in which the prophet warns Babylon:

> Look, the day of the Lord is coming — cruel, with fury and burning anger — to make the earth a desolation and to destroy its sinners. Indeed, the stars of the sky and its constellations will not give their light. The sun will be dark when it rises, and the moon will not shine.

Other Old Testament passages employ similar language in connection with God's final judgment (e.g., Isa. 24:23; 34:4; Ezek. 32:7-8; Joel 2:10, 31; 3:14-16; Amos 5:20; 8:9; Zech. 14:6). New Testament writers sometimes embrace this same imagery (e.g., Acts 2:20; Rev. 6:13; 8:12).

Whichever view is correct – and they all have merit – the return of Jesus in power is the central theme of this portion of the Olivet Discourse: "and they will see the Son of Man coming on the clouds of heaven with power and great glory (Matt. 24:30).

In Chapter 4, we addressed the return of Jesus on (or with) the clouds of heaven. This harkens back to Daniel 7, in which the Son of Man approaches the Ancient of Days to receive an everlasting kingdom. Just as clouds often accompany *theophanies*, or appearances of Yahweh in the Old Testament, these clouds appear with Jesus in his transfiguration and ascension. No mere puffy white vapors that drift across peaceful summer skies, the clouds of heaven upon which Jesus returns are the same dark, lightning-filled clouds that envelop the *Shekinah* glory on Mount Sinai and hover over the temple at its dedication.

Matthew 26:62-64

The high priest stood up and said to him, "Don't you have an answer to what these men are testifying against you?" But Jesus kept silent. The high priest said to him, "I charge you under oath by the living God: Tell us if you are the Messiah, the Son of God."

"You have said it," Jesus told him. "But I tell you, in the future you will see the Son of Man seated at the right hand of *Power* and coming on the clouds of heaven [emphasis added]."

Here, the Son of Man isn't merely coming on the clouds of heaven with power, as in Matthew 24:31. He's "seated at the right hand of Power" (Matt. 26:64). We should carefully note the distinction Jesus makes in his words to his disciples on the Mount of Olives and his words to the high priest that result in a charge of blasphemy. Jesus tells his disciples he's "coming with power;" he tells Caiaphas he's "seated at the right hand of Power."

For the disciples, Jesus assures them of his return in power. The same divine power by which he is raised from the dead accompanies him at his return, when he finally brings the kingdom of God in fullness. This is meant to comfort them, cheer them, and encourage them to persevere while they await his return.

For Caiaphas and the other religious leaders, however, Jesus' claim to be seated at the right hand of Power is meant to instill both anger and fear in them. To be seated at the right hand of Power – "Power" being another title for Yahweh – is to claim the same authority as God; that is, to claim deity. This is what enrages Caiaphas so that he tears his robes and cries "blasphemy" (Matt. 26:65). If there were ever any hesitation on Caiaphas' part to call for Jesus' crucifixion, it dissolves in the revelation of Jesus as God incarnate.

But Jesus intends to reveal more than his deity. He warns members of the Sanhedrin, and their high priest, that rejecting the Son of Man brings divine judgment upon their heads. Jesus is coming one day in power to resurrect and judge all people. But he's also coming to judge the nation of Israel, which has rejected its Messiah. This happens in A.D. 70 with the destruction of the temple, the overthrow of Jerusalem, and the scattering of the Jewish people.

The Olivet Discourse of Matthew 24-25, and Jesus' words to Caiaphas in Matthew 26, are closely related, but they don't necessary describe the same chronological events. Much of the Olivet Discourse is fulfilled in A.D. 70, but the physical, visible, personal return of Jesus is still to come.

SUMMARY

Today, Jesus is seated at the Father's right hand in heaven, where he serves as our mediator and intercessor. This exalted position illustrates his power as creator, sustainer, and redeemer. It also bears testimony to his humility in the Incarnation, and his submission to the Father in the eternal covenant of redemption. The Word of God, who spoke the universe into existence, became a creature for our sake – taking on human flesh without surrendering his deity.

As the God-Man, Jesus is the power of God; manifests his omnipotence in miracles ranging from raising the dead to forgiving sins; declares his power over Satan, sin, and death through his resurrection; ministers during his time on earth by the power of the Holy Spirit; sends that same Spirit after his ascension to empower his followers to do greater works than he does – that is, greater in number and scope; and establishes his kingdom in power. Everything about Christ's earthly ministry demonstrates his divine power. And yet he isn't finished.

One day, at the Father's command, Jesus rises from his place in the throne room of heaven and returns to earth. The one who possesses all authority in heaven and on earth comes to finish the work of redemption as he raises the dead, judges all people, casts the evil one into hell, purges the cosmos of sin and its stain, and creates new heavens and a new earth. This is power – all power, or omnipotence. Just as Yahweh rides a cherubim-propelled chariot-throne across the skies in Ezekiel's day, Jesus rides the clouds of heaven as he returns to earth to fully and finally set things right. Truly, the Son of Man returns in power.

REVIEW

Key takeaways from this chapter

1. Jesus tells his disciples he is "coming on the clouds of heaven with *power* and great glory" (Matt. 24:30, emphasis added). The Greek word translated "power" is *dynamis*, which essentially means "power" but also may denote acts of power, such as miracles, or, on occasion, a person's ability. Our English word "dynamite" is a derivative. Yet, dynamite's power to destroy is quite different from God's power to create, heal, judge, and restore. The return of Jesus demonstrates divine power to set all things right.

2. *Power* is a name for God, as Jesus makes clear in his confrontation with Caiaphas, the high priest: "you will see the Son of Man seated at the right hand of Power and coming on the clouds of heaven" (Matt. 26:64).

3. While we may witness God's power in many ways, his power is manifested personally in Jesus, the eternal second person of the triune Godhead (Col. 2:9). Jesus claimed to possess all *authority* in heaven and on earth (Matt. 28:18). Thus, Jesus has the same divine power the Father and the Spirit possess.

4. We may make several observations about the power of Jesus in light of the New Testament:

(a) Jesus is the power of God. Through the Incarnation, Jesus manifests the power of God in human flesh.

(b) Jesus manifests omnipotence in his miracles. He demonstrates this power in miraculous deeds, from raising the dead to forgiving sins.

(c) Jesus declares his power as Messiah through his resurrection.

(d) Jesus ministers in the power of the Holy Spirit, the co-equal, co-eternal third person of the Trinity.

(e) Jesus promises to send the Holy Spirit, who empowers Christians to share the gospel message.

(f) Christ's kingdom comes in power.

(g) Jesus returns in power.

5. Just as Yahweh rides a cherubim-propelled chariot-throne across the skies in Ezekiel's day, Jesus rides the clouds of heaven as he returns powerfully to earth to fully and finally set things right.

DISCUSS

Questions for personal or group study

1. How is God's power different from the power of nature, animals, and humans? What does the term "omnipotent" mean with respect to God's power?

2. In what ways does Jesus manifest the power of God?

3. Read 1 Corinthians 6:14 and 15:20. How does the resurrection power of Jesus guarantee our future resurrection?

4. How would you define the kingdom of God? What are several New Testament truths that help us understand the kingdom in practical terms?

5. Read Matthew 24:29-31. What do you think Jesus means by "the powers of the heavens will be shaken" at his return? How does his coming "on the clouds of heaven with power and great glory" overshadow these heavenly powers?

* * *

_____ A _____

Jesus wears a crown of thorns
to the cross. But he wears all
the diadems of heaven and
earth when he returns
in glory.

_____ Ω _____

"KING OF KINGS AND LORD OF LORDS"

JESUS IS RETURNING VICTORIOUSLY

*I*t has all the markings of defeat: betrayal, false accusations, wrongful imprisonment, a kangaroo court, a politically motivated judge, excessive abuse, and the most excruciating death known at the time. Jesus of Nazareth hangs naked on a Roman cross, about to breathe his last. Satan is set to achieve what he has monomaniacally pursued since the days of Eden: the death of mankind, and especially mankind's divine agent.

The evil one stands on the cusp of victory. But Jesus says something that turns the tables. Mustering sufficient breath in his overtaxed lungs, the Son of God declares, "It is finished." Then he bows his head and dies (John 19:30).

The Greek word translated "it is finished" is *tetelestai*. The word has many applications. Merchants often use it as an accounting term that means "paid in full." With this simple statement – possibly the "loud cry" of Mark 15:37 – Jesus declares that the debt of mankind's sin, owed to his Father in heaven, has been wiped away. Warren Wiersbe writes:

> When he gave Himself on the cross, Jesus fully met the righteous
> demands of a holy law; He paid our debt in full. None of the Old

Testament's sacrifices could take away sins; their blood only *covered* sin. But the Lamb of God shed His blood, and that blood can *take away* the sins of the world (John 1:29; Heb. 9:24-28).[1]

But those gathered around the cross may understand Jesus' words differently. To the Roman soldier, *tetelestai* is a declaration of military conquest. To the Jew, *tetelestai* is the statement from the high priest on the Day of Atonement when the final sacrifice has been offered.

In every case, *tetelestai* signals victory – a paid-in-full debt, a battlefield rout, a covering of sin.

There's more. The verb *teleo*, from which *tetelestai* is derived, denotes the completion of a task. In religious contexts, it bears the overtone of fulfilling one's obligations. Perhaps that's why John notes of Jesus, "Having loved his own who were in the world, he loved them *to the end*" (*eis telos*, John 13:1). Later, Jesus tells his Father, "I have glorified you on the earth by *completing* (*teleiosas*) the work you gave me to do" (John 17:4). So now, on the brink of death, the Son of Man declares that he has finished the redemptive work for which he was sent.[2]

Paul and the writer of Hebrews echo this truth as they write that Jesus' death took place once for all; that is, it's a finished work (Rom. 6:10; Heb. 7:27; 9:12; 10:10). Further, John twice records the expression "It is done" from the lips of Jesus in heaven as our Savior prepares to banish sin forever from the created order (Rev. 16:17; 21:6).

Much is finished in Jesus' work on the cross. As Matthew Henry points out, *tetelestai* is "a comprehensive word, and a comfortable one." Henry lists eight ways in which *it is finished* may be applied: (1) to the malice and enmity of Jesus' persecutors; (2) the counsel and commandment of his Father concerning his sufferings; (3) all the types and prophecies of the Old Testament; (4) the ceremonial law; (5) sin; (6) his sufferings; (7) his earthly life; and (8) the work of man's redemption and salvation.[3]

As we look back on Christ's finished work, we should also look forward. As the acorn contains the oak, Christ's death on the cross encapsulates the future fruit of redemption. From his heavenly vision, John records the words of Jesus, "It is done! I am the Alpha and the Omega, the beginning and the end. I will freely give to the thirsty from the spring of the water of life" (Rev. 21:6). Christ's own thirst on the cross results in streams of living waters for future generations (cf. John 7:37-38).

We can't know what Satan is thinking when he hears the words of Jesus. Perhaps the evil one believes *tetelestai* to be the ravings of a delirious man who's lost too much blood. Maybe the words are a vicious sarcasm offered to Jesus' heavenly Father. Maybe they're nothing more than relief that death, and the end of pain, is near.

But Jesus' simple declaration before he bows his head in death is a cry of victory. Satan gets the message on Sunday morning, when this same Jesus, whose body has lain wrapped in burial clothes and been anointed with spices, emerges victoriously from a borrowed tomb.

The resurrection of Jesus assures not only that our sin debt is paid in full, but the consequences of sin are being rolled back. Spiritual death gives way to regeneration. Alienation from God surrenders to the Spirit's indwelling. Guilt fades as justification takes its place before the heavenly bar. Abandonment is removed and adoption is conferred. Hell is poorer and heaven rejoices.

Through his finished work, Jesus defeats Satan, sin, and death for us. We are more than conquerors through the one who loved us (Rom. 8:37). The resurrection is a great victory for Jesus and his followers; a stunning blow for the evil one, evil spirits, and rebellious humans.

The victory is full and final, but not finally realized. That is, Satan still roams the earth like a lion, seeking whom he may devour (1 Pet. 5:8). Evil runs rampant through the streets of our cities and the hearts of sinful and fallen people. Sorrow, pain, aging, and death continue to claim every human life – eventually, if not suddenly.

But at the return of Jesus, the victory is fully realized. Satan, evil spirits, and the unrepentant wicked are cast into hell. The righteous are rewarded and granted access to the New Jerusalem. The whole creation, which today groans beneath the weight of human rebellion, is purged of sin and its stain, giving way to new heavens and a new earth, where righteousness dwells (Rom. 8:22; 2 Pet. 3:10-13).

THE GARDEN AND THE CROSS

To more fully appreciate the victorious return of Jesus, we need to look back at what he suffers on the cross, and even further back to what necessitates the cross: Adam's fall in the Garden of Eden.

The garden

Consider human life at the very beginning. God has finished his work of creation and declares everything "very good indeed" (Gen. 1:31). He has set Adam and Eve in the Garden of Eden and given them the privilege of tending it. He has made available to them the garden's abundant produce, restricting only their access to the tree of the knowledge of good and evil. Genesis 2 ends with a depiction of innocence: "Both the man and his wife were naked, yet felt no shame" (Gen. 2:25).

That's all about to change as the evil one – depicted as "the serpent" – appears unannounced. We pick up the story in Genesis 3:

> Now the serpent was the most cunning of all the wild animals that the LORD God had made. He said to the woman, "Did God really say, 'You can't eat from any tree in the garden'?"
>
> The woman said to the serpent, "We may eat the fruit from the trees in the garden. But about the fruit of the tree in the middle of the garden, God said, 'You must not eat it or touch it, or you will die.'"
>
> "No! You will not die," the serpent said to the woman. "In fact, God knows that when you eat it your eyes will be opened and you will be like God, knowing good and evil." The woman saw that the tree was good for food and delightful to look at, and that it was desirable for obtaining wisdom. So she took some of its fruit and ate it; she also gave some to her husband, who was with her, and he ate it. Then the eyes of both of them were opened, and they knew they were naked; so

they sewed fig leaves together and made coverings for themselves
(Gen. 3:1-7).

Satan appears suddenly in the garden as *the serpent*. We are not to
suppose this is a talking snake. Rather, it's likely that the evil one, a
fallen spirit being, breaks into the physical realm as an anointed
guardian cherub. This remarkably beautiful member of the divine
council comes for the express purpose of deceiving Eve (2 Cor. 11:3).[4]
The father of lies employs several tactics that flow from his evil
nature.

First, Satan comes disguised. The evil one is a beast, a dragon, an
insidious monster who inhabits the spiritual realm. Yet when he
breaks through into the physical world, he wears seductive costumes
that appeal to our flesh. This isn't lipstick on a pig; it's a transforma-
tive disguise that attracts us to him and masks his wiles.

The evil one possesses great knowledge of the truth, but he holds
no affection for it. Making himself a beautiful friend, he is nevertheless a sworn enemy of the truth, and he wishes to make us his allies.
As Paul makes clear, Satan comes to us as "an angel of light" (2 Cor.
11:14).

Second, Satan catches us alone. Since God has yet to create Eve when
he gives Adam the command not to eat of the tree of the knowledge of
good and evil (Gen. 2:16-17), Adam likely relays this warning to his
wife, for she is well aware of it. While Eve has no reason to doubt
Adam's truthfulness, the serpent approaches her because she's in a
more vulnerable position than her husband, having received the
Lord's instructions second-hand. Further, the serpent catches Eve
when she's by herself (Gen. 3:1).

Satan often lies to us when we're alone, away from the spiritual
support of fellow believers. He tempts Jesus when the Savior is
isolated in the wilderness (Matt. 4:1-11; Mark 1:12-13; Luke 4:1-13).
He privately stirs up David's heart to number his troops (1 Chron.
21:1). And – we all know this – he comes to us when we're alone, and
especially when we're tired, hungry, or lonely.

Third, Satan casts doubt. Note the question he poses to Eve: "Did

God really say, 'You can't eat from any tree in the garden'?" (Gen. 3:1).
It's a misquote of Genesis 2:16-17: "And the LORD God commanded
the man, 'You are free to eat from any tree of the garden, but you must
not eat from the tree of the knowledge of good and evil, for on the
day you eat from it, you will certainly die.'"

Satan's subtle turn of a phrase is sufficient to cast doubt in Eve's
mind, for she replies, "We may eat the fruit from the trees in the
garden. But about the fruit of the tree in the middle of the garden,
God said, 'You must not eat it or touch it, or you will die'" (Gen.
3:2-3).

Eve responds correctly to the serpent, with one caveat: she tells the
serpent she's forbidden to eat of the tree *or touch it*. Lois Tverberg
offers insight into Eve's exaggeration of God's word:

> Eve was probably trying to be faithful to God in her conversation with
> Satan, but when she told the serpent God's regulations regarding the
> tree, she overstated what God had said by saying that they must not
> even touch it or they will die. She was exaggerating for God's sake, by
> making his rule more strict than it really was....
>
> We must be ever mindful that our own zeal does not cause us to go
> beyond God, as we put words in God's mouth. We need to always
> speak to let God's truth be known.[5]

Eve's well-intended overstatement opens the door for Satan's next
tactic.

Fourth, Satan caters to falsehood. When Eve stretches God's prohibi-
tion regarding the tree, and then truthfully reports the penalty of
death, Satan pounces: "No! You will certainly not die" (Gen. 3:4). The
serpent craftily tells Eve she will not die for touching the tree. Eve
knows this, but now she's caught in her exaggerated statement. If the
serpent confirms she won't die for touching the tree, maybe she won't
die for eating from it, either. "At that point, [Satan's] temptations
gained credibility in her mind because he corrected her own misstate-
ment."[6]

Fifth, Satan caricatures the truth. With a foothold in Eve's mind, the

serpent convinces her there are no consequences for disobedience –
at least not drastic ones. What's more, he sells her on the notion that
rebellion holds great advantages. Look at what Satan says next about
the fruit on the forbidden tree: "In fact, God knows that when you eat
it your eyes will be opened and you will be like God, knowing good
and evil" (Gen. 3:5).

God certainly knows Eve's eyes will be opened, and he knows she
will gain the capacity to explore good and evil. The Lord is omniscient; that is, he knows all things perfectly. But God also is omnipotent and immutable. That means he is all-powerful and unchanging.
He is beyond reproach, unable to sin, perfect in holiness, and, by his
very nature, he remains this way forever. Eve, on the other hand, isn't
God, and the knowledge of sin is bound to wreck her.

There is more truth than falsehood in the serpent's words. Yet the
father of lies spins such a subtle web of deception that the first
humans are about to plunge themselves, their descendants, and the
whole world under a curse. It doesn't take long.

Eve sees that the tree is good for food, delightful to gaze upon, and
desirable for obtaining wisdom. So, she takes some of its fruit and eats
it. She also gives some to Adam, and he partakes. The consequences
are immediate and dramatic: "Then the eyes of both of them were
opened, and they knew they were naked; so they sewed fig leaves
together and made coverings for themselves" (Gen. 3:7).

Truly, the eyes of Adam and Eve are opened, but their first vision
is not divine omniscience. Rather, it's an exposure of their nakedness,
which they find necessary to cover. They have lost the radiant perfection of glorified bodies and must look with shame on their corruptible flesh. It must have horrified them, for they sought to shield their
bodies as if trying to deny the effects of the Fall.

The Lord confronts Adam and Eve, who are quick to confess –
and equally swift to pass the buck. Adam blames Eve, and Eve pins it
on the serpent. God then curses the serpent, as well as the ground,
and he announces the consequences of human rebellion against their
creator (Gen. 3:14, 16-19).

But the Lord also comes in grace, delivering a message of doom (for the serpent) and hope (for mankind): "I will put hostility between you [the serpent] and the woman, and between your offspring and her offspring. He will strike your head, and you will strike his heel" (Gen. 3:15).

This is the first of more than four hundred messianic references in the Old Testament.[7] God promises that a future male descendant of Eve will "strike" – that is, crush, smite in pieces, greatly injure – the head of the serpent, while the serpent will strike the deliverer's heel.

Many additional Old Testament prophecies paint a more complete picture of a virgin-born redeemer who is God in human flesh. Jesus of Nazareth is the fulfillment of these prophecies. In fact, Jesus makes it clear he has come to destroy the works of the devil (John 12:31; 16:11; 1 John 3:8).

Because of Jesus' death on the cross and his resurrection, he delivers the fatal blow to Satan's dominion over mankind (Acts 10:38; 26:15-18; Eph. 4:8; Col. 2:15; Jas. 4:7). At his future return, Jesus vanquishes the father of lies and casts him into hell, a place prepared for him and his angels (Matt. 25:41; Rev. 20:10).

The cross

With Adam's fall, along with the promise of a future redeemer who crushes the head of Satan, we are propelled forward to the cross, on which Jesus – the last Adam – pays our sin debt in full.

Consider the following bridges between Adam and Jesus, and how they connect the garden and the cross.

Jesus is the last Adam (1 Cor. 15:45). Adam is created a perfect being with dominion over the earth. Yet, he falls into sin and fails in his mission as federal head of the human race. In contrast, Jesus is the uncreated creator of all. He adds sinless humanity to his deity via the miracle of the virgin birth so that he is fully divine and fully human. He overcomes fierce temptation at the hands of the same serpent that woos Eve in the garden. Where Adam fails, Jesus triumphs. Through his victory over Satan, Jesus is now the one who rightfully has dominion over the earth, and who brings many sons and daughters into the ever-expanding kingdom of God.

Jesus encounters the same serpent that visited Eden. Satan comes to Eve in the garden, where food, drink, and comfort are bountifully supplied. But the evil one comes to Jesus in the wilderness, after the Savior has fasted for forty days, and where the necessities of human life are sparse. Satan's goal is the same in the garden and the wilderness: to dethrone the first and last Adams. The first Adam stumbles; the second succeeds as he stands on Scripture to combat the evil one. Later, Jesus' struggle with temptation becomes even more intense. In the Garden of Gethsemane, he sweats drops of blood over the prospect of becoming sin for us (Luke 22:44; 2 Cor. 5:21).

Jesus wears a crown of thorns as a result of Adam's sin. Adam is the crowning achievement of God's creation, and God endows Adam with dominion over the earth. But Adam forfeits his crown for a chance to enlarge God's kingdom for himself – a strategic blunder of cosmic proportions. The earth falls under a curse, which includes the emergence of thorns and thistles. To retake dominion from Satan the usurper, Jesus wears a crown of thorns and is mocked as a powerless king. The way of victory is the way of the cross.

Jesus is offered a scepter, a symbol of sovereignty, that reminds us of the rule God originally gave to Adam and Eve (Gen. 1:26-28). Not long before Jesus' crucifixion, Roman soldiers take him into Pilate's residence. There, they strip him and dress him in a scarlet robe. They twist together a crown of thorns, place it on his head, and put a staff – a crude scepter – in Jesus' right hand. Then, they kneel before Jesus and mock him: "Hail, king of the Jews!" After that, they remove the scarlet robe, put his own clothes back on him, and lead him to the cross (Matt. 27:27-31).

The soldiers fail to understand they are mocking a true king, one whose kingdom is not of this world (John 18:36). One day, however, the kingdom of the world becomes the kingdom of our Lord and of his Christ, and he will reign forever and ever (Rev. 11:15). As God the Father declares to his Son: "Your throne, God, is forever and ever, and the scepter of your kingdom is a scepter of justice" (Heb. 1:8; cf. Ps. 45:6-7).

Jesus hangs naked on a cross, which harkens back to the garden where Adam and Eve discover their nakedness and seek to cover it with leaves. Considering the sinful shame of Adam and Eve, God clothes the first humans with animal skins. Likely, these are the skins of sacrificial animals as God teaches Adam and Eve about the seriousness of sin – it requires death – and the necessity of blood atonement. This first covering in the garden sets in motion an entire system of animal sacrifice fulfilled on the cross, where the Lamb of God takes away the sin of the world (John 1:29).

Jesus is forsaken, just as Adam and Eve are banished from God's presence. Sin brings alienation from God. Spiritual death is the cold darkness of the human spirit – the uninhabited holy of holies in our mortal bodies. Death of the soul is the slow agony of experiencing life in the flesh. Physical death is the separation of the material part of man from the immaterial. Each of these deaths – of spirit, soul, and body – is a type of banishment. And as he who knew no sin becomes sin for us (2 Cor. 5:21), Jesus embraces this agony and cries out, "My God, my God, why have you forsaken me?" (Matt. 27:46 ESV).

Jesus becomes sin for us because Adam births sin for us. The apostle Paul explains it this way: "If by the one man's trespass, death reigned through that one man, how much more will those who receive the overflow of grace and the gift of righteousness reign in life through the one man, Jesus Christ" (Rom. 5:17). Adam's sin marks the end of innocence. From that point forward, all people are naturally born sinners because they inherit Adam's sin nature. But Christ's sacrifice on the cross marks the end of death. Those who trust in Jesus experience three types of new life: new life in the spirit (regeneration); new life in the soul (sanctification); and new life in the body (glorification).

Jesus hangs on a tree because Adam hangs humanity on a tree. The first humans are granted free access to all the trees in Eden, except one. Their fascination with the tree of the knowledge of good and evil contributes to their fall and ushers in the curse of all creation. Much later, Jesus hangs on a tree at Calvary, becoming a curse for us. Under

Old Testament law, anyone guilty of a capital crime and hung on a tree is under God's curse (Deut. 21:22-23).

Paul picks up on this in Galatians 3:13 to show us that Jesus' sacrificial death removes the curse: "Christ redeemed us from the curse of the law by becoming a curse for us." What's more, the day is coming when those who have trusted in Jesus will see the curse of creation removed and the tree of life offered freely to all the redeemed (Rev. 22:2-3).

God's work of redemption, completed in the death, burial, and resurrection of Jesus, turns spiritual death into spiritual life; makes the darkened mind the mind of Christ; and guarantees the future glorification of the corruptible earthly body. Even the curse of this sinful and fallen world is reversed one day in the creation of new heavens and a new earth (2 Pet. 3:10-13; Rev. 21-22).

What Jesus suffers on the cross is reminiscent of what happens in the Fall in the Garden of Eden. In fact, the Fall necessitates the cross. And while bystanders at the base of Golgotha may think they are witnessing brutal justice applied to a presumptuous king, they are in fact eyewitnesses of a glorious reversal of fortune.

Yes, Jesus suffers terribly. The serpent has struck his heel. Yet, three days later, when Jesus rises triumphantly from the grave, he crushes the serpent's head with that same bruised heel. What's more, he begins the process of reversing mankind's death of body, soul, and spirit, restoring the created order to the pristine perfection of Eden before the Fall.

But it takes the glorious return of Christ to complete this gracious act of divine intervention.

THE GLORIOUS RETURN AND THE GARDEN RESTORED

John's vision of the returning Christ reveals marvelous truths about the Lord's conquest of sin and his restoration of righteousness. Stand with John on the Isle of Patmos and share his experience:

Then I saw heaven opened, and there was a white horse. Its rider is called Faithful and True, and with justice he judges and makes war. His eyes were like a fiery flame, and many crowns were on his head. He had a name written that no one knows except himself. He wore a robe dipped in blood, and his name is called the Word of God. The armies that were in heaven followed him on white horses, wearing pure white linen. A sharp sword came from his mouth, so that he might strike the nations with it. He will rule them with an iron rod. He will also trample the winepress of the fierce anger of God, the Almighty. And he has a name written on his robe and on his thigh: King of Kings and Lord of Lords (Rev. 19:11-16).

John captures many details that show how Christ's glorious return sets in motion his final battle with sin, thus paving the way for a restored Eden. Let's examine a few of these features.

Jesus rides a white horse from heaven. This is in stark contrast to Jesus' triumphal entry into Jerusalem, in which the Son of Man rides a borrowed donkey (Matt. 21:1-10). A horse is used for war; a donkey, for peace. A horse is a symbol of conquest; a donkey, a vehicle of humility. Jesus comes humbly the first time as the Suffering Servant, but he rides with the clouds of heaven victoriously as the conquering king in his return to earth. This illustrates that Jesus has won complete victory over Satan, sin, and death. The pristine Garden of Eden is about to be restored as the last Adam regains what the first Adam lost – dominion over the earth, and immortality.

The horse's color is significant. White signifies victory, and "Christ now goes to his final triumph."[8] Kendall Easley adds, "Christ is a conquering King, a picture of the victorious Lord at the end of the age. It is not Caesar who holds the balance of the world's power, but Jesus the Lord."[9]

As one commentary notes:

The white horse is a sign of His coming triumph. It was customary for a triumphant Roman general to parade on the Via Sacra, a main thoroughfare of Rome, followed by evidences of his victory in the form of booty and captives (cf. 2 Cor. 2:14). The white horse is thus a symbol of Christ's triumph over the forces of wickedness in the world.[10]

Jesus is called "Faithful and True." The Lord is not merely a proclaimer of faithfulness and truthfulness, or even an exemplar of these qualities. Rather, he *is* divine faithfulness and truth incarnate. As Matthew Henry notes, "He is faithful and true to his covenant and promise, he is righteous in all his judicial and military proceedings, he has a penetrating insight into all the strength and stratagems of his enemies, he has a large and extensive dominion, for he is King of kings, and Lord of lords."[11]

Despite the names Jesus' opponents call him – a demon-possessed Samaritan (John 8:48), a blasphemer (Matt. 26:65), and an illegitimate child (John 8:41), to name a few – he is "the way, the truth, and the life" (John 14:6). He has promised to return, and now he proves once again that he keeps his word. The wicked are judged, the righteous vindicated. Satan, the father of lies who wrecks innocence in the Garden of Eden, is soon destroyed by the very Word who created all things and declared them good. The lie that plunges mankind into ruin gives way to the Truth who sets people free. Eden wilts under the corruption of sin. The new Eden blooms with life-giving truth.

With justice, Jesus judges and makes war. Since Adam's fall, mankind has rushed to judgment and war, but rarely with justice in mind. Adam and Eve are quick to pass the buck when God questions them about their disobedience. Their firstborn son, Cain, murders his brother, and human history launches into a descending spiral of violence from that point forward.

God delivers justice in the garden as he curses the serpent and pronounces sin's consequences on Adam and Eve. He also promises a redeemer who ultimately – and justly – crushes the serpent's head.

God always judges with perfect justice, seasoned with grace. We see it in the flood in Noah's day, as the Lord waits for more than a century for the world's wicked to repent. We see it in Sodom and Gomorrah, where Lot and his family are granted an escape, and where Abraham petitions on behalf of any righteous people left in those communities. We see it in the cycle of judges God gives the Israelites, and in the sacrificial system in which the death of a spotless animal atones for human transgression. Ultimately, we see God's perfect justice in the death of his Son, who offers his sinless life on the cross to take away our sin.

Warfare is a constant in the human experience. From the earliest pages of Scripture through the day of Christ's future return, people take up the sword against one another and, ultimately, against Christ. Thomas Aquinas developed a just war theory in the 13th century. It set out conditions for determining whether a war should be waged and, if it could be justified, how it should be fought. But for the most part, people have engaged in warfare with impunity, seeking to wipe out rivals, conquer vast tracts of land, or even murder their own citizens. God's campaign against the Canaanites comes only after a four-century wait, until there is no redeeming spark in their beliefs or practices.

But when Christ returns, he wages a perfectly just war. The holy one of God always confronts sin head on and with relentless purpose. He battles Satan in the wilderness and sends the evil one packing (Matt. 4:1-11). He drives the money changers from the temple in his zealousness to make God's house a house of prayer (Matt. 21:13). He pronounces woes on the religious leaders of his day for their greed, pride, and hypocrisy, wondering aloud how they possibly can escape the fires of hell (Matt. 23:33). And he wages war with Satan in a most unique battle plan, laying down his life for his friends (John 15:13).

The Son of God is neither weak nor aloof. His holiness demands justice. His sovereignty commands warfare against the ungodly who seek to usurp his throne. At his triumphant return, he wages a solitary war – the angels and saints who accompany him are but observers – destroying all who stand on the wrong side of divine justice.

In the wake of sin, Eden blushes with shame, hardship, guilt, and banishment. But in the new heavens and earth, Christ makes all things new (Rev. 21:5). And the tree of life, refused to Adam and Eve in their fallen state, is now available to all for the healing of nations and the end of the curse (Rev. 22:2-3).

Jesus' eyes are like a fiery flame, and he wears many crowns. In the garden, God sends cherubim with flaming swords to prevent Adam and Eve from reentering Eden. The blazing weapons depict the holiness of God as he separates sinners from intimate fellowship with him. The first parents once shared that holiness – a passion for God and his perfection. But now they experience the cutting edge of holiness as they rebel against their creator.

The blazing eyes of Jesus describe his piercing holiness, as well as his omniscience. In John's vision of the risen Lord in Revelation 1:13-14, he sees "one like the Son of Man" with "eyes like a fiery flame." And in the opening lines of the letter to the church at Thyatira, Jesus describes himself as "the one whose eyes are like a fiery flame" (Rev. 2:18).

There is an Old Testament tie here. The angel who appears to Daniel to tell him what will become of the Israelites in the last days has "eyes like flaming torches" (Dan. 10:6). While this is not the preincarnate Christ, it is a holy angel who engages in battle in the unseen world and whose appearance strikes fear in the eyes of mortals like Daniel. Perhaps the Jewish readers of Revelation are reminded that God has not abandoned his people, whether they are in exile in Babylon or scattered throughout the Roman Empire.

Jesus also wears many crowns. These crowns are not *stephanoi*, or garlands of victory, such as those placed on the heads of athletes, but *diadema*, or royal crowns fit for the King of kings. In John's day, monarchs who claimed authority over more than one country wore more than one crown. The kings of Egypt wore the *Pshent*, or united crowns of Upper and Lower Egypt. When Ptolemy Philometer entered Antioch in the second century B.C., he wore a triple crown: two for Egypt and a third for Asia.[12]

The seven diadems on the seven heads of the dragon (Rev. 12:3), and the ten diadems on the ten horns of the beast from the sea (Rev. 13:1), are usurpers' crowns. The wearers of these crowns claim authority to which only Christ is entitled. And here, Jesus wears the "many crowns" as radiant proof that he alone possesses all authority in heaven and on earth (Matt. 28:18).

The psalmist writes that God crowned Adam with glory and honor and made him ruler over creation (Ps. 8:5-8). But the first human being fell through disobedience, and the created order fell with him. Adam lost dominion over the earth, and usurpers have been claiming it as their own ever since. In contrast, Jesus – the last Adam – faithfully carries out his role as the Son of Man. Being obedient unto death on a cross, Jesus reclaims what Adam lost. One day, every knee bows and every tongue confesses that Jesus Christ is Lord (Phil. 2:5-11).

The writer of Hebrews elevates a quote from Psalm 8, taking what was written about Adam before the Fall to its fulfillment in Christ. In so doing, the writer anticipates a future exercise of dominion over all things:

> For he [God] has not subjected to angels the world to come that we are talking about. But someone somewhere has testified:
> What is man that you remember him,
> or the son of man that you care for him?
> You made him lower than the angels for a short time;
> you crowned him with glory and honor
> and subjected everything under his feet.
>
> For in subjecting everything to him, he left nothing that is not subject to him. As it is, we do not yet see everything subjected to him. But we do see Jesus — made lower than the angels for a short time so that by God's grace he might taste death for everyone — crowned with glory and honor because he suffered death (Heb. 2:5-9).

Jesus wears a crown of thorns to the cross. But he wears all the diadems of heaven and earth when he returns in glory.

Jesus has a name written that no one knows except himself. When Adam falls, his banishment from Eden severs mankind's face-to-face fellowship with God. As such, much of what could be known of God is hidden from Adam – and from us. For sinful and fallen human beings, the Lord has not revealed everything about himself and his plan. At the same time, we must realize that because Christ is infinite, certain unknowable aspects of his attributes will always remain. "Humans, even in their eternal glorified condition, may only know what he chooses to reveal, and his secret name reminds us of this."[13]

In Deuteronomy 29:29, we're told, "The hidden things belong to the LORD our God, but the revealed things belong to us and our children forever, so that we may follow all the words of this law." When other nations see Israel defeated in battle, and its people carried into captivity, they assume God has cancelled the covenant between himself and his people. But they fail to see that the Lord, who keeps his promises, is working through human history to bring his people to repentance so they may enjoy unending fellowship with him.

In a letter to the church at Pergamum, Jesus promises the victor a white stone inscribed with a new name that no one knows except the one who receives it (Rev. 2:17). In the fulfillment of this pledge, disciples are made like our Lord. His own name is to become ours. One day, we will know what Adam could have known about God – not just intellectually, but experientially. As John writes, "Dear friends, we are God's children now, and what we will be has not yet been revealed. We know that when he appears, we will be like him because we will see him as he is" (1 John 3:2-3).

Adam bore the untarnished image of God. And the high priest bore the inscribed words, "Holy to the LORD," on the miter on his brow (Exod. 28:36-38). The 144,000 on Mount Zion have the name of Jesus and God the Father on their foreheads (Rev. 14:1). And the day is coming when we see the Lamb's face, and his name is on our foreheads (Rev. 22:4). Eden is restored, and the triune God is revealed to us in new and glorious ways.

He wears a robe dipped in blood. There is considerable disagreement among Bible commentators as to whose blood stains the robe of Jesus. Is it Jesus' own blood? The blood of the martyrs? Or, is it the blood of the wicked who oppose Christ at his return? Could it be all of these?

Leon Morris argues that Christ's own blood is in view:

> This is surely a reference to Calvary; Christ overcame by shedding his
> blood.... It is not impossible that both ideas are in mind [Christ's
> blood and the blood of his enemies], but it is more than difficult to
> hold that John writes of blood without a thought of the blood shed on
> the cross. In this book he repeatedly makes the point that it is in his
> capacity as the 'Lamb as though slain' that Christ conquers. He over-
> came, not by shedding the blood of others, but by shedding his own.
> Besides, at this point the battle has not yet been joined, nor the wine-
> press trodden.[14]

Other commentators point to Isaiah 63 as the prophetic basis for
Christ's vengeance on the ungodly:

> Who is this coming from Edom in crimson-stained garments from
> Bozrah – this one who is splendid in his apparel, striding in his
> formidable might? It is I, proclaiming vindication, powerful to save.
> Why are your clothes red, and your garments like one who treads a
> winepress? I trampled the winepress alone, and no one from the
> nations was with me. I trampled them in my anger and ground them
> underfoot in my fury; their blood spattered my garments, and all my
> clothes were stained. For I planned the day of vengeance, and the year
> of my redemption came (Isa. 63:1-4).

This leads some interpreters to write that the blood on Jesus' robe
is "probably not his own, but the blood of his enemies. In this respect,
John's vision draws on the fearful dialogue of Isaiah 63:1-6."[15]

But perhaps it's best to see the blood-stained robe as both
prophetically fulfilled and anticipatory. In Isaiah 63, the blood is not
Messiah's own, but the blood of his foes – a foretelling of what occurs
in Revelation 19:15-21. In other words, Isaiah predicts what is about
to happen to Jesus' enemies at his return.

In Revelation 19:13, however, the blood on Jesus' robe could be his
own – a reminder of his shed blood at Calvary, even for the sake of

the ungodly who trample on it. That blood symbolizes Christ's victory over Satan, sin, and death, and his authority to rule with a rod of iron. Now, the conquering Jesus sheds the blood of others – not of the godly, as the forces of the antichrist do, but the blood of the ungodly. The blood of Jesus is redemptive; the blood of his enemies is retributive.

In the garden, Adam tries to usurp God's authority. The result is a bloody mess. An animal sacrifice has to be offered to atone for his sin and to provide clothing to cover his nakedness. On the cross, the Lamb of God hangs naked as he bleeds out his life, not to temporarily cover sin, but to take it away. On the clouds of heaven, Christ returns, wearing garments that remind us of his bloody sacrifice on our behalf, and fulfilling the prophecy of Isaiah 63 to take vengeance on those who trample the blood of Jesus and kill the Lord's faithful followers.

His name is called the Word of God. In his Gospel account, John tells us of the person and work of Jesus as the incarnate Word (John 1:1-18). He is eternal, divine, distinct from the Father and yet equal with him. He is the creator of everything. He added sinless humanity to his deity in the Incarnation and thus pitched his tent with sinful and fallen people. Though rejected by his own, he is the true source of light and life. And to those who trust in him, he grants the right to be God's adopted children. He is God revealed in human flesh.

Warren Wiersbe writes, "A word is made up of letters, and Jesus Christ is 'Alpha and Omega' (Rev. 21:6; 22:13). He is the 'divine alphabet' of God's revelation to us…. Just as the Word was the Father's Agent in Creation (John 1:1-3), so the Word is His Agent for judgment and consummation."[16]

In Eden, Adam and Eve walk with the eternal Word, by whom they were created. But sin banishes them from intimacy with God. For their own protection, they are denied access to the tree of life, which would seal them forever in a fallen state. Eden, the intersection between God's unseen realm and the physical world he created, is no longer freely available to sinful people. But in the Incarnation, God once again breaks into the physical realm through the virgin birth of the eternal Son. As John writes, "No one has ever seen God. The one and only Son, who is himself God and is at the Father's side – he has revealed him" (John 1:18).

And now, in Revelation 19, the Word of God again appears – not to create, suffer, or die, but to gloriously claim the prize he won through his sinless life and sacrificial death on the cross. He comes for us – the redeemed he has purchased with his own blood. He reverses the curse that Adam's sin wrought on mankind and his environment. He judges the wicked, casts them out, purges the physical realm of sin and its stain, and creates new heavens and a new earth. Put simply, the Word restores Eden.

The armies in heaven follow Jesus on white horses, wearing pure white linen. It's important to note that John sees more than one army; he sees *armies* in heaven. This indicates that both angels and saints accompany Jesus in his return. The host, or armies, of heaven in Scripture often are supernatural beings (Deut. 33:2; 1 Kings 22:19; Ps. 68:17; Luke 2:13). What's more, angels play a key role in Christ's second advent (Zech. 14:5; Matt. 13:41; 25:31; Luke 9:26; 2 Thess. 1:7). But redeemed people in heaven also follow Jesus back to earth as he executes judgment on the wicked and takes his rightful place in the kingdom (1 Thess. 3:13; 2 Thess. 1:10).

Angels in Scripture sometimes are depicted wearing white (John 20:12). The saints also are clothed in white robes, signifying both the righteousness of Christ and their good deeds (Rev. 6:11; 7:13-14; 19:8; cf. Phil. 3:9). Their robes remain spotless, for it is the Word of God, wearing a blood-stained robe and wielding a sword, who wages war against the enemies of God and God's people.

In the Garden of Eden, the Word is rejected as Adam and Eve seek their own path of fulfillment. In the Incarnation, the Word becomes flesh, only to be despised and rejected by those who should have recognized the time when God visited them (Isa. 53:3; Luke 19:44; John 1:11). In the Garden of Gethsemane, the disciples desert Jesus (Matt. 26:56). In the courtyard outside the high priest's home, Peter denies Jesus three times (Matt. 26:69-75). On the cross, Jesus cries out, "My God, my God, why have you abandoned me?" (Matt. 27:46).

But what a spectacular turn of events we see in the return of Jesus.

The despised one now leads armies of angels and saints in his triumphant reentry of earth's atmosphere. The deserted one now leads enthusiastic hordes riding in his wake on white horses. The denied one is surrounded by hosts of heavenly and earthly creatures who acclaim him as worthy of all praise. The malicious betrayal of the Son of God since the days of Eden is now eclipsed by the unified armies of heaven riding victoriously behind their glorious king.

Jesus strikes the nations with a sharp sword and rules them with an iron rod. This is the same double-edged sword John sees in the opening vision on Patmos (Rev. 1:16) and revealed in Christ's letter to Pergamum (Rev. 2:12, 16). It should be clear this is figurative language describing the powerful spoken word of our Savior.

The word translated "sword" in Revelation 19:15 is *rhomphaia* and is used of an unusually long sword, or even a spear, indicating a piercing action. John may be referring to Isaiah 11:4, where a future Davidic king will "strike the land with a scepter from his mouth, and he will kill the wicked with a command from his lips." John also may have Hebrews 4:12 in mind. There, the "word of God is living and effective and sharper than any double-edged sword." No doubt, the spoken word of Christ, which has the power to create (see Gen. 1:3 ff; John 1:3; Col. 1:16), also has the power to judge.

As for ruling with an iron rod, John draws from previous Scriptures to symbolize Christ's justice as he rules the earth. In Revelation 2:26-27, John quotes the messianic prophecy of Psalm 2:9: "You will break them [the nations] with an iron scepter; you will shatter them like pottery." And in Revelation 12:5, John sees the Son "who is going to rule all nations with an iron rod."

The word *rule* may be rendered "tend as a shepherd." But in this context, it means ruling in a punitive way. "He, who would have *shepherded* them with pastoral rod and with the golden scepter of His love, shall dash them in pieces, as refractory rebels, with 'a rod of iron.'"[17]

While the Lord entrusts all people with an ability to make choices for which they are held accountable, those who rebel against God and persecute his people are not permitted to perpetually harm the saints or blaspheme their creator.

The dominion granted Adam in the Garden of Eden is revoked as a penalty for sin (Gen. 1:26, 28; 2:15; 3:23-24). Access to the tree of life is denied. A cursed ground yields its fruit stubbornly to the man formed out of it, and who returns to it one day. But the returning Christ, who created the tree of life, and who is life himself, rides a white horse from heaven to earth, reclaiming the dominion mankind forfeited in rebellion. The Chief Shepherd tends to his sheep, who return with him in white robes, riding white horses. And he violently *shepherds* the wicked who oppose his rule.

Jesus tramples the winepress of the fierce anger of God, the Almighty. This reference is rooted deeply in Old Testament imagery. We see it in Isaiah 63:2-3, as a future Davidic king judges the nations; in Jeremiah 51:33, as God punishes Babylon; in Lamentations 1:15, as God judges Judah; and in Joel 3:13, as the Lord judges the nations. We also see the imagery in Revelation 14:14-20, where Christ, or a delegated angel, harvests the earth's wicked. Perhaps Revelation 14 and 19 are two descriptions of the same event.

In any case, the color of crushed grapes vividly depicts the blood Christ shed on Calvary for our sins, as well as the blood about to be shed when the victorious king returns to take vengeance on those who reject him and revile his people. The treading of the winepress points to the complete overthrow of those who resist Christ at his second coming.

Adam's rebellion in Eden results in bloodshed – that is, the death of an innocent animal to atone for his sin (Gen. 3:21), and the slaughter of countless animals going forward in countless ceremonies to cover mankind's guilt before a holy and offended God. But the shed blood of the Lamb of God – to which these animal sacrifices point – does not merely atone for our sins; it takes our sins away (John 1:29; Heb. 9:26). And now, the conquering king, with a robe stained in his own blood, returns to earth to demand the blood of those who reject his life-giving sacrifice.

The fierce anger of God, the Almighty, has always been directed against sin. By his grace, he has redirected it to sacrificial animals and, ultimately, to the life of his Son on the cross. Having satisfied the

Father's wrath against sin through his substitutionary death, the resurrected and glorified Jesus now returns to exact justice on those who trample his blood and thus reject his Father's gracious offer of redemption.

Jesus has a name written on his robe and on his thigh. Unlike the written name known only to Jesus in Revelation 19:12, the name John now sees written on Jesus' robe and thigh are clear for everyone to see: "King of Kings and Lord of Lords" (Rev. 19:16). These are in fact two titles. In the only other place they appear together in Revelation, the order is reversed (Rev. 17:14). Elsewhere in the Bible, these titles often are ascribed separately to God. But now they appear together, etched indelibly on the God-Man as he returns victoriously to earth.

Kendell Easley notes, "The Caesars were fond of being called *king* (Greek *basileus*) and *lord* (Greek *kyrios*). Jesus is King over earth's kings, Lord over all other lords, demonstrated beyond question in his ultimate victory over 'the kings of the earth' (Rev. 19:19)."[18]

The name that Jesus bears brings to mind references such as Daniel 2:47, in which Nebuchadnezzar acknowledges, "Your God is indeed God of gods, Lord of kings, and a revealer of mysteries." It also recalls the words of Moses to the Israelites in Deuteronomy 10:17: "For the LORD your God is the God of gods and the Lord of lords, the great, mighty, and awe-inspiring God." Paul also uses these titles for God in 1 Timothy 6:15: "He is the blessed and only Sovereign, the King of kings, and the Lord of lords, who alone is immortal and who lives in unapproachable light, whom no one has seen or can see, to him be honor and eternal power."

The first man to exist is named *Adam.* While that name is not written on his forehead or borne elsewhere on his body, it is imprinted *in* the first human being. God speaks everything into existence until the sixth day of creation. Then, he reaches down in the dirt and forms Adam from it. In fact, the name *Adam* is related to *adamah,* the Hebrew word for "ground" or "soil." Unlike all other creatures, Adam is made in the image, or likeness, of God (Gen. 1:26-27). That is, he bears the divine stamp of the creator in his body, soul, and spirit. So does Eve. And so does every human being from that time forward.

Through sin, Adam loses his special relationship with God. He and Eve are banished from Eden. The curse of sin falls on all the earth and its inhabitants. And all people inherit Adam's tendency to live independently of God. It seems hopeless, except for God's promise of a future redeemer (Gen. 3:15).

This redeemer comes to earth two thousand years ago, bearing the name *second*, or *last*, Adam (1 Cor. 15:45-49; cf. Rom. 5:12-19; 1 Cor. 15:21-22). For the first time since the days of Adam, a man appears on earth who has no human father. The eternal Son of God steps aside from his privileged place at the Father's right hand and humbles himself, taking on human flesh, becoming a man who shares fully in our humanity.

Jesus claims many names for himself, from "Son of Man" to "good shepherd" to "I AM." His eyewitnesses call him many names as well, from "Christ" to "rabbi" to "illegitimate child." As he hangs on the cross, a name is inscribed above him: "Jesus of Nazareth, the King of the Jews" (John 19:19). In reaction to this name, the religious leaders scoff in unbelief. But Jesus *is* the true king. The last Adam – God in human flesh – performs the ultimate kingly act in sacrificing his life for his subjects.

And now, John sees Jesus returning from heaven in victory, with "King of kings and Lord of lords" emblazoned on his clothing. All those who assign derisive names to Jesus, and all those who ascribe good but inadequate names to the last Adam, now see him clearly as he is. Citizens of his kingdom wear white robes and ride triumphantly behind him. Meanwhile, those who reject the last Adam as King of kings find themselves at the wrong end of his sword.

In every way, the victorious return of Jesus brings back Eden by the way of the cross. The tree of life, denied sinful humans in the garden, is made accessible again in the new heavens and earth only because the eternal Son of God became a curse for us on a tree at Calvary.

REVIEW

Key takeaways from this chapter

1. In declaring on the cross, "It is finished," Jesus makes it clear he has completed the redemptive work for which the Father sent him. Even though there are many ways in which the Greek *tetelestai* may be interpreted – a paid-in-full debt, a battlefield rout, a covering of sin – there is little doubt that Jesus employs the term as a cry of victory. Satan gets the message three days later when this same Jesus, whose brutalized body has lain wrapped in burial clothes and anointed with spices, emerges victoriously from a borrowed tomb.

2. To more fully appreciate the victorious return of Jesus, we need to look back at what he suffers on the cross, and even further back to what necessitates the cross – Adam's fall in the Garden of Eden. God's promise to the first humans to send a redeemer (Gen. 3:15) is fulfilled in Jesus. Because of his death, burial, and resurrection, Jesus delivers a fatal blow to Satan's dominion over mankind. At his future return, Jesus vanquishes the father of lies and casts him into hell, a place prepared for him and his angels.

3. Scripture connects Adam and Jesus – and thus, Eden and the cross – in many ways. For example:

(a) Jesus is the last Adam;

(b) Jesus encounters the same serpent who visited Eden;

(c) Jesus wears a crown of thorns as a result of Adam's sin;

(d) Jesus is offered a scepter that reminds us of the rule God originally gave to Adam and Eve;

(e) Jesus hangs naked on a cross, which reminds us of the garden where Adam and Eve discover their nakedness and seek to cover it;

(f) Jesus is forsaken, just as Adam and Eve are banished from God's presence;

(g) Jesus becomes sin for us because Adam births sin for us;

(h) Jesus hangs on a tree because Adam hangs humanity on a tree.

4. In his vision of the returning Christ (Rev. 19:11-16), John captures many details that show how the Lord's second coming sets in motion his final battle with sin, thus paving a way for a restored Eden. Consider:

(a) Jesus rides a white horse from heaven;

(b) He is called "Faithful and True";

(c) He judges and makes war with justice;

(d) His eyes are like a fiery flame;

(e) He has a name written no one knows except himself;

(f) He wears a robe dipped in blood;

(g) His name is called the Word of God;

(h) Armies in heaven follow him on white horses;

(i) He strikes the nations with a sharp sword and rules them with a rod of iron;

(j) He tramples the winepress of the fierce anger of God, the Almighty;

(k) He has a name written on his robe and on his thigh: "King of Kings and Lord of Lords."

5. In every way, the victorious return of Jesus brings back Eden by the way of the cross. The tree of life, denied sinful humans in the garden, is made accessible again in the new heavens and earth only because the eternal Son of God became a curse for us on a tree at Calvary.

DISCUSS

Questions for personal or group study

1. What are some different ways the Greek word *tetelestai* – "It is finished" – may have been interpreted by the eyewitnesses of Jesus' crucifixion? How do you think Jesus meant this cry from the cross to be understood?

2. Read Genesis 3:1-7; 2 Corinthians 11:3; and Revelation 20:2. Who is *the serpent* that appears to Eve in the Garden of Eden? Why is it wrong to think of the serpent as a mere "talking snake"? And what are several tactics the serpent employs in Eden to tempt Eve that he still uses today?

3. Read 1 Corinthians 15:45-49. Why does Paul refer to Jesus as "the last Adam"? In the context of Paul's writing on the resurrection, what do human beings have in common with the first Adam and the last Adam?

4. Read Revelation 19:11-16. How does the horse Jesus rides from heaven compare with the donkey he rode into Jerusalem on Palm Sunday (Matt. 21:1-10)? What are some names and titles that accompany Jesus at his return? And why are they significant?

5. In Revelation 19:13, John writes that Jesus wears a robe dipped in blood. Whose blood is on the robe? How does that connect with what John records a couple of verses later: "He will also trample the winepress of the fierce anger of God, the Almighty" (v. 15).

* * *

———————— A ————————

The swift coming of Jesus
produces a great divide. Some
are taken and some are left.
But all are called to be
prepared.

———————— Ω ————————

"I AM COMING LIKE A THIEF"

JESUS IS RETURNING SUDDENLY

On January 17, 1950, eleven men wearing navy blue coats and chauffeurs' caps entered a Brink's Armored Car depot in Boston. Covering their faces with rubber Halloween masks, the men surprised several Brink's employees and tied them up in the company's counting room.

The thieves filled fourteen canvas bags with cash, coins, checks, and money orders — in total, more than 2.7 million dollars' worth of loot weighing more than half a ton — then sped away in a getaway car. It was the largest robbery in U.S. history up to that time. And it proved to be the perfect crime — almost.

Mastermind Anthony "Fats" Pino, a career criminal, and his ten fellow thieves staked out the depot for eighteen months before pulling off the heist. During the thirty-minute caper, they injured no one, and they left almost no clues. The gang members promised to stay out of trouble. They further vowed not to touch the stolen loot for six years, when the statute of limitations would expire.

They nearly made it, except for the antics of one man, Joseph "Specs" O'Keefe, who left his share with another gang member in order to serve a prison sentence for a different burglary. While imprisoned, O'Keefe wrote bitterly to his cohorts, demanding money and hinting that he might talk if he didn't get what he wanted. The group sent a hitman to rub out O'Keefe, but the would-be assassin was caught before completing the job. The wounded O'Keefe made a deal with the FBI to testify against his cronies.

Eight of the Brink's robbers were caught, convicted, and given life sentences. Two others died before they could face prosecution. Only a small part of the money was ever recovered; the rest is fabled to be tucked away in the hills north of Grand Rapids, Minnesota. Hollywood immortalized the heist in a 1978 film, *The Brink's Job*, starring Peter Falk.[1]

As the Brink's story illustrates, successful thieves employ at least two tactics: they plan meticulously, and they leverage the element of surprise. Whether it's Butch Cassidy's celebrated robbery of the San Miguel Valley Bank in 1889,[2] D. B. Cooper's audacious hijacking of a Boeing 727 jet in 1971,[3] or the nearly perfect Brink's job, the success of any theft requires a great deal of thought and swift execution.

So, when Jesus tells his followers he's coming back like a thief (Rev. 16:15), we should understand that his return to earth is carefully planned and flawlessly executed. In fact, Jesus, Paul, and Peter all compare Christ's second coming to the actions of a thief.

Not that Jesus fancies himself a mobster or relishes the thought of conducting his own Brink's heist. He's coming to take what's rightfully his, not lavish himself with ill-gotten gain. Further, we may clearly distinguish Jesus from false teachers, whom he describes as thieves that come to steal, kill, and destroy (John 10:10). In short, Jesus applies a thief's exhaustive planning and precise execution to the manner in which he returns one day.

Let's explore a section of the Olivet Discourse (Matt. 24-25) in which Jesus addresses the suddenness of his return. Then, we'll see how Jesus uses parables to illustrate the thief-like elements of that coming day. It should become clear that Jesus warns us to be ready, for both the rescue of the righteous and the judgment of the wicked are swift and sure.

THE SUDDENNESS OF JESUS' RETURN

We begin with an excerpt from the Olivet Discourse in which Jesus applies history, prophecy, and an analogy to underscore the suddenness of his return.

Matthew 24:36-44

Now concerning that day and hour no one knows — neither the angels of heaven nor the Son — except the Father alone. As the days of Noah were, so the coming of the Son of Man will be. For in those days before the flood they were eating and drinking, marrying and giving in marriage, until the day Noah boarded the ark. They didn't know until the flood came and swept them all away. This is the way the coming of the Son of Man will be. Then two men will be in the field; one will be taken and one left. Two women will be grinding grain with a hand mill; one will be taken and one left. Therefore be alert, since you don't know what day your Lord is coming. But know this: If the homeowner had known what time the thief was coming, he would have stayed alert and not let his house be broken into. This is why you are also to be ready, because the Son of Man is coming at an hour you do not expect.

Jesus takes his disciples back to the story of Noah and likens his return to that dramatic historical event. In the days before the flood, "they" – that is, unbelievers who rejected Noah's prophetic message – ate, drank, and married. There's nothing inherently sinful about these activities. What's striking, however, is that the wicked are condemned for disregarding Noah's warnings and living as if there were no consequences of their actions.

In his second epistle, Peter connects the same unbelieving attitude with "scoffers" in the last days, who insist that "all things continue as they have been since the beginning of creation" (2 Pet. 3:3-4). Like those in Noah's day, scoffers in the end times experience the suddenness and certainty of divine judgment (2 Pet. 3:5-7).

Of those in Noah's day, Jesus says, "They didn't know until the flood came and swept them all away. This is the way the coming of the Son of Man will be" (Matt. 24:39). We should note here that the wicked do not perish for lack of information. Noah is "a preacher of righteousness" (2 Pet. 2:5). And it's clear that in the last days, despite an abundance of gospel proclamations, the wicked harden their hearts against the sincere warnings of God's heralds. They even blaspheme God as he rains down judgment on them (Rev. 16:8-11). In other words, the wicked perish in spite of God's grace, not because of its absence.

Leon Morris notes:

> The purposes of God are worked out quite irrespective of what puny humans think about them. Jesus is saying that people will in this way continue to be about their normal business right up to the time of his coming. That will be the critical point; after that it will be too late, just as it was too late for the antediluvians when the Flood came. *The coming of the Son of man* will be just as abrupt, just as unexpected, just as decisive as the coming of the Flood was.[4]

Jesus goes on to tell his disciples, "Then two men will be in the field; one will be taken and one left. Two women will be grinding grain with a hand mill; one will be taken and one left" (Matt. 24:40-41). Again, these are ordinary human activities in which believers and unbelievers engage, just like eating, drinking, and marrying in the days before the flood.

But the suddenness of Christ's return results in separation. Some experience divine blessing; others, divine judgment. Bible commentators differ as to whether the ones "taken" are raptured followers of Jesus (1 Thess. 4:13-17) or the wicked summoned before the great white throne (Rev. 20:11-15). It seems more likely the redeemed are kept secure as Christ delivers the wicked to justice, but either scenario is possible.

That's because Jesus' point is to stress the suddenness of his return. Those who choose to live without God have their desire cemented in everlasting damnation when the great day comes. "It will be the portion of the godless to be without God," writes Morris.[5]

"Therefore be alert," Jesus says, "since you don't know what day your Lord is coming" (Matt. 24:42). Jesus then draws an analogy: "But know this: If the homeowner had known what time the thief was coming, he would have stayed alert and not let his house be broken into" (v. 43). Jesus is coming as a thief, but "the way, the truth, and the life" is no criminal (John 14:6).

Jesus' point is clear: the thief carefully plots his actions and then executes his plan with cat-like quickness. Surprise overcomes only those who are unprepared. But the homeowner who knows the imminent threat of thieves locks his doors, secures his possessions, guards his loved ones, and stays vigilant so that when the thief comes, the homeowner is not caught off-guard.

There's a message here for believers and unbelievers alike. The swift coming of Jesus produces a great divide. Some are taken and some are left. Some are secure and some perish. Some are rewarded and some are punished. But all are called to be prepared. The wicked are called to repent, and God's delay in brandishing judgment is for their benefit (2 Pet. 3:9). There is heaven to gain and hell to avoid. For the redeemed, they, too, are to be ready, as a bride is to eagerly prepare for the coming of the bridegroom (Matt. 25:1-13). There are rewards to gain and shame to avoid (1 Cor. 3:11-15; 1 John 2:28).

Since Jesus depicts unbelievers as having no regard for God, it should not surprise us that Christ's return catches them off-guard. But for followers of Jesus, there is no excuse. That's why Jesus closes this section of the Olivet Discourse with these words: "This is why you are also to be ready, because the Son of Man is coming at an hour you do not expect" (Matt. 24:44).

JESUS' PARABLES ON THE SUDDENNESS OF HIS RETURN

There are well over a hundred parables in the Bible, but the most beloved are the thirty-plus parables Jesus shares with us. While he's not the first to use this form of teaching,[6] Jesus endows his parables with unparalleled originality and spiritual depth. In fact, more than one-third of all his recorded sayings are parables.

Two Greek words are translated "parable" in the New Testament: *parabole* (forty-eight times), meaning "to represent or stand for something," and *paroimia* (four times in John), meaning "an adage, dark saying, proverb, a presentation deviating from the usual means of speaking." At its most basic meaning, a parable consists of one object or idea laid beside another for the purpose of comparison.

Several of Jesus' parables address the suddenness of his future return in glory.

A faithful and wise servant

Matthew 24:45-51 reads:

Who then is a faithful and wise servant, whom his master has put in charge of his household, to give them food at the proper time? Blessed is that servant whom the master finds doing his job when he comes. Truly I tell you, he will put him in charge of all his possessions. But if that wicked servant says in his heart, "My master is delayed," and starts to beat his fellow servants, and eats and drinks with drunkards, that servant's master will come *on a day he does not expect him and at an hour he does not know.* He will cut him to pieces and assign him a place with the hypocrites, where there will be weeping and gnashing of teeth [emphasis added].

This parable comes on the heels of Jesus' exhortation to be ready for his return, since no one – not even Jesus – knows the day and hour it is to occur (Matt. 24:36-44). A parallel account is recorded in Luke 12:42-46, with an additional warning:

And that servant who knew his master's will and didn't prepare himself or do it will be severely beaten. But the one who did not know and did what deserved punishment will receive a light beating. From everyone who has been given much, much will be required; and from the one who has been entrusted with much, even more will be expected (Luke 12:47-48).

Jesus directs this parable at his disciples, especially those with leadership responsibilities. Much is expected of those Christ has entrusted with his kingdom. A day of reckoning is coming, and some who claim to serve the Lord ultimately prove themselves counterfeits.

Being a member of a Christian community doesn't guarantee a reward, nor does it secure salvation. As the parable of the sower teaches us, some people believe for a while and then fall away – expressing a shallow intellectual or emotional faith that withers beneath the heat of testing or persecution (Matt. 13:1-9).

In a similar way, a church leader may gain quite a following, only to discover on judgment day he is cut to pieces and assigned a place with the hypocrites. The New Testament epistles are replete with warnings against those who sneak in the side door of the church and wreak havoc on the Shepherd's flock (e.g., Acts 20:29-31; 2 Cor. 11:12-15; 2 Pet. 2:1-10).

As Trent Butler comments, "Fake discipleship – discipleship without dedication to Jesus – does not fool the Lord. He will exact the punishment deserved. The servant unprepared for the master's return finds himself suffering the flogging and punishment any unfaithful servant would endure."[7]

Ten virgins

Matthew 25:1-13 reads:

At that time the kingdom of heaven will be like ten virgins who took their lamps and went out to meet the groom. Five of them were foolish and five were wise. When the foolish took their lamps, they didn't take oil with them; but the wise ones took oil in their flasks with their lamps. When the groom was delayed, they all became drowsy and fell asleep.

In the middle of the night there was a shout: "Here's the groom! Come out to meet him."

Then all the virgins got up and trimmed their lamps. The foolish ones said to the wise ones, "Give us some of your oil, because our lamps are going out."

The wise ones answered, "No, there won't be enough for us and for you. Go instead to those who sell oil, and buy some for yourselves."

When they had gone to buy some, the groom arrived, and those who were ready went in with him to the wedding banquet, and the door was shut. Later the rest of the virgins also came and said, "Master, master, open up for us!"

He replied, "Truly I tell you, I don't know you!"

Therefore be alert, because you don't know either the day or the hour (see also Luke 12:35-38).

The central theme of this parable is readiness for the return of Christ. Like the bridegroom in first-century Galilean society, Jesus most assuredly is coming, but he's coming suddenly and catches the unprepared by surprise.

The central character in this parable is the bridegroom (Christ), who is delayed in coming for his bride (the church). Scripture often refers to the church as the bride and Christ as the bridegroom (Matt. 9:15; Mark 2:19-20; Luke 5:34-35; John 3:29). Believers are "betrothed" to Jesus, who promises to come one day and take them to his Father's house (John 14:1-3).

A general understanding of first-century Jewish wedding customs is helpful in navigating this parable. Chapter 14 provides details of the *erusin*, or betrothal period to which Jesus refers in this parable.

In Jesus' day, if a young man acquires sufficient means to provide a marriage dowry, his parents select a girl for him, call in a "friend of the bridegroom" to represent them (see John 3:29), and begin negotiations with the bride's father, who also has selected a representative.

If an agreement is reached, congratulations are exchanged, coffee or wine is brought out, and everyone drinks as a seal of the marriage covenant. Later, the families of the bride and groom meet. The young man gives the young woman either a gold ring, some article of value, or simply a document in which he promises to marry her, saying, "See by this ring (or this token) thou art set apart for me, according to the law of Moses and of Israel." The young man then leaves his bride-to-be, promising to return once he has prepared a place for her.

Returning to his father's house, and under his father's supervision, he prepares a wedding chamber. The period of betrothal normally lasts a year or more, and it only may be broken by obtaining a bill of divorce. While the bridegroom works on the wedding chamber, the bride prepares herself, remaining chaste, and covering her face with a veil in public to show she's pledged to be married.

At long last, the father tells his son all is ready; the night of the wedding approaches. The groom dresses as much like a king as possible. If he's wealthy enough, he wears a gold crown; otherwise, it's a garland of fresh flowers. The bride, meanwhile, goes through an elaborate and costly adorning. Every effort is made to make her complexion glossy and shining like marble. Her dark locks of hair are braided with gold and pearls, and she is decked with all the precious stones and jewels her family has inherited from previous generations.

The groom sets out from his father's house in a nighttime procession – often very late, adding to the drama. Wedding guests bearing torches accompany him to the bride's home. The bride steps out to meet the groom, receives the blessing of her relatives, and proceeds with the groom to his father's home.

A grand procession follows them. Invited guests light their lamps, join the march, and swell the ranks of those headed for the marriage feast. Along the route, family members hand out ears of parched grain to the children, musical instruments are played, and there is dancing and shouts of "Behold, the bridegroom comes!"

At last, they reach their destination, where the specially built wedding chamber is prepared. In time, the bride and groom enter the suite and shut the door. For up to seven days they stay inside, alone. Meanwhile, an extended celebration breaks out. In the end, the bride and groom emerge, leave the father's house, and set out to establish their own home.

This is the Galilean context in which Jesus' disciples hear the parable. The details of the groom going away, preparing a place, and promising to return are well-known to them, as are the elements of delay and surprise.

Jesus tells this parable to prepare them for what's ahead. After his imminent suffering, death, and resurrection, Jesus returns to his Father, prepares a place in heaven for believers, and then calls his bride to meet him at his return. Many who hold a dispensational premillennial view of the end times point to this event as the *rapture*, in which followers of Jesus are "caught up" to meet him in the air (1 Cor. 15:50-57; 1 Thess. 4:13-18).

According to this view, the seven-day honeymoon depicts seven years the church is in heaven while tribulation takes place on earth. And the departure from the father's house after the honeymoon pictures the glorious appearing of Christ when he returns to earth with the saints, sits on the throne of David, and rules the earth with his queen.

For historical premillennialists and amillennialists, this parable foretells a general resurrection of all people at Christ's second coming. Glorified believers go up to meet Jesus in the air – like ancient citizens going out from their city to welcome a visiting king – and accompany him in his victorious return to earth. Meanwhile, unbelievers – the foolish virgins – are denied entrance into the kingdom.

There are other interpretations besides these, but we should be careful not to impose unnecessary details on this parable. Remember that parables are designed to communicate a simple truth – in this case, the truth of Jesus' sudden return and the necessity of being prepared. Details help round out the story, or make it more engaging, but they don't necessarily contribute to its meaning.

It's interesting to note that the bride is not mentioned in this parable. While Scripture often refers to Christ's church as his bride, the focus in this parable is on the bridegroom and the virgins, or attendants. It's not necessary for believers to be represented as both bride and bridal attendants, or this would present difficulties Jesus did not intend.

Therefore, it's probably best to see the virgins as people who profess faith in Jesus, claim to know him, and anticipate his return. Some are "wise" and some are "foolish." There is at least a degree of goodwill in the foolish as well as in the wise. The difference is in the depth of their commitment, which is evident by their readiness for the bridegroom's coming.

The wise virgins are those who truly know Christ, understand that his coming may be delayed, and thus prepare with an abundance of oil, which could represent the seal of the Holy Spirit. They may slumber while the bridegroom tarries – even Christ's closest followers could not stay awake one hour while he prayed in Gethsemane – yet they persevere and are welcomed into the marriage feast.

The foolish virgins are those who profess to know Christ but lack a genuine relationship with him. They carry their lamps – an outward profession of faith – but they're not truly committed to the bridegroom or fully invested in his purpose. They fall asleep. Their reserve of oil runs out. And when the bridegroom comes, their lamps are dark and cold.

While there are various opinions about the meaning of the oil – a symbol of the Holy Spirit, love, joy, conscience – at the very least, we may consider it the inward grace of Christ that has enduring character. Whereas God's grace is given to all in a general sense, only those who have entered into a relationship with him receive his Spirit, who, like the oil of the wise, is abundant and sufficient.[8]

When the bridegroom comes at last, the foolish virgins realize their lamps are going out, so they ask the wise to share. The response of the wise virgins is important in two respects. First, they deny the request – not out of selfishness or a judgmental nature, but because all ten virgins would then be undone.

Second, the wise virgins tell the foolish to buy their own reserves of oil. This does not imply that salvation may be purchased, only that the foolish need to acquire salvation the same way the wise did. Salvation has one source: Christ.

When the bridegroom comes, the wise are ready. They join the wedding procession, lamps blazing, and are welcomed into the feast. The foolish come too late, after the door is shut, and thus are excluded. Just as the wicked are denied entrance into the ark in Noah's day once God seals the door, unbelievers at the return of Christ are denied entrance into his kingdom.

Today, believers and unbelievers populate the visible church. In a day to come, God separates those who merely profess to know Christ from those who truly do. Some may hold a form of godliness while denying God's power (2 Tim. 3:5). Others may protest, "Lord, Lord, didn't we prophesy in your name, drive out demons in your name, and do many miracles in your name?" To these, Jesus replies, "I never knew you. Depart from me, you lawbreakers!" (Matt. 7:22-23).

In summarizing this parable, we may not improve on the closing words of Jesus: "Therefore be alert, because you don't know either the day or the hour" (Matt. 25:13).[9]

A man on a journey

Mark 13:32-37 reads:

Now concerning that day or hour no one knows — neither the angels in heaven nor the Son — but only the Father.
  Watch! Be alert! For you don't know when the time is coming.
  It is like a man on a journey, who left his house, gave authority to his servants, gave each one his work, and commanded the doorkeeper to be alert. Therefore be alert, since you don't know when the master of the house is coming – whether in the evening or at midnight or at the crowing of the rooster or early in the morning. Otherwise, when *he comes suddenly* he might find you sleeping. And what I say to you, I say to everyone: Be alert [emphasis added]!

This parable comes in Mark's account of the Olivet Discourse (Mark 13; cf. Matt. 24-25; Luke 21:5-36). As in Matthew 24:36, Jesus states that no one – including himself – knows the exact time of his return. In his humanity, Jesus at times purposefully lays aside the exercise of his deity. Although fully divine as well as fully human, Jesus could have known and revealed the day and hour of his return. But he has left heaven and come to earth for a higher purpose – to lay down his life for us in obedience to the Father – and the details of the consummation of his kingdom are of lesser importance.

As followers of Jesus, we shouldn't sweat these details; rather, we should always be ready to share our faith with others (1 Pet. 3:15), and be ready for Christ's imminent return. Even prior to his ascension, Jesus reminds his disciples that it's not their business to know "times or periods that the Father has set by his own authority" (Acts 1:7).

Having set aside the finer points of his return, Jesus moves on to a parable that accentuates our need to be alert for that approaching day. He tells his disciples, "Watch!" and he uses the phrase "be alert" four times in these verses. The clear focus of this parable is a stern warning to be on guard because Christ could come back at any time. This parable shares some features with the parables of the talents (Matt. 25:14-30) and minas (Luke 19:12-27), yet retains its uniqueness.

Like the doorkeeper of his master's house, followers of Jesus always must be vigilant in light of his return. This means engaging in kingdom business – using our time, talents, spiritual gifts, and other resources to advance the gospel – and protecting the flock from savage wolves at the door (cf. Matt. 7:15; Acts 20:29).

Jesus mentions four specific times the master might return: evening, midnight, the crowing of the rooster, and dawn. These are Roman night watches with which his listeners are familiar. And they stress the disciplined nature of a vigil.

Regardless of when Jesus returns, he should not catch us off-guard. The Lord does not say about the master, "*if* he comes suddenly," but "*when* he comes suddenly." The alert doorkeeper, and the watchful Christian, have no reason to fear the swiftness of the master's return.

"Watch!" is the final and most important word in Mark's account of the Olivet Discourse, according to James Edwards. Jesus' words ring true through the corridors of time: "What I say to you, I say to everyone: 'Watch!'" (Mark 13:37 NIV). Edwards writes, *"To everyone* designates a wider audience than the Twelve. This is the word of Jesus to the Twelve, the word of Mark to his readers, and the word of the Spirit to believers in every age."[10]

The homeowner

Luke 12:39-40 reads:

But know this: If the homeowner had known at what hour the thief was coming, he would not have let his house be broken into. You also be ready, because the Son of Man is coming at *an hour you do not expect* [emphasis added].

Luke places this parable right after another parable about servants who wait expectantly for their master to return from a wedding banquet (Luke 12:35-38). These servants are blessed for being alert, hearing the master's knock – even in the middle of the night or near dawn – and opening the door. In fact, these faithful servants find themselves reclining at the table with their master, who then, in a dramatic twist, serves them.

Taken together, these parables underscore Jesus' exhortation to "Be ready for service and have your lamps lit" (Luke 12:35). Literally, the phrasing is, "Let your loins be girded," an idiom for tying up loose outer clothing in readiness for action (cf. Exod. 12:11 KJV).

The second parable invites servants to consider a homeowner's perspective. Perhaps Jesus is subtly making the point that his followers are both servants of Christ *and* joint heirs with him (Rom. 8:16-17). In any case, the duty of both servants and home-owners is the same: be ready.

No responsible master would leave his house unguarded, espe-cially if he knew a thief was headed for his property. In a similar way, Christ is returning like a thief – suddenly and unexpectedly – and his followers, likened both to faithful servants and responsible homeowners, should "gird their loins" and be ready, for most certainly he is coming.

As Darrell Bock points out, "There is spiritual exposure in lack of preparedness. The thief image suggests that the risks of unpreparedness are great."[11]

WHY JESUS USES PARABLES

In Matthew 13, Jesus' disciples ask him why he teaches in parables. His answer is revealing.

First, Jesus says he uses parables because the mysteries, or secrets, of God's kingdom have been given to the disciples but not to others (Matt. 13:11). Jesus spends three years with the apostles, teaching them the necessity of his death, burial, and resurrection. Others are taught the mystery of the kingdom in parables and, if they incline their hearts toward God, come to understand.

Second, those who receive the gospel of the kingdom benefit from the truths revealed in Jesus' parables, while those who insist on a political and military Messiah are no longer to be trusted with the Scriptures – a clear reference to the Jewish religious leaders of the day (Matt. 13:12).

Third, those who already reject Jesus as Messiah are so hard of heart, they cannot understand these simple parables. Just as the Israelites in Isaiah's days reject God – leading to judgment – so the unbelieving Jews of Jesus' day would face judgment in the destruction of the temple in A.D. 70, as well as judgment after the kingdom comes in power (Matt. 13:13-15).

As Matthew Henry writes:

A parable, like the pillar of cloud and fire, turns a dark side towards Egyptians, which confounds them, but a light side towards the Israelites, which comforts them, and so answers a double intention. The same light directs the eyes of some, but dazzles the eyes of others.[12]

Fourth, Jesus' parables, especially those regarding the kingdom of heaven, reveal spiritual truths the prophets of old could only see in shadow form. The apostles should rejoice that they are witnessing the coming of the kingdom in mystery (Matt. 13:16-17).

Finally, Jesus' parables fulfill prophecy. The psalmist writes that Messiah would "declare wise sayings; I will speak mysteries from the past" (Ps. 78:2). That's exactly what Jesus does (Matt. 13:35; see also Deut. 29:29; Rom. 16:25; 1 Cor. 2:7; Eph. 3:9; and Col. 1:26).

OTHER SCRIPTURAL WARNINGS

Paul, James, and Peter all record warnings about the suddenness of Christ's return. In each case, the authors stress the need for followers of Jesus to live ethically and expectantly. Consider the following examples.

1 Thessalonians 5:1-11

About the times and the seasons: Brothers and sisters, you do not need anything to be written to you. For you yourselves know very well that the day of the Lord will come *just like a thief in the night.* When they say, "Peace and security," then sudden destruction will come upon them, like labor pains on a pregnant woman, and they will not escape. But you, brothers and sisters, are not in the dark, for this day to surprise you like a thief. For you are all children of light and children of the day. We do not belong to the night or the darkness. So then, let us not sleep, like the rest, but let us stay awake and be self-controlled. For those who sleep, sleep at night, and those who get drunk, get drunk at night. But since we belong to the day, let us be self-controlled and put on the armor of faith and love, and a helmet of the hope of salvation. For God did not appoint us to wrath, but to obtain salvation through our Lord Jesus Christ, who died for us, so that whether we are awake or asleep, we may live together with him. Therefore encourage one another and build each other up as you are already doing [emphasis added].

Paul borrows from the language of Jesus in warning that the Lord is returning "just like a thief in the night" (1 Thess. 5:2). And he echoes Christ's exhortation to be ready at all times. Believers are to "stay awake and be self-controlled" (v. 6). While unbelievers ignore the clear signs of impending judgment – "like labor pains on a pregnant woman" (v. 3) – they cannot escape the wrath of God. But believers should take heart. Thanks to Christ's finished work of redemption, we may eagerly anticipate a different outcome in which we "live together with him" (v. 10).

Titus 2:11-14

For the grace of God has appeared, bringing salvation for all people, instructing us to deny godlessness and worldly lusts and to live in a sensible, righteous, and godly way in the present age, while we wait for the blessed hope, the appearing of the glory of our great God and Savior, Jesus Christ. He gave himself for us to redeem us from all lawlessness and to cleanse for himself a people for his own possession, eager to do good works.

While Paul does not explicitly point to the sudden return of Christ in this passage, he teaches it elsewhere (1 Thess. 5:2). Consistent with that teaching, the apostle here exhorts followers of Jesus to deny worldly lusts and to live in a godly way "while we wait" for his return, which catches the unfaithful off-guard.

Note Paul's use of "appeared" and "appearing" in verses 11 and 13. God's grace already has appeared universally – not just his general grace by which all people live and breathe, but his particular grace in the person and work of Jesus. The phrase "bringing salvation for all people" is not a cry for universalism. Rather, Paul's point is that "salvation is universally offered to all without exception."[13]

Next, Paul points to the future "appearing of the glory of our great God and Savior, Jesus Christ." The first appearance of Jesus is one of humility, servanthood, and suffering. The second appearance is one of glory, sovereignty, and victory. While there is some debate as to whether the phrase "great God and Savior" refers to two persons – the Father and the Son – or to Jesus alone, it makes the most sense to understand Paul's words as a reference to Jesus, who alone is returning in glory.

James 5:7-9

Therefore, brothers and sisters, be patient until the Lord's coming. See how the farmer waits for the precious fruit of the earth and is patient with it until it receives the early and the late rains. You also must be patient. Strengthen your hearts, because the Lord's coming is near.

Brothers and sisters, do not complain about one another, so that you will not be judged. Look, the judge stands at the door!

James admonishes believers to be patient until the Lord returns, especially those suffering at the hands of the wealthy wicked, who face certain condemnation on the day of judgment (see Jas. 5:1-6). The word "coming" in verse 7 translates the Greek *parousia*, which basically means "presence" and is applied in secular Greek to the arrival of a dignitary. Early Christians consistently used *parousia* to refer to the coming of Jesus at the end of history to judge the wicked and deliver the saints (e.g., Matt. 24:37, 39; 1 Cor. 15:23; 1 Thess. 2:19; 3:13; 4:15; 5:23; 2 Thess. 2:8). This is the meaning James intends here.

While we wait for the Lord, we are to expect and endure suffering at the hands of those who reject Christ, knowing that a great reversal of fortune is promised at the Lord's return. At the same time, we are not to seek revenge against those who abuse us, for vengeance belongs to the Lord (cf. Rom. 12:19).

James points to the farmer, who has planted his crops and now waits for the early and late rains to produce "the precious fruit of the earth" (Jas. 5:7). There is little else the farmer can do but trust in the providence of God. James may be directing his readers back to Deuteronomy 11:14, where God, in response to his people's obedience, promises to "provide rain for your land in the proper time, the autumn and spring rains, and you will harvest your grain, new wine, and fresh oil."

In a similar way, Christians should endure suffering, hardship, and temptation with an eye toward the day when Christ returns and sets things right. James bases this encouragement on the nearness of the Lord's coming. The verb James uses in verse 8 – *engizo*, "is near" – occurs elsewhere in the New Testament in reference to the kingdom of God and to Christ's second coming. For example, Jesus often equates his earthly ministry with the nearness of the kingdom (Matt. 3:2; 4:17; 10:7; Mark 1:15; Luke 10:9-11). And both Paul and Peter remind us of the nearness of the Lord's return (Rom. 13:12; 1 Pet. 4:7).

But what are we to make of the fact that two thousand years have passed and Christ is yet seated in heaven, having delayed the *parousia*? Didn't Jesus and the New Testament writers declare the nearness of the second coming?

Douglas Moo offers valuable insight into this question:

What is crucial is to understand this "nearness" in the appropriate temporal framework: salvation history. With the death and resurrection of Jesus and pouring out of the Spirit, the "last days" have been inaugurated. This final age of salvation will find its climax in the return of Christ in glory. But – and here is the crucial point – the length of the age is unknown. Not even Jesus knew how long the "last days" would last (cf. Mark 13:32). What this means is that the return of Christ, as the next event in the salvation-historical timetable, is, from the time of the early church to our own day, "near," or "imminent."[14]

So, every generation of Christians should realize the *parousia* could occur at any moment. That insight should guide our values and behavior. We need to be patient and stand firm, for the Lord's coming *is* near. There's more about the nearness of Christ's return in Chapter 15.

In verse 9, James urges us not to complain about one another, or turn our suffering at the hands of the wicked into internal squabbles. Just as evil people face a day of reckoning, Christians have their appointment at the judgment seat of Christ (Rom. 14:10; 2 Cor. 5:10). "Look," James writes, "the judge stands at the door!"

1 Peter 4:7-11

The end of all things is near; therefore, be alert and sober-minded for prayer. Above all, maintain constant love for one another, since love covers a multitude of sins. Be hospitable to one another without complaining. Just as each one has received a gift, use it to serve others, as good stewards of the varied grace of God. If anyone speaks, let it be as one who speaks God's words; if anyone serves, let it be from the strength God provides, so that God may be glorified through Jesus Christ in everything. To him be the glory and the power forever and ever. Amen.

Peter writes, "The end of all things is near" (1 Pet. 4:7). This picks up on the theme of preceding verses, in which the apostle reminds us that the wicked "will give an account to the one who stands ready to judge the living and the dead" (v. 5). But believers are not to stand idly, gloating in anticipation of the day when the enemies of God get their comeuppance. Rather, we are to remember that we, too, have a summons to appear before Christ's holy bench. Therefore, we're to be alert, sober-minded for prayer, loving, hospitable, and faithful stewards of our spiritual gifts.

Thomas Schreiner comments, "The realization that God is bringing history to a close should provoke believers to depend on him, and this dependence is manifested in prayer, for in prayer believers recognize that any good that occurs in the world is due to God's grace."[15]

Like James, who writes that "the Lord's coming is near" (Jas. 5:8), Peter says the "end of all things is near." They are on the same page. The reason both writers focus on the nearness of Christ's return is that the death, resurrection, and ascension of Jesus inaugurated the last days (1 Cor. 10:11; 1 John 2:18). Other New Testament writers also sound the call to be alert for the imminent coming of Jesus (Rom. 13:11-12; Phil. 4:5; Heb. 10:23-25; Rev. 1:3; 22:10).

The nearness of the end, and the transience of the evil world system in which we live, should inspire Christians to make our lives count. It's interesting that Peter does not urge us to engage in bizarre behavior like predicting the date of Christ's return, disposing of earthly assets, going off the grid, and hunkering down in a secluded bunker, only to emerge on cloudless nights to gaze into the heavens for signs of the *parousia*. Rather, he tells us to live ordinary lives with extraordinary valor.

It reminds us of what Martin Luther once said when asked what he would do if the end were to come that day. He replied that he would plant a tree and pay his taxes. What he meant, of course, was that he lived every day in light of the end. So, he would faithfully fulfill the obligations the day demanded.[16]

2 Peter 3:10-13

But the day of the Lord will come like a thief; on that day the heavens will pass away with a loud noise, the elements will burn and be dissolved, and the earth and the works on it will be disclosed. Since all these things are to be dissolved in this way, it is clear what sort of people you should be in holy conduct and godliness as you wait for the day of God and hasten its coming. Because of that day, the heavens will be dissolved with fire and the elements will melt with heat. But based on his promise, we wait for new heavens and a new earth, where righteousness dwells.

Peter picks up the language of both Jesus and Paul, likening the return of Christ to the coming of a thief (cf. Matt. 24:42-44; 1 Thess. 5:2). And he goes further, revealing the work of Jesus to purge our fallen world of sin and its stain, and to create new heavens and a new earth. A thief depends on surprise, hoping to escape undetected with his loot in tow. In contrast, while the Lord's coming is sudden, every eye will see him and every person will bear witness of his work to set things right (Rev. 1:7).

When Peter writes that the day of the Lord "will come," he's emphasizing the certainty of Christ's *parousia*. False teachers have cast a shadow over Christian confidence in this event, arguing that "all things continue as they have been since the beginning of creation" (2 Pet. 3:4). Peter points out the historical evidence against such foolishness – namely, the global flood in the days of Noah – and urges his readers to look ahead, when God opens a storehouse of fire "for the day of judgment and the destruction of the ungodly" (v. 7). There is to be no doubt among believers that the Lord's return, while seemingly delayed, is certain.

And there's good reason for resting in God's timing:

> Dear friends, don't overlook this one fact: With the Lord one day is like a thousand years, and a thousand years like one day. The Lord does not delay his promise, as some understand delay, but is patient with you, not wanting any to perish but all to come to repentance (2 Pet. 3:8-9).

Peter offers no specific signs of the Lord's sudden return, although other Scriptures provide general descriptions of circumstances in the last days. For example:

- The preaching of the gospel to all nations (Mark 13:10; cf. Matt. 24:14)
- Great tribulation (Mark 13:7-8; cf. Matt. 24:15-22; Luke 21:20-24)
- False prophets who perform signs and wonders (Mark 13:22; cf. Matt. 24:23-24)
- Signs in the heavens (Mark 13:24-25; cf. Matt. 24:29-30; Luke 21:25-26)
- The coming of the man of sin (2 Thess. 2:1-10; 1 John 2:18; Rev. 13)
- The salvation of Israel (Rom. 11:12, 25-27)[17]

These signs are general in nature, like the redness of the sky at dawn or dusk, and the budding of fig trees (Matt. 16:2-3; Luke 21:29-31). But Peter's point is that Christ's return provides no advance warning. Believers must be ready for their master's return, while unbelievers must repent while there is still time.

When Christ returns, Peter notes three significant events: (1) "the heavens will pass away with a loud noise;" (2) "the elements will burn and be dissolved;" and (3) "the earth and the works on it will be disclosed" (v. 10). We discuss these events in more detail in Chapter 13.

But we should note that the apostle is describing cataclysmic acts of judgment on the physical world similar to God's judgment through a universal flood in the days of Noah. In the case of the second coming, however, God's instrument is fire, not water. And the result is not a fresh start with still-fallen creatures, but a renovation of the material order that purges the world of sin and its curse and populates this new world with redeemed people who are fully conformed to the image of Christ (2 Cor. 5:17; 1 John 3:2).

One final note in this section: In the Book of Revelation, John warns that the events heralding the second coming "must soon take place" (Rev. 1:1; cf. Rev. 22:6). We must hear the words of prophecy and keep what is written because "the time is near" (Rev. 1:3). Three times in the book's final chapter, Jesus declares, "I am coming soon" (Rev. 22:7, 12, 20). We explore the nearness of Christ's return in Chapter 15.

SUDDENLY, BUT WE DON'T KNOW WHEN

Jesus is returning to earth like a thief in the night. Behind the realization that Christ's second coming is sudden lies the fact that we do not, and cannot, know exactly when this occurs. Jesus himself make this clear:

Matthew 24:36 – "Now concerning that day and hour no one knows — neither the angels of heaven nor the Son — except the Father alone."

Matthew 24:44 – "This is why you are also to be ready, because the Son of Man is coming at an hour you do not expect."

Matthew 25:13 – "Therefore be alert, because you don't know either the day or the hour."

Mark 13:32-33 – "Now concerning that day or hour no one knows — neither the angels in heaven nor the Son — but only the Father. Watch! Be alert! For you don't know when the time is coming."

Luke 12:40 – "You also be ready, because the Son of Man is coming at an hour you do not expect."

Since no one knows the exact time of his return, Jesus exhorts us to "be ready," "be alert," and "watch." In the meantime, we should make no effort to pinpoint the moment of Christ's *parousia*, as some counterfeit forms of Christianity do. Nor should we read this morning's headlines into the Scriptures, as if we may discern a general time of the Lord's return – perhaps the week, month, or year.

If Jesus tells his listeners even *he* doesn't know the day or the hour of the second coming, we should not be obsessed with seeking information even the Son of God did not find it necessary to obtain in his human nature.

It does raise a question, however: If Jesus retains his deity in the Incarnation – adding sinless humanity to his eternally divine nature – how can he say he doesn't know his date with destiny? Certainly, Jesus was and is God. He does not surrender his divine nature by becoming the God-man. After all, we see Jesus knowing and doing things only God can do: receiving worship, forgiving sins, raising the dead, claiming the divine name "I AM," and knowing people's thoughts.

At the same time, Jesus voluntarily limits himself by taking on human flesh. He appears in one, and only one, location at a time. He gets tired, hungry, and thirsty. He experiences pain. He dies. As the fully divine Son of God, Jesus could have made bread of stones. He could have gone without sleep. He could have avoided the suffering of the cross, or come down from the cross, as he was chided to do, stunning the Roman soldiers and Jewish leaders with divine bravado. But in order to identify fully with us in our humanity, Jesus chose not to leverage his deity to make his life easier.

As the writer of Hebrews notes, Jesus is "made lower than the angels for a short time so that by God's grace he might taste death for everyone" (Heb. 2:9). Further, Jesus "had to be like his brothers and sisters in every way, so that he could become a merciful and faithful high priest in matters pertaining to God, to make atonement for the sins of the people" (Heb. 2:17).

So, when Jesus says he doesn't know the time of his return, he's taking on the form of a servant (Phil. 2:7-8). Since no other human being knows the time of Jesus' return – that information is the Father's alone (Matt. 24:36) – Jesus voluntarily restricts his knowledge on that point. It also demonstrates Jesus' complete submission to the Father, who sends him to be the Savior of the world (see John 5:30; 6:38; 8:28-29).

Not only that, but can you imagine how we might conduct ourselves today if Jesus pinpointed the date and time of his return? Some of us might live in abandonment to fleshly desires, only to repent at the last moment, trusting Jesus to save us "as through fire" (1 Cor. 3:15). Others might use this information for financial gain, rebalancing our retirement portfolios and acquiring or disposing of assets to make the most of our final days on earth. Some might even stop paying mortgages and taxes since the world is on a collision course with fiery judgment.

If we learn that Christ's return is a long way off, we might live with little sense of anticipation; after all, we'll be long gone when Christ rides a white horse and comes back with the clouds of heaven. On the other hand, if we know the Lord's coming is at hand – say, a week or a month away – we might be gripped with panic over unfinished spiritual business. Or, we might hide ourselves from the unbelieving world, which gladly takes advantage of our perceived vulnerability.

Thank God that Jesus, in his deity, chose not to communicate certain truths to his own human nature, and that Jesus, in his humanity, was contented to trust certain truths to his Father alone.

Evidently, even knowing the proximate time of divine acts doesn't necessarily result in righteous living. Noah preaches for more than a century while building the ark. And when God finally closes the doors of the seaworthy vessel and seals Noah and his family inside, there is no greater number of converts than when Noah began his ambitious construction project.

The Amorites have four centuries to repent, but instead, they fill up the measure of God's wrath (Gen. 15:16). When God promises Abram and Sarai a son in their lifetimes, they grow impatient because of their advancing age and take matters into their own hands. When Jesus tells the religious leaders of his day that judgment is imminent, they don't fall on their knees in worship; they tear their clothes, grit their teeth, and cry out for his crucifixion.

So, lest we're too hard on those depicted in Scripture as unrepentant, we should heed the warnings of Jesus that his coming is going to be swift, sudden, and sure. As Wayne Grudem writes, "the point of these passages is that Jesus is telling us that we *cannot* know when he is coming back. Since he will come at an unexpected time, we should be ready at all times for him to return."[18]

REVIEW

Key takeaways from this chapter

1. When Jesus tells his followers he is coming like a thief (Rev. 16:15), we should understand that his return to earth is both carefully planned and flawlessly executed. There is the unmistakable element of surprise. Jesus, Paul, and Peter all compare the second coming to the actions of a thief.

2. In his teaching on the second coming, Jesus applies history,

prophecy, analogies, and parables to underscore the suddenness of his return. And he makes it clear that the exact time of his return is known only to the Father.

3. The swift coming of Jesus produces a great divide. Some are taken and some are left. Some are secure and some perish. Some are rewarded and some are punished. But all are called to be prepared. The wicked are called to repent, and God's delay in brandishing judgment is for their benefit (2 Pet. 3:9). There is heaven to gain and hell to avoid. The redeemed are to be ready as well. There are rewards to gain and shame to avoid (1 Cor. 3:11-15; 1 John 2:28).

4. Every generation of Christians should realize the *parousia* – the appearing of Jesus with the clouds of heaven – could occur at any moment, and that realization should guide our values and behavior. We need to be patient and stand firm, for the Lord's coming is near. As James writes, "Look, the judge stands at the door!" (Jas. 5:9).

5. In 2 Peter 3:10-13, the apostle describes cataclysmic acts of judgment on the physical world similar to God's judgment through a universal flood in the days of Noah. In the case of the second coming, however, God's instrument is fire, not water. And the result is not a fresh start with still-fallen creatures, but a renovation of the material order that purges the world of sin and its curse and populates this new world with redeemed people who are fully conformed to the image of Christ (2 Cor. 5:17; 1 John 3:2).

DISCUSS

Questions for personal or group study

1. Jesus says he's coming like a thief (Rev. 16:15). He also describes false teachers as thieves (John 10:10). In what ways are the activities of Jesus and false teachers similar to those of thieves? And in what ways are the thief-like activities of Jesus and false teachers clearly different?

2. Read Matthew 24:36-44. How are the events that precede the return of Jesus similar to activities in the days of Noah before the flood? Consider also 2 Peter 3:3-7.

3. Several of Jesus' parables address the suddenness of his future return in glory. Match the following parables with the corresponding key points (a, b, c) Jesus makes:

A faithful and wise servant (Matt. 24:45-51)
Ten virgins (Matt. 25:1-13)
The homeowner (Luke 12:39-40)

(a) Like a first-century Galilean bridegroom, Jesus is coming suddenly and catches the unprepared by surprise.

(b) Like a home invader, Jesus is coming as a thief – suddenly and unexpectedly.

(c) Being a member of a Christian community doesn't guarantee a reward, nor does it secure salvation.

4. In the following passages, what do the New Testament writers tell us we should do as we wait for the Lord's return?

- 1 Thessalonians 5:1-11
- James 5:7-9
- 1 Peter 4:7-11
- 2 Peter 3:10-13

5. What are the advantages of *not* knowing the day and hour of the Lord's return?

* * *

SECTION III: HEAR ME

THE REASONS FOR JESUS' RETURN

As followers of Jesus eagerly anticipate his return and obey his command to be ready, we may rightly ponder why Jesus is returning at all. What's lacking in his first coming that necessitates his return? Don't we meet him in heaven at the moment of death? What could be better than that?

But Jesus and the apostles make it clear our Lord has unfinished business on earth. When he returns in glory, he establishes his kingdom in fullness; resurrects and judges all people; glorifies the saints; sentences unbelievers to outer darkness; casts Satan and demons into hell; and creates new heavens and a new earth.

Christ's mission as Suffering Servant is accomplished in the Incarnation and the sacrifice of his sinless life on our behalf. His role as King of kings and Lord of lords plays out in his triumphant return on a white horse, accompanied by heavenly armies of angels and redeemed people.

———————— A ————————

One day, the kingdom of God
comes gloriously as the
Lion of Judah returns
to claim his throne.

———————— Ω ————————

"YOUR KINGDOM COME"

JESUS IS RETURNING TO ESTABLISH HIS KINGDOM IN FULLNESS

*I*n the 1972 film *The Candidate*, idealistic attorney Bill McKay allows himself to become the Democratic nominee in a campaign for U.S. Senate against a seemingly unbeatable Republican incumbent. McKay, played deftly by Robert Redford, has no chance of winning. But entering the race offers him a forum for his views on civil rights, legal aid, and the environment.

A handsome and charismatic figure, McKay eschews backroom deals and compromises – until his campaign begins to gain traction. The probability of an upset victory looms larger with each passing day. But to win, McKay must choose between his integrity and his ambition. The more he moderates his views, the higher his poll numbers rise. And when he gets support from his father, who once served as governor, as well as an endorsement from a labor-union chief, McKay rockets into a near tie with his opponent.

Increasingly, we see McKay's inner conflict overshadow his political skirmishes. The story reveals the costs – financial, political, emotional, and moral – of running for public office. Has McKay ultimately sold out for a Senate seat he's not sure he wants?

McKay wins the election. And in a memorable final scene, the newly elected senator escapes the victory party and pulls his campaign manager aside. "What do we do now?" he asks. A throng of reporters descends on McKay, and we're left wondering how his question is answered.

"What do we do now?"

That's a question on the minds of Jesus' followers after his stunning victory over the grave. His resurrection has transformed the disciples from fearful to exuberant. For a period of forty days, Jesus teaches them about the kingdom of God. As a result, they seem eager to march Jesus into Jerusalem to claim the throne. But there's an inner conflict in the disciples between their ambitions and their deference to the king. So they ask, essentially, "What do we do now?"

Take a moment to read the opening verses of Acts 1:

I wrote the first narrative [the Gospel of Luke], Theophilus, about all that Jesus began to do and teach until the day he was taken up, after he had given instructions through the Holy Spirit to the apostles he had chosen. After he had suffered, he also presented himself alive to them by many convincing proofs, appearing to them over a period of forty days and speaking about the kingdom of God.

While he was with them, he commanded them not to leave Jerusalem, but to wait for the Father's promise. "Which," he said, "you have heard me speak about; for John baptized with water, but you will be baptized with the Holy Spirit in a few days."

So when they had come together, they asked him, "Lord, are you restoring the kingdom to Israel at this time?"

He said to them, "It is not for you to know times or periods that the Father has set by his own authority. But you will receive power when the Holy Spirit has come on you, and you will be my witnesses in Jerusalem, in all Judea and Samaria, and to the ends of the earth."

After he had said this, he was taken up as they were watching, and a cloud took him out of their sight. While he was going, they were gazing into heaven, and suddenly two men in white clothes stood by them. They said, "Men of Galilee, why do you stand looking up into heaven? This same Jesus, who has been taken from you into heaven,

will come in the same way that you have seen him going into heaven"
(Acts 1:1-11).

The resurrected Jesus spends forty days with the apostles,
presenting himself alive "by many convincing proofs ... and speaking
about the kingdom of God" (Acts 1:3). We should not miss the significance of Luke's record. Jesus has risen bodily from the dead. His
appearances to the apostles and other believers confirm his victory
over Satan, sin, and death (see 1 Cor. 15:3-7). Equally important, his
teaching is anchored in the kingdom of God.

No doubt, the apostles have a concept of the kingdom. Based on
the Hebrew Scriptures, a messianic king from the line of David is
coming to sit on the throne and rule over a never-ending kingdom in
which justice, peace, and righteousness reign (e.g., 2 Sam. 7; Isa. 9).
Many in Israel believe Jesus *is* this king – until he speaks about a
kingdom "not of this world" (John 18:36); until he focuses his righteous anger, not on Roman occupiers, but on hypocritical Jewish religious leaders; and until he allows himself to be betrayed, falsely
accused, beaten, and crucified. The cross is the end of his followers'
messianic hopes – or so they think.

But three days later, Jesus rises spectacularly from the grave. The
hope of a Davidic king and the restoration of his earthly rule is
revived. The risen Jesus is indeed the promised king, and his kingdom
most certainly is on the cusp of universal greatness. That's why it
makes sense when the apostles ask, "Lord, are you restoring the
kingdom to Israel at this time?" (Acts 1:6).

But Jesus' response isn't what they expect: "It is not for you to
know times or periods that the Father has set by his own authority"
(Acts 1:7).

Jesus' followers see his resurrection as proof that the glory of
ancient Israel is about to be restored. They still don't get it. The
Savior's focus, at least for now, is not on the date of his earthly
enthronement, but on the Father's promise to baptize his Son's
followers with the Holy Spirit. While Jesus must return to his Father
for a time, the apostles are to serve as eyewitnesses of his finished

work of redemption, starting in Jerusalem and then fanning out to Judea, Samaria, and the ends of the earth (Acts 1:4-5, 8).[1]

Surely, if God is faithful to send his promised Messiah to redeem fallen sinners, he plans to reveal his Son's kingdom in fullness. But when? When does Messiah sit on David's throne (Jer. 23:5-6; Luke 1:32-33)? When do the nations come to Jerusalem and pay homage to the King of kings (Isa. 2:2; Mic. 4:1-5)? When does the earth experience such universal peace that the wolf and lamb lie down together, and the child plays fearlessly atop the cobra's lair (Isa. 9:6-7; 11:6-9)?

The answer, of course, is when Jesus returns.

WHAT IS THE KINGDOM OF GOD?

The terms "kingdom of God," "kingdom of heaven," and "kingdom" (with reference to the kingdom of God/heaven) appear nearly 150 times in Scripture. None of these references offers a simple, straightforward definition of the kingdom, yet the kingdom is the primary focus of Jesus' teaching. Many of his parables describe the kingdom. The apostles preach the "gospel of the kingdom." And end-times prophecies point us toward the day when God's kingdom comes in fullness.

When we turn to the Scriptures, however, we find a perplexing diversity of statements about the kingdom, many of them focusing on the now vs. future aspects of the kingdom of heaven. For example:

- The kingdom is a present spiritual reality (Rom. 14:17); at the same time, it's a future inheritance that God gives people when Christ returns in glory (Matt. 25:34).
- The kingdom is a realm into which Christians already have entered (Col. 1:13); then again, it's a future realm we enter when Christ comes back (Matt. 8:11; 2 Pet. 1:11).
- The kingdom is to be ushered in with great glory (Matt. 13:41-43; 24:30); yet, its coming is without signs (Luke 17:20-21).

- The kingdom is present and at work in the world (Luke 13:18-21); still, Jesus tells Pilate, "My kingdom is not of this world" (John 18:36).
- The kingdom is both a present reality (Matt. 12:28) and a future blessing (1 Cor. 15:50-57).
- The kingdom is an inner, spiritual, redemptive blessing that can only be experienced through the new birth (John 3:3; Rom. 14:17); yet, one day it involves world government (Rev. 11:15).
- People enter the kingdom now (Matt. 21:31) and in the future (Matt. 8:11).
- The kingdom is a gift God gives the redeemed in the future (Luke 22:29-30), and yet it must be received in the present (Mark 10:15).

How do we reconcile these seemingly contradictory teachings? By setting aside our modern notion of a kingdom as a geographical boundary over which a king rules. As George Ladd explains:

The primary meaning of both the Hebrew word *malkuth* in the Old Testament and of *basileia* in the New Testament is the rank, authority and sovereignty exercised by a king. A *basileia* may indeed be a realm over which a sovereign exercises authority; and it may be the people who belong to that realm and over whom authority is exercised; but these are secondary and derived meanings. First of all, a kingdom is the authority to rule, the sovereignty of the king. [2]

The kingdom of God is the primary focus of Jesus' teaching. Many of his parables describe the kingdom. Jesus says the "good news of the kingdom" will be proclaimed in all the world before his return (Matt. 24:14). And end-times prophecy points to the day when God's kingdom comes in fullness.

So, what is the kingdom of God? Simply stated, *the kingdom is God's reign, his authority to rule over all.* As Burk Parsons notes:

> When Jesus taught about the kingdom of God, He primarily taught about the nature of the kingdom so that his followers might understand that in His first coming He established and inaugurated God's kingdom, that, through the Holy Spirit, He is now expanding and increasing God's kingdom, and that one day He will return to judge all people. When He does return, He will bring the full and final consummation of God's kingdom; establish the new heaven and earth; conquer His and our enemies; save all who are true Israel and united to Him by faith; dry every tear from our eyes; and fully and finally eradicate sin and death. All these Christ secured on the cross and manifested in His victorious resurrection.[3]

CREATION, FALL, REDEMPTION, RESTORATION

Perhaps the kingdom of God is best understood in light of the biblical account of creation, fall, redemption, and restoration. In the beginning, God creates everything and declares it "very good indeed" (Gen. 1:31). Initially, all creatures in the invisible and visible realms serve their creator faithfully. There is universal peace throughout God's kingdom.

But Satan leads an angelic revolt against the Lord and his authority. Then, under the influence of the evil one, Adam falls, and a competing kingdom on earth rises up in opposition to God – a kingdom over which Satan reigns.

In reply, God promises a virgin-born redeemer who will crush the serpent's head (Gen. 3:15). The Old Testament expands this view with roughly four hundred prophecies and foreshadows of a coming Messiah. When the Son of God comes to earth, he invades the rebel kingdom and picks a fight with its ruler (see Matt. 12:28-29; 16:13-20).

Jesus' sinless life, death, burial, and resurrection brings salvation to sinful humans. And his promised return one day completely reverses the effects of the Fall and restores the created order to its pristine perfection.

THE KINGDOM IN THE OLD AND NEW TESTAMENTS

In a broad sense, the kingdom of God – which Matthew also calls *the kingdom of heaven* – is the rule of an eternal, sovereign God over the universe. He creates everything, visible and invisible (Col. 1:15-16). And as the all-knowing, all-powerful, everywhere-present creator, he sits enthroned as sovereign king.

In the Old Testament, the kingdom is revealed as God's rule over creation. The writers depict God as a king whose sovereignty extends to the ends of the earth (Ps. 47:2, 7; 95:3-5). This means the Lord orchestrates the rise and fall of nations (2 Chron. 20:6; Job 12:23; Ps. 22:28). Further, benevolence and justice characterize his rule (Ps. 99:4).

Yahweh is the undeniable monarch of creation, as the psalmist writes: "The LORD has established his throne in heaven, and his kingdom rules over all" (Ps. 103:19). Even the pagan king Nebuchadnezzar declares, "His kingdom is an eternal kingdom, and his dominion is from generation to generation" (Dan. 4:3). So, God's kingdom actually includes all that exists.

The Old Testament writers understand that God's purposes are to be worked out in the unfolding of human history. Even so, the Old Testament picture of the kingdom of God is incomplete, pointing to the works of the coming Messiah.[4]

So, when we get to the New Testament, Jesus and the writers of Scripture use a more narrow definition, depicting the kingdom of God as a spiritual rule over those who willingly submit to Christ's authority. Jesus declares that repentance is necessary to be a citizen of the kingdom (Matt. 4:17). And in Jesus' nighttime encounter with Nicodemus, Jesus makes it clear that being "born again," or "born from above," is necessary for entrance into the kingdom (see John 3:1-8).

Rebellious angels and humans are necessarily excluded from God's kingdom. They are usurpers, rebels, tyrants, who would never accept the Lord as king (see Jesus' parables in Matt. 21:33-45; 22:1-14). Conversely, those who acknowledge the kingship of Jesus, and surrender to his sovereignty over their lives, are willing subjects of the kingdom.

Throughout the Gospels, Jesus preaches about the kingdom and tells parables to reveal what the kingdom is like. Early in his ministry, he declares that the kingdom "has come near" (Matt. 4:17), meaning that where Jesus is present, the kingdom of God is present.

His miracles – turning water into wine, calming the seas, raising the dead, and casting out demons – validate his authority to rule. He is the creator with absolute power over the elements in the visible and unseen realms. Further – and it's vital we grasp this truth – Jesus' miracles provide a window into the future, when the kingdom in its fullness banishes death, grief, crying, and pain (Rev. 21:4).

It's that future fulfillment we now await – the literal rule of Christ on earth after his return. Daniel writes, "the God of heaven will set up a kingdom that will never be destroyed" (Dan. 2:44; cf. 7:13-14). Other prophets foretell the same truth.

For example, Obadiah declares, "the kingdom will be the LORD's" (Obad. 1:21). In that day, "the earth will be filled with the knowledge of the LORD's glory, as the water covers the sea" (Hab. 2:14). Citizens of the kingdom will shout, "Come, let's go up to the mountain of the LORD, to the house of the God of Jacob. He will teach us about his ways so we may walk in his paths" (Mic. 4:2). Zechariah writes, "On that day the LORD will become King over the whole earth — the LORD alone, and his name alone" (Zech. 14:9).

The kingdom of God has always existed as God's sovereign rule over creation. In Old Testament times, this rule is experienced mostly through God's providence. Then, with the coming of Messiah, the kingdom is revealed as a present reality, with Jesus ruling in the hearts of willing subjects. Finally, the kingdom is a future promise, realized when Jesus comes in glory and sits on David's throne. By fiat, he reverses the curse that has held creation under its spell for so long.

THE MYSTERY OF THE KINGDOM

It may help our understanding of the kingdom of God to see it as a mystery, which Jesus addresses in his parables (Matt. 13:11). The Greek *mysteria* means what we can know only by divine revelation. This has particular value in helping us understand the already/not yet quality of the kingdom. That is, some aspects of the kingdom are experienced in the present, while others await future fulfillment.

First-century Jews are looking for a political and military kingdom based on their understanding of the Hebrew Scriptures. They largely ignore the prophecies in Isaiah 53 and elsewhere of a Suffering Servant and thereby reject Jesus, who declares that his kingdom "is not of this world," meaning his kingdom is distinct from the fallen system over which the evil one rules (John 18:36; 2 Cor. 4:4).

So, the mystery of the kingdom is that it must first come without fanfare in the Lamb of God, who takes away the sin of the world (John 1:29). The kingdom is present where Jesus is present – on the earth briefly two thousand years ago, and today in the hearts of believers. One day, the kingdom comes in fullness as the Lion of Judah returns to claim his throne, judge all people, cast the usurper (Satan) and his followers into the lake of fire, and create new heavens and a new earth (2 Pet. 3:10-13; Rev. 19:11-16; 21-22).

As we await the full revealing of the kingdom, Christians should pray, as John entreated, "Come, Lord Jesus!" (Rev. 22:20).

THE KING'S AGENDA

As we look for the return of the king, it may help to briefly survey his unfinished business.

The king returns in glory. As angels tell the apostles who watch Jesus ascend into heaven: "Men of Galilee, why do you stand looking up into heaven? This same Jesus, who has been taken from you into heaven, will come in the same way that you have seen him going into heaven" (Acts 1:11).

Jesus is returning personally, physically, visibly, and gloriously. He begins his parable of the sheep and goats with these words: "When the Son of Man comes in his glory, and all the angels with him ...." (Matt. 25:31). Paul tells the Thessalonians, "For the Lord himself will descend from heaven with a shout, with the archangel's voice, and with the trumpet of God ...." (1 Thess. 4:16). And, drawing from Old Testament prophecies, John declares, "Look, he is coming with the clouds, and every eye will see him, even those who pierced him. And all the tribes of the earth will mourn over him" (Rev. 1:7; cf. Isa. 19:1; Dan. 7:13; Zech. 12:10).

In his ascension, Jesus reclaims the glory he shared with the Father before the world existed (John 17:5). His coronation takes place as he ascends to the throne and sits at the Father's right hand, with all authority given to him in heaven and earth (Matt. 28:18; Mark 16:19; Acts 2:33; Rom. 8:34; Heb. 12:2). When he returns, he bears that same divine glory as "King of Kings and Lord of Lords" (Rev. 19:16).

The king sits on the throne of David. The messianic prophecies of Isaiah are stunning. Time and again, we are given the promise of a faithful king who brings back the kingdom of God (e.g., Isa. 2:1-5; 9:1-7; 11:1-9). It appears this promise stands as a potential reality for each generation of King David's descendants. But as Judah's kings rise and fall, none fulfills the messianic hopes. The promises pass from generation to generation and slowly fade from view.

This is the void into which Jesus is born. The basic claim of the four Gospels is that Jesus is the promised, faithful king from the line of David. As Tim Mackie writes, "Those ancient poems and prophetic stories created a giant 'help wanted: Messiah needed' sign, Jesus arrived to apply for the job, and successfully."[5]

Today, Jesus is seated on the throne in heaven, at the Father's right hand (Heb. 1:3; 8:1; 12:2). But when he returns to earth in glory, he brings the throne of God with him (Dan. 2:44; Matt. 25:31; Luke 1:32; Rev. 22:1, 3). Then, Jesus' prayer that the Father's will be done on earth as it is in heaven is fulfilled (Matt. 6:10). The king arrives and sits on David's throne, fulfilling God's promises to Abraham and David. And with the king, the kingdom comes in fullness.

The king judges. Bible commentators differ as to the order of final judgment. Dispensational premillennialists, for example, see multiple resurrections and judgments spanning more than a thousand years, beginning with the rapture of the church and the judgment seat of Christ, and ending with the resurrection of the wicked, who stand before the great white throne. Others, like amillennialists, see Scripture revealing a general resurrection of the dead, followed immediately by final judgment; the judgment of the sheep and goats (Matt. 25:31-46), the judgment seat of Christ (Rom. 14:10; 2 Cor. 5:10), and the great white throne judgment (Rev. 20:11-15) all are depictions of the same event from different perspectives.

What these and other views share in common, however, is the firm conviction that all people, as well as Satan and evil spirits, are subject to final judgment with everlasting consequences. And in all cases, Jesus rules as judge (John 5:22). Believers are judged and rewarded for their faithful stewardship. The wicked are judged and punished in varying degrees for their works against the king and his kingdom. Satan and the angels who rebelled with him are cast into the lake of fire, a place prepared especially for them (Matt. 25:41).

Unlike even the most noble earthly kings, Jesus judges in perfect righteousness (Acts 17:30-31; 2 Tim. 4:8; Rev. 19:11). His final judgment evaluates human and angelic works, resulting in everlasting rewards and punishments.

For Satan and rebellious angels, their eternal destiny was determined long ago. There is no salvation for them. Jesus did not come in the likeness of sinful and fallen angels; rather, he came in the likeness of sinful and fallen humans. Even so, there appears to be varying degrees of wickedness, and thus varying degrees of judgment, even among fallen angels (see 2 Pet. 2:4; Jude 6).

For people who receive the gift of eternal life, final judgment is not to determine *where* they spend eternity, but *how* (see Chapter 9). The same may be said of those who reject the Son of God. They join Satan and demons in the lake of fire, yet they do not experience hell in exactly the same way. Jesus punishes Adolf Hitler and the law-abiding atheist according to what's written about them in the books (see Rev. 20:12), yet they share a common destiny in outer darkness.

The king purges his kingdom. When Jesus returns, he not only resurrects and judges all people, he removes evil from the earth. Old and
New Testament saints receive glorified bodies, similar to the body
Jesus bears when he rises from the dead. These new bodies no longer
suffer the effects of the Fall. They're not prone to sickness, frailty,
aging, and death. Rather, they are what Paul describes as "spiritual"
bodies – bodies fully empowered and preserved by the Holy Spirit
(1 Cor. 15:44). They are bodies fit for everlasting life with Jesus in a
perfectly restored earth.

At the same time, people who have rejected God's gracious offer of
salvation are sent away, out of the kingdom and into outer darkness
(Matt. 7:21-23; 22:1-14; 25:31-46; Rev. 20:11-15; 21:8, 27; 22:15).
Though the wicked continue to exist for all eternity, they are
prevented from entering the kingdom of God.

Satan and the angels who rebelled with him also are banished to
the lake of fire (Matt. 25:41; Rev. 20:10). The "god of this age" (2 Cor.
4:4) may no longer lay claim to the people and elements of his rogue
kingdom; rather, he shares outer darkness with them.

Finally, Jesus expunges sin and its stain from the created order.
Peter describes this coming event as a purging by fire – a complete
global cleansing comparable to the flood in Noah's day, yet better by
far because it permanently banishes sin from God's kingdom
(2 Pet. 3:5-13).

The king restores Eden. Before the Fall, earth served as an intersection between the unseen realm, where God dwells, and the physical
world he created. Adam and Eve enjoyed intimate, face-to-face
communion with God, who evidently met with them in the cool of
the evening and walked alongside them (see Gen. 3:8).

But sin ruined everything. Adam and Eve are exiled from Eden.
The earth comes under a curse, grudgingly yielding its fruit. Rather
than bear a promised redeemer, the first parents birth a murderer.
And before long, there's hardly a righteous person to be found on the
face of the earth. Even the flood doesn't improve the wickedness of
the human heart. As Paul notes, the whole creation groans with labor

pains, waiting to be set free from the bondage of decay (Rom. 8:21-22).

But new heavens and a new earth are coming (2 Pet. 3:13; Rev. 21-22; cf. Isa. 65:17; 66:22). In what Jesus calls "the renewal of all things" (Matt. 19:28), he cleanses creation of sin and its stain and makes all things new (Rev. 21:5). The Greek word John uses for "new" when he describes "a new heaven and a new earth" is *kainos*, which means not only recently made, or fresh, but "of a new kind, unprecedented" (Rev. 21:1).[6] In other words, Jesus doesn't annihilate the world he created and start again from scratch; he redeems the world, clearing out all the effects of the Fall and restoring the sinless perfection of Eden.

When the King of kings returns, he sets everything right.

WHAT DO WE DO NOW?

In *The Candidate*, John McKay's stunning political victory spurs him to ask, "What do we do now?" The apostles in Acts 1 seem equally baffled as they gaze upward, watching Jesus ascend from the Mount of Olives and then vanish from view.

Jesus has come quietly and unassumingly, born to a teenage mother in a Near Eastern village. A most unlikely candidate for king, Jesus lives his life humbly, refusing coronation on numerous occasions, hiding his identity as Messiah until just the right moment, and then surrendering that sinless life on a Roman cross. The kingdom he has proclaimed is lost, or so it seems.

But his resurrection three days later makes good on his promise to conquer the grave, and it seals his identity as Lord and Messiah (Acts 2:36). Forty days later, standing on the Mount of Olives, Jesus is moments away from a *Shekinah*-glory escort to his coronation in heaven. He's been preparing his followers for this day, assuring them of the advantage of his ascension.

The Holy Spirit – another Counselor like himself – is coming to indwell and empower them (see John 14:16-17; 16:7-15). But before Jesus goes and the Spirit comes, Jesus passes the torch of proclaiming the kingdom of God to his followers. The gospel of the kingdom is in their hands now – and, by extension, in ours.

The kingdom – God's authority to rule – has always existed because the king has always existed. Satan rebels against God's authority, cobbling together a competing kingdom of fallen angels and sinful humans. But Jesus comes at just the right time to invade Satan's kingdom, binding the strong man and plundering his goods (Matt. 12:29; Gal. 4:4). Then, defeating Satan, sin, and death through his finished work on the cross, Jesus ascends to the Father's right hand, where he is crowned king.

What do we do now? While we await the king's return, we proclaim the gospel of the kingdom. And when Jesus comes back, he casts everything and everyone in opposition to his rightful rule into outer darkness. The created order, which has groaned for millennia beneath the weight of sin (Rom. 8:22), is made new – not new in kind, but new in quality. Sin and its curse are banished. The old is gone. The new has come.

In the Lord's prayer, Jesus tells the Father, "Your kingdom come. Your will be done on earth as it is in heaven" (Matt. 6:10). While God's subjects in heaven always act in perfect harmony with their creator's will, the same may not be said on earth, where the Fall has ruined everything and rebellion is rampant.

But Jesus is made a curse for us so we might be redeemed from the curse (Gal. 3:13). Now crowned king, and seated at the Father's right hand as our mediator and intercessor, Jesus awaits word from the Father to come and fetch his bride. When that day – the day of the Lord – arrives, Eden is restored. And just as in the beginning, when God's will was done perfectly in heaven and on earth, so it will be once again.

REVIEW

Key takeaways from this chapter

1. Between Jesus' resurrection and ascension, he appears to many people and teaches them about the kingdom of God. They seem eager

for Jesus to sit on David's throne, and they ask if he's about to restore the kingdom to Israel. But Jesus says it's not for them to know the timing of such details. Rather, when the Holy Spirit empowers them, they are to take the gospel of the kingdom to the ends of the earth.

2. The terms "kingdom of God," "kingdom of heaven," and "kingdom" (with reference to the kingdom of God/heaven) appear nearly 150 times in Scripture. While none of these passages offers a straightforward definition, we may state simply that *the kingdom is God's reign, his authority to rule over all.*

3. In the Old Testament, the kingdom is revealed as God's rule over creation. When we get to the New Testament, Jesus and the writers of Scripture use a more narrow definition, depicting the kingdom of God as a spiritual rule over those who willingly submit to Christ's authority. When Christ returns, the kingdom comes in fullness as Jesus sits on the throne of David and rules over a restored earth.

4. Jesus addresses the mystery of the kingdom in his parables. The mystery is that the kingdom must first come without fanfare in the Lamb of God who takes away the sin of the world. One day, the kingdom comes gloriously as the Lion of Judah returns to claim his throne, judge all people, cast Satan and his followers into the lake of fire, and create new heavens and a new earth.

5. King Jesus has an ambitious agenda when he returns. Specifically, the king:

(a) Returns in glory

(b) Sits on the throne of David

(c) Judges

(d) Purges his kingdom

(e) Restores Eden

DISCUSS

Questions for personal or group study

1. What's the difference between the "kingdom of God" and the "kingdom of heaven"? Why do you think Matthew is the only Gospel writer to prefer the term "kingdom of heaven"?

2. How different do you think our lives would be today if Jesus had answered the disciples' question about the restoration of his kingdom (see Acts 1:6)? How might knowing the date of Jesus' return be a disadvantage to the church?

3. What are some of the seemingly contradictory statements we find about the kingdom in the New Testament? How might we reconcile them?

4. Try telling, briefly, the story of the kingdom of God in four parts, considering the biblical narrative of: (1) creation, (2) fall, (3) redemption, and (4) restoration.

5. Briefly describe five items on Jesus' agenda when he brings the fullness of the kingdom of God at his return.

* * *

9

"ALL WHO ARE IN THE GRAVES"

JESUS IS RETURNING TO RESURRECT AND JUDGE ALL PEOPLE

*I*n 1789, two years after he signed the U.S. Constitution, Benjamin Franklin wrote a letter to French scientist Jean-Baptiste Leroy. The 83-year-old Franklin, reflecting on his role in history and, perhaps, wrestling with the inevitability of his own mortality, penned, "Our new Constitution is now established, and has an appearance that promises permanency; but in this world nothing can be said to be certain, except death and taxes."

Franklin died the next year. And while his famous quip about death and taxes isn't original – it dates back to a line from English dramatist Christopher Bullock in 1716 – Franklin is credited with popularizing the thought.

The famous quote sometimes has been wrongly attributed to Mark Twain. Meanwhile, numerous writers have sought to improve it. For example, Will Rogers once said, "The difference between death and taxes is death doesn't get worse every time Congress meets." And in a line from the 1991 film *Bill & Ted's Bogus Journey*, the Grim Reaper raps, "You might be a king or a little street sweeper, but sooner or later you dance with the reaper."

Finally, in a 2013 BizarroComics.com strip, the Grim Reaper

stares across a desk at an IRS auditor and sighs, "I suppose this was inevitable."[1]

Whether we consider death in light-hearted or graver ways (pun intended), we can't escape the truth that one day we breathe our last. But what then? Everyone who's thought seriously about this question has an answer – or at least an opinion.

Those who embrace a naturalistic worldview say death is the end of our existence. We may live on in the memories of loved ones. Meanwhile, our contributions to mankind – or our crimes against humanity – may outlive us, but our consciousness ends permanently and irreversibly once we stop breathing.

Tibetan Buddhists believe the spirits of the departed embark on a journey lasting forty-nine days and divided into three stages. At the conclusion of the third stage, a person either enters *nirvana* – a place of liberation from the cravings that cause suffering – or returns to earth for rebirth.

Jehovah's Witnesses believe most of the departed (except for the 144,000 of the anointed class) go into a state of soul sleep until a future date with destiny. At that time, many of the dead are resurrected and given an opportunity to prove themselves worthy to enter an eternal paradise on earth.

But Scripture paints a different picture. At physical death, the immaterial part of human beings – that is, our souls and spirits – enters an intermediate state, either with Jesus in heaven or in torment in *hades*. Meanwhile, our lifeless bodies await future resurrection, at which time our souls and spirits reunite with our resurrected bodies so we may stand before Jesus in final judgment.

The whole person – body, soul, and spirit – has a date on the docket with the highest court in the universe. As the writer of Hebrews notes, "it is appointed for people to die once — and after this, judgment" (Heb. 9:27).

Jesus states this in John 5:28-29:

> ... a time is coming when all who are in the graves will hear his [the Son of Man's] voice and come out — those who have done good

things, to the resurrection of life, but those who have done wicked things, to the resurrection of condemnation.

Jesus doesn't mean living a good life merits heaven and living a wicked life automatically results in hell. Quite the contrary. Just a few verses earlier, Jesus lays out the requirements for eternal life: "Truly I tell you, anyone who hears my word and believes him who sent me has eternal life and will not come under judgment but has passed from death to life" (John 5:24). Our Lord, and the New Testament writers, make it clear that salvation is by grace alone, through faith alone, in Christ alone (Rom. 10:9-10; Eph. 2:8-9; Tit. 3:5).

Even so, every person who has ever lived is going to be physically resurrected and stand in judgment before Christ, to whom all judgment has been given (John 5:22). When does this final judgment take place? At the return of Christ.

WHY RESURRECTION IS NECESSARY

If physical death is not the end of our existence, what happens to our bodies? Why does the Bible speak of future resurrection? And if the immaterial part of us – our souls and spirits – separates from our bodies at death and resides either in a state of blessedness with the Lord (2 Cor. 5:8; Phil. 1:23) or apart from him in torment (Luke 16:19-31), what need is there for resurrection?

First, it's important to note that God created Adam and Eve to live forever in their bodies. That's his intent for us as well. But sin ruins everything. It affects our ability to relate to a holy God. It corrupts our minds, emotions, and wills. It brings a curse on the material universe. And it results in spiritual and physical death.

As a consequence of Adam's sin, all people suffer, age, and die. Nature itself is in the throes of a struggle with entropy. So, if Jesus paid our sin debt in full, it means he not only restores believers to a right relationship with him; he also reverses the effects of the Fall, including physical death and a cursed environment.

A Christian's salvation is completed in *glorification*, the resurrec-

tion and perfection of his or her body, which is made like the body of
the risen Jesus. This final chapter in redemption is so certain that Paul
refers to it in the past tense, along with God's foreknowledge, predestination, calling, and justification (Rom. 8:29-30). Followers of Jesus
ultimately see him as he is – in unveiled, radiant glory – and become
like him.

But what about those who reject Christ? What purpose does their
future resurrection serve? It enables them to experience what they
want – everlasting existence on their own terms, apart from God.
They love darkness, as Jesus says, and ultimately get what they crave
(John 3:19). As Adam and Eve are banished from the presence of God
in the Garden of Eden, so unbelievers are expelled from the new
heavens and earth into what Jesus calls "outer darkness" (Matt. 22:13;
25:30).

JESUS: FIRSTBORN AND FIRSTFRUITS

Our future resurrection is pinned to the resurrection of Jesus. King
David prophesies that the grave cannot hold the coming Messiah
(Ps. 16:10), a fact to which Peter and Paul attest as fulfilled in Jesus
(Acts 2:24-36; 13:33-39). Jesus predicts his return from the grave
(Matt. 12:39-40; 16:21; John 2:18-22), and this claim is common
knowledge (Matt. 27:62-64). Jesus' bodily ascension into heaven is a
foretaste of his personal, physical, and visible return one day
(Acts 1:11).

As the resurrected Savior, Jesus is sometimes called the "firstborn"
from the dead. The adjective *prototokos* (firstborn) is found nine times
in the New Testament and is used in both literal and figurative senses.
For example, a reference to Jesus as Mary's firstborn son appears in
Luke 2:7. Meanwhile, Hebrews 11:28 refers to the firstborn of
Egyptian families that the avenging angel destroys.

But in metaphorical contexts, the meaning of "firstborn" signifies
the person of Jesus Christ. Paul depicts him as the firstborn over all
creation (Col. 1:15). This does not mean, as some suggest, that Jesus
is a created being, for if Paul had intended that, he could have used the

Greek word *protoktisis* (first-created) rather than *prototokos* (firstborn). Rather, the apostle is describing Jesus as "the initial representative of a regenerate communion of believers who would continue throughout eternity."[2]

In Revelation 1:5, John uses "firstborn from the dead" to exalt Jesus as the prime example of resurrected members of his body, the church. Put simply, Jesus is the foremost of those raised from the dead. Based on his physical resurrection, Jesus is declared the powerful Son of God (Rom. 1:4). His work of redemption is complete, and we have the confident expectation of our own resurrection and glorification one day.

G. K. Beale notes that "firstborn" refers to the high, privileged position Christ has as a result of his resurrection from the dead:

> Christ has gained such a sovereign position over the cosmos, not in the sense that he is recognized as the first-created being of all creation or as the origin of creation, but in the sense that he is the inaugurator of the new creation by means of the resurrection.[3]

In addition to "firstborn," Jesus also is depicted as "firstfruits." Like the first grain taken from the fields and offered to the Lord in the Jewish feast of firstfruits, Jesus is the first to pass through death and emerge victoriously, ensuring that the full harvest of believers is gathered one day (see 1 Cor. 15:20-28).

The resurrection of Christians is pinned inextricably to the resurrection of Christ. As Paul writes:

> For if the dead are not raised, not even Christ has been raised. And if Christ has not been raised, your faith is worthless; you are still in your sins. Those, then, who have fallen asleep in Christ have also perished. If we have put our hope in Christ for this life only, we should be pitied more than anyone. But as it is, Christ has been raised from the dead, the firstfruits of those who have fallen asleep (1 Cor. 15:16-20).

Jesus is the "firstborn" and the "firstfruits" of the dead. That is, he's

the first to rise from the dead in glory, never to die again, and the
foremost of those raised from the cold grip of the last enemy to be
abolished: death (1 Cor. 15:26).

THE BELIEVER'S RESURRECTION

It's comforting to keep in mind that when Christ died, he redeemed
our bodies, souls, and spirits. Our salvation doesn't stop with the
forgiveness of sins, the declaration of our right standing with God in
Christ, and the sanctifying work of the Holy Spirit, although these are
unfathomable gifts of grace. Rather, the redemptive work of Christ
finds its ultimate fulfillment in future resurrection and glorification,
when the effects of sin are completely removed, and believers are fully
conformed to the image of Christ.

Equally comforting is the Lord's promise that neither death nor
hades threatens his children again. John, who hears Christ assure him
that Jesus holds the keys of death and *hades*, later bears witness to the
fact that these enemies are thrown into the lake of fire (Rev. 20:14). In
our glorified bodies, we no longer sin, nor are we drawn to rebellion
against God. As a resulting benefit, we have no reason to fear death,
for it is but a distant memory God banishes from the realm of
possibility.

One day, death and *hades* are forced to give up their treasure.
Christ uses his keys to open the graves and call the dead to life. *Hades*,
the temporary abode of the dead, swallows the deceased no more. As
Paul writes triumphantly for the believer:

> For the Lord himself will descend from heaven with a shout, with the
> archangel's voice, and with the trumpet of God, and the dead in Christ
> will rise first. Then we who are still alive, who are left, will be caught
> up together with them in the clouds to meet the Lord in the air, and so
> we will always be with the Lord. Therefore encourage one another
> with these words (1 Thess. 4:16-18).

But how, exactly, does this work? Two passages of Scripture are most helpful in answering this question: 1 Corinthians 15:50-58 and 1 Thessalonians 4:13-18. In these passages, Paul describes our future resurrection as a "mystery," a secret hidden in the past but now revealed.

In the resurrection of the just, Jesus descends from heaven and calls the "dead in Christ" to rise first (1 Thess. 4:16). The souls and spirits of the redeemed with Jesus in heaven are reunited with their resurrected bodies, which are glorified, or made incorruptible and immortal (1 Cor. 15:52-54). This happens in "the twinkling of an eye" and causes us to rejoice that death has been "swallowed up in victory" (1 Cor. 15:52, 54).

Immediately after this, followers of Jesus who are alive and remain on the earth are caught up physically to "meet the Lord in the air" (1 Thess. 4:17). Our earthly bodies are instantly transformed into glorified bodies, without experiencing physical death. Both resurrected saints and living followers of Jesus who are "caught up together with them in the clouds" are assured they will "always be with the Lord" (4:17). When Christ returns to earth, the glorified saints return with him (1 Thess. 3:13; Rev. 19:14), along with the holy angels (Matt. 16:27; 2 Thess. 1:7).

What are these glorified bodies like? Paul uses differentiations within the created order as analogies for the similarities and differences between our earthly bodies and our resurrected ones (1 Cor. 15:35-44). For example, the wheat seed planted in the ground must die in order to spring to life with a stalk and heads of grain. There is continuity in kind – it remains wheat – but advancement in form.

In a similar manner, our earthly bodies are "sown in corruption, raised in incorruption" (1 Cor. 15:42). That is, our earthly bodies waste away and are prone to death, but our resurrected bodies are impervious to decay. Our earthly bodies are "sown in dishonor, raised in glory" (15:43). This means, as Paul tells the Philippians, Christ "will transform the body of our humble condition into the likeness of his glorious body" (Phil. 3:21).

In addition, our earthly bodies are "sown in weakness, raised in power" (1 Cor. 15:43), another way of saying that our present inability to avoid all types of infirmities will give way to health and vitality in glorification. Finally, our earthly bodies are "sown a natural body, raised a spiritual body" (15:44). The bodies we now inhabit – animal-like, soulish – are incapable of perfect holiness, but our resurrected bodies are under the full control of the Holy Spirit.

The best way to understand glorification is to examine the post-resurrection life of Jesus. He is raised in a physical body (Luke 24:39-40; John 2:18-22), and thus he eats (Luke 24:41-43). He shows people his hands, feet, and side, complete with nail and spear prints in them (Luke 24:39; John 20:27).[4] Further, we see people clutch Jesus' feet and worship him (Matt. 28:9).

Jesus' resurrected body no doubt retains physical characteristics. At the same time, he is able to vanish from sight in one place and appear in another (Luke 24:31-36). He evidently is able to pass through locked doors (John 20:19). And, finally, he ascends physically into heaven, a preview of the visible and personal manner in which he is to return (Acts 1:9, 11).

While we struggle to fully understand the qualities of Jesus' resurrected body, we may rest assured that our glorified bodies are physical, fully controlled by the Spirit, and free of sin and its consequences. In essence, we are restored to the sinless perfection Adam and Eve enjoyed in Eden before the Fall, along with face-to-face fellowship with God.

THE UNBELIEVER'S RESURRECTION

There is less in Scripture about the resurrection of the wicked than there is about the glorification of the just. Nevertheless, the Bible gives us enough information to know that those who reject Christ are physically resurrected one day and separated forever from God.

Daniel gives us the clearest Old Testament glimpse of the resurrection of the wicked, and their everlasting destiny: "Many who sleep in the dust of the earth will awake, some to eternal life, and some to disgrace and eternal contempt" (Dan. 12:2). Job and Isaiah also offer insights into future resurrection (Job 19:25-27; Isa. 26:19).

In the New Testament, Jesus tells us a day of reckoning is coming for all people, an event that begins with resurrection (John 5:28-29). The New Testament writers confirm final judgment of the wicked in numerous places, a judgment that presupposes resurrection (Acts 10:42; 17:31; 2 Thess. 1:6-9; Heb. 9:27; 1 Pet. 4:5; 2 Pet. 3:7).

We've surveyed the resurrection of life, also known as the "first resurrection" (John 5:29; Rev. 20:5-6). Let's look now at the resurrection of judgment, which leads to "the second death, the lake of fire" (Rev. 20:14).

It is reasonable, but by no means certain, to conclude that the wicked of all ages are the last to be resurrected, depending on how one interprets Revelation 20. John writes, "The rest of the dead did not come to life until the 1,000 years were completed" (Rev. 20:5). These dead, great and small, stand before a great white throne and are judged according to their works (Rev. 20:11-13).

Prior to this judgment, Satan is thrown into the lake of fire (Rev. 20:10). Presumably, demons are cast there at this time as well (see Matt. 25:41). Then, death and *hades* are cast into hell (Rev. 20:14). This lends credence to the view that the wicked are the last to be resurrected because no one dies physically anymore (death), and there is no need for an intermediate abode of the dead (*hades*). Last, the wicked, whose names are not found written in the book of life, are thrown into the lake of fire and experience the second death (Rev. 20:14-15).

But what kind of resurrected bodies do the wicked receive? Scripture offers no details like the ones Paul lays out for believers in 1 Corinthians 15. Even so, we may offer a few observations about the resurrected bodies of the damned:

- They are physical bodies, reunited with the souls and spirits of the wicked in *hades*.
- They are prepared for everlasting separation from God in hell. Scripture does not support the false doctrines of

annihilationism (the wicked ultimately cease to exist) or
universalism (everyone ultimately is saved).

- They cannot be what Paul describes as "spiritual" bodies in
  1 Corinthians 15:44, for the wicked have rejected Christ
  and thus are void of the indwelling Holy Spirit.
- They experience the second death – that is, the lake of fire –
  in which they are doomed forever for existence, but not for
  true life, for they are in outer darkness, cut off from the
  Source of Life.

WHAT IF THERE'S NO CORPSE?

Every person is physically resurrected one day, summoned before
Christ on his throne of glory, and ushered into eternity, either in a
glorified body similar to the body Christ had when he rose from the
dead, or in a physical body prepared for everlasting existence in outer
darkness.

But what about those whose bodies have been cremated, lost at
sea, ravaged in warfare, or otherwise ruined beyond recovery? The
God who names the stars (Isa. 40:26) is fully capable of tracing every
human atom and resurrecting every person ever conceived, and then
fashioning that body for everlasting life with God or everlasting existence apart from him.

Resurrection must take place for Christ to set things right. The
salvation of believers depends on Jesus' finished work at Calvary,
purging sin and its consequences from their whole being, and
restoring in eternity what was sacrificed in time for the sake of Jesus.

A young woman beheaded for professing faith in Christ must
experience the resurrection power of Jesus, whose brutalized body
burst forth from the grave in health and wholeness. The child who
dies in his mother's womb, never to draw his first breath, must experience the joys of childhood and the embrace of a loving Father. And
the faithful bond-servant of Christ whose physical vigor erodes with
the ravages of time must experience the vitality of being a new
creation once again.

Equally important, the punishment of the wicked demands resurrection, for their sins are not confined to their souls and spirits. Jesus' story of Lazarus and the rich man illustrates the truth that we reap in eternity what we sow in time.

In the resurrection of the wicked, the rich man could forever seek the creature comforts he denied Lazarus (Luke 16:19-31). The one who traffics in human lives may find himself forever on the run as a marked man. And the false teacher who, for personal gain, proclaims "another Jesus," "a different spirit," and "a different gospel" (2 Cor. 11:4), may find his sensual cravings forever unsatisfied, while he seeks to escape the haunting eyes of those he wooed into hell.

While outer darkness may seem unreasonably harsh, everyone who experiences everlasting existence apart from Christ has chosen it. The rich man in Jesus' parable confesses to being in torment, but he shows no willingness to repent of his sin. The resurrected wicked summoned before the great white throne watch in stunned silence as books are opened, revealing no evidence of a desire for Christ (Rev. 20:11-15). Even those who dare to offer a word in their own defense are proven to be lawbreakers whom Jesus never knew (Matt. 7:21-23).

When judgment falls on the wicked, it does not produce repentance, for that is the goal of God's kindness, restraint, and patience now (Rom. 2:4). In body, soul, and spirit, the resurrected wicked remain, throughout eternity, what they have proven to be on this side of the grave.

Like a black hole, the second death permits no escape. The gentle touch of the Savior's hand, the Spirit's still, small voice calling the lost to repentance, the joy of an intimate relationship with the God of the universe – these have been rejected and are not welcome in the second death. Worse, there is no second chance. The second death, experienced in an indestructible body devoid of the Spirit, is final and irrevocable.

EVERYONE'S DAY OF RECKONING

One day, every person is resurrected and summoned before Christ in final judgment. While salvation is a gift of God, received by grace alone, through faith alone, in Christ alone, our lifestyles *reflect* our beliefs. That is, our words and deeds reveal our citizenship, either in the kingdom of God or in the domain of the evil one.

Put another way, our works count for something. Heaven is not the same for every believer, nor do all those who reject Christ experience hell identically. Our final, personal, individual judgment before Christ is his way, as the righteous judge, of setting things right for eternity.

Our short stay on earth is a dress rehearsal for life beyond the grave. One day, we all stand before Jesus to give an account of what we did with the gospel, as well as our time, talents, opportunities, and other gifts God has entrusted to us. This results in varying degrees of reward for believers, and varying degrees of punishment for unbelievers.

Followers of Jesus stand in a different judgment than those who reject Christ. Paul tells us that Christians are summoned to the judgment seat of Christ (Rom. 14:10-12; 2 Cor. 5:10). At the same time, John is given a glimpse of the great white throne, upon which Jesus sits to judge those whose names are not written in the Lamb's book of life (Rev. 20:11-15).[5]

THE JUDGMENT SEAT OF CHRIST

The judgment seat of Christ is where Christians, and perhaps believers of all eras, stand before Jesus to receive his evaluation of our lives. The result is everlasting reward, in greater or lesser degrees, based on our faithfulness to walk the path of good works God set for us in eternity past (Eph. 2:10). Paul writes about this judgment in several places:

Romans 14:10-12 – "But you, why do you judge your brother or sister? Or you, why do you despise your brother or sister? For we will all stand before the judgment seat of God. For it is written: *As I live, says the Lord, every knee will bow to me, and every tongue will give praise to God.* So then, each of us will give an account of himself to God."

1 Corinthians 3:11-15 – "For no one can lay any foundation other than what has been laid down. That foundation is Jesus Christ. If anyone builds on that foundation with gold, silver, costly stones, wood, hay, or straw, each one's work will become obvious. For the day will disclose it, because it will be revealed by fire; the fire will test the quality of each one's work. If anyone's work that he has built survives, he will receive a reward. If anyone's work is burned up, he will experience loss, but he himself will be saved – but only as through fire."

2 Corinthians 5:10 – "For we must all appear before the judgment seat of Christ, so that each may be repaid for what he has done in the body, whether good or evil."

The Greek word translated "judgment seat" is *bema,* a bench or platform from which public or judicial pronouncements are made. Pilate sits on the *bema* (Matt. 27:19; John 19:13), as do Herod (Acts 12:21 – "throne") and Gallio (Acts 18:12-17 – "tribunal"). Paul does not specify the exact time of this judgment. However, it's reasonable to conclude that it is tied to our resurrection, rather than to our death, so that the full impact of our earthly lives – an impact that continues after our departure from earth – may be fully evaluated and rewarded.

This judgment does not determine a believer's eternal destiny, for that is fixed on this side of death with his or her decision to trust in Christ. Rather, the *bema* judgment is where Christ rewards his followers based on how faithfully they manage the time, talents, spiritual gifts, and other good things they are given. All Christians are winners. Jesus has secured our eternal lives through his finished work on the cross. But not every Christian is rewarded equally.

Jesus urges his followers to lay up treasure in heaven, where it is kept safe and endures (Matt. 6:20). Paul informs us that our works of faithfulness – which he likens to gold, silver, and precious stones – are refined in the fires of judgment and emerge purified (1 Cor. 3:11-15). And in the Book of Revelation, Jesus reminds us that our faithfulness is rewarded (Rev. 2:23; 22:12).

In fact, the New Testament mentions at least five crowns, or rewards, believers may send ahead of them to heaven:

- The crown of righteousness, for those who love the appearing of Jesus and live as if he could return at any moment (2 Tim. 4:7-8)
- The incorruptible crown, for those who persevere in their Christian walk (1 Cor. 9:24-27)
- The crown of life, or the martyr's crown (Rev. 2:10)
- The crown of rejoicing, or the soul-winner's crown (1 Thess. 2:19-20)
- And the crown of glory, for those who shepherd the flock faithfully (1 Pet. 5:1-4)

WHY THE *BEMA* JUDGMENT?

In 1 Corinthians 4:1-5, Paul describes God's purpose for the *bema* judgment, as well as our proper perspective on it:

> A person should think of us in this way: as servants of Christ and managers of the mysteries of God. In this regard, it is required that managers be found faithful.... It is the Lord who judges me. So don't judge anything prematurely, before the Lord comes, who will both bring to light what is hidden in darkness and reveal the intentions of the hearts. And then praise will come to each one from God.

This judgment is a full disclosure of our words and deeds, as Christ uncovers even our secret conversations, as well as our thoughts, intentions, and motivations. Like a purging fire, Christ's impartial evaluation of our lives burns away our worthless works and purifies our righteous ones. For believers who have built well upon the foundation of their faith, they receive a "well done" from Christ and are given greater positions of authority and greater degrees of responsibility in his eternal kingdom (Matt. 25:21, 23).

Those who have squandered their Christian lives watch as their worthless works are consumed in the fires of judgment. Paul reminds such unfaithful believers, "If anyone's work is burned up, he will experience loss, but he himself will be saved – but only as through fire" (1 Cor. 3:15). John warns his readers to remain faithful to Christ, lest they be ashamed at his coming (1 John 2:28).

The judgment seat of Christ serves as a divine assessment of a Christian's deeds or lifestyle rather than the determination of his or her eternal destiny. As Daniel Hays writes:

> Having been saved by grace through faith (Eph. 2:8-9), Christians are nevertheless committed to working out their faith through deeds (e.g., Gal. 5:6; Eph. 2:10; Phil. 2:12-13; 1 Thess. 1:3). Believers are accountable for individual actions and are not exempt from doing good. Eschatology and ethics are bound tightly together. The judgment seat of Christ fulfills God's impartial justice, since not all believers live with the same degree of devotion to Christ. Christians are individually accountable for what they do in this mortal body.[6]

THE GREAT WHITE THRONE

The great white throne, described in Revelation 20:11-15, is unique among the thrones of God in Scripture. It stands alone. It offers no hope, grace, or mercy. It calls no one to repentance. It prompts no one to sing. It fulfills no covenant promises. It surrounds itself with no rainbows, flaming torches, seas of glass, or heavenly creatures. It is perhaps the most solemn image of God's throne in the Bible, for it depicts the time and place where Christ – the creator, redeemer, and judge – meets face-to-face with the wicked, who must now give an account of their lives. It is the last stop on the road to hell.

Joseph Seiss writes, "We read of no white robes, no spotless linen, no palms, nothing but naked sinners before the naked majesty of enthroned Almightiness, awaiting their eternal doom."[7]

As unbelievers stand before this throne – alone, without a defense, and with no escape – John notes that "books were opened. Another book was opened, which is the book of life, and the dead were judged according to their works by what was written in the books" (Rev. 20:12). What are these books, and how many are there? What is different about the book of life that it should be named, while the others are mentioned as a group without distinction?

God keeps a record of our lives and holds us accountable for how we manage the time, talents, relationships, and other gifts he has entrusted to us. He knows our thoughts, which form the action plans for good and evil deeds (Matt. 5:27-28). He hears our words, which reveal the true nature of our hearts and for which we must give an account (Matt. 12:33-37).

In various places, the Bible depicts God's record of our lives as contained in heavenly books. No person escapes the creator's interest or avoids a day of reckoning with him, as Seiss comments:

> Myriads of human beings have lived and died of whom the world knows nothing; but the lives they lived, the deeds they wrought, the thoughts and tempers they indulged, still stand written where the memory of them cannot perish. Not a human being has ever breathed earth's atmosphere whose career is not traced at full length in the books of eternity.[8]

The books that record the unbelievers' deeds are opened in order to show them at least two truths: the full extent of their lifelong wickedness, and the failure of their good deeds to earn God's favor.

THE BOOK OF LIFE

In addition, there is a search for unbelievers' names in the book of life, where their eternal bliss in the presence of Christ may have been secured by faith. But no, their names are missing. As a result, they are banished to outer darkness, or hell.

There are six references to the book of life in Revelation, including two verses that speak of the Lamb's book of life (Rev. 13:8; 21:27). We should not assume these are two separate books: the book of life and the Lamb's book of life. Because John stresses Christ's finished work at Calvary to secure our salvation, he calls the roster of the redeemed both "the book of life" and "the Lamb's book of life." Followers of Jesus may rest assured of our salvation. Our names were recorded in this book "from the foundation of the world" (Rev. 13:8). What's more, they were secured in the redemptive work of Christ foreordained in eternity past (see Acts 2:23; 1 Pet. 1:18-21).

What's so special about the book of life that would concern unbelievers? Its pages list no good deeds, no legacy of charitable acts, no meritorious service worthy of everlasting life. It seems there's no reason the names of the wicked are excluded. If they could scour the pages, they would see the names of people great and small – leaders, foot soldiers, neighbors, family members. To the mind of the damned, the listing makes no sense.

There is ample room in the book for every person's name, and yet their names are missing. Why? An entry in this book is not achieved through human effort but through simple surrender. Those written in the book of life have washed their robes in the blood of the Lamb, and he has written their names with his own blood. Those who would not have the Lamb will not have life. They are thrown into the lake of fire. The difference is that the wicked have pleaded their own righteousness while the righteous have pleaded the blood of the Lamb.

There are no doubt degrees of punishment in hell just as there are varying rewards in heaven. Eternity in hell is not the same for the mass murderer as for the law-abiding citizen, but it is outer darkness nonetheless.

Jesus saves some of his most graphic depictions of hell for the most religious people of his day. He tells the Jewish leaders they will receive greater condemnation because they know the Scriptures, which point to Jesus, yet persist in their hypocritical and destructive work against the kingdom of God (Matt. 23:13-15). He tells the story of Lazarus and the rich man in front of the Pharisees to illustrate that wealth and privilege are not entitlements God owes a self-righteous person; rather, heaven awaits those who humbly trust in him for salvation (Luke 16:19-31).

What a comfort it is for believers to know their names are written in the book of life, and what a shock it must be for countless unbelievers who discover before the great white throne that their names are absent from heaven's roll. On earth, their deeds earned a place in many great volumes – books of valor, conquest, heroics, feats, discoveries, inventions, charities, religious quests, political coups, scientific breakthroughs, medical advances, social progress, military campaigns, community activism, and legendary leadership.

Perhaps their names are inscribed on grand buildings, or chiseled into monuments, or painted on the hulls of ocean-going vessels. At the very least, the newspapers noticed their entrance into the world and their departure from it. Somewhere, their names are inscribed in family trees or scribbled in the opening pages of family Bibles. How can it be that the God who created all people does not ensure their names are in his book of life?

There must be some mistake. "Lord, Lord, didn't we prophesy in your name?" some cry out. "Didn't we drive out demons in your name, and do many miracles in your name?" The one seated on the throne does not deny they invoked his name on numerous occasions, no doubt producing some earthly good. But Jesus reveals he has no relationship with them when he utters the seven most tragic words in human history: "I never knew you: depart from me" (Matt. 7:23 KJV).

ANYONE NOT FOUND

Revelation 20:15 is as clear as Scripture can be: "And anyone whose name was not found written in the book of life was thrown into the lake of fire."

There is but one way a person's name is entered into the book of life: God writes it there and never blots it out. Just as he chooses believers in Christ before the foundation of the world, he keeps those who belong to him and never lets them go.

Many debate whether God's election is anchored simply in divine foreknowledge or in hard determinism, or even fatalism. No doubt, much about the will of God is beyond our understanding. Yet it appears that God's sovereignty includes his decision to entrust all people with an ability to make choices for which he holds them responsible. No one is denied a place in the book of life, and no one's name is entered there without their assent.

As the wicked pass through the gates of hell in Dante's epic poem *Inferno*, they are greeted with these words: "Abandon hope, all you who enter here." They remind the damned that once inside, there is no escape from the fiery torments they have brought upon themselves.

Charles Swindoll writes:

> Though the details of Dante's fictional picture of heaven, hell, and purgatory range from the fantastic to the heretical, he was right about this: the final destination of the wicked features a one-way entrance. All hope vanishes beyond; there will be no escape from the lake of fire.... The facts of eternal punishment are set forth without a hint of hope ... because no hope exists apart from God.[9]

EVERY KNEE WILL BOW

Paul writes to the Philippians that one day "every knee will bow – in heaven and on earth and under the earth – and every tongue will confess that Jesus Christ is Lord, to the glory of God the Father" (Phil. 2:10-11). Believers' knees bow in humble adoration and, like the elders before heaven's throne, the redeemed may cast any crowns placed upon their heads at Jesus' feet (Rev. 4:10). Unbelievers' knees bow in grudging acknowledgement that while they have their way and live forever apart from Jesus, he is the ultimate master with the authority to rule over the human heart.

It's a common expression at funerals that the deceased have "gone on to their eternal reward." Meant to comfort mourners that their loved ones are "in a better place," the statement glosses over the deeper truth that indeed all people ultimately are repaid for their lives on earth.

The "reward" may be our Savior's greeting: "Come, you who are blessed by my Father, inherit the kingdom prepared for you from the foundation of the world" (Matt. 25:34), followed by the bliss of authority in the presence of the Lord in the new heavens and new earth.

Or, the "reward" may be the words of the one seated on the throne of his glory: "Depart from me, you who are cursed, into the eternal fire prepared for the devil and his angels" (Matt. 25:41).

Ultimately, all people get the eternal destiny they choose, based on their acceptance or rejection of Christ. In addition, people spend eternity as close to, or as far away from, their creator as they desire based on how they lived out their acceptance or rejection of the Savior.

Jesus reminds us in the Book of Revelation that when he returns, he is going to set things right: "Look, I am coming soon, and my reward is with me to repay each person according to his work" (Rev. 22:12). His words should prompt all people to search their hearts and take stock of their treasure.

REVIEW

Key takeaways from this chapter

1. At the return of Christ, every person who has ever lived is going to be physically resurrected and stand in judgment before Christ, to whom all judgment has been given (John 5:22).

2. The judgment seat of Christ is where Christians, and perhaps believers of all eras, stand before Jesus to receive his evaluation of their lives, resulting in varying degrees of reward for their faithfulness. In contrast, the wicked of all times stand one day before the great white throne. There, it is shown that their names are absent from the book of life. They are given varying degrees of punishment in hell.

3. Our future resurrection as Christians is pinned to the resurrection of Jesus. He is both the "firstborn" from and the "firstfruits" of the dead – the first to rise from the dead in glory, never to die again, and the foremost of those raised from the cold grip of the last enemy to be abolished: death.

4. While we may struggle to fully understand the qualities of Jesus' resurrected body, we may rest assured that our glorified bodies are physical, fully controlled by the Spirit, and free of sin and its consequences. In essence, we are restored to the sinless perfection Adam and Eve enjoyed in Eden before the Fall, along with face-to-face fellowship with God.

5. There is less in Scripture about the resurrection of the wicked than there is about the glorification of the just. Nevertheless, the Bible gives us enough information to know that those who reject Christ are resurrected one day and separated forever from God.

DISCUSS

Questions for personal or group study

1. If salvation is by grace alone, through faith alone, in Christ alone, why do our works matter?

2. Why do you think we stand in final judgment *after* our resurrection, which could be hundreds of years from now, rather than immediately after our death?

3. Read 1 Corinthians 15:35-38. How does Paul use a grain of wheat as an analogy for believers' present and future bodies?

4. How do the bodies of glorified saints differ from the bodies of resurrected unbelievers?

5. Do you agree with the statement, "Everyone gets the eternal destiny they choose"? Why or why not?

* * *

——————— A ———————

Glorification is the final act of
God's redemptive work, in
which he raises our lifeless
bodies from the grave and
restores us to a state that's
better than the original.

——————— Ω ———————

"SO THAT MORTALITY MAY BE SWALLOWED UP BY LIFE"

JESUS IS RETURNING TO GLORIFY THE SAINTS

*M*emphis Belle is one of the most celebrated aircraft of World War II. Named after the girlfriend of chief pilot Robert Morgan, the lumbering B-17F Flying Fortress carried the first U.S. crew to complete twenty-five combat missions over Europe before returning to America, where the airmen were hailed as heroes during a three-month tour to sell war bonds and raise morale.

Based in Bassingborne, England, Belle coursed through flak-filled skies over France and Germany in 1942-43. The ten-man crew battled Nazi fighter planes and delivered its payload before returning to base through the same menacing skies. The crew's survival through more than two dozen missions was rare indeed. The Army Air Forces lost thirty thousand airmen in battles against Nazi Germany. During the heaviest fighting, U.S. bomber-crew airmen had a one-in-four chance of survival.

The plane's exploits were featured in a 1944 documentary and retold a generation later in a major motion picture.

For a time after the war, however, Memphis Belle sat outdoors, neglected, until an ambitious restoration project began, requiring more than one hundred workers and thousands of hours to scrape paint, bend metal, and fabricate parts. In May of 2018, on the seventy-fifth anniversary of Belle's historic twenty-fifth mission, the fully restored legend was reintroduced to the public at the National Museum of the U.S. Air Force at Wright-Patterson Air Force Base in Ohio.

Today, Belle stands as sleek as when she first rolled off the assembly line, a testament to the people who recognized her intrinsic value and labored to restore her glory for generations to come.[1]

In a manner of speaking, followers of Jesus are like Memphis Belle. We make our way through perilous times as we live in a sinful and fallen world. We age, get sick, break bones, endure disappointment, suffer crushing defeats, and sometimes are persecuted for our faith. Christ does not offer us an easy path to everlasting life, but in his work of salvation, he promises to bring us home one day and then fully restore us – body, soul, and spirit.

That's what *glorification* means. It's the final act of God's redemptive work, in which he raises our lifeless bodies from the grave and restores us to a state that's better than the original. That's because we have incorruptible bodies that never again bear the flak of sin or experience death.

This final work of redemption is yet to come, when Christ appears from heaven to fetch his bride. Indeed, Jesus is returning to glorify the saints.

WHAT IS GLORIFICATION?

Glorification is the final stage in God's work of salvation. It is the crowning achievement of sanctification, in which Christians are fully conformed to the image of Christ. It's the perfection of the body, rejoined with soul and spirit in resurrection, as well as the restoration of the universe to its original state (see Chapter 13).

Put another way, glorification is the means by which God fully reverses the effects of the Fall, purging sin and its stain from the created order. It involves the return of Jesus, the future resurrection and judgment of all people, and the creation of new heavens and a new earth.

For the most part, when Christians talk about glorification, we're referring to our future resurrection, at which time we receive incorruptible bodies similar to the body Christ had when he rose from the dead. In this respect, Wayne Grudem provides an excellent summary:

> Glorification is the final step in the application of redemption. It will happen when Christ returns and raises from the dead the bodies of all believers for all time who have died, and reunites them with their souls, and changes the bodies of all believers who remain alive, thereby giving all believers at the same time perfect resurrection bodies like his own.[2]

Even so, glorification is more than this. It is multidimensional, involving time and eternity, individuals and the believing community, saints and their Savior, resurrection of people, and the regeneration of earth. To better understand glorification, let's first define "glory" according to Scripture. Then, let's see how glorification works now, then at our death, resurrection, and the installation of new heavens and a new earth.

THE MEANING OF GLORY

To understand glorification, we should first explore the meaning of "glory," which translates a number of biblical words. One such word is the Hebrew *kabod*, which refers to an individual's display of splendor, wealth, and pomp.[3]

When used to describe God, however, it does not point to a singular attribute, but to the greatness of his whole nature. For example, Psalm 24:7-10 depicts God as the "King of glory," attended by his hosts and distinguished by his infinite splendor and beauty:

> Lift up your heads, you gates!
>   Rise up, ancient doors!
>   Then the King of glory will come in.
>   Who is this King of glory?

The Lord, strong and mighty, the Lord, mighty in battle.

Lift up your heads, you gates!

Rise up, ancient doors!

Then the King of glory will come in.

Who is he, this King of glory?

The Lord of Armies, he is the King of glory.

In the New Testament, the Greek word *doxa* carries the meaning of honor, splendor, brilliance, fame, and glory.[4] God is the "glorious Father" (Eph. 1:17) and the "God of glory" (Acts 7:2). In the Incarnation, Jesus bears "the glory as the one and only Son from the Father" (John 1:14).

While sometimes used to describe the honor of human beings, "glory" often connects the glory of Jesus with that of God the Father, particularly in his resurrection. For example, Jesus prays that the Father would glorify him as he glorifies the Father (John 17:1-5). Peter declares that God has glorified Jesus by raising him from the dead (Acts 3:13-15; 1 Pet. 1:21). Paul notes of Jesus, "Therefore we were buried with him by baptism into death, in order that, just as Christ was raised from the dead by the glory of the Father, so we too may walk in newness of life" (Rom. 6:4).

Paul also sees Christ's glorification in his ascension; Jesus is "taken up in glory" (1 Tim. 3:16). Further, the apostles preach that Christ is now exalted at the right hand of God (Acts 2:33; 5:31). And, when he returns, his appearance is glorious (Tit. 2:13).

William Mounce writes:

Because God is so glorious, it is only natural that his people want to ascribe "glory" to him. For this reason, there are many doxologies (ascriptions of glory to God) in the NT. Furthermore, every part of our lives should reflect the fact that the glorious God lives in us – even our eating and drinking.[5]

The Bible tells us there is glory now, glory in death, glory in resurrection, and glory in the restoration of the cosmos.

GLORY NOW

It is our Christian duty to glorify God. As we honor the Father, Son, and Holy Spirit for their divine attributes and redemptive work, we replicate God's glory in our thoughts, words, and deeds. This requires more than mere reflection. Consider how the moon, which generates no light, reflects the brilliance of the sun. In a similar way, all of God's creation declares his glory, including his eternal power and divine nature (Ps. 19:1; Rom. 1:20).

But followers of Jesus have something more: the *Shekinah* glory residing in our human spirits; thus, we radiate God's eternal light from within. This should lead us to shine in such a way that others see our good works and give glory to our Father in heaven (Matt. 5:16).

As we exalt God in our lives, he begins the glorification process in us. Peter writes:

His divine power has given us everything required for life and godliness through the knowledge of him who called us by his own glory and goodness. By these he has given us very great and precious promises, so that through them *you may share in the divine nature*, escaping the corruption that is in the world because of evil desire (2 Pet. 1:3-4, emphasis added).

Peter doesn't mean believers become little gods or acquire the unique qualities of deity such as eternality, omnipotence, omniscience, and omnipresence. Rather, he seems to be saying we participate in God's moral excellence and one day are morally perfected.

The ESV Study Bible notes:

"Divine nature" uses terms familiar to Peter's Hellenistic readership to help them understand the idea of transformation into the image of Christ. Peter emphasizes the moral focus of the believer's transformed life. At conversion, Christians are delivered from the **corruption** of this world, which is rooted in **sinful desire**.[6]

The Lord's divine nature in us produces an added benefit: the assurance that the sanctifying work of the Holy Spirit continues until glorification comes in its fullness at the return of Christ. As John writes, "Dear friends, we are God's children now, and what we will be has not yet been revealed. We know that when he appears, we will be like him because we will see him as he is" (1 John 3:2).

GLORY IN DEATH

There's a sense in which the physical death of the saints is a glorious event. As the psalmist pens, "The death of his faithful ones is valuable in the Lord's sight" (Ps. 116:15). Paul agonizes over the inevitability of his death, not because he fears it, but because being present with the Lord would leave fellow believers without his tutelage.

"For me, to live is Christ and to die is gain," he writes to the Philippians. "Now if I live on in the flesh, this means fruitful work for me; and I don't know which one I should choose. I am torn between the two. I long to depart and be with Christ – which is far better – but to remain in the flesh is more necessary for your sake" (Phil. 1:21-24).

In a similar passage, Paul writes:

So we are always confident and know that while we are at home in the body we are away from the Lord. For we walk by faith, not by sight. In fact, we are confident, and we would prefer to be away from the body and at home with the Lord. Therefore, whether we are at home or away, we make it our aim to be pleasing to him (2 Cor. 5:6-9).

To pass through the portal of death, followers of Jesus leave their earthly bodies behind (but not abandoned, as we see shortly). Our souls and spirits pass into the presence of God in heaven, where a place is prepared for us (John 14:1-3). There, we glorify God in ways previously unknown, since he endows us with moral and spiritual perfection. We worship around the throne in heaven. And we experience the liberation of sin from our thoughts, words, and deeds.

This is what's known as the *intermediate state*, which falls between our physical death and future resurrection. The New Testament teaches that upon death, believers' souls and spirits separate from our lifeless bodies and enter into the presence of God in heaven. There we enjoy intimate fellowship with our Lord while awaiting the future resurrection and glorification of our bodies (John 5:28-29; 1 Cor. 15:51-58; 1 Thess. 4:13-18).

We see magnificent glimpses into the throne room of heaven through the visionary eyes of John in the Book of Revelation: the triune Godhead; an emerald-colored rainbow surrounding a glorious throne; living creatures; elders; angels; and redeemed people from every tribe, language, people group, and nation. The combined voices of all creatures in heaven, on earth, under the earth, and in the sea proclaim, "Blessing and honor and glory and power be to the one seated on the throne, and to the Lamb, forever and ever!" (Rev. 5:13).

We may be tempted to stop here, as if heaven is the final destination in life's long journey. It *is* breathtaking. But it gets even better. Heaven, a place so awe-inspiring that Paul is not allowed to speak the inexpressible words he hears while visiting there (2 Cor. 12:4), nevertheless is a temporary home for those who rest in the Lord until he returns to earth and brings us with him.

Meanwhile, it may be helpful to lay out several biblical truths about the intermediate state of glory in heaven for followers of Jesus:

- The Father, Son, and Holy Spirit reside in heaven, yet they have immediate access to earth (Matt. 3:16-17; Mark 16:19; Acts 9:3-6).
- God's will is done completely in heaven – and one day will be done on earth (Matt. 6:9-11).
- Angels surround the throne in heaven (Matt. 18:10), as do majestic heavenly creatures and redeemed people (Rev. 4-5).
- The heavenly throne is the heart of God's authority and majesty (Mark 16:19).
- Heaven is the place from which Satan fell and in which he has no future part (Luke 10:18; Rev. 20:10).

- Heaven is where believers' names are written down,
  providing assurance of everlasting life (Luke 10:20;
  Heb. 12:23).
- Christ is preparing a place for believers in heaven and will
  take us there one day (John 14:3), bringing us back to earth
  with him when he returns (Rev. 19:11-16).
- Our citizenship is in heaven (Phil. 3:20).
- Our inheritance is in heaven – imperishable, undefiled, and
  unfading (1 Pet. 1:4).
- Jesus came from heaven (John 3:31; 6:38, 42), ascended
  there after his finished work on the cross (Luke 24:51;
  Eph. 4:10; Heb. 4:14), and will descend from heaven one day
  to resurrect and glorify believers (1 Cor. 15:51-58; 1 Thess.
  4:16-17).
- God brings heaven and earth together one day and dwells
  with us (Rev. 21:3-4).
- Nothing profane enters heaven – or the new heavens and
  new earth (Rev. 21:27 - 22:5).

Upon physical death, we experience moral and spiritual perfection in heaven while we await the resurrection and glorification of our bodies. Paul writes, "But now he has reconciled you by his physical body through his death, to present you holy, faultless, and blameless before him …." (Col. 1:22). We are declared righteous when we place our faith in Christ, and we are made righteous in soul and spirit when we meet him in death.

Paul further notes, as he urges us to be faithful in this life:

"He will also strengthen you to the end, so that you will be blameless in the day of our Lord Jesus Christ" (1 Cor. 1:8).

"For he chose us in him, before the foundation of the world, to be holy and blameless in love before him" (Eph. 1:4).

"And I pray this: that your love will keep on growing in knowledge and every kind of discernment, so that you may approve the things that are superior and may be pure and blameless in the day of Christ, filled with the fruit of righteousness that comes through Jesus Christ to the glory and praise of God" (Phil. 1:9-11).

Jude adds, "Now to him who is able to protect you from stumbling and to make you stand in the presence of his glory, without blemish and with great joy ...." (Jude 24).

Accompanying our moral and spiritual purity in heaven is a fullness of knowledge. Not that we become omniscient, for that is an exclusive attribute of God. However, our present, incomplete understanding is transformed into a deeper comprehension of all things. Paul encourages the Corinthians with these words: "For now we see only a reflection as in a mirror, but then face to face. Now I know in part, but then I will know fully, as I am fully known" (1 Cor. 13:12).

GLORY IN RESURRECTION

The glory we experience now as Christ lives in and through us, and the glory we experience in death as our souls and spirits ascend into heaven, are partial works of glorification. But full glorification for followers of Jesus takes place when he calls our bodies from the grave and gives us incorruptible bodies like the body he bore when he rose from the dead. Physical resurrection is the apogee of personal glorification, for in it we shrug off the last vestiges of sin, which have clung to our mortal bodies. In glorification, the effects of the Fall are fully and finally reversed.

At the return of Christ, all who have died in the Lord are resurrected.[7] Their souls and spirits, which are in heaven with Jesus, are reunited with their bodies, resulting in complete personal glorification; the body, soul, and spirit are fully conformed to the image of Christ and thus free of any effects of the Fall. Christians alive on the earth at the return of Christ are instantly transformed as they are given glorified bodies; their souls and spirits are perfected at the same time.

Three New Testament passages describe the transformation to which all Christians may look forward.

Philippians 3:20-21

Paul writes, "Our citizenship is in heaven, and we eagerly wait for a Savior from there, the Lord Jesus Christ. He will transform the body of our humble condition into the likeness of his glorious body, by the power that enables him to subject everything to himself." The Greek word *summorphon* ("likeness") indicates that our bodies become similar in form to that of the resurrected Christ.

The CSB Study Bible notes, "Physical bodies will become glorified bodies in the image of Christ. Salvation has three stages: conversion, moral perfection at death, and the transformation of the body through resurrection at the second coming of Christ."[8]

2 Corinthians 5:1-5

To the church in Corinth, Paul pens these words:

For we know that if our earthly tent we live in is destroyed, we have a building from God, an eternal dwelling in the heavens, not made with hands. Indeed, we groan in this tent, desiring to put on our heavenly dwelling, since, when we are clothed, we will not be found naked. Indeed, we groan while we are in this tent, burdened as we are, because we do not want to be unclothed but clothed, so that mortality may be swallowed up by life. Now the one who prepared us for this very purpose is God, who gave us the Spirit as a down payment (2 Cor. 5:1-5).

Paul compares our mortal body to an earthly tent, and our resurrection bodies to a heavenly palace. Further, he likens glorification to putting on new clothes that never wear out. The word "naked" is a reference to the human soul and spirit apart from bodily existence. While we are very much alive, conscious, and blessed in heaven, Paul emphasizes that it's far better to be resurrected and glorified, since that is the completion of our salvation and the total reversal of sin in our lives.

While we "groan in this tent," God gives us the Holy Spirit as his guarantee of future glorification. The apostle's tent analogy is fitting, since Paul made tents while living in Corinth (Acts 18:3), and the Corinthians likely sold tents to sailors or used them for housing visitors attending the Isthmian Games.[9]

1 Corinthians 15:35-49

While Paul devotes the entire fifteenth chapter to resurrection, he draws a comparison between our present bodies and our resurrection bodies in verses 35-49:

But someone will ask, "How are the dead raised? What kind of body will they have when they come?" You fool! What you sow does not come to life unless it dies. And as for what you sow — you are not sowing the body that will be, but only a seed, perhaps of wheat or another grain. But God gives it a body as he wants, and to each of the seeds its own body. Not all flesh is the same flesh; there is one flesh for humans, another for animals, another for birds, and another for fish. There are heavenly bodies and earthly bodies, but the splendor of the heavenly bodies is different from that of the earthly ones. There is a splendor of the sun, another of the moon, and another of the stars; in fact, one star differs from another star in splendor. So it is with the resurrection of the dead: Sown in corruption, raised in incorruption; sown in dishonor, raised in glory; sown in weakness, raised in power; sown a natural body, raised a spiritual body. If there is a natural body, there is also a spiritual body. So it is written, **The first man Adam became a living being**; the last Adam became a life-giving spirit. However, the spiritual is not first, but the natural, then the spiritual.

The first man was from the earth, a man of dust; the second man is from heaven. Like the man of dust, so are those who are of the dust; like the man of heaven, so are those who are of heaven. And just as we have borne the image of the man of dust, we will also bear the image of the man of heaven (1 Cor. 15:35-49).

Let's look a little closer at this passage.

Paul begins with two questions: "How are the dead raised?" and "What kind of body will they have when they come?" (1 Cor. 15:35). Evidently, many Corinthian believers fail to understand how their material bodies – with their tendency toward death and decay – can possibly live forever.

The apostle's first question deals with the seeming impossibility that mortal men and women have any hope of escaping the finality of death. The Sadducees, a leading sect of first-century Judaism, deny the resurrection. Many Greek philosophers understand a human being to have a divine soul of pure fire that, in this life, is imprisoned in a body; at death, the soul escapes from that prison, returns to the divine fire from which it came, and becomes one of the stars.

Thus, the idea of physical resurrection is abhorrent to the Greek mind. For them, the goal is to endure until death, at which time they discard the body with a sigh of "good riddance."[10]

These Jewish and pagan influences evidently lead many Christians in Corinth to doubt the possibility of a glorious future beyond the inevitability of an earthly demise.

The second question addresses the uncertainty of how a corruptible physical body can ever be restored. Paul assures the Corinthians that resurrection is not reconstruction. While there is both continuity and identity in resurrection – yes, it's us, and we have physical bodies – our future bodies are significant improvements over the present ones.

"You fool!" Paul writes. "What you sow does not come to life unless it dies. And as for what you sow – you are not sowing the body that will be, but only a seed, perhaps of wheat or another grain. But God gives it a body as he wants, and to each of the seeds its own body" (1 Cor. 15:36-38).

This is the first of three analogies from nature Paul employs to explain how God takes the bodies of the deceased and prepares them for everlasting glory. A seed of wheat is distinct from the roots, stalk, and fruit, yet there is continuity between them all, and the final product comes from the seed. A fully mature stalk of wheat comes from a wheat seed; the seed of a dandelion or an apple has never been shown to produce wheat.

In a similar manner, our earthly bodies, like the seed, go into the ground at death. But in the resurrection, God raises them up into fully mature, completely healthy, everlasting bodies that retain our individual identities.

Kenneth Bailey writes:

The seed is a "body" that first must die. That body dies naked (bare) and *God gives it a new body* different from the one that dies, and yet it is the same in that each seed has "its own body." There is both continuity and discontinuity in this parable. God brings about resurrection *and* transformation.[11]

Perhaps unknowingly, Paul echoes Jesus' prediction of his crucifixion – a prediction John records much later: "Truly I tell you, unless a grain of wheat falls to the ground and dies, it remains by itself. But if it dies, it produces much fruit" (John 12:24). Christ's death on the cross secures salvation for us. And in his resurrection, he is "the first-fruits of those who have fallen asleep" (1 Cor. 15:20). That is, he is the first to rise from the dead in a glorified body, paving the way for our future resurrection and glorification. Followers of Jesus do not need to worry about our skin and bones turning to dust in the tomb because God brings us back to life one day.

Next, Paul writes, "Not all flesh is the same flesh; there is one flesh for humans, another for animals, another for birds, and another for fish" (1 Cor. 15:39). Paul uses the word "flesh" (Greek *sarks*) several times in this verse to make a point. Human beings share with animals the reality of physical death and corruption, even though our body types are suited for different earthly environments.

In his third example from nature, Paul notes, "There are heavenly bodies and earthly bodies, but the splendor of the heavenly bodies is different from that of the earthly ones. There is a splendor of the sun, another of the moon, and another of the stars; in fact, one star differs from another star in splendor" (1 Cor. 15:40-41). The word "splendor" in Greek is *doxa*, which means "glory." The splendor of the heavenly bodies has to do with brightness, while the word *doxa*, when applied to people, often carries the idea of honor, reputation, or esteem.

In any case, the sun "dies" in the evening, only to rise the next morning. The stars, moon, and planets "die" at sunrise, but they return at sunset to illuminate the night sky. In a similar way, believers in all levels of honor and reputation die physically, but God most certainly raises them from the dead in glory, just as reliably as he causes the sun, moon, and stars to fulfill their created purposes each day.

With that as a backdrop, Paul differentiates between the mortal body and the immortal one. "So it is with the resurrection of the dead," he writes (1 Cor. 15:42). Our bodies therefore are:

Sown in corruption, raised in incorruption (v. 42). Physical death is the result of living in a perishable body. We simply wear out. Even death by natural causes means the fittest body can't live forever. And we should note that those raised from the dead in Scripture – from the son of the widow at Zarephath to Lazarus – died a second time because they did not receive glorified bodies.

However, God fashions our future resurrection bodies so they are immune to sickness, disease, aging, and decay. Put another way, our glorified bodies are guaranteed to last as long as Jesus' resurrected body endures – forever.

Sown in dishonor, raised in glory (v. 43). Paul may be thinking ahead to verses 47-49 in depicting our earthly bodies as dishonorable. The first man, Adam, left us a legacy of dishonor. He willfully disobeyed God, made excuses for his sin, and even implicated God in the process. As a result, Adam passed on to us a sin nature – a natural tendency to live independently of God, which manifests itself in sin and shame in every human life.

Our earthly rap sheets are exceedingly long and disgraceful. Standing in sharp contrast, however, are believers' resurrection bodies, which are raised in glory. They no longer bear the stamp of sin, and thus they radiate the Christlike qualities of holiness, integrity, reliability, and wisdom.

Sown in weakness, raised in power (v. 43). The Greek word rendered "weakness" is *astheneia* and means "frailty," "sickness," or "disease." Our present earthly bodies cannot overpower the effects of living in a sinful and fallen world. Ultimately, the curse of sin is victorious over the healthiest human specimens, and we all succumb to death in a thousand awful ways.

But our resurrection bodies are raised in power. The Greek *dynamis* means "might," "strength," or "ability." Often in the New Testament, it is connected with miraculous power, particularly with respect to the power of God and the miracles of Jesus. Our glorified bodies are powered by God, who destroys every trace of sin plaguing our earthly bodies.

Sown a natural body, raised a spiritual body. (v. 44). Paul distinguishes between the bodies we now possess and the bodies we put on in glorification. Today, we have a *soma psychikos*, or a "natural body." This means more than just flesh and blood, however. It refers to a living human being who belongs to the natural world. But in resurrection, we receive a *soma pneumatikos*, or a "spiritual body." This means the Holy Spirit preserves and directs our glorified bodies.

Commenting on this verse, Kenneth Bailey writes:

In the resurrection the believer will have a Spirit-constituted physical body. The brokenness and decay of the old body will be gone. The new body will be a physical body like the resurrected body of Christ. Such a truly glorious vision and promise calls for an exuberant hymn of victory.[12]

In verses 47-49, Paul summarizes by contrasting the "first man" (Adam) and the "second man" (Jesus). While God forms Adam from the ground, and he becomes a "man of dust," Jesus is from heaven –

eternal and otherworldly. In our present bodies, we resemble Adam in that we "have borne the image of the man of dust." However, in the resurrection, "we will also bear the image of the man of heaven."

Our glorification in resurrection is not a lengthy process. Rather, Paul reveals to us a mystery: "We will not all fall asleep, but we will all be changed, in a moment, in the twinkling of an eye, at the last trumpet" (1 Cor. 15:51b-52a). Whether we are raised from the dead or instantly transformed as living Christians on earth into glorified believers, the promise of Christ's return should cause us to rejoice, as Paul does: "But thanks be to God, who gives us the victory through our Lord Jesus Christ!" (v. 57).

GLORY IN RESTORATION

The glorified body of Jesus easily navigates a world still under the curse of sin. After his emergence from the tomb, Jesus eats, travels, speaks with befuddled eyewitnesses of his resurrection, passes through closed doors, transports himself instantly from one location to another, and finally launches from the Mount of Olives into heaven.

Our resurrected bodies will have many of these same capabilities. Yet, the redemptive work of God isn't finished at our resurrection. The world in which we now live was not always cursed, nor will it always be cursed. A day is coming when our sovereign Lord makes all things new (Rev. 21:5).

That's the subject of Chapter 13, in which we explore Christ's creation of new heavens and a new earth. There, the Lord fashions an environment custom-made for our glorified bodies. But first, let's survey several passages of Scripture that address glorification.

KEY PASSAGES ON GLORIFICATION

Romans 8:11

And if the Spirit of him who raised Jesus from the dead lives in you, then he who raised Christ from the dead will also bring your mortal bodies to life through his Spirit who lives in you.

The Holy Spirit's presence in our lives serves as God's mark of ownership on us, along with his guarantee to finish the good work he began in us (Phil. 1:6). The climax of this work is glorification – the transformation of our corruptible bodies into incorruptible bodies like Christ's resurrected body. This occurs when Jesus retrieves our corpses from the graves at his return.

Or, if we're alive on earth at his coming, he converts our mortal bodies into glorified ones. The Christian's body still dies today because of sin's destructive power, but the indwelling Spirit assures us that, just as he imparts new spiritual life to us now, he delivers new physical life one day.

The Greek verb *egeiro* (to raise) is used several times in the Gospels to depict getting up after awakening from sleep (Matt. 1:24; 8:25; 25:7). More importantly, it describes people who are known to be dead, such as Jairus' daughter (Mark 5:22-24, 35-43) and Lazarus (John 12:1, 9, 17), being raised to life.

But the core usage of *egeiro* has to do with Jesus being raised from the dead. Except for Philippians 1:17 ("will cause me"), the New Testament epistles only use this verb to depict the resurrection of Jesus.[13] In fact, Paul employs the term more than thirty times in Romans and 1 Corinthians to make it clear that Jesus is the firstfruits of the resurrection and thus is qualified to raise us from the dead when he returns in glory.

Romans 8:16-17, 23

The Spirit himself testifies together with our spirit that we are God's children, and if children, also heirs – heirs of God and coheirs with Christ – if indeed we suffer with him so that we may also be glorified with him.... Not only that, but we ourselves who have the Spirit as the firstfruits – we also groan within ourselves, eagerly waiting for adoption, the redemption of our bodies.

The indwelling Holy Spirit confirms our relationship with the Father. We may rest assured that we are his adopted sons and daughters, elevated to the status of coheirs with the eternal Son of God. We are joined to Jesus now in suffering, but just as certainly we are united with him in a glorious future.

As Jesus is in glory now, so we will be, as Paul captures in another passage: "And most certainly, the mystery of godliness is great: He was manifested in the flesh, vindicated in the Spirit, seen by angels, preached among the nations, believed on in the world, taken up in glory" (1 Tim. 3:16). One day, we also are taken up in glory.

Until the day Christ comes for us, he gives us the Holy Spirit as the "firstfruits," or the down payment of our inheritance. While in our earthly tents, we may groan with hardship, aging, sickness, and encroaching death, but these only serve as reminders of the glories to come. Just as a farmer's firstfruits are the initial harvest of his ripened crops, the Holy Spirit offers believers a foretaste of the abundant blessings to come, including living in God's presence forever.

Paul uses "adoption" in a unique way in this passage. In other places, he makes it clear that believers already are adopted as sons and daughters of God. At the same time, we anticipate the completion of our adoption when the full effects of redemption are realized in glorification. Paul refers to this as the revelation of God's sons (Rom. 8:19) and the glorious freedom of God's children (Rom. 8:21).

Warren Wiersbe writes:

We are waiting for "the adoption," which is the redemption of the body when Christ returns (Phil. 3:20-21). This is the thrilling climax to "the adoption" that took place at conversion when "the Spirit of adoption" gave us an adult standing in God's family. When Christ returns, we shall enter into our full inheritance.[14]

Romans 8:29-30

For those he foreknew he also predestined to be conformed to the image of his Son, so that he would be the firstborn among many brothers and sisters. And those he predestined, he also called; and those he called, he also justified; and those he justified, he also glorified.

Paul ties together God's work of redemption, which spans time and eternity. Those whom God has always foreknown and predestined, he draws to himself and declares righteous in time, and ultimately glorifies in future resurrection — the final act of salvation that extends unbroken into eternity future.

The word "glorified," as applied here, means to admit to a state of bliss, or to beautify.[15] Surely, when Christ calls our corpses out of the graves and transforms them into glorious bodies, we experience not only the newness of life in perfection, but the incomprehensible joy that accompanies it. And we experience first-hand what John hears declared from the throne room of heaven: "He will wipe away every tear from their eyes. Death will be no more; grief, crying, and pain will be no more, because the previous things have passed away" (Rev. 21:4).

But perhaps the most noteworthy feature of this golden chain of redemption in Romans 8:29-30 – foreknowledge, predestination, calling, justification, glorification – is that Paul depicts the redeemed as "glorified." Note the past tense. No follower of Jesus has yet experienced resurrection and glorification. We, along with our departed brothers and sisters in heaven, await the return of Jesus to make this a reality. And yet, Paul is so certain of our future glorification that he links it to the already accomplished work of foreknowledge, predestination, calling, and justification.

John Witmer notes:

> … not a single person is lost. God completes His plan without slippage. "Glorified" is in the past tense because this final step is so certain that in God's eyes it is as good as done. To be glorified is another way of saying that God's children will be "conformed" to His Son; and that is God's ultimate "purpose." No longer will they "fall short of the glory of God" (Rom. 3:23).[16]

1 Corinthians 15:51-54

> Listen, I am telling you a mystery: We will not all fall asleep, but we will all be changed, in a moment, in the twinkling of an eye, at the last trumpet. For the trumpet will sound, and the dead will be raised incorruptible, and we will be changed. For this corruptible body must be clothed with incorruptibility, and this mortal body must be clothed with immortality. When this corruptible body is clothed with incorruptibility, and this mortal body is clothed with immortality, then the saying that is written will take place: **Death has been swallowed up in victory.**

Paul discloses a "mystery," a truth that would remain secret apart from divine revelation. Not every believer is to experience physical death, but all Christians may eagerly anticipate the miraculous transformation of our corruptible bodies into incorruptible ones. This occurs at "the last trumpet," or Christ's return for us (see also 1 Thess. 4:13-17).

The change is more than dramatic; it's instantaneous. Paul says it takes place "in a moment," using the Greek word *atomas*, which signifies the smallest possible division of something, in this case, time. The phrase "in the twinkling of an eye" further describes the quickness with which our mortal bodies are made like the glorified body of Jesus.

The Greek word *rhipe* (twinkling) is used only here in the New Testament. It is employed in classical Greek to depict the rush of a storm, the flapping of wings, the buzz of a gnat, and the twinkling of stars. Generally, it describes very rapid movement.[17]

Paul uses the metaphor of putting on clothing to describe the manner in which our bodies are transformed. Our corruptible bodies must be clothed with incorruptibility, and our mortal bodies must be clothed with immortality. This is an apt depiction of glorification because humans naturally possess neither incorruptibility nor immortality. These must come from God, "who alone is immortal and who lives in unapproachable light" (1 Tim. 6:16).

Just as believing sinners are clothed in the righteousness of Christ now, we look forward to the day when he drapes us in his incorruptibility and immortality. When this occurs, then Isaiah's prophecy is fulfilled: "Death has been swallowed up in victory" (1 Cor. 15:45; cf. Isa. 25:8).

The seeming victories of Satan in the Garden of Eden, and on many subsequent occasions, are reversed on the cross and eradicated by the empty tomb. From the vantage point of glorification, Paul could echo a victorious taunt: **"Where, death, is your victory? Where, death, is your sting?** The sting of death is sin, and the power of sin is the law. But thanks be to God, who gives us the victory through our Lord Jesus Christ!" (1 Cor. 15:55-56; cf. Hos. 13:14).

Philippians 3:21

He will transform the body of our humble condition into the likeness of his glorious body, by the power that enables him to subject everything to himself.

Paul encourages his readers to imitate him, and to follow the example of mature believers around them, for enemies of the cross abound. With tears, Paul reminds the Philippian Christians that false teachers are destined for everlasting separation from God. They are preoccupied with Jewish dietary laws, thus making a god of their bellies. They focus inappropriately on the genitals as they glorify circumcision. And they are slavishly devoted to earthly things (Phil. 3:17-19).

But just as the Philippians are proud of their Roman citizenship, Paul urges them to embrace the greater citizenship of heaven. From there, a Savior far superior to Caesar is returning one day (3:20). When he comes, a miraculous transformation takes place. By the same power he exhibits in resurrection (3:10) and applies in kingly rule, Jesus transforms our earthly bodies into heavenly bodies modeled after his.

The "body of our humble condition" (3:21) refers to the frailty of our mortal existence. Every day, followers of Jesus experience the consequences of living in a fallen world. We stumble, break bones, get sick, age, and grow inevitably weaker by the day. But when Christ returns on the clouds of heaven, in the glory of his Father and in the presence of his holy angels, he renews our frail bodies, making them victorious over the effects of the Fall.

Paul uses the Greek word *metaschematisei* (transform) to describe the work of Jesus in our resurrected bodies. It means to change the outward form of something; to remodel or transfigure.[18] It's similar to *metamorphoo*, which describes Jesus' transfiguration (Matt. 17:2; Mark 9:2), as well as the spiritual transformation that believers experience on this side of heaven (Rom. 12:2; 2 Cor. 3:18).

Our future glorification is not a change in identification, but in form. As Christ's glorified body is physical and identifiable, so is ours. Yet, his resurrected body exhibits astonishing characteristics that serve as the template for our glorified selves.

1 John 3:2

Dear friends, we are God's children now, and what we will be has not yet been revealed. We know that when he appears, we will be like him because we will see him as he is.

The world may not think much of Christians. That's because unbelievers don't know God, nor can they fathom the love the Father has lavished on those who trust in him, calling them his children (1 John 3:1). As adopted sons and daughters of God, we should look beyond the hardships that naturally come with bearing the name of Christ and catch a glimpse of our glorious inheritance.

Living in the light of eternity should prompt us to consider four truths John shares with us. First, God finishes what he starts, even though he hasn't revealed all the details of our glorification. Second, Jesus is returning for us; John doesn't say "if," but "when he appears." Third, we become like Jesus in our resurrected bodies – transformed, clothed in his immortality, free of the weight of sin's curse. Fourth, we are going to see him as he is. Just as Peter, James, and John catch a glimpse of Christ's radiance on the Mount of Transfiguration (Matt. 17:1-7; Mark 9:2-8), we have all eternity to bask in his unveiled glory.

John writes, "what we will be has not yet been revealed." The word "revealed" comes from the Greek verb *phaneroo*. It denotes the act of making visible or disclosing something not readily seen. In several places, it refers to the appearing of Jesus – in the Incarnation (1 Tim. 3:16; 1 John 1:2; 3:8), after his resurrection (Mark 16:12, 14; John 21:1), and at his second coming (Col. 3:4, 1 John 2:28; 3:2).[19]

In fact, John uses the word again later in verse 2: "We know that when he *appears* ...." In other words, we may take comfort in knowing that when Jesus returns, we both understand his resurrection power and experience it ourselves.

But the apostle doesn't stop here. He's told us what we *are* and what we *will be*. Before moving on, he tells us what we *should be*: "And everyone who has this hope in him purifies himself just as he is pure" (1 John 3:3).

SUMMARY

The writer of Hebrews exhorts Christians to "run with endurance the race that lies before us, keeping our eyes on Jesus, the source and perfecter of our faith" (Heb. 12:1-2). Just as Jesus "endured the cross, despising the shame, and sat down at the right hand of the throne of God" (v. 2), we should live our often-grueling earthly race with a heavenly perspective.

The world was not always fallen, nor will it always be so. Despite the constant struggle against Satan's temptations, the world's charms, and the shadow of encroaching death, followers of Jesus should live in joyful anticipation of a victorious and never-ending future when we see Jesus as he is and are made like him.

The finish line of faith hovers just beyond our reach, spurring us to continue our pursuit. Meanwhile, the God who has known us throughout eternity promises to carry us across the goal, finishing the good work he began in us (Phil. 1:6).

Future glorification is as certain as the other elements of salvation. It is the completion of God's gracious work of breathing new life into our dead spirits, redeeming us from the slave market of sin, declaring us in right standing before him, and adopting us as his children. Just as God's creation of all things was "very good indeed" (Gen. 1:31), his redemption of fallen humans and his restoration of the sin-stained universe to innocence one day stand forevermore as a testimony to his goodness, faithfulness, and love.

For now, Christians are not promised an earthly walk in the park, but an arduous race through enemy territory. If we're living faithfully, we may expect hardship, shunning, persecution, and pain – not health, riches, fame, and ease. Christ is not the means to an end; he is the end himself, accessed through a narrow gate (Matt. 7:13) and pursued down a path of good works he laid out for us ahead of time (Eph. 2:10). He walks with us, however, urging our faithfulness while we "go through many hardships to enter the kingdom of God" (Acts 14:22).

In the end, we may rejoice with Paul that "the sufferings of this present time are not worth comparing with the glory that is going to be revealed in us" (Rom. 8:18).

REVIEW

Key takeaways from this chapter

Consider these summary statements on glorification:

1. Glorification is the final act of God's redemptive work, in which he raises our lifeless bodies from the grave and restores us to a state that's better than the original. That's because we have incorruptible bodies that never again suffer the ravages of sin or experience death.

2. There is glory now. As we honor the Father, Son, and Holy Spirit for their divine attributes and redemptive work, we replicate God's glory in our thoughts, words, and deeds. Thus, God enables us to share in the divine nature (2 Pet. 1:3-4). This doesn't mean we become little gods. Rather, we participate in God's moral excellence, knowing that one day we are morally perfected.

3. There is glory in death. When we breathe our last, followers of Jesus leave our earthly bodies behind. Our souls and spirits pass into the presence of God in heaven, where we glorify God in ways previously unknown as he endows us with moral and spiritual perfection.

4. There is glory in resurrection. Full glorification for followers of Jesus takes place when he calls our bodies from the grave and gives us incorruptible bodies like the body he bore when he rose from the dead. Resurrection is the apogee of personal glorification, for in it we shrug off the last vestiges of sin, which have clung to our mortal bodies. In glorification, the effects of the Fall are fully and finally reversed.

5. There is glory in restoration. Jesus refers to this as "the renewal of all things, when the Son of Man sits on his glorious throne" (Matt. 19:28). Peter urges us to wait for "new heavens and a new earth, where righteousness dwells" (2 Peter 3:13). And in John's vision of the world to come, he sees "a new heaven and a new earth" (Rev. 21:1). All of these passages refer to the future glorification of the created order, a world purged of sin and its stain, where the pristine innocence of all creation is restored.

DISCUSS

Questions for personal or group study

1. In what ways is glorification the final act of God's redemptive work?

2. Briefly describe how glorification works in the following stages:

- In our Christian duty now to honor the Father, Son, and Holy Spirit
- In death
- In resurrection
- In the new heavens and new earth, or what Jesus calls "the renewal of all things"

3. Read 1 Corinthians 15:35-52 and consider:

- How does Paul use a seed as an analogy for our mortal bodies and for what becomes of them in resurrection (vv. 36-38)?
- What hope do we have in death that animals do not possess (v. 39)?
- How does the rising of the sun, moon, and stars give us hope of God's faithfulness to redeem our mortal bodies (vv. 40-41)?
- How does Paul contrast our earthly bodies with our heavenly ones (vv. 42-44)?
- How quickly are we transformed when Christ calls us from the grave (vv. 51-52)?

4. What do you think Paul means when he says we are "raised a spiritual body" (1 Cor. 15:44)?

5. Read Hebrews 12:1-2. How should we live today in light of our future glorification?

* * *

"THROWN INTO THE LAKE OF FIRE"

JESUS IS RETURNING TO SENTENCE UNBELIEVERS

*I*n Dante Alighieri's *The Divine Comedy*, a man, assumed to be Dante himself, is taken on a guided journey through hell, purgatory, and paradise. The Roman poet Virgil leads the man through hell and purgatory, while Beatrice, the woman to whom Dante dedicates most of his poetry, introduces him to paradise.

The author describes hell as consisting of nine concentric circles, which mark a descending scale of human sins: limbo, lust, gluttony, greed, wrath, heresy, violence, fraud, and treachery. Above the entrance to hell are inscribed these words: "Abandon all hope, ye who enter here."

Dante's allegorical masterpiece is breathtaking in places, even if it fails the test of biblical fidelity. Those haunting words – "Abandon all hope" – ring true as they remind the damned that once in hell, there's no escape from the fiery torments they have brought upon themselves.

We can think of Christ's sentencing of unbelievers to hell as the first stage in cosmic renewal. Surely, Jesus' finished work of redemption brings new life to those once dead in trespasses and sins (Eph. 2:1). But Jesus also promises to restore creation to sinless perfection in what he calls "the renewal of all things" (Matt. 19:28). In this, he purges the cosmos of sin and its stain and restores Eden, where citizens of his kingdom have free access to his throne (see 2 Pet. 3:10-13; Rev. 21-22).

But in order to banish sin from the new heavens and earth, Christ must judge wicked humans and angels, and remove both them and the negative influences they left in their wake. For evil human beings, the day of reckoning comes when they stand before the great white throne, which we addressed in Chapter 9.

In this chapter, we turn our attention to what happens after Revelation 20:15, where John records, "And anyone whose name was not found written in the book of life was thrown into the lake of fire." But first, we should examine one Hebrew word and two Greek words that give us a clearer picture of life beyond the grave.

SHEOL AND THE AFTERLIFE

While the doctrines pertaining to life beyond the grave are not fully developed in the Old Testament, there's ample evidence that the souls of people survive death. A key term used to describe the intermediate state of the deceased is the Hebrew word *sheol*.

Old Testament writers use *sheol* sixty-five times, usually to describe the abode of the dead. It should be noted, however, that *sheol* is an enigmatic term that simply can mean "death" (1 Sam. 2:6; Job 7:9; Ps. 88:3; Isa. 38:10). In either case, *sheol* communicates the reality of human mortality and, to a lesser degree, the impact of one's life on his or her destiny. That's because there is no clear distinction in the Old Testament between the final destiny of the righteous and the wicked in *sheol*.

Ancient Israelites believed in life beyond the grave, borne out in such passages as Isaiah 14:9-15, where *sheol* contains "the spirits of the departed," and 1 Samuel 28:13, where the deceased prophet Samuel temporarily appears as "a spirit form coming up out of the earth," presumably from *sheol*.

While the Old Testament consistently refers to the body as going to the grave, it always refers to the soul or spirit of a person as going to *sheol*, according to Robert Morey.

One source of confusion is the manner in which the King James Version translates *sheol*, according to Morey: "The KJV translates *Sheol* as 'hell' 31 times, 'grave' 31 times, and 'pit' three times. Because of this inconsistency of translation, such groups as the Adventists ... and Jehovah's Witnesses have taught that *Sheol* means the grave."[1]

Fortunately, Morey adds, lexicons and rabbinic literature consistently understand *sheol* as the place where the souls and spirits of persons go at death.

In fact, the first occurrence of *sheol* in the Old Testament (Gen. 37:35) cannot possibly mean "grave." As Jacob holds the bloodied remnants of Joseph's coat, he laments about his deceased boy, "I will go down to *Sheol* to my son, mourning."

Whatever else *sheol* may mean, in this passage it cannot mean Joseph's grave, for Jacob believes his son has been devoured by wild animals and thus has no grave. Jacob could not be buried in a common grave with Joseph.

According to the context, Jacob anticipates being reunited with Joseph in the underworld. He speaks of going "down" because it is assumed that *sheol* is the place of departed spirits, likely a hollow place in the center of the earth.

There are other factors about *sheol* to consider.

First, when Old Testament writers want to identify the grave, they often use the Hebrew word *kever*, which is contrasted with *sheol*. *Kever* is the fate of the body, while *sheol* is the fate of the soul. In addition, the Hebrew word *bor* appears sixty-five times in the Old Testament. Often translated "pit," it also may mean "well," "dungeon," "cistern," or "grave," terms associated with the physical realm.

Second, in the Septuagint, the Greek translation of the Old Testament, *sheol* is never translated as *mneema*, the Greek word for "grave."

Third, *sheol* is depicted as "under the earth" or "the underworld," while graves in Old Testament times tend to be built as sepulchers above the earth, in caves, or in holes in the earth.

Finally, while bodies are lifeless in the grave, those in *sheol* are viewed as conscious.

God's revelation in Scripture is progressive, meaning that as we move through the Bible, God reveals additional truths that build on the others. With this in mind, we see the concept of *sheol* develop throughout the Old Testament. While it is described as dark (Lam. 3:6), as well as a place of helplessness (Ps. 88:4), trouble, and sorrow (Ps. 116:3), God is both present in *sheol* (Ps. 139:8) and able to deliver from it (Ps. 16:10; 49:15).

This leads some commentators to argue there are two or more compartments in *sheol*, some for the wicked and some for the righteous. Later Jewish literature describes these divisions, in which people experience a foretaste of their final destiny. Enoch, for example, encounters four "hollow places" in which four different classes of the dead are held until final judgment (see 1 Enoch 22, an ancient Jewish work not part of the biblical canon). Jesus' story of Lazarus and the rich man appears to draw from this depiction, applying the Greek word *hades* to the realm of the dead (Luke 16:19-31).

Other Bible interpreters contend that *sheol* is only for the wicked, because God rescues the spirits of the righteous from *sheol* and takes them to a place of blessedness. The biblical accounts of the ascensions of Enoch and Elijah to heaven, for example, are cited to support the belief that the righteous under the Old Covenant could be taken directly into God's presence at the end of their earthly lives (see Gen. 5:24; 2 Kings 2:1-12). It should be noted, however, that neither of these Old Testament figures experiences physical death before their journeys into heaven.

Whether righteous people in the Old Testament went directly to heaven, or rested in a blissful compartment of *sheol*, Jesus indicates that "torment" and "Abraham's side" are in view of each other (Luke 16:23).

After Christ's passion, it becomes clear that the souls and spirits of his followers enter heaven immediately upon death. Paul writes: "So we are always confident and know that while we are at home in the body we are away from the Lord. For we walk by faith, not by sight.

In fact, we are confident, and we would prefer to be away from the body and at home with the Lord" (2 Cor. 5:6-8). Evidently, the souls of unbelievers remain in *sheol*, where they await resurrection and final judgment.

HADES AND THE AFTERLIFE

Hades is a Greek god whose name means "The Unseen." He is depicted as lord of the underworld (the abode of the dead). In ancient times, *hades* often was used to describe the place where *shades*, or disembodied spirits of the deceased, roamed. So, it should come as no surprise that Jesus and the New Testament writers borrow from the familiar term *hades* to describe the realm of departed spirits. What's more, they cut through the mythology to present a more accurate picture of the afterlife.

The word *hades* appears ten times in the New Testament, forming a linguistic bridge from the Old Testament view of life beyond the grave (in *sheol*) to the New Testament position. In coming to a biblically faithful understanding of *hades*, it's important to state what the word does *not* mean.

First, *hades* does not mean death, because the Greek word *thanatos* is used for death in the New Testament. Further, death (*thanatos*) and *hades* appear side-by-side in Revelation 1:18, so we may distinguish them.

Second, *hades* cannot mean the grave, because the Greek noun *mneema* depicts the place where bodies of the deceased are buried. Appearing forty times in the New Testament, *mneema* often is translated "grave" or "tomb" (e.g., Matt. 27:60-61; Acts 13:29).

Third, *hades* cannot mean hell, the place of final punishment for the wicked, because the Greek word *gehenna* is used for hell in the New Testament, along with other terms like "outer darkness," "eternal fire," and "lake of fire." Further, *hades* is cast into the lake of fire in Revelation 20:14.

Fourth, *hades* is not heaven, the intermediate state of Christian souls between death and resurrection, because the Greek word *ouranos* depicts heaven.

While *hades* is used consistently in the Septuagint as the Greek equivalent of the Hebrew term *sheol*, this does not mean *hades* should be limited to the Old Testament understanding of the afterlife. As mentioned previously in our discussion of *sheol*, God reveals additional truths as we move through the Bible. The New Testament picks up where the Old Testament leaves off by further developing our understanding of what happens to the soul and spirit after death.

During the period between the Old and New Testaments, the Jewish concept of *sheol* progressed to the point where it was believed that *sheol* had two distinct compartments: torment, and paradise (Abraham's "bosom" or "side").

This rabbinic understanding of *sheol* is the basis for Jesus' story of Lazarus and the rich man, in which Jesus uses the Greek word *hades* (Luke 16:19-31). The rich man dies and finds himself tormented in *hades*. Angels, on the other hand, carry Lazarus to Abraham's side, presumably the other compartment of *hades*, or heaven itself. The point of the parable is not to give us a road map of the afterlife, but to warn those unprepared for death.

The conversation between Abraham and the rich man, the description of the rich man's consciousness and suffering, and the impassable gulf between the two main characters in this story provide further details about *hades* that build on the Old Testament understanding of life beyond the grave.

Nevertheless, we should acknowledge that *hades* is a somewhat flexible term whose precise meaning depends on context. Consider:

- In Matthew 11:23-24 and Luke 10:15, Jesus uses *hades* to depict the destruction of Capernaum.
- In Matthew 16:18, Jesus assures his followers that the shadowy afterlife (*hades*) cannot overpower his church because he has come to conquer sin and death.

- In Luke 16:19-31, Jesus describes the rich man's torment in *hades*, where a great chasm separates the rich man from Lazarus and Abraham.
- In Acts 2:25-31, Peter quotes from Psalm 16:8-11 to make it clear that Jesus, unlike David, did not remain among the dead in *hades*, but rose from the dead without his flesh suffering corruption.
- In Revelation 1:18, Jesus holds the keys of death and *hades*, meaning he has authority over death and its consequences.
- Finally, in Revelation 20:13-14, death and *hades* are personified as giving up their dead. Then, death and *hades* are thrown into the lake of fire. There is no more physical death, and no more temporary abode for the wicked dead in *hades*.

Citing Ephesians 4:8-9 and 1 Peter 3:18-22, some New Testament commentators believe Jesus escorted the Old Testament saints from *hades* into heaven during the days between his death and resurrection. Other interpreters dispute this, arguing that saints under the Old Covenant entered heaven immediately after death.

In any case, the New Testament describes the souls and spirits of all believers *after* Christ's resurrection as entering heaven directly upon death (Phil. 1:23). There, believers are present with the Lord (2 Cor. 5:6-8), worshiping with the angelic hosts of heaven and other redeemed people at the altar of God (Heb. 12:22-23; Rev. 6:9-11).

Meanwhile, the souls and spirits of deceased unbelievers continue to populate *hades*, awaiting resurrection and final judgment, at which time they stand before the great white throne and are cast into *gehenna*.

GEHENNA AND THE AFTERLIFE

The ultimate destiny of the wicked is the same habitation created for Satan and demons: *gehenna*. It's a place in English we call "hell," and a place Jesus and the New Testament writers describe in various ways, among them: destruction (Matt. 7:13); outer darkness (Matt. 8:12); blazing furnace (Matt. 13:42, 50); eternal fire (Matt. 18:8; 25:41); the unquenchable fire (Mark 9:43); wrath (Rom. 2:5, 8; Rev. 14:10); the blackness of darkness (Jude 13); the second death (Rev. 2:11; 20:14; 21:8); and the lake of fire (Rev. 19:20; 20:10, 14, 15; 21:8).

While *sheol* and *hades* generally depict the temporary abode of the dead, *gehenna* and its associated terms describe the place of everlasting future punishment for those whose names are not written in the book of life (Rev. 20:15).

The term *gehenna* is derived from the Valley of Hinnom. Located southwest of Jerusalem, this steep, rocky valley is the scene of human sacrifices to pagan deities (2 Kings 23:10; 2 Chron. 28:3; 33:6). Jeremiah declares it the "Valley of Slaughter" (Jer. 7:31-34 ESV). To the Jewish mind, the images of fire and destruction become appropriate representations of the ultimate fate of idol worshipers.

Jesus seizes rabbinic language connected with *gehenna*, such as "unquenchable fire" and "never-dying worms," to impress upon his listeners that their choices in this life have everlasting consequences. In fact, of the twelve uses of *gehenna* in the New Testament, eleven come from the lips of the Messiah. The only exception is James 3:6, in which the author cautions against the tongue's dangerous potential. The tongue, he writes, "stains the whole body, sets the course of life on fire, and is itself set on fire by hell."

Traditionally, these passages are understood to speak of final judgment, with Jesus using images from everyday life to warn about a place of everlasting separation from God. It should be noted, however, that hell does not undermine God's omnipresence, since the idea of separation in hell is set in the context of relationship, intimacy, or fellowship.

Scripture teaches that those who worship the beast are tormented forever "in the sight of the holy angels and in the sight of the Lamb" (see Rev. 14:9-11). As Alan Gomes notes, "In hell, God is completely absent in terms of his presence to bless, but is only present to impart suffering and pain to the sinner."[2]

A scriptural summary of *gehenna* reveals the absence of all good and the misery of an unshakeable evil conscience. John MacArthur suggests that Jesus' depiction of hell as a place where the unbeliever's "worm does not die" could be emblematic of an eternally accusing conscience (Mark 9:48; cf. Isa. 66:24).[3]

Or, as Timothy Phillips explains, "The 'undying worm' has often been interpreted as the soul's internal torment, coveting and grieving what has been lost" – a regret that "is compounded, since the reprobate are not penitent but locked into their rebellion."[4]

It gets worse. The most terrifying aspect of hell is complete and final alienation from God and others. As Ralph Powell notes, "This is the worst possible punishment to which anyone could be subject: to be totally and irrevocably cut off from God and to be at enmity with all those who are around oneself." Another painful consequence is to be at odds with oneself – "torn apart from within by an accusing sense of guilt and shame."[5]

Some commentators see Jesus speaking of *gehenna* in more limited terms. Steve Gregg, for example, argues that Jesus may have used *gehenna* literally to warn first-century Jews that they are about to suffer fiery judgment for their rejection of the Messiah at the hands of the Romans – a judgment that falls hard on Jerusalem and its inhabitants in A.D. 70.[6]

This is not to deny the existence of hell as a place of everlasting separation from God, since other texts speak of resurrection, final judgment, and fiery punishment for the wicked. But it is to encourage us to carefully consider Scripture's context so we do not glean more from a text than is warranted.

In the end, the divine wrath of hell is the necessary response of an eternally holy God to the rejection of his gracious provision for sin. As Powell notes, "When the only remedy for human sin is rejected and all appeals of a loving, seeking God for the reconciliation of rebellious sinners are refused, there is no other course of action which God himself can pursue but to leave the sinner to his self-chosen destiny."[7]

IS HELLFIRE LITERAL?

We might ask: When Jesus and the New Testament writers depict hell, are we to take the lake of fire literally or figuratively? Godly scholars stand on both sides of the debate. Charles Spurgeon, for example, spoke of hell's fire as real:

> Now, do not begin telling me that that is metaphorical fire: who cares for that? If a man were to threaten to give me a metaphorical blow on the head, I should care very little about it; he would be welcome to give me as many as he pleased. And what say the wicked? "We do not care about metaphorical fires." But they are real, sir – yes, as real as yourself. There is a real fire in hell, as truly as you have now a real body – a fire exactly like that which we have on earth in everything except this – that it will not consume, though it will torture you. You have seen the asbestos lying in the fire red hot, but when you take it out it is unconsumed. So your body will be prepared by God in such a way that it will burn forever without being consumed; it will lie, not as you consider, in metaphorical fire, but in actual flame.[8]

St. Augustine, regarded as the greatest church father of western Christendom,[9] held to a literal view of hell. So did Thomas Aquinas and Jonathan Edwards.

However, William Crockett expresses a different view, one shared by such theologians as John Calvin, W. G. T. Shedd, and J. I. Packer:

> Christians should never be faced with this kind of embarrassment – the Bible does not support a literal view of a burning abyss. Hellfire and brimstone are not literal depictions of hell's fictions, but figurative expressions warning the wicked of impending doom.[10]

Theologian Charles Hodge adds:

> There seems no more reason for supposing that the fire spoken of in Scripture is to be a literal fire, than that the worm that never dies is

literally a worm. The devil and his angels who are to suffer the vengeance of eternal fire, and whose doom the finally impenitent are to share, have no material bodies to be acted upon by elemental fire.[11]

Wicked humans, however, *do* possess material bodies following their resurrection, although they are not glorified bodies like those of resurrected saints. The damned in hell are complete human beings, having bodies and souls that experience torment. In fact, the Greek words John employs for "torment" and "tormented" in Revelation 14:9-11 and 20:10 come from *basanizo*, which means "to vex with grievous pains (of body or mind)."[12] Likewise, another lexicon says *basanizo* means "to torture, torment," and may apply to either physical or mental pain or distress.[13]

So, the fires of hell, whether literal or figurative, are designed to inflict torment on the whole person. This torment in hell is experienced from the inside out. As Alan Gomes writes:

> It will not arise from God boiling sinners in a cauldron or turning them over slowly on a rotisserie spit, as vulgar, cartoonish depictions would have it. Rather, they will suffer the natural consequences of rejecting God and his goodness toward them, in which they will experience the pain of complete abandonment, remorse unmingled with comfort, and the relentless torments of their own consciences, which will burn forever but never finally consume. This cup they will drink to the full, experiencing unmitigated pain in both body and spirit.[14]

When considering the flames of hell, remember that the Bible uses fire metaphorically many times. Daniel sees the throne of God in heaven as "flaming fire; its wheels were blazing fire" (Dan. 7:9). James describes the tongue as an appendage that "sets the course of life on fire, and is itself set on fire by hell" (Jas. 3:6).

So, it may be that the Bible's depiction of hell in such graphic terms is God's way of explaining an indescribable place in language we can understand. Whether literal or metaphorical, the fires of hell are to be avoided at all costs, and the blood of Jesus is to be pleaded for forgiveness of sins while there is yet time.

IS HELL FOREVER?

Do hell's inhabitants experience suffering without end?

Anglican cleric John Stott, who wrote the influential book *Basic Christianity*, found the idea of eternal suffering in hell so repugnant, he rejected it in favor of annihilationism – the view that the wicked do not experience an eternity of suffering in hell; rather, they are extinguished after death, perhaps suffering first in hell for a period of time.

Those who embrace the idea of body and soul ceasing to exist after a time of punishment in hell point out that the "fire" and "worm" to which Jesus refers in Mark 9:47-48 are indeed eternal, but the body and soul are destroyed: "It is better for you to enter the kingdom of God with one eye than to have two eyes and be thrown into hell, where their worm does not die, and the fire is not quenched." Proponents of this view further cite Jesus' words in Matthew 10:28: "Don't fear those who kill the body but are not able to kill the soul; rather, fear him who is able to *destroy* both soul and body in hell [emphasis added]."

In response, we should consider two observations. First, the rabbinic understanding of these terms is that the bodies and souls of the wicked are eternal, not just the fires and worms.[15]

Second, the term *destroy* in Matthew 10:28 does not mean "annihilated." As *Thayer's Greek-English Lexicon* defines the word *apollumi*, it means "to be delivered up to eternal misery." In every instance where the word *apollumi* is found in the New Testament, something other than annihilation is described.[16] For example, people do not pass into nonexistence when they are "dying of hunger" (Luke 15:17), and wineskins don't vanish into thin air when they burst and "are ruined" (Matt. 9:17). In each of these instances, New Testament writers use the term *apollumi*.

While rejecting annihilationism, other Christian leaders favor the idea of suffering in the afterlife as a prerequisite for heaven. This may be in hell, or in an intermediate state such as purgatory. Augustine, sometimes wrongly called "the father of purgatory," was never completely convinced of the need for purging sins after death. Nevertheless, he conceded the possibility. He once wrote:

> Of those who suffer temporary punishments after death, all are not doomed to those everlasting pains which are to follow that judgment; for to some ... what is not remitted in this world is remitted in the next, that is, they are not punished with the eternal punishment of the world to come.[17]

Augustine appeared to believe there may be real, but temporary, punishment for those destined for heaven. Meanwhile, eternal punishment is reserved for the unsaved.

Even so, Jesus' teachings on "outer darkness," "eternal fire," and "eternal punishment" support the concept of *gehenna* as a place of conscious, everlasting separation from God. There is no scriptural provision for temporal post-mortem punishment to pay the debt owed an eternally holy God. Nor does there appear to be a temporary state of suffering after death to prepare the adopted sons and daughters of God for heaven.[18]

Paul describes heaven – not purgatory, nor time in hell followed by heaven – as the intermediate state between death and resurrection for followers of Jesus. In 2 Corinthians 5, Paul describes two mutually exclusive states for Christians. While we live now on earth in our bodies, we are absent from the Lord. And when we are "away from the body" in death, we are "at home with the Lord" (2 Cor. 5:8).

If there's an interim step between death and heaven, the Bible makes no mention of it, and we would do well to rest in the plainly stated promises of God's word. For those who die in the Lord, heaven can't wait, nor should it. At the same time, Scripture offers no hope for the unbeliever – no second chance. As the writer of Hebrews makes clear, "it is appointed for people to die once — and after this, judgment" (Heb. 9:27).

The final section in this chapter ("But why *eternal?*") offers a deeper exploration of the everlasting nature of both heaven and hell.

THE GOODNESS OF HELL

Hell is an awful prospect for anyone. C. S. Lewis once shuddered at the concept of hell: "There is no doctrine which I would more willingly remove from Christianity than this, if it lay in my power."[19]

But the notion of a loving God and the doctrine of hell are perfectly compatible. There is nothing of one that cancels out the other. Jesus speaks frequently on hell and alludes to it in parables. He tells certain religious leaders they are headed for hell. He warns his listeners about this place where the worm does not die and the fire is not quenched. He refers to hell as "outer darkness." And he says hell is prepared for Satan and evil spirits, yet he makes it clear that many people are going to spend eternity there. (See Appendix II for a listing of key Bible verses on hell.)

So, in what possible way is hell good?

First, hell is good because it's a place God prepared for the one who wrecked the goodness of creation – and the very goodness of beings made to be God's imagers. The Greek word rendered "prepared" in Matthew 25:41 is *hetoimazo*. It means to make the necessary preparations, or to get everything ready. The term is drawn from the oriental custom of sending servants ahead of kings on their journeys to level the roads and make them passable. So, with hell, the Lord has made everything ready for the god of this age – the king of a corrupt and rebellious kingdom – to end his journey in outer darkness.

Second, hell is good because it affirms God's justice. If God only had the attributes of benevolence and mercy, hell would be an unreasonable reading of Scripture. But God is infinitely holy and perfectly just. To sin against him offends his very nature – and all people have sinned (Rom. 3:23). For those who reject Christ's payment for their sins on the cross and thus spend eternity apart from him, justice also demands punishment relative to their deeds. Human beasts like Hitler, Stalin, and Pol Pot are responsible for the slaughter of millions of people whose lives ended in starvation, torture, human experimentation, or execution. How can the mere death of these tyrants by any means satisfy divine justice?

If we accept the doctrine of universalism – the view that every human, and perhaps every fallen angel, ultimately makes it to heaven – we must admit that Osama bin Laden and Mother Teresa are feasting at the same banquet table. At the same time, if we embrace the dogma of annihilation, we struggle to explain how temporal suffering in the afterlife pays an eternal debt. Without the existence of hell, life indeed is cruel, and life's creator is eternally unjust.

Third, hell is good because it affirms free will. While we may debate whether humans have libertarian free will, or whether we simply make decisions within predetermined boundaries, there is little question among Christians that God allows us to make choices for which he holds us accountable. In a world where God refuses to grant humans real choices, there is no freedom to love God.

If we view life fatalistically, God is a cruel puppet master who manipulates us before discarding us like broken toys. But the biblical concept of hell carries with it the clear teaching that people choose to spend eternity apart from Christ. As C. S. Lewis so poignantly penned, "[T]he doors of Hell are locked on the inside."[20] Without hell, our choices have no real meaning or lasting consequences.

Fourth, hell is good because it implies heaven. Many atheists attack the idea that a good God would send people to hell for eternity as payment for temporal sins. But they are less likely to contest the idea of a God – if he could possibly exist – who welcomes people into eternal bliss merely for being the recipients of his grace.

Freud argued that heaven is a product of wishful thinking. But if that's so, how does one explain the fact that many religions embracing heaven also have clear doctrines of hell? We are invited to join God in this life, and in the life to come, by his grace through faith. We may reject him and enter eternity on our own terms, but we cannot take God with us or it would cease to be hell.

While it's troubling to consider eternity in "outer darkness," the Bible is clear that hell is a place people choose to live independently of

God – forever. We do not see the rich man repent of his sin after finding himself in torment in *hades* (Luke 16:19-31), nor do we see those before the great white throne asking to be nearer to Jesus (Rev. 20:11-15). Indeed, the blasphemers and unrepentant in the Book of Revelation hide themselves from the presence of God, preferring death under a deluge of rocks to life in the light of Christ (Rev. 6:15-17).

A final caution: When we say hell is good, we don't mean to gloat over those who enter eternity without Christ, no matter how wicked they may be. The Lord himself does not delight in the death of the ungodly (Ezek. 18:23; 33:11). Rather, he took the human condition so seriously that he sent his Son to save us from ourselves – and from his wrath.

Why did God have to take on our humanity to save us? Why couldn't he simply forgive our sins without judging them? Why couldn't he remove our sins and their consequences by granting forgiveness without a cost?

Throughout the centuries, Christian thinkers have pondered these questions, perhaps no one more deeply than Anselm, the archbishop of Canterbury from A.D. 1093 to 1109. In *Why the God-Man?*, Anselm makes the point that because God is an infinitely perfect being, our sin against him incurs an infinite debt that must be satisfied in order for God to remain just. Only a being who is infinitely worthy can pay that debt. Yet, because humans sin, a human must satisfy the debt.

Therefore, Anselm argued, the infinitely holy Son of God – very God of very God – added sinless humanity to his deity via the miracle of the virgin birth. In taking on a human nature and living a sinless life, he could pay the sinner's debt. The infinite worth of Jesus' divine nature makes the atonement he offered in his humanity sufficiently worthy to pay the infinite debt of sin.[21]

These marvelous truths may help us grasp the audacity of God's love for fallen human beings, as well as understand why those who trample on the Son of God and regard as profane his blood deserve everlasting separation from him (Heb. 10:29).

THE ETERNAL FIRE: MATTHEW 25:41

In Matthew 24-25, Jesus is on the Mount of Olives with his disciples, responding to their questions about the future destruction of the temple and the end of the age. He closes out the Olivet Discourse with the parable of the sheep and goats, revealing the preparation of a final place of judgment for Satan, evil spirits, and unbelievers. A key verse reads: "Then he [the Son of Man] will also say to those on the left, 'Depart from me, you who are cursed, into the eternal fire prepared for the devil and his angels!'" (Matt. 25:41).

The central theme of this parable is that Christ separates believers from unbelievers at his return. Jesus also makes it clear that all angelic and human rebels are banished from his presence. This passage deals with human works, not as a condition of salvation, but as evidence of one's regard for the Son of Man.

Distinct places are prepared for the sheep and goats. Jesus tells the sheep, "Come, you who are blessed by my Father; inherit the kingdom prepared for you from the foundation of the world" (Matt. 25:34). God's kingdom – his reign, or authority to rule – has always existed and must be entered by faith.

Christ has known his sheep from eternity past and has prepared a special place of honor for them. This honor is bestowed when the kingdom of the world becomes "the kingdom of our Lord and of his Christ, and he will reign forever and ever" (Rev. 11:15). God's kingdom is not an afterthought. Its citizens are elect from eternity past. After Christ's return, Satan, sin, and death are fully and finally banished, and Christ makes everything new (2 Pet. 3:10-13; Rev. 21-22; cf. Isa. 65:17).

As for the goats, Jesus says, "Depart from me, you who are cursed, into the eternal fire prepared for the devil and his angels" (Matt. 25:41). In contrast to the sheep, who are welcomed into Christ's kingdom, the goats are banished to a singular place prepared for Satan and evil spirits.

The idea of banishment is consistent throughout the New Testament with respect to those who reject Christ. Jesus calls false prophets "lawbreakers," declares that he never knew them, and commands them to depart from him (Matt. 7:23). Paul writes of the day when Christ "takes vengeance with flaming fire on those who don't know God and on those who don't obey the gospel of our Lord Jesus. They will pay the penalty of eternal destruction from the Lord's presence and from his glorious strength" (2 Thess. 1:8-9). And at the great white throne judgment, the judge throws the wicked into the lake of fire (Rev. 20:15).

Note in Jesus' words to the goats that hell is a place "prepared for the devil and his angels." Jesus does not tell the goats that hell is prepared for *them*, but for another race of beings – rebellious angels. There's no hint of redemption for the evil one and his angelic cronies. Christ did not come in the likeness of sinful and fallen angels, but in the likeness of sinful and fallen people. Salvation is God's exclusive gift to humans, a gift denied to the evil one and fallen angels. More on this in Chapter 12.

Nevertheless, those who reject Christ occupy the same place of everlasting punishment as Satan. Just as saints enjoy everlasting life in the presence of the triune God and God's holy angels, unbelievers experience banishment in hell, along with "the god of this age" (2 Cor. 4:4) and his angelic minions. Unbelievers don't care about being heirs of God's kingdom because they have no regard for the king. And so, by their choice, the goats depart into eternal fire.

This judgment is final and everlasting. The sheep gladly accept eternal life as the ultimate act of God's grace. The goats, however, depart in stunned silence to hell. There is no higher court to which they may appeal. No second chance. No calls for clemency. No end to the consequences of their sin; that is, no annihilation, and no universal salvation. Just the stark reality of eternity in outer – and utter – darkness.

Jesus clearly teaches a final judgment, as well as a final destination, for all people. God has prepared a place of blessing for those who submit willingly to his Son's kingship. It's a place of rest, peace, security, and joy in the presence of the triune God, his holy angels, and other heavenly beings. At the same time, those who reject the Lord's gracious provision for their sin, and who rebel against his kingship, are cast into a place not prepared for them, but a place where they nevertheless suffer the same fate as the ones for whom hell is created: Satan and evil spirits. Together, they all go to a place of eternal punishment, while the redeemed enjoy eternal life.

BUT WHY *ETERNAL*?

We should clarify that only God is truly eternal. That is, only the uncreated Father, Son, and Holy Spirit share the attribute of being without beginning or end. So, in what sense are we to understand the final destinies of the sheep, goats, Satan, and evil spirits as *eternal*?

The Greek word rendered "eternal" in this passage is *aionios*, which generally means "without beginning or end, that which always has been and always will be."[22] In some contexts, *aionios* may be rendered "without beginning" or "without end, never to cease, everlasting." R. T. France says the word "may convey either the sense of 'going on forever' or that of 'belonging to the age to come.'"[23]

Moses Stuart points out that the Greek words *aion* and *aionios* are applied sixty times in the New Testament to designate the continuance of the future happiness of the righteous, and twelve times to depict the continuance of the future misery of the wicked. He thus asks, "by what principles of interpreting language does it become possible for us to avoid the conclusion that *aion* and *aionios* have the same sense in both cases?"[24]

Since these places of blessing and punishment are *prepared*, they must have come into existence; that is, God must have created them. Surely, the earthly kingdom in which the sheep enjoy everlasting life, and into which God brings his heavenly throne, is created (and ultimately renovated; see 2 Pet. 3:10-13). So, the concept of *eternal life* means not only "without end;" it also signifies a *quality* of life as we enjoy unbroken fellowship with the one who truly is eternal.

Many Scriptures address the qualitative nature of eternal life with Christ. Jesus' words in John 5:24 are one example: "Truly I tell you, anyone who hears my word and believes him who sent me *has* eternal life and will not come under judgment but has passed from death to life [emphasis added]." Believing sinners receive eternal life now, as a present reality, passing from spiritual death into new life in Christ. As Paul puts it, "For you died, and your life is hidden with Christ in God" (Col. 3:3).

This is eternal life in the qualitative sense. Followers of Jesus do not become eternally existing beings; only God is without beginning and end. But because we have entered into a covenant relationship with the Son of God, his eternal life is bound to ours. And thus, as long as Jesus lives, we live, too (John 14:19).

But there's more. This qualitative aspect of eternal life is permanent and irrevocable, thus everlasting. That is, those who receive eternal life through faith in Jesus enjoy the never-ending benefits of our covenant relationship with him. We look forward to the new heavens and new earth, where we enjoy face-to-face fellowship with our creator for all eternity.

Perhaps there is a similar sense in which Satan, evil spirits, and wicked people enter into both qualitative and quantitative "eternal punishment." God certainly foreknows their banishment to the lake of fire, and they stand condemned today (John 3:18; 16:11). Just as believers are foreknown, elected, and predestined outside of time – one might say in eternity past – so Satan, evil spirits, and unbelievers are foreknown as those who reject God and thus destined to spend eternity apart from him.

Wicked angels and unbelieving people live today as renegades, outside the intimate fellowship that believers in Christ and holy angels enjoy with God. Thus, they presently reap everlasting punishment in a qualitative sense. They experience never-ending punishment, in the quantitative sense, when they are cast into outer darkness after final judgment. So, their eternal punishment is foreknown, determined, experienced now in spiritual darkness, and without end.

Finally, when we think of the fires of hell, we should not disconnect them from the presence of God. Remember that God often is associated with fire throughout Scripture. He appears to Moses in a burning bush (Exod. 3). His presence radiates through the pillar of fire and cloud during the Israelites' forty years in the desert. He comes down on Mount Sinai in fire (Exod. 19:18). The writer of Hebrews depicts him as a "consuming fire" (Heb. 12:29). John's vision of heaven shows the seven spirits – or seven-fold Spirit – blazing like fire before the throne in heaven (Rev. 4:5). Further, John sees those who worship the beast being tormented with fire and sulfur in the sight of the holy angels and in the sight of the Lamb (Rev. 14:10).

The fires with which God is associated provide holy angels and believing sinners with light, warmth, protection, and guidance. These same fires torment rebellious angels and unrepentant sinners. In some respects, the blazing brilliance of hellfire is the backside of heaven's *Shekinah* glory. It continuously reveals the holiness of God and perpetually sears the blackened hearts of the damned. The fires of heaven and hell are not two distinct fires. They share the same divine source but have very different effects on the righteous and the wicked.

REVIEW

Key takeaways from this chapter

1. We should think of Christ's sentencing of unbelievers to hell as the first stage in cosmic renewal. Jesus' finished work of redemption brings new life to those once dead in trespasses and sins (Eph. 2:1). At the same time, Jesus promises to restore creation to sinless perfection in what he calls "the renewal of all things" (Matt. 19:28), which necessitates the banishing of wicked humans and angels.

2. The Bible offers several key terms that give us a picture of life beyond the grave:

(a) *Sheol* – a Hebrew term used sixty-five times in the Old Testament to describe the abode of the dead.

(b) *Hades* – a Greek word seen ten times in the New Testament with flexible meanings, but often used as a synonym for *sheol*.

(c) *Gehenna* – a Greek term appearing twelves times in the New Testament and meaning (with one exception) the place of everlasting future punishment of wicked humans and fallen angels.

3. Scholars disagree as to whether the fires of hell, as depicted in Scripture, are literal or figurative. It may be that the Bible's description of hell in such graphic terms is God's way of explaining an indescribable place in language we can understand. Whether literal or metaphorical, the fires of hell are to be avoided at all costs, and the blood of Jesus is to be pleaded for forgiveness of sins while there is yet time.

4. Annihilationism and universalism are false teachings that seek to skirt the biblical truth that hell's inhabitants reside there eternally. Jesus' parable of the sheep and goats (Matt. 25:31-46) employs the Greek word *aionios* – "without end, never to cease, everlasting" – to depict both the nature of life with Christ and existence apart from him in hell.

5. The notion of a loving God and the doctrine of hell are, in fact, compatible. Put another way, hell is good for the following reasons:

(a) It's a place God prepared for Satan, the one who wrecked the goodness of creation and the very goodness of beings made to be God's imagers.

(b) It affirms God's justice.

(c) It affirms free will.

(d) It implies heaven.

While it's troubling to consider eternity in "outer darkness," the Bible is clear that hell is a place people choose in order to live independently of God.

DISCUSS

Questions for personal or group study

1. What are the differences between *sheol, hades,* and *gehenna*?

2. How might you respond to the person who argues that the Old Testament says nothing about the afterlife?

3. What terms besides *gehenna* do Jesus and the New Testament writers use to describe the eternal destiny of the wicked?

4. Read Matthew 25:41 and Revelation 20:10-15. For whom did Jesus say hell is prepared? Who ends up being cast into the lake of fire?

5. Do you think it's fair for God to punish someone eternally for sins committed in a single lifetime? Why or why not?

* * *

———— A ————

Despite common beliefs that the evil one welcomes willing sinners into a never-ending fraternity kegger beyond the grave, hell is the final stop on Satan's long descent into ruin.

———— Ω ————

"THE ETERNAL FIRE PREPARED FOR THE DEVIL"

JESUS IS RETURNING TO CAST SATAN AND DEMONS INTO HELL

The Souza-Baranowski Correctional Center in Massachusetts is well into its third decade of operation and has yet to report a breakout. The center has earned its reputation as the most technologically advanced and secure prison in the world – even more secure than Russia's notorious Black Dolphin Prison, or the ADX prison in Colorado, dubbed the "Alcatraz of the Rockies."

Roughly six hundred corrections officers guard Souza-Baranowski's fifteen hundred prisoners. But just to be sure, the omniscient eye of a robotic watchman carefully monitors every inch of the facility. More than forty graphic-interfaced computer terminals drive a keyless system that controls every aspect of the prison, from doors to the water supply. If that's not enough, three hundred and seventy high-definition cameras record everything at all times. Plus, a taut-wire fence and microwave detection system guard the perimeter.

If you think you can simply snip a few wires or pull the plug on the entire system, think again. Souza-Baranowski is one of the only U.S. prisons designed to run entirely on solar and hydroelectric power. Oh, and for anyone trying the old-school method of digging out, the prison was built using the highest-strength concrete and tool-resistant steel available. Hollywood blockbuster *Escape Plan* to the contrary, not even Arnold Schwarzenegger and Sylvester Stallone could bust out of this place.[1]

A prison of this stature isn't built overnight. It requires careful planning, thorough research, an advanced grasp of the sciences, and special insight into the minds of the world's most diabolical criminals. For most inmates, Souza-Baranowski is their final stop; once inside, their fates are sealed.

Imagine the far greater mind of God that designed *gehenna*, the everlasting lake of fire and sulfur prepared for the devil and his angels (Matt. 25:41), and a place into which they are cast to be tormented day and night forever (Rev. 20:10). This inescapable prison, which the world's unbelievers share (Rev. 20:15), is both a fascinating and terrifying place.

Satan may rule a kingdom of evil spirits and rebellious people today. He may even prowl the earth like an uncaged lion. But he lays no claim to hell. And despite common beliefs that the evil one welcomes willing sinners into a never-ending fraternity kegger beyond the grave, hell is the final stop on Satan's long descent into ruin. There, in the presence of God and his holy angels, the party ends. The evil one gets his comeuppance and forever loses the autonomy he thought he possessed.

In many snapshots of Satan throughout the Bible, it may appear he is an unbeatable foe. He entices the first man and woman to sin, thus plunging the human race into a cataclysmic fall, and placing the created order under a curse. He openly accuses God's servants of unworthiness. He destroys Job's property, kills his family, takes away his health, and turns his wife against him. He tries wiping out the Israelites so there is no chosen people through whom Messiah comes, and then he inspires King Herod to try killing the newborn king in Bethlehem. He harasses Jesus and the apostles, causes serious illnesses, controls Jesus' betrayer, spreads spiritual blindness, deceives millions, divides the church, prowls the earth like a lion, and leads an all-out blitz against Christ and his church in the last days. We may wonder when all of this ends.

But end it does. God's judgments have spanned human history.

They begin in the expulsion of Adam and Eve from the garden (Gen. 3), and they end at a great white throne (Rev. 20). The Day of the Lord is coming, an event about which the Old Testament prophets and New Testament writers repeatedly warn (e.g., Isa. 2:6-22; Amos 5:18-19; Rom. 2:1-3). Jesus emphatically tells us a day is coming when all people are resurrected and judged, resulting in everlasting life or never-ending damnation (John 5:28-29).

But human beings are not the only ones to receive final judgment. Jesus makes it clear that a place is prepared for the evil one and his minions. A day has been set when Christ judges Satan and banishes him forever into the lake of fire. So, let's consider Satan's final date with destiny as we explore key passages of Scripture, most notably Matthew 25:41 and Revelation 20:1-3, 10.

A FIRE PREPARED AND ETERNAL: MATTHEW 25:41

In Chapter 11, we surveyed Jesus' parable of the sheep and goats to show that hell is a never-ending place of punishment for rebellious people. Even so, it was not originally intended for them, but for Satan and evil spirits. A key verse in the parable reads, "Then he [the Son of Man] will also say to those on the left, 'Depart from me, you who are cursed, into *the eternal fire prepared for the devil and his angels!*'" (Matt. 25:41, emphasis added).

We noted in the previous chapter that distinct places are prepared for the sheep and goats. Jesus tells the sheep, "Come, you who are blessed by my Father; inherit the kingdom prepared for you from the foundation of the world" (Matt. 25:34). God's kingdom – that is, his reign, or authority to rule – has always existed and must be entered by faith.

Christ has known his sheep from eternity past and has prepared a place of honor for them. This honor is bestowed when the kingdom of the world becomes "the kingdom of our Lord and of his Christ, and he will reign forever and ever" (Rev. 11:15).

As for the goats, Jesus says, "Depart from me, you who are cursed, into the eternal fire prepared for the devil and his angels"

(Matt. 25:41). In contrast to the sheep, who are welcomed into Christ's kingdom, the goats are banished to a place prepared for the evil one and the rebellious spirits that followed him.

So, while Jesus directs his parable to human beings, he also pulls back the curtain on the ultimate destiny of rebel angels. But what is the Lord telling us about that fateful day? Let's briefly examine three key words Jesus employs in Matthew 25:41.

Eternal. The Greek word is *aionios* and occurs seventy-one times in the New Testament. It often means without beginning or end. While this most accurately describes an attribute of God, who alone has always existed, it's commonly applied to God's gift of salvation, with a particular emphasis on his eternal purpose in redemption.

For example, Jesus tells us in John 3:36, "The one who believes in the Son has eternal life, but the one who rejects the Son will not see life; instead, the wrath of God remains on him." The eternally existing Son of God grants believers an unbreakable relationship with him. Followers of Jesus receive a *quality* of life – life in Christ – that goes on without end. This life always has existed in the eternal triune Godhead. Many other passages use *aionios* to depict eternal life in this way (e.g., Matt. 19:29; John 3:16; 4:14; 5:24; 6:40; 17:3; Acts 13:48; Rom. 6:23; 1 Tim. 1:16).

But *aionios* also can mean without end, never to cease, or never-ending. It's a *quantity* of life. From a human perspective, it captures the idea of salvation. Although God foreknew, elected, and predestined us in eternity past, we enter the realm of everlasting life by God's grace through faith in real time. In a similar manner, God determined the necessity of the "eternal fire" of hell in eternity past but brought it into existence as a place of future, never-ending punishment for Satan and evil spirits.

So, by "eternal" in Matthew 25:41, Jesus does not mean hell has always existed. Rather, he fashioned the lake of fire as a place of never-ending torment for the evil one.

Fire. This comes from the Greek *pyr* and refers to literal or figurative fire, or even lightning. *Pyr* occurs seventy-one times in the New Testament and may signify natural combustion (e.g., Matt. 13:40;

John 15:6), supernatural punishment (e.g., Matt. 18:8; Luke 17:29; Rev. 8:7; 20:14-15), or the presence of God (e.g., Acts 2:3; 7:30; Rev. 4:5).

As we learned in Chapter 11, there is some debate as to whether the fires of hell should be understood literally or figuratively. But clearly, from all biblical descriptions of hell, we may rest assured that the lake of fire is a place of unending punishment in the presence of God, who is "a consuming fire" (Heb. 12:29; cf. Deut. 4:24).

Paul offers a graphic portrayal of hellfire in 2 Thessalonians 1:7-9. There, he describes the justice of God in afflicting unbelievers who have persecuted the saints:

> This will take place at the revelation of the Lord Jesus from heaven with his powerful angels, when he takes vengeance with *flaming fire* on those who don't know God and on those who don't obey the gospel of our Lord Jesus. They will pay the penalty of eternal destruction from the Lord's presence and from his glorious strength ....

So, we may conclude that the words of Jesus in Matthew 25:41 about "eternal fire" refer to never-ending divine justice for Satan, fallen angels, and humans who reject the gospel message. But there's one more word we need to consider.

Prepared. Jesus says the eternal fire was "prepared for the devil and his angels." The Greek word employed here is *hetoimazo* and means to prepare, make ready, or provide. It occurs forty times in the New Testament and may be linked with personal or impersonal objects. Regarding personal preparation, Paul writes that God has cleansed believers and prepared us for good works (2 Tim. 2:21). And, as we look forward to the return of Christ, we are to make ourselves ready for the wedding of the Lamb (Rev. 19:7; 21:2).

From a perspective of impersonal objects, we hear John the Baptist crying out, "Prepare the way for the Lord; make his paths straight" (Matt. 3:3; cf. Isa. 40:3). Near the end of Jesus' earthly ministry, he gives his disciples instructions for preparing the Passover meal (Matt. 26:17-19). During this meal, Jesus assures his disciples that he is going away to prepare a place for them in heaven (John 14:2-3). And, as we anticipate our own future, we can only imagine the glorious gifts "God has prepared ... for those who love him" (1 Cor. 2:9).

So, in the context of Jesus' revelation of hell in the parable of the sheep and goats, we may note a stark contrast. Just as Jesus has prepared a place in heaven for his sheep, he has made ready a place in eternal fire for the goats – a place specifically primed for the devil and his angels. This means hell is a created place – a real destination where evil, disembodied spirits (Satan and demons), and resurrected unbelievers share "the second death" in never-ending torment (Rev. 20:14). Whether the fires of hell are literal or figurative, they represent God's wrath and the consequences of rebellion against his holiness.

THE ABYSS: REVELATION 20:1-3

Before Satan is cast into the lake of fire to be tormented forever, he is imprisoned for a thousand years:

> Then I saw an angel coming down from heaven holding the key to the abyss and a great chain in his hand. He seized the dragon, that ancient serpent who is the devil and Satan, and bound him for a thousand years. He threw him into the abyss, closed it, and put a seal on it so that he would no longer deceive the nations until the thousand years were completed. After that, he must be released for a short time (Rev. 20:1-3).

The Greek word *abyssos*, rendered "abyss," "pit," or "bottomless pit" in many English translations, occurs nine times in the New Testament. In most cases, it refers to a place of temporary confinement for certain evil spirits. For example, in Jesus' encounter with Legion, the demons who possess the Gerasene man beg Jesus not to banish them to the *abyss* – no doubt a place evil spirits fear (Luke 8:31).

Later, both Peter and Jude refer to a place where particularly nasty evil spirits are kept in reserve for judgment. Peter uses the Greek *tartaroo* (transliterated "Tartarus" in 2 Pet. 2:4 HCSB). Jude describes it as a place where certain rebellious spirits are kept in "eternal chains in deep darkness" (Jude 6).

In the Book of Revelation, demonic "locusts" and a murderous beast emerge from the *abyss*, and Satan is cast there for a time (Rev. 9:1-11; 11:7; 20:1-3). The only exception seems to be Romans 10:7, where Paul uses *abyss* as a synonym for the grave (or perhaps the underworld), contrasting Jesus' descent into it with the Savior's ascension into heaven.[2]

Note several characteristics of the abyss.

First, the abyss is under God's sovereign control. An angel must be given the key for the shaft to the *abyss*, for the angel has no authority to open it on his own (Rev. 9:1; 20:1). The beast, upon whom the "Mother of Prostitutes" rides, comes up from the *abyss*, only to go to destruction (Rev. 17:5, 8). Demons fear the *abyss* and seek to avoid it, although Jesus has the final say (Luke 8:31). Finally, Satan is seized, bound, and thrown into the *abyss* for a thousand years – a sentence he may neither appeal nor shorten (Rev. 20:1-3). Bible commentators debate whether the thousand years are to be taken literally or figuratively, but they agree the evil one's unfettered freedom is revoked for a lengthy period of time.

We also may note the humiliating nature of Satan's detention in these verses. It is not God the Father, the exalted Son of God, or the Holy Spirit who deals with the evil one in this passage. Nor do Michael the archangel or Gabriel swoop in to play the role of cosmic warden. Rather, an unnamed angel is dispatched to lock Satan in the abyss. This may be the same unidentified "star" that unlocked the *abyss* to release the locust plague in Revelation 9:1-2. In any case, sending an anonymous angel to lock up the "anointed guardian cherub" is the ultimate cosmic burn (cf. Ezek. 28:14).

Second, the abyss is a place of confinement. Like Satan, evil spirits seem to desire freedom to prowl the earth (1 Pet. 5:8). They crave autonomy – independence from God, and both the ability and opportunity to oppose him. In the *abyss*, however, they are kept under lock and key. Jude describes it as a place where some evil spirits are "kept in eternal chains in deep darkness" (Jude 6). The image we're left with is of a manacle that binds a captive's hands to the prison wall.[3] No doubt, the expression "chains" is used figuratively, since evil spirits are non-corporeal beings and physical chains cannot bind them. Nevertheless, they are imprisoned, and God, who is spirit (John 4:24), knows full well how to keep spirits he created in their place.

Note the significance of the seal the angel places on the *abyss*. There are about sixty references to seals in the Bible, denoting marks of authenticity, possession, and authority. Scrolls often are sealed (Jer. 32:7-15; Rev. 5:1-7). So are a den of lions and the tomb of Jesus (Dan. 6:16-17; Matt. 27:62-66). Only authorized persons may remove seals. And when God seals a person or place, it is his prerogative – and only his – to determine its permanence. For Christians, the most personally significant seal is one that human eyes cannot see. It is the secret work of the Holy Spirit, placing God's mark of ownership on us and ensuring that the work of redemption is completed (2 Cor. 1:22; Eph. 1:13-14; 4:30).

The seal on the *abyss* is secure for a thousand years. It is an unbreakable seal, far more impregnable than the one Pilate ordered, soldiers guarded, and Satan endorsed over the tomb of Jesus, "which was burst on the resurrection morn."[4] As Grant Osborne notes, "The abyss is [Satan's] Alcatraz, and God is in complete control."[5]

Third, the abyss is a place of temporary punishment. Satan is kept there for a thousand years, only to be cast into the lake of fire to be tormented night and day forever (Rev. 20:10). Like *hades*, the abode of the dead where the wicked go between physical death and final judgment, the *abyss* is imprisonment – with no parole – for evil spirits. Ultimately, both "death" and "Hades" are cast into the lake of fire, for they are temporary states of punishment and are no longer needed after final judgment (Rev. 20:14).

Similarly, once Satan, evil spirits, and wicked people are cast into hell, the *abyss* serves no further purpose. Though temporary, the *abyss* is a place of genuine punishment, for confinement prevents Satan and evil spirits from carrying out their wicked campaign against God and God's people.

Fourth, the abyss houses Satan and evil spirits, not people. The departed spirits of human beings reside in a temporary place called *sheol* in the Old Testament and *hades* in the New Testament. Followers of Jesus go directly into his presence in heaven upon physical death, where they await resurrection, glorification, and everlasting life in the new heavens and new earth (2 Cor. 5:1-10; Phil. 1:21-24; 2 Pet. 3:10-13; Rev. 21-22). But nowhere in Scripture are people described as being in the *abyss*.

Death and *hades*, which John personifies in Revelation 20:14, clearly impact all humanity. But believers should take heart. The risen Christ holds the keys of death and *hades* (Rev. 1:18) and ultimately casts them both into the lake of fire (Rev. 20:14).

Fifth, the purpose of Satan's confinement in the abyss is to prevent him from deceiving the nations. This is clearly stated in Revelation 20:3. The angel places a seal on the *abyss* so the evil one "would no longer deceive the nations until the thousand years were completed."

The binding of Satan in the *abyss* curtails his ability to deceive. It does not necessarily stop the residual influence of his evil work on human beings. And it certainly doesn't put an end to sin. But it's a much-welcomed incarceration.

We should note that the evil one is prohibited from deceiving the "nations." The Greek word *ethnos* appears more than 160 times in the New Testament with two basic meanings: "nation" and "Gentile." In the former sense, it signifies a body of people united by kinship, culture, and common traditions, such as the Israelites or a Gentile people group. But nations, even Gentile ones, consist of individuals. So, when Jesus commands us to "Go, therefore, and make disciples of all *nations*," he's not referring to geographical boundaries or political entities but "in the sense of every single people group in the world" (Matt. 28:19, emphasis added).[6]

So, John's use of *ethnos* in this passage likely refers to people in general, although it could be a reference to unbelievers in the last days.

In Revelation 12, Michael the archangel and his angels engage in fierce battle with the dragon and his angels. Michael's army emerges victorious and, as a result, the dragon – "the ancient serpent, who is called the devil and Satan, *the one who deceives the whole world"* – is thrown out of heaven down to earth (Rev. 12:9, emphasis added). While heaven rejoices, earth's inhabitants are placed on notice "because the devil has come down to you with great fury, because he knows his time is short" (Rev. 12:12).

In Revelation 13, the dragon empowers two human beings to lead the nations astray. We're introduced to the beast from the sea and the beast from the earth. Together with the dragon, they present a powerful counterfeit trinity capable of garnering a loyal worldwide following. We read in verses 12-14 that the purpose of the false prophet's "great signs" are to deceive the earth's inhabitants so they worship the beast from the sea.

When the angel confines Satan to the *abyss* in Revelation 20:1-3, the evil one is no longer able to deceive the nations. That's not the end of the story, however. A few verses later, an unrepentant Satan is released. He picks up where he left off, deceiving the nations and gathering them for battle (20:7-9). Clearly, the evil one's millennial sentence is meant to give the nations a respite from his trickery.

Finally, the abyss is a reverse image of heaven. Just as "Every good and perfect gift is from above, coming down from the Father of lights" (Jas. 1:17), the *abyss* spews nothing but wickedness from below. As Walter Elwell and Barry Beitzel point out:

> This is in keeping with the metaphor and the picture throughout Revelation in which the Dragon and the Beast attempt to duplicate the power and glory reserved for God alone. Just as heaven is a source of all that is worthwhile, the bottomless pit is the source of all that is evil.[7]

Kendall Easley makes a key point as we struggle with the chronology of Satan's rise and fall as depicted in the Book of Revelation: "However we interpret the binding of Satan in Revelation 20, we must never lose the essential New Testament teaching that his primary defeat was in the death and resurrection of Jesus, and his ultimate defeat is already certain."[8]

The evil one's temporary imprisonment in the *abyss* in some ways mirrors the intermediate confinement of wicked people in *hades*. When unbelievers die physically, their souls and spirits depart to *hades*, where they are held until their future resurrection and arraignment before the great white throne (Rev. 20:11-15). Upon their conviction in final judgment, Christ banishes them to the lake of fire.

Similarly, Satan experiences an intermediate state when imprisoned in the *abyss*. After a thousand years, he's released for a short time, proving his impenitent nature through immediate rebellion. Swiftly and decisively, he is cast into hell to be tormented night and day forever and ever. So, Satan and the wicked follow a similar pattern: rebellion, imprisonment, arraignment, conviction, sentencing.

As Christ is the second Adam, freeing his followers from the bonds of death and *hades*, Satan is the prototype of wicked humans, experiencing temporary confinement in the underworld before being cast eternally, and irrevocably, into the lake of fire.

To summarize, we may see Satan's downfall in three stages: from heaven to earth (Rev. 12:7-9); from earth to the *abyss* (Rev. 20:1-3); and from the *abyss* to the lake of fire (Rev. 20:10).

THE LAKE OF FIRE AND SULFUR: REVELATION 20:10

After Satan's release from the *abyss*, he proves himself unreformed and undeterred. The evil one immediately returns to his life of crime, setting out to deceive the nations once again and gather them for battle against Christ and his followers. As soldiers of this newly formed axis of evil surround the encampment of the saints, fire from heaven consumes them (Rev. 20:7-9). Then, we read:

> The devil who deceived them was thrown into the lake of fire and sulfur where the beast and the false prophet are, and they will be tormented day and night forever and ever (Rev. 20:10).

In this verse, John describes Satan's ultimate destination as "the lake of fire and sulfur." In Matthew 25:41, Jesus calls it "the eternal fire prepared for the devil and his angels." Jesus and the New Testament writers also describe this place as "outer darkness," "eternal punishment," and "the second death" (e.g., Matt. 22:13; 25:46; Rev. 21:8). But there's an even more descriptive term for this place: *gehenna*, or hell.

As we noted in Chapter 11, the Hebrew *sheol* and Greek *hades* generally depict the temporary abode of the dead. However, *gehenna* and its associated terms describe a place of everlasting future punishment, not only for Satan and evil spirits, but also for those whose names are not written in the book of life (Rev. 20:15).

The noun *gehenna* originally referred to the Valley of Hinnom. Located southwest of Jerusalem, this steep, rocky valley is the scene of human sacrifices to pagan deities (2 Kings 23:10; 2 Chron. 28:3; 33:6). A particular part of the valley is called Tophet, which means "fire-stove," where Israelite children are burned as offerings to the false gods Moloch and Baal. Jeremiah declares it the "Valley of Slaughter" (Jer. 7:31-34 ESV). To the Jewish mind, the images of fire and destruction become appropriate representations of the eventual fate of idol worshipers.

Jesus seizes rabbinic language connected with *gehenna*, such as "unquenchable fire" and "never-dying worms" (cf. Isa. 66:24) to impress upon his listeners that their choices in this life have everlasting consequences. In fact, of the twelve uses of *gehenna* in the New Testament, eleven come from the lips of the Messiah.

It's probable that Jesus uses *gehenna* on only four occasions: in the Sermon on the Mount (Matt. 5:22, 29, 30); in urging the disciples not to fear men (Matt. 10:28; Luke 12:5); in a discourse on relationships (Matt. 18:9; Mark 9:43, 45, 47); and in his denunciation of the scribes and Pharisees (Matt. 23:15, 33). Traditionally, these passages are understood to speak of final judgment, with Jesus using images from everyday life to warn about a place of everlasting punishment.

It's also important to understand *who* and *what* are cast into the lake of fire. The beast and the false prophet are tossed there (Rev. 19:20). So is Satan (Rev. 20:10), as is anyone whose name is not found written in the book of life (Rev. 20:15). This includes cowards, unbelievers, the vile, murderers, the sexually immoral, sorcerers, idolaters, and all liars – meaning the unrepentant wicked (Rev. 21:8; cf. 1 Cor. 6:9-10; Gal. 5:19-21; Eph. 5:5). Ultimately, death and *hades* also are banished to hell, since there is no longer any need for physical death or a temporary spiritual existence in the underworld (Rev. 20:14).

John describes the evil one's torment as enduring "day and night forever and ever." This phrase may be considered metaphorically as "without intermission" or "unceasingly." As surely as Christ's kingdom is "forever and ever" (Rev. 11:15), so is the length of Satan's punishment. The same divine fire that comes down from heaven in judgment of wicked people now engulfs the ultimate rebel (Rev. 20:9; cf. 2 Kings 1:10, 12).

The fires of hell devour, but do not annihilate, Satan, evil spirits, and wicked humans. For unbelieving people, hell transforms the temporary consequences of sin, such as physical death and disembodiment in *hades*, into permanent and unalterable punishments such as the second death, darkness, and separation from the intimacy God offers all people through his Son's finished work on the cross.

As Paul writes, those who don't know God and those who do not obey the gospel "pay the penalty of eternal destruction from the Lord's presence ...." (2 Thess. 1:9). Perhaps this divine act of judgment is the first step in what Peter describes as God's work of creating new heavens and a new earth. He first purges sin and its stain from the created order, and then restores the earth, skies, and outer space to their former pristine condition (2 Pet. 3:10-13; Rev. 21-22).

For Satan, hell is the final humiliation for the one-time guardian cherub. The "god of this age" (2 Cor. 4:4) is stripped of his kingdom. The deceiver of the whole world (Rev. 12:9) discovers he's the victim of his own ruse. The one who would set his throne above the stars of God (Isa. 14:13) is crushed beneath the Messiah's heel (Gen. 3:15). The one who commanded a vast army (Rev. 20:8) becomes a prisoner of war. And the one who received the worship of adoring hordes (Rev. 13:4) now spends eternity as a reviled despot. From the throne room of heaven, to the underworld, to the *abyss*, and finally to the lake of fire, the ancient serpent is defanged, defeated, dethroned, and despised.

COULD SATAN BE SAVED?

Scripture is clear that Satan's eternal destiny is the unrelenting lake of fire. It's the place into which the antichrist, the false prophet, and all unbelievers are cast as well. It does not appear there is any reversal of fortune for those in hell. Nevertheless, some in the early church took a different view.

Clement of Alexandria, for example, thought there was hope for the devil based on God's limitless mercy. Clement's pupil, Origen, took it a step further. He argued for *apocatastasis*, or the idea that all things made by God return to him. He once wrote, "We believe that the goodness of God through Christ will restore his entire creation to one end, even his enemies being conquered and subdued."[9]

In Origen's view, everyone – including Satan, evil spirits, and the most wicked humans – ultimately submit to God's sovereignty and are saved. Thus, Satan ceases to be evil and his angelic nature is restored.

Origen's view never gained much traction. Jerome and Augustine countered it. And the Council of Constantinople II in A.D. 553 anathematized the idea that the demonic could revert to the angelic in nature.[10] Graham Cole summarizes, "The darkness won't extinguish the light. The destiny of the darkness is its destruction. Fallen angels will experience the eternal fire. The devil may be the prince of this world. Be that as it may, in the next he has no kingdom."[11]

Satan cannot be *saved* – that is, restored to angelic holiness – for at least three reasons.

First, God has decreed that Satan will not be saved. The Lord has prepared the fires of hell for Satan and rebellious angels, who are cast into hell to be tormented night and day forever and ever – an unceasing suffering. Scripture offers no salvation to unbelieving humans beyond the grave, or to Satan at any point after his rebellion. The biblical account is straightforward. The evil one rebelled, God prepared the lake of fire for him, and in the end God casts him into this place of unrelenting torment.

Second, Satan would refuse salvation if offered. Satan's rebellion, committed in the perfection of the created order, and done with superior knowledge, wisdom, and power, was such that it is irrevocable. Nothing in Scripture hints at the possibility of Satan seeing the error of his ways and repenting. He knows his time is short, yet rather than repent – as humans facing their own mortality are urged to do – he turns up the heat to wreak as much havoc as possible on God's reputation and God's people. After a thousand years in the *abyss*, Satan is neither contrite nor converted. His first act after being released is not to repent, but to lead a global rebellion.

Third, there is no provision for salvation for Satan and fallen angels. Jesus did not come in the likeness of sinful angels, but in the likeness of sinful human beings. Forgiveness of sins, eternal life, adoption as children of God, and much more are reserved only for those whose salvation was secured in the sinless life, death, burial, and resurrection of Jesus, the God-Man. As the writer of Hebrews notes:

> Now since the children have flesh and blood in common, Jesus also shared in these, so that through his death he might destroy the one holding the power of death — that is, the devil — and free those who were held in slavery all their lives by the fear of death. For it is clear that he does not reach out to help angels, but to help Abraham's offspring. Therefore, he had to be like his brothers and sisters in every way, so that he could become a merciful and faithful high priest in matters pertaining to God, to make atonement for the sins of the people (Heb. 2:14-17).

A REAL PLACE

Jesus is clear that *gehenna* is a real place prepared for Satan and evil spirits. It's a place of separation, darkness, torment, hopelessness, and regret (but not repentance). And yet it's a place fully within the scope of God's omnipresence, for Satan and demons are tormented in the presence of God and his holy angels, as are the wicked followers of the beast (Rev. 14:10).

God designed hell as a final destination for Satan and rebellious angels. There is no hope of redemption for them. Not now. Not ever. But there *is* hope for us. Christ came in the likeness of sinful men and women, living a perfect life as the God-Man, and offering that life on the cross to the Father as an acceptable payment for our sin debt.

Christ's eternal life pays an eternal debt we owe an eternally offended God. Jesus' death took the place of ours. His resurrection secured the keys of death and *hades* so that he is the firstfruits of the righteous dead; we have his promise of future resurrection and glorification (1 Cor. 15:20-23).

Every person lives forever. But where, and how, are the key questions. And these questions are answered in our response to the most important question Jesus ever posed: "Who do you say that I am?" (Matt. 16:15). Many people answer wrongly today. They regard Jesus merely as a good man, a prophet, or perhaps even a god. But it's not good enough to have a high opinion of Jesus. We must answer as Peter did, "You are the Messiah, the Son of the living God" (Matt. 16:16).

That declaration must not be one of facts alone. Even demons declare Jesus the Son of God (Matt. 8:28-29; cf. Jas. 2:19). What makes Peter's bold statement redemptive are two biblical truths: the Father's initiative in revealing his Son (Matt. 16:17), and Peter's response in faith, which goes beyond mere intellectual assent.

Satan and demons both believe *and* continue to rebel. Unsaved people may believe facts about Jesus, while living the serpent's lie of thinking they can make themselves like God. Only those who hear the gospel and believe – entrusting their lives to Christ and surrendering all claims to their own autonomy – have truly passed from death to life (John 5:24). This is our hope. This is God's promise. And it's ours exclusively; Satan and evil spirits have only the lake of fire in their future.

If we read chapters 12 and 20 of Revelation together, we gain a concise history of the evil one: (1) The dragon begins in the heavens (12:3); (2) he tries unsuccessfully to destroy Christ at his incarnation (12:4-5); (3) he is thrown to the earth for a season and deceives the nations (12:12); (4) he is cast into the *abyss* for a thousand years (20:3); (5) he is released for a short time and resumes his work of deceiving the nations (20:7-8); finally, (6) he is thrown into the lake of fire and sulfur to be tormented forever (20:10).[12]

The same holy fire that lights the way for Israelites crossing the desert; that resides in the holy of holies above the mercy seat; and that blazes in the human spirits of the redeemed finally engulfs Satan, evil spirits, and human unbelievers. The holiness of God warms; it also burns.

REVIEW

Key takeaways from this chapter

1. Satan may rule a kingdom of evil spirits and rebellious people today. He may even prowl the earth like an uncaged lion. But he lays no claim to hell. And despite common beliefs that the evil one welcomes willing sinners into a never-ending fraternity kegger beyond the grave, hell is the final stop on Satan's long descent into ruin.

2. In the parable of the sheep and goats, Jesus says hell is a place "prepared for the devil and his angels" (Matt. 25:41). This means hell is a created place – a real destination where evil, disembodied spirits (Satan and demons) and resurrected unbelievers share "the second death" in never-ending torment (Rev. 20:14).

3. Before Satan is cast into the lake of fire to be tormented forever, he is sent for a time to the *abyss*, a place of temporary imprisonment where the evil one and certain demons are kept under lock and key. Incarceration doesn't reform Satan, however. After a thousand years, he's released, and immediately he leads a final rebellion against God and God's people.

4. While the Hebrew *sheol* and Greek *hades* generally depict the temporary abode of the dead, *gehenna* and its associated terms describe a place of everlasting future punishment, not only for Satan

and evil spirits, but also for those whose names are not written in the book of life.

5. Despite the views of some in the early church, Satan cannot be *saved* – that is, restored to angelic holiness – for at least three reasons:

(a) God has decreed that Satan will not be saved;

(b) Satan would refuse salvation if offered; and

(c) there is no provision for salvation for Satan and fallen angels.

DISCUSS

Questions for personal or group study

1. If Jesus says hell is prepared for "the devil and his angels," why do people end up in this place of everlasting punishment?

2. Do you believe the Bible teaches that the fires of hell are literal or figurative?

3. Name several characteristics of the *abyss*.

4. Why do you think Satan is granted a short reprieve from the *abyss* before he's cast into the lake of fire?

5. Why has God provided redemption for sinful people but not for Satan and demons?

* * *

"THE RENEWAL OF ALL THINGS"

JESUS IS RETURNING TO CREATE NEW HEAVENS AND A NEW EARTH

*A*ll works of art suffer the ravages of time. Museum curators and patrons go to great lengths to preserve masterpieces left in their care. When we see Vincent van Gogh's *The Starry Night*, or Michelangelo's *David*, we appreciate the care with which these timeless treasures have been handled.

At the same time, some classic paintings and sculptures have fallen into such disarray that they require the expert touch of restorers. And even then, their work often attracts controversy. For example, art lovers continue to debate whether the restoration of the frescoes in the Sistine Chapel between 1980-1994 was a triumph or a travesty.

Sometimes, however, it's plain to see when a restoration effort has run horribly off the rails. Take the statue of Virgin Mary and Child Jesus in front of the Church of Sainte-Anne des Pins in Sudbury, Canada. Vandals lopped off the head of Jesus, prompting local artist Heather Wise to sculpt a new head of clay. When she placed the new head on the existing stone body, perhaps the only happy person was Matt Groening, creator of *The Simpsons*. The restored head resembled Maggie Simpson far more than the Son of God. The faithful were so horrified by the artist's sincere yet faltering effort, the original stone head was recovered and put back in place.[1]

Whether expert or amateur, art restorers do their best to refresh works of art while retaining the aesthetic character of the original. No one is under the illusion of improving the masterpiece, for that is the domain of the artist alone.

When we consider the greatest work of art ever completed – God's creation of all things out of nothing – we know we're viewing a masterpiece desperately in need of restoration. We live in a world that groans beneath the weight of sin, and we long for the day when Jesus returns to make all things new (Rom. 8:22; Rev. 21:5). Many try to remake the world in their image – dictators and revolutionaries, for example – while the evil one has claimed this fallen world as his own.

It's only going to get worse until Jesus – the original artist of the cosmos – returns to set things right. Yes, Jesus is returning to create new heavens and a new earth. But we should not suppose that he is *merely* – if we may use that term – sending us back to the Garden of Eden. Rather, the creator causes the new heavens and earth to retain the qualities of creation as "very good indeed" (Gen. 1:31) and then goes beyond "good." Only the God of creation can improve on perfection.

Let's begin with a look at heaven as a bridge between our earthly existence now and the new heavens and earth to come. Then, let's see why the new heavens and earth, not heaven alone, constitute a better final destination. Finally, we'll explore three passages of Scripture that describe this divine restoration project.

IS HEAVEN OUR FINAL HOME?

Is heaven the final destination of all who rest in Jesus? Or do we spend eternity someplace else?

In 2 Corinthians 5, Paul describes two mutually exclusive states of existence for Christians. While we are "at home in the body we are away from the Lord." And when we are "away from the body" we are "at home with the Lord" (5:6, 8).

Let's unpack this marvelous truth. The New Testament teaches that upon death, believers' souls and spirits separate from our lifeless bodies and enter the presence of God in heaven (see Phil. 1:21-24). There we enjoy intimate fellowship with our Lord while awaiting the future resurrection and glorification of our bodies (John 5:28-29; 1 Cor. 15:51-58; 1 Thess. 4:13-18).

We see magnificent glimpses into the throne room of heaven through the eyes of John in the Book of Revelation: the triune Godhead; an emerald-colored rainbow surrounding a glorious throne; living creatures; elders; angels; and redeemed people from every tribe, language, people, and nation. The combined voices of all creatures in heaven, on earth, under the earth, and in the sea proclaim, "Blessing and honor and glory and power to the one seated on the throne, and to the Lamb, forever and ever!" (Rev. 5:13).

We may be tempted to stop here, as if heaven is the final destination in life's long journey. It *is* breathtaking. But it gets better. Heaven, a place so awe-inspiring that Paul is not allowed to speak the inexpressible words he hears while visiting there, nevertheless is a temporary home for those who rest in the Lord until he returns to earth and brings us with him.

As Randy Alcorn writes:

> The intermediate Heaven is *not* our final destination. Though it will be a wonderful place, the intermediate Heaven is not the place we were made for – the place God promises to refashion on a resurrected Earth. We must not lose sight of our true destination. If we do, we'll be confused and disoriented in our thinking about where, and in what form, we will spend eternity.[2]

What should we know, then, about heaven?

THREE HEAVENS

While rabbis in ancient times envisioned as many as seven heavens, the Bible generally uses the Hebrew word *shamayim* and the Greek word *ouranos* in three ways:

- Of the atmospheric heaven, or the sky (Gen. 1:8). It's where the birds fly (Mark 4:32), the clouds carry storms (Luke 12:54, 56), and the rain falls (Jas. 5:18).
- Of the stellar heaven(s), where the moon and stars shine (Ps. 8:3; Heb. 11:12).
- Of the domain of God, or his dwelling place (1 Kings 22:19; Luke 20:4).

The Scriptures also speak of the "heavens" as a metaphor for where Christ reigns with his church (Eph. 2:6), as well as the unseen spiritual realm that evil beings inhabit (Eph. 6:12). The context determines the word's proper meaning.

For our purposes, we're concerning ourselves with what Paul calls the "third heaven," or "paradise," the domain of God (2 Cor. 12:2). It is the intermediate state between death and resurrection for Christians, giving way ultimately to everlasting life on a restored earth.

KEY TRUTHS ABOUT HEAVEN

The New Testament reveals many truths about this intermediate state. Further, it shows us a seamless transition from the intermediate state to the eternal state as the intersection between heaven and earth is restored, with God bringing down his throne to rest among the redeemed. Consider several key truths regarding heaven.

First, the Father, Son, and Holy Spirit reside in heaven, yet they have immediate access to earth. This is seen, for example, in Matthew's account of Jesus' baptism, where all three members of the Trinity appear together (Matt. 3:16-17).

Second, God's will is done completely in heaven – and one day will be done on earth as well. In his model prayer, Jesus expresses this desire for God's kingdom to come in its fullness (Matt. 6:9-10).

Third, angels surround the throne in heaven, as do majestic heavenly creatures and redeemed people. Angels assigned to watch over "little ones" continually view the face of God the Father (Matt. 18:10). Meanwhile, John is granted a vision of God's throne in heaven, around which stand a countless host of angels, living creatures, and elders (Rev. 4-5).

Fourth, the heavenly throne is the heart of God's authority and majesty. Jesus takes his place as exalted king there immediately after his ascension (Mark 16:19).

Fifth, heaven is the place from which Satan fell, according to Jesus (Luke 10:18). Further, the evil one has no hope of regaining his exalted position; rather, he is cast into the lake of fire prepared for him and rebellious angels (Matt. 25:41; Rev. 20:10).

Sixth, heaven is where believers' names are written down, providing assurance of everlasting life. Jesus tells his followers to rejoice because of their inclusion in heaven's roll call (Luke 10:20). And the writer of Hebrews urges us to look toward "a festive gathering" that includes "myriads of angels" and "the assembly of the firstborn whose names have been written in heaven" (Heb. 12:22-24).

Seventh, Christ is preparing a place for believers in heaven and one day takes us there (John 14:1-3). Ultimately, he brings us back to earth with him when he returns (Rev. 19:11-16).

Eighth, our citizenship is in heaven. Paul writes that all believers "eagerly await a Savior from there, the Lord Jesus Christ," who will "transform the body of our humble condition into the likeness of his glorious body" (Phil. 3:20-21).

Ninth, our inheritance is in heaven. We are coheirs with Jesus of the world to come (Rom. 8:17), and that inheritance is "imperishable, undefiled, and unfading, kept in heaven" for us (1 Pet. 1:4).

Tenth, Jesus came from heaven (John 3:31; 6:38, 42), ascended into heaven after his finished work on the cross (Luke 24:51; Eph. 4:10; Heb. 4:14), and will descend from heaven one day to resurrect and glorify believers (1 Cor. 15:51-58; 1 Thess. 4:16-17).

Eleventh, God brings heaven and earth together one day and dwells with us. As John sees and hears in his vision of the new heavens and earth:

Look, God's dwelling is with humanity, and he will live with them. They will be his peoples, and God himself will be with them and will

be their God. He will wipe away every tear from their eyes. Death will
be no more; grief, crying, and pain will be no more, because the
previous things have passed away (Rev. 21:3-4).

Finally, nothing profane enters heaven – or the new heavens and
new earth. In John's depiction of the New Jerusalem, he notes,
"Nothing unclean will ever enter it, nor anyone who does what is
detestable or false, but only those written in the Lamb's book of life."
Further, there is no more curse, and no more night, "because the Lord
God will give them light, and they will reign forever and ever
(Rev. 21:27 – 22:5).

BETTER BY FAR

As wonderful as the intermediate heaven is, our ultimate destiny is
the new heavens and new earth, which Peter and John describe as a
place of righteousness and restored innocence (2 Pet. 3:10-13;
Rev. 21-22). Christ returns, resurrects and judges all people, establishes his kingdom in fullness, creates new heavens and a new earth,
and gives us roles to play in the administration of his eternal
kingdom.

John begins Revelation 21 with these words: "Then I saw a new
heaven and a new earth …." There are two words translated "new" in
the Greek New Testament: *neos* and *kainos*. *Neos* is an adjective
describing the age of something or someone. But John uses *kainos*,
which means "different from the usual, impressive, better than the
old, superior in value or attraction."[3]

In effect, *kainos* refers quality, not time. It suggests fresh life arising
from the decay of the old world. This theme is consistent throughout
Revelation, for we encounter "the new Jerusalem" (3:12), "a new
name" (2:17), "a new song" (5:9; 14:3), and "everything new" (21:5); in
each case, *kainos* is employed.

This should help us understand that God does not annihilate the
old order of things and start again from scratch. Rather, he purges the
sinful and fallen cosmos and restores it to its pristine beauty. As

German Lutheran theologian Franz Delitzsch writes, "Jehovah creates a new heaven and new earth which so fascinate by their splendor, so satisfy every wish, that all remembrance of the first, of wishing them back again, is utterly out of the question."[4]

Jesus calls this work "the renewal of all things," or "the Messianic Age" (Matt. 19:28). Peter explains it as a cleansing and renewing by fire, and he employs *kainos*, as John does, to describe the world to come (2 Pet. 3:10-13).

The new heavens and new earth stand in stark contrast to Eden after the Fall. God is fully revealed, and we are glorified so that our natural desire is for the intimacy Adam and Eve originally experienced in the garden. God sets his throne among us, and we do not flee from his presence with the shame that drove Adam and Eve to hide among the trees. There is personal contact with our sovereign creator. We call him *Abba* – father; an expression of familial intimacy – and he calls us his children. There is security, joy, and unending peace. God is with us and we never again experience the consequences of separation from the one who is our life.

While the intermediate heaven is the joyous aim of all who trust in Jesus, the new heavens and new earth are better by far. Satan, sin, and death – three enemies that Christ conquered through his finished work on the cross – are banished to the lake of fire, along with all those who reject God's provision for eternal life. God wipes the tears from his children's cheeks and declares that the former things – death, grief, crying, and pain – have passed away (Rev. 21:4).

J. I. Packer writes:

As life in the "intermediate" or "interim" state between death and resurrection is better than life in this world that preceded it, so the life of resurrection will be better still. It will, in fact, be best. And this is what God has in store for all his children."[5]

GLORY IN RESTORATION

When we read the post-resurrection accounts of Jesus' life, we see that his glorified body is able to navigate the ravages of a world still under the curse of sin. Jesus eats our food, travels our roads, speaks with befuddled eyewitnesses of his death and resurrection, passes through closed doors, transports himself effortlessly from one location to another, and finally launches from the Mount of Olives into heaven.

Our resurrected bodies are destined to have many of the same capabilities. Yet there's still something missing in God's redemptive work. The world in which we live is still fallen, a reminder of the full effects of sin. So, a day is coming when our sovereign Lord reverses the curse and makes all things new (Rev. 21:5).

Jesus refers to this as "the renewal of all things, when the Son of Man sits on his glorious throne" (Matt. 19:28). Peter urges us to wait for "new heavens and a new earth, where righteousness dwells" (2 Pet. 3:13). And in his vision of the world to come, John says he sees "a new heaven and a new earth; for the first heaven and the first earth had passed away, and the sea was no more" (Rev. 21:1). These passages refer to the future glorification of the created order, a world purged of sin and its stain, where the pristine innocence of all creation is restored.

Salvation is God's work of conquering Satan, sin, and death. It stands to reason that he not only purges our bodies of the effects of the Fall; he also purifies the cosmos under sin's curse. Because people are stewards of the creation, Adam's sin reaps devastating consequences for himself, his progeny, and the world in which we now live.

The Lord spells out the curse in Genesis 3:14-19. The serpent, once a glorious herald of God's goodness, is consigned to "eat dust" in the underworld beneath man's feet. Satan's offspring are at odds with the children of God. Satan himself is to bite the heel of a future redeemer, who in turn crushes the evil one's head. The pains of childbirth intensify. Conflict arises between husband and wife – and by extension, between men and women. The fruit of the earth is harvested with great difficulty as thorns and thistles arise. Work becomes laborious. And death is inevitable, for man is dust, and to dust he returns.

Since that fateful day in Eden, sin has ruined everything. Adam and Eve's first child – perhaps thought to be the promised redeemer of Genesis 3:15 – turns out to be a murderer. Men begin taking multiple wives and boasting of tribal violence. Humans become so corrupt that God destroys all but one family in a global flood. Then, survivors build a lofty tower at Babel in naked rebellion against God. The Egyptians enslave the Israelites for more than four hundred years, while the Lord delays giving his chosen people the Promised Land. Why the long wait? So the sins of the Amorites, who live in the land, reach full measure. After their release from captivity, the Israelites whine and rebel, and thus they are made to wander in the wilderness for forty years.

Once settled in the Promised Land, God's chosen people fail to completely purge it of wickedness. They demand a king, divide them-selves into two kingdoms, fall into idolatry and injustice, and are carried off into captivity – the northern kingdom to Assyria, the southern kingdom to Babylon. The *Shekinah* glory leaves the temple and never returns until God in human flesh, Jesus of Nazareth, appears and declares himself Messiah. Rather than being honored as king, he is betrayed and arrested, falsely tried, convicted, and hung naked on a Roman cross. Even after the Lord rises triumphantly from the dead and ascends into heaven, his followers are treated with the same disdain shown their Savior.

Along with this legacy of moral evil, let's not forget the parallel record of so-called natural evil: droughts, famines, floods, hurricanes, tornadoes, plagues, infestations, earthquakes, electrical storms, tsunamis, volcanoes, diseases, meteorites ... and on it goes.

No wonder Paul laments, "For we know that the whole creation has been groaning together with labor pains until now" (Rom. 8:22). But there's hope surrounding this verse:

> For I consider that the sufferings of this present time are not worth comparing with the glory that is going to be revealed in us. For the

creation eagerly waits with anticipation for God's sons to be revealed. For the creation was subjected to futility – not willingly, but because of him who subjected it – in the hope that the creation itself will also be set free from the bondage to decay in the glorious freedom of God's children.... Not only that, but we ourselves who have the Spirit as the firstfruits – we also groan within ourselves, eagerly waiting for adoption, the redemption of our bodies (Rom. 8:18-21, 23).

Just as Christians look forward to receiving glorified bodies, we delight in knowing that the corrupted world in which we live is going to be redeemed one day as well. Peter writes that it is going to happen like this:

But the day of the Lord will come like a thief; on that day the heavens will pass away with a loud noise, the elements will burn and be dissolved, and the earth and the works on it will be disclosed.... Because of that day, the heavens will be dissolved with fire and the elements will melt with heat. But based on his promise, we wait for new heavens and a new earth, where righteousness dwells (2 Pet. 3:10, 12-13).

John describes it this way:

Then I saw a new heaven and a new earth; for the first heaven and the first earth had passed away, and the sea was no more. I also saw the holy city, the new Jerusalem, coming down out of heaven from God, prepared like a bride adorned for her husband. Then I heard a loud voice from the throne: Look, God's dwelling is with humanity, and he will live with them. They will be his peoples, and God himself will be with them and will be their God. He will wipe away every tear from their eyes. Death will be no more; grief, crying, and pain will be no more, because the previous things have passed away (Rev. 21:1-4).

Millard Erickson writes:

Humanity's original dwelling was in the paradisiacal setting in the Garden of Eden; their final dwelling will also be in a perfect setting – the New Jerusalem. Part of the glorification of the human will be the provision of a perfect environment in which to dwell. It will be perfect for the glory of God will be present.[6]

After Christ returns, he resurrects and judges all people. He creates new heavens and a new earth, where the triune God resides forevermore with redeemed people. Our eternal home is earth the way God made it and intended it to be – sinless, perfect, and fruitful in the presence of his unveiled glory.

OUR ETERNAL HOME

Now, let's look at three New Testament passages that help us grasp the promise of our eternal home.

Matthew 19:28

Jesus said to them, "Truly I tell you, in the renewal of all things, when the Son of Man sits on his glorious throne, you who have followed me will also sit on twelve thrones, judging the twelve tribes of Israel."

This verse comes in the context of Jesus' instructions to his disciples about possessions and the kingdom of heaven. The disciples have just witnessed Jesus' encounter with the rich young ruler, whose love of wealth goads him to walk away from the Lord's invitation to eternal life (Matt. 19:16-22).

Jesus tells the disciples how hard it is for a rich person, like the young ruler, to enter the kingdom. Those who invest their lives and resources in the corrupt and fleeting domain of the evil one have no regard for the eternal king who offers them so much more.

Wealth itself is morally neutral. The Bible urges us to work hard, invest wisely, and enjoy the fruits of our labors. In that regard, wealth is a blessing. But it also may be a curse in that it becomes a barrier to those seeking to enter the kingdom of God. As R. C. Sproul notes, "Wealth can be a god, and as such it must be set aside if one is to follow God. This is no easy step."[7]

Since we're all worldly beings, made of dust and prone to embrace the creature comforts the evil one offers, the disciples ask in amazement, "Then who can be saved?" (Matt. 19:25). Perhaps this reflects the Jewish tradition that equates riches with God's blessing. If those viewed as most blessed by God are unlikely to make it, how does anyone else stand a chance?

Jesus responds, "With man this is impossible, but with God all things are possible" (Matt. 19:26). The Son of God left heaven and pitched his tent with us to show us there is a better kingdom than the one we now inhabit, and to present himself as the door into that kingdom. Salvation is totally of the Lord, and the Spirit is the one who regenerates hearts.

Peter says to Jesus, "See, we have left everything and followed you. So what will there be for us?" (Matt. 19:27). He seems to be asking how the disciples would be compensated for their voluntary poverty if wealthy people could enjoy their earthly riches and also be welcomed into the kingdom.

Jesus offers Peter a longer view – a glimpse of the world to come. There, Christ sits on his glorious throne, and the apostles – mostly blue-collar workers, not the world's rich and famous – sit on thrones as well, ruling over the twelve tribes of Israel. This delayed reward in "the renewal of all things" is far better than the riches of this world (Matt. 19:28).

The word "renewal" (Gr. *paligenesia*) comes from two Greek words that together mean "new genesis" or "coming back from death to life."[8] This Greek noun appears only twice in the New Testament – Matthew 19:28 and Titus 3:5 – but the concept of regeneration goes beyond this single word, embracing the ideas of being "born again" (John 3:3; 1 Pet. 1:23), "born of the Spirit" (John 3:5), becoming a "new creation" (2 Cor. 5:17; Gal. 6:15), and experiencing a "new birth" (1 Pet. 1:3).

In Matthew 19:28, *palingenesia* refers to God's ultimate renovation of the cosmos, while in Titus 3:5, it speaks of the work of the Holy Spirit, bringing back to life a dead human spirit, "a radical change of heart and mind resulting in renewed devotion to God and Christ."[9]

So, when Jesus invites his disciples to look toward "the renewal of all things," they understand this in the context of their earthly experiences, not just their need of spiritual rebirth. Indeed, the Bible speaks comprehensively about God's work of redemption embracing not just the spiritual realm but the fallen physical world as well.

Randy Alcorn writes:

> God has his hands on the earth. He will not let go – even when it requires that his hands be pierced by nails. But his incarnation and those nails secured him to Earth and its eternal future. In a redemptive work far larger than most imagine, Christ bought and paid for our future and the earth's.[10]

A couple of final observations before moving on. Jesus tells the apostles that "everyone who has left houses or brothers or sisters or father or mother or children or fields because of my name will receive a hundred times more and will inherit eternal life" (Matt. 19:29). This promised hundred-fold reward assures all followers of Jesus that he compensates us for temporal loss with everlasting gain – and with compounding interest that grows without end.

Jesus then remarks: "But many who are first will be last, and the last first" (Matt. 19:30). In the renewal of all things, many of the world's great men and women – the wealthy, powerful, influential, and elite, including the rich young ruler and the unbelieving religious leaders Jesus encounters – will find themselves "last." They will discover they are judged and excluded from the kingdom of heaven.

Meanwhile, the "last" of this world – the shunned and dispossessed who have followed Christ – are honored and invited to feast at the Lamb's banquet table. Like those at Jesus' right hand in the parable of the sheep and goats, they hear their master say, "Come, you who are blessed by my Father; inherit the kingdom prepared for you from the foundation of the world" (Matt. 25:34).

2 Peter 3:10-13

> But the day of the Lord will come like a thief; on that day the heavens will pass away with a loud noise, the elements will burn and be dissolved, and the earth and the works on it will be disclosed. Since all these things are to be dissolved in this way, it is clear what sort of people you should be in holy conduct and godliness as you wait for the day of God and hasten its coming. Because of that day, the heavens will be dissolved with fire and the elements will melt with heat. But based on his promise, we wait for new heavens and a new earth, where righteousness dwells.

Before Jesus introduces us to new heavens and a new earth, he must first deal with the sinful corruption of the universe as we know it. This "day of the Lord" comes suddenly and unexpectedly, the way a thief uses the element of surprise to plunder the goods of unsuspecting victims. But, once that day comes, the Lord introduces it with great fanfare.

Jesus declares, "Heaven and earth will pass away" (Matt. 24:35). The writer of Hebrews picks up Old Testament language that describes heaven and earth wearing out like clothing (Heb. 1:11; cf. Ps. 102:26; Isa. 51:6). And the prophet Isaiah offers a similar view: "All the stars in the sky will dissolve. The sky will roll up like a scroll, and its stars will all wither as leaves wither on the vine, and foliage on the fig tree" (Isa. 34:4).

The heaven and earth to which biblical writers refer are the entire created order: the earth, the sky, and space, but not God's throne in heaven, for sinless perfection always has reigned there. The Hebrew has no word for "universe," so the phrase "heaven and earth" are meant to depict the full physical realm.

But do the fires of judgment annihilate or refine? This is a key question about which Bible commentators disagree. And it's a question that's central to our understanding of 2 Peter 3:10-13 and John's vision of "a new heaven and a new earth; for the first heaven and the first earth had passed away" (Rev. 21:1).

Some notable commentators see the fleeing of earth and heaven as the *uncreation* of the universe. They believe earth and heaven are not refashioned; they go completely out of existence. That's why John writes that "no place was found for them" (Rev. 20:11). This view is known as the *annihilation and replacement* model.

"This is nothing less than the sudden, violent termination of the universe," writes John MacArthur.[11] American theologian Donald Barnhouse comments:

> There is to be an end of the material heavens and earth which we know. It is not that they are to be purified and rehabilitated, but that the reverse of creation is to take place. They are to be uncreated. As they came from nothing at the word of God, they are to be sucked back into nothingness by the same word of God.[12]

But is this the case? Does the universe, which Christ spoke into existence out of nothing and declared "very good indeed," truly return to nothingness? Many Bible commentators argue against the annihilation and replacement model in favor of the so-called *renewal* position.[13] Consider the following arguments against annihilation of the physical realm and in favor of restoration at Christ's return.

First, Jesus speaks of this event as "the renewal of all things" (Matt. 19:28), not the annihilation and replacement of all things.

Second, the words Jesus, Peter, and John use to describe this event do not mean heaven and earth vanish into nothingness. We examine Peter's use of "pass away," dissolved," and "disclosed" in more detail shortly. Meanwhile, we've already noted that Peter and John's use of "new" is the Greek *kainos*, which means new in quality, not recreated *ex nihilo*.

Third, the annihilation of the present heavens and earth would run contrary to God's promise to restore the cosmos. The flood of

Genesis 9 shows the earth completely covered with water but not uncreated. In a similar way, Peter compares the destruction of the present heaven and earth by fire with the destruction of the earth by water in Noah's day (see 2 Pet. 3:5-7).

Fourth, annihilation of the cosmos would cast doubt on Christ's work of redemption, which necessarily includes the cosmos. After dying for our sins, Jesus rises physically from the dead as the "first-fruits" of all believers who have died (1 Cor. 15:20). While Christ's glorified body is a significant improvement over his pre-passion body, it is still *his* body, which the Father renovates in resurrection.

So, we should not think God's work of salvation removes all traces of our existence. Paul certainly doesn't teach this (see 1 Cor. 15). There must be continuity between the old and the new. While our resurrected bodies are meant to last forever in a glorified state, we retain our unique identities, personalities, and interests – only, they are purged of sin's stain. The same holds true for the fallen world in which we live. In the *palingenesia*, trees, hills, and birds retain their properties, yet they are restored to mint condition.

Fifth, annihilation implies that God's good creation is not fixable. Although God declares his entire creation "very good indeed" (Gen. 1:31), he allows rebellious angels and wicked people to poison it. But God has abandoned neither his creatures nor their environment. He enters the physical realm as the God-Man, lives among us, and redeems us. Satan does not get the last word in the destiny of the cosmos.

When people trust in Christ and become new creations (2 Cor. 5:17), they do not cease to exist momentarily and then emerge as different persons with new DNA; rather, they are transformed qualitatively as the indwelling Spirit gives them new desires, perspectives, and outlooks.

Sixth, to annihilate the present heavens and earth and start over from scratch would cede ground to Satan. In effect, the Lord would be compromising with the evil one. Sure, Satan would spend eternity in hell, along with fallen angels and rebellious humans. But it would be a partial victory for the father of lies in that he was able to permanently undermine God's good creation.

These are important truths to keep in mind. In Randy Alcorn's seminal book, *Heaven*, he points out that God has never given up on his original creation. Yet, somehow, we've managed to overlook an entire biblical vocabulary that makes this point clear.

Alcorn invites us to consider the words "reconcile," "redeem," "restore," "recover," "return," "renew," "regenerate," and "resurrect." Each of these biblical words begins with re-, corresponding to the Greek prefix *ana*. In each case, the prefix suggests a return to an original condition that was ruined or lost.

For example, "reconciliation" means the restoration of a prior friendship or unity. "Renewal" means to make new again, restoring to an original state. And "resurrection" means becoming physically alive again, after death has occurred. As Alcorn notes, "God is the ultimate salvage artist. He loves to restore things to their original condition – and make them even better."[14]

Theologian Albert Wolters makes a fascinating observation:

> … all of Jesus' miracles (with the one exception of the cursing of the fig tree) are miracles of *restoration* – restoration to health, restoration to life, restoration to freedom from demonic possession. Jesus' miracles provide us with a sample of the meaning of redemption: a freeing of creation from the shackles of sin and evil and a reinstatement of creaturely living as intended by God.[15]

To summarize, Peter is not arguing in favor of the annihilation of the universe at Christ's return. He's saying the fires of judgment are intended to remove the dross from a fallen world and purify what remains. In a similar way, we must remember that salvation is holistic; it's intended for the full human being – body, soul, and spirit. God is not going to uncreate what he created and called "very good." He's going to redeem believing humans and restore our sin-wrecked environment.

With that in mind, let's explore key words and phrases Peter uses in this passage.

The heavens will pass away with a loud noise (2 Pet. 3:10). The phrase "the heavens," here and in verse 12, refers to the atmospheric and interstellar realms – the physical space in which earth hangs and moves. To "pass away" comes from the Greek *parerchomai*. While it may mean to "pass by," "neglect," or even "come near," in this context it means "to perish."[16] This does not imply the uncreation of the physical world, as we noted earlier. Rather, it means the Lord purges the physical realm in such a way as to remove the last vestiges of sin. Put another way, the world as we know it today is forever changed for the better.

The words "loud noise" come from the Greek *rhoizedon*. In classical Greek, it depicts the whistling of an arrow; the sound of a shepherd's pipe; the rush of wings; the splash of water; the hissing of a serpent; even the sound of filing.[17]

This is a day Jesus describes in the Olivet Discourse (see Matt. 24:35). It's going to be a noisy day, accompanied by the whooshing, crackling, rumbling sounds of a raging wildfire that consumes physical materials and even the air surrounding them. Some commentators believe the "loud noise" depicts the archangel's voice and the trumpet of God that accompany Christ's return (see 1 Thess. 4:16).

The elements will burn and be dissolved (2 Pet. 3:10), and *the elements will melt with heat* (v. 12). The Greek word for "elements" is *stoicheia* and literally means "ones in a row," as in letters of the alphabet or numbers in a sequence. In this context, it likely refers to the basic components that make up the universe, including air, earth, fire, and water.[18] However, some interpreters see the *elements* in this passage as the sky and heavenly bodies orbiting in outer space, or as the destruction of rebellious angelic forces.

The word translated "dissolved" is used several times in these verses (2 Pet. 3:10, 11, 12). It comes from the Greek root *lyo* and generally means to loosen or free any person or thing tied or fastened; to loosen one bound; or to loosen, undo, or dissolve anything bound, tied, or compacted together.[19] In the application of these three verses,

Peter is describing the unraveling of the world's physical elements, perhaps even at the atomic level that binds them together, setting the stage for Christ to refashion them into new heavens and a new earth.

Note how Peter writes "the elements will burn and be dissolved" (2 Pet. 3:10); "all these things are to be dissolved in this way" (v. 11); and "the heavens will be dissolved with fire" (v. 12). This dissolution seems to involve the whole physical universe. Paul writes that Christ holds all things together (Col. 1:17). So, it makes sense that when he creates new heavens and a new earth, Jesus first loosens the bonds of creation, purges them of the stain of sin right down to the atomic level, and then refashions the universe in pristine perfection.

The earth and the works on it will be disclosed (2 Pet. 3:10). Due to ancient manuscript variations, English translations of the New Testament render the Greek *heyrisko* in various ways: "disclosed" (CSB); "laid bare" (NIV); "exposed" (ESV); and "burned up" (KJV; NASB 1995). In context, "disclosed" or one of its synonyms is preferable to "burned up." As Peter Davids points out, "The picture is indeed that of stripping off everything that stands between the eye of God and the earth."[20]

This appears to be God's goal in bringing the fires of judgment. He consumes the dross of human activities that for centuries has hardened into an impermeable shell between sinful people and the unblinking eye of God, who is "a consuming fire" (Heb. 12:29). This exposure by fire calls to mind the flood in Noah's day. It engulfs the whole earth, involves both the heavens and what lies beneath the earth's crust, exposes human and angelic rebellion, and makes way for a fresh start.

The difference is that the fires of judgment on the day of the Lord result in a *permanent* renovation of the created order. Satan, *hades*, and death are banished to the lake of fire, along with all those who stubbornly reject the gracious ark of God's salvation and prefer to sink into the stormy seas of hell.

But based on his promise, we wait for new heavens and a new earth, where righteousness dwells (2 Pet. 3:13). Followers of Jesus should eagerly anticipate the day of the Lord, for it brings vindication. The promise in the Garden of Eden of a virgin-born redeemer (Gen. 3:15); the promise of a Suffering Servant who takes away our sins (Isa. 53); the promise of a Davidic king who rules the world in righteousness (Ps. 2; 89; 110; 132; Isa. 9:6-7; 11:1-5; Jer. 23:5-6; 33:14-26; Ezek. 34:23-31; 37:24-28; Amos 9:11-13; Mic. 5:2-6; Zech. 9:9-10; Matt. 2:1-12); the promise of a returning Savior to set things right (John 14:3; Rev. 22:12); and the promise of all things being made new (Isa. 65:17-25; Rev. 21:5) – these are completely fulfilled with the destruction of the fallen world and the introduction of new heavens and a new earth.

God's goal isn't limited to the demolition of evil. His promise to us is not only to remove evil, but to reward and honor his followers, even making us partakers of the divine nature (2 Pet. 1:4). The promise of new heavens and a new earth is revealed in Isaiah 65:17 ("For I will create new heavens and a new earth") and Isaiah 66:22 ("For just as the new heavens and the new earth, which I will make, will remain before me — this is the LORD's declaration — so your offspring and your name will remain").

Evil has so permeated God's good creation that a radical renewal is necessary. Paul looks forward to this in Romans 8:21: "the creation itself will also be set free from the bondage to decay into the glorious freedom of God's children." The renewed creation is not a place where God's will is *sometimes* evident, but where it's *always* manifest (see Matt. 6:10).

It's not that we don't look forward to the return of Christ; it's that we don't look forward to it as often or as intently as we should. Peter exhorts us to fix our gaze on the return of Christ, the banishment of evil, and the restoration of Eden as the intersection between the throne of God and the land of his loyal subjects.

Righteousness dwells in the new heavens and earth. The righteousness of Christ, the eternal Son of God, is ever-present because the "sun of righteousness" dwells with us (Mal. 4:2). He is our righteousness, and all thoughts of human good melt away in his presence. All that is unrighteous, unholy, and ungodly is banished to the lake of fire. Satan, demons, and all unbelievers get what they've always wanted: the opportunity to exist apart from the grace of God. It is existence but not life. It is darkness, fire, and never-ending suffering as those separated from God agonize over their decision to be their own gods.

Meanwhile, those Christ has redeemed not only enjoy eternity with the righteous one; they actually *become* righteous. Believing sinners are declared in right standing before God in his work of *justification*. In *sanctification*, the indwelling Holy Spirit works tirelessly to conform us to the image of Christ. But it's not until *glorification* – our physical resurrection and receipt of an incorruptible body untainted by sin – that we actually become "the righteousness of God" (2 Cor. 5:21). Indeed, righteousness – true righteousness – dwells in the new heavens and new earth, which John sees in some detail in his visions from Patmos.

Revelation 21-22

The final chapters of Scripture offer details about what Jesus describes as "the renewal of all things" (Matt. 19:28) and what Peter portrays as "new heavens and a new earth" (2 Pet. 3:13). Volumes have been written on Revelation 21-22. Space does not permit a full exploration here. So, let's consider just three components of our future life in the new heavens and new earth: the descent of New Jerusalem; the lifting of the curse; and the restoration of Eden.

The descent of New Jerusalem

In the opening musical theme of the 1960s sitcom *Green Acres*, Oliver Wendell Douglas, the attorney-cum-farmer who compels his wife to move with him from New York to Hooterville, declares:

Green Acres is the place to be
Farm livin' is the life for me
Land stretchin' out so far and wide
Keep Manhattan, just give me that countryside

Douglas' wife, Lisa, is not convinced:

New York is where I'd rather stay
I get allergic smelling hay
I just adore a penthouse view
Dahling I love you but give me Park Avenue[21]

Whether we enjoy the bustling streets of major cities or the deafening silence of a solitary life off the grid, Christians are born again to be city folks. That's because God is preparing a massive city in heaven that descends to earth one day and welcomes all of us to its streets of gold.

John introduces us to New Jerusalem:

Then I saw a new heaven and a new earth; for the first heaven and the first earth had passed away, and the sea was no more. I also saw the holy city, the new Jerusalem, coming down out of heaven from God, prepared like a bride adorned for her husband (Rev. 21:1-2).

Much of Revelation 21:1 – 22:5 offers a virtual tour of our future home. This massive metroplex – a cube[22] covering 1,400 miles in height, width, and depth – is the same shape as the holy of holies in the ancient tabernacle and temple. It serves as the place where God's name, that is, his very presence, resides.

Unlike the holy of holies, however, there is no veil in New Jerusalem separating the divine presence from human mediators, who are required to enter with atoning blood to cover their sins, and then the sins of the people. Christ, the one mediator between God and people (1 Tim. 2:5), passed through the veil in heaven with his own blood to take away our sins and offer direct access to the Father. As the writer of Hebrews notes:

Therefore, brothers and sisters, since we have boldness to enter the sanctuary through the blood of Jesus — he has inaugurated for us a new and living way through the curtain (that is, through his flesh) —

and since we have a great high priest over the house of God, let us draw near with a true heart in full assurance of faith, with our hearts sprinkled clean from an evil conscience and our bodies washed in pure water. Let us hold on to the confession of our hope without wavering, since he who promised is faithful (Heb. 10:19-23).

What Christians experience now in the spiritual realm – intimacy with God through worship, Bible reading, and prayer – gives way to a fuller expression of true life as we encounter God face-to-face in our glorified bodies. We truly see God as he is, and become like him (1 John 3:2). This is how God created people in the beginning and intended them to be. Adam's fall resulted in banishment from Eden and the withdrawal of God's paradise. But New Jerusalem is God's final answer to sin, Satan, and death. Yahweh once again resides with us, and we are invited to join him in everlasting life as he designed it and always envisioned it to be.

Note some key features of New Jerusalem.

New Jerusalem is a holy city (Rev. 21:2, 10). Humans have built many great cities over the centuries, from ancient Babylon to modern-day Tokyo. But New Jerusalem is unique in that it is a city built without hands. The writer of Hebrews tells us Abraham saw New Jerusalem from afar. He may have lived in tents as a foreigner in the Promised Land, but "he was looking forward to the city that has foundations, whose architect and builder is God" (Heb. 11:10).

New Jerusalem is a holy city because it is the city of God. It is his home, his dwelling place, and he invites us to live there forever with him. It is a holy place because God is holy – set apart, unique, perfect, and righteous. God's *otherness* sets him apart from all creatures. He is eternal, all-knowing, all-powerful, everywhere present, unchanging, and transcendent. Wherever God visits creation, that place is holy ground, as Moses and Joshua experienced (Exod. 3:5; Josh. 5:15).

In our future resurrection and glorification, we are fully conformed to the image of Christ. We are perfected in body, soul, and spirit, prepared to take up everlasting residence in the city of God, and fulfilling what Peter could only exhort us to do: "... do not be conformed to the desires of your former ignorance. But as the one who called you is holy, you also are to be holy in all your conduct; for it is written, **Be holy, because I am holy**" (1 Pet. 1:14-16; cf. Lev. 11:44).

New Jerusalem comes down out of heaven from God (Rev. 21:2, 10). The Bible describes the third heaven – beyond the atmosphere and outer space – as God's dwelling place, where he rules from his throne. Sometimes, he grants sinful humans a glimpse into the throne room.

The prophet Isaiah is given a vision of the Lord, who is seated on a high and lofty throne. Seraphim declare his superlative holiness – "Holy, holy, holy is the LORD of Armies." The foundations shake, the heavenly temple is filled with smoke, and all the prophet can cry is, "Woe is me, for I am ruined" (Isa. 6:1-5).

Paul is "caught up" to the third heaven, where he hears "inexpressible words, which a human being is not allowed to speak." The "extraordinary revelations" are so otherworldly, Paul writes that "a thorn in the flesh was given to me, a messenger of Satan to torment me so that I would not exalt myself" (2 Cor. 12:2-10).

Of course, John provides us with the most detailed view into paradise. One vision features the Lord on his throne; twenty-four robed elders on thrones of their own; the seven-fold Spirit of God; a sea of glass; four living creatures who repeat the praise of Isaiah 6: "Holy, holy, holy;" the Lamb of God who is worthy to take the scroll from the one seated on the throne; an innumerable host of angels; and "every creature in heaven, on earth, under the earth, on the sea, and everything in them" declaring praise to the one seated on the throne, and to the Lamb (Rev. 4-5).

Now, near the end of John's visions, he sees the throne room of God – off-limits to sinful human beings since the Fall – *coming down* out of heaven (Rev. 21-22). Like Isaiah and Paul, John is overwhelmed. He falls down to worship at the feet of the angel who has shown him all of this, and he's immediately rebuked. "Don't do that!" the angel cries. "Worship God!" (22:8-9).

New Jerusalem comes down out of heaven because God's throne sits above and beyond the created order. It comes down because God is higher and holier than those created in his image. It comes down because God is restoring Eden, the intersection of the physical and spiritual realms. It comes down because God is gracious, merciful, and kind. He does all the work of creation, redemption, and restoration. He condescends to bring heaven down to earth for his glory and our everlasting enjoyment.

We should note that while God dwells with human beings on a new earth, he does not cease to reside in the third heaven at the same time. That is, heaven – the unseen realm where God abides – does not melt into the new earth, sky, and space. God is omnipresent. He cannot be confined to a single location although he may be fully present in any location.

We recall that Jesus' deity was not confined to his humanity, although the Son of Man was fully human. The *Shekinah* glory in the burning bush, the pillar, the chariot of fire, and the holy of holies represented the full presence of God, but not the complete presence of God. God also is transcendent, which means while he abides with us on the new earth, he continues to transcend the earthly sphere and reside in the unseen realm with angels, as he did before. This does not diminish his presence with us, and it should not cause us to doubt that we will enjoy God fully in our glorified states.

New Jerusalem is described as the bride, the wife of the Lamb (Rev. 21:2, 9). Old Testament writers sometimes liken Israel to the Lord's wife. Yahweh refers to himself as Israel's husband in order to communicate his special love for the nation. For example, the prophet Isaiah says to Judah, "Indeed, your husband is your Maker – his name is the LORD of Armies – and the Holy One of Israel is your Redeemer; he is called the God of the whole earth" (Isa. 54:5).

But the nation proves to be an unfaithful spouse, spiraling into spiritual adultery, forsaking the Lord and his commandments, and running into the arms of false gods. The northern kingdom of Israel is first, and the Lord sends her "a certificate of divorce" and sends her away – a reference to the Assyrian invasion (Jer. 3:8; cf. 2 Kings 17:5-7). Judah is next, unless she repents, Yahweh warns.

And yet, the Lord invites his people back: "Return, unfaithful

Israel. This is the LORD's declaration. I will not look on you with anger, for I am unfailing in my love.... I will not be angry forever" (Jer. 3:12). God promises to do what the Mosaic Law could never do: restore a broken marriage between a faithful husband and an unfaithful wife who has married another.

Another illustration of God's unfathomable goodness is found in the story of the prophet Hosea, whom God commands to marry a prostitute. When she persists in immorality, the Lord directs Hosea to buy her back. Hosea's grace toward an unfaithful wife pictures God's grace toward rebellious people.

In the New Testament, Christ is the bridegroom, and the church is his bride. Jesus makes this clear in his teaching. For example, when the disciples of John the Baptist ask Jesus why his followers don't fast as they do, Jesus replies, "Can the wedding guests be sad while the groom is with them? The time will come when the groom will be taken away from them, and then they will fast" (Matt. 9:15).

Jesus' parables of the wedding banquet and the ten virgins also reveal truths about the special relationship between Christ and his followers (Matt. 22:1-14; 25:1-13). Even John the Baptist understands the role of Messiah as bridegroom to his church: "He who has the bride is the groom. But the groom's friend [John], who stands by and listens for him, rejoices greatly at the groom's voice. So this joy of mine is complete. He must increase, but I must decrease" (John 3:29-30).

Paul further touches on this truth: "For I am jealous for you with a godly jealousy, because I have promised you in marriage to one husband – to present a pure virgin to Christ" (2 Cor. 11:2).

So, if *true* Israel – comprised of Old and New Covenant believers – is the virgin bride and faithful wife of the Lamb, in what way is it connected to New Jerusalem in Revelation 21? The city is pictured as a bride because it houses the redeemed and takes on their character. Old and New Covenant believers are fully conformed to the image of Christ. That is, they see Jesus as he is and become like him (1 John 3:2).

Jesus promises to prepare a place for us in heaven (John 14:3). He further promises that wherever he lives, we also will live (John 14:19). We enter heaven disembodied in the intermediate stage between physical death and resurrection. But now, in Revelation 21, the redeemed in heaven are resurrected and glorified saints. We are perfected in holiness and ready to descend from heaven with our bridegroom. The marriage supper of the Lamb has taken place in heaven (Rev. 19:7-9), and now the groom and his bride are presented as entering their eternal state in the celestial city that comes down from God out of heaven.

Some commentators believe the church, or a single body of Old and New Covenant saints, constitutes New Jerusalem, and therefore we are to read Revelation 21 symbolically. Proponents of this view cite 1 Corinthians 3:16, in which Paul reminds us that our bodies are temples of the Holy Spirit. Peter also describes Christians as living stones, being built into a spiritual house for a holy priesthood to offer spiritual sacrifices unto God, with Jesus as the chosen and honored cornerstone (1 Pet. 2:4-6).

So, it may be possible that glorified saints of all time provide the perfect habitation for Christ as he descends to earth and dwells among his people. Just as a bridegroom leaves his father's home and establishes a new home with his bride, Jesus one day descends from heaven to earth with the redeemed and fully establishes his kingdom on earth, with God's people providing a pure and everlasting habitation for their Savior.

If we embrace this view, we should be careful not to take the symbolism too far. Jesus is not leaving the Father and the Holy Spirit behind in heaven when he creates new heavens and a new earth. The triune Godhead inhabits the throne room in heaven today, and no doubt the three persons of the Trinity are the ruling dignitaries in Eden restored.

With all that Scripture says about New Jerusalem, it's best to understand the city both as a literal metropolis and as a reference to the people of God. As Alan Gomes points out:

So, the NJ [New Jerusalem] refers to the people in [Rev.] 21:9-10, when the angel shows John the NJ as a bride. But it is a place in 21:3, which speaks of God as dwelling there; in 21:24, 26, when people "inherit" it; and in 21:24, 26, when the text describes the nations as entering it.[23]

New Jerusalem is arrayed with God's glory. John writes of New Jerusalem, "Her radiance was like a precious jewel, like a jasper stone, clear as crystal" (21:11). The most significant quality of New Jerusalem is stated at the outset: it is the radiance of God, the sign of his visible presence.

As in the burning bush, the pillar of cloud and fire, the *Shekinah* glory in the holy of holies, and the brilliance of Jesus' presence on the mount of transfiguration, God is light, and in him there is no darkness at all (1 John 1:5). Isaiah foretells the work of the divine warrior who penetrates the earth's spiritual darkness (Isa. 59:17-21). As a result, Isaiah exults, "Arise, shine, for your light has come, and the glory of the LORD shines over you" (Isa. 60:1).

In a similar fashion, Ezekiel sees the glory of God returning through the eastern gate of the temple, from which the glory had earlier departed. He describes it in these terms: "I saw the glory of the God of Israel coming from the east. His voice sounded like the roar of a huge torrent, and the earth shone with his glory" (Ezek. 43:2).

God's glory always is depicted as radiant. John seems to pick up on the prophecies of Isaiah and Ezekiel and apply them to their ultimate fulfillment in the glorious return of Christ with his saints. Further, he compares the light proceeding from God to that of the jasper jewel.

In Revelation 4:2-3, John sees a throne set in heaven. The one seated on the throne looks like a jasper and carnelian stone. And now, in Revelation 21:11, the bride has a similar radiance. What could be more perfect than the glory of God shining through his people?

Charles Swindoll writes that when John compares the brilliant glory of God to a jasper stone – the Greek word is *iaspis* – he probably doesn't mean the modern stone that comes in a variety of colors, but rather an unblemished, perfectly clear diamond that refracts the blazing glory of God. "Nothing on earth begins to compare to what God has prepared for us, since any choice of words fails to capture the breathtaking intensity of His glory."[24]

New Jerusalem is a vast cube-shaped structure in which the number twelve plays a prominent role and ornamentation is abundant (Rev. 21:12-21). In these verses, John describes the exterior of New Jerusalem, turning to the interior in verses 22-27. The city is laid out in a cube. Its length, width, and height are 12,000 stadia, or about 1,400 miles, in each direction. The wall surrounding the city is 144 cubits, or more than two hundred feet, thick.

Bible commentators are divided as to whether these dimensions are to be understood literally or figuratively. Those who argue for a symbolic representation point out that the repeated use of the number twelve depicts the majesty, vastness, and perfection of the Lamb's bride, not physical dimensions.

However, a literal understanding should not be rejected. Christ is returning to earth personally and physically. He is creating new heavens and a new earth – real places. And he has promised to bring us back with him – in glorified bodies, no less. The totally refurbished heavens and earth may easily accommodate a city housing billions of people and spanning a space roughly equivalent to the eastern half of the United States.

It's important to note the cube shape of the city, which corresponds to the holy of holies in the temple. Since John sees no temple in the city (Rev. 21:22), we may infer that the whole city is the temple, or more specifically, the true holy of holies, where the triune Godhead resides in undiminished glory. Just as our bodies are temples of the Holy Spirit now (1 Cor. 3:16), New Jerusalem – the bride of the Lamb – is corporately the spiritual household built up for God's habitation with redeemed people (see Eph. 2:19-22; 1 Tim. 3:15; Heb. 3:6; 1 Pet. 2:4-5).

The ancient cities of Babylon and Nineveh were designed in the shape of a square. They had substantial length and width but lacked equivalent height. But the city of God surpasses these human endeavors in its harmony, being cube-shaped, which in the ancient world symbolized supreme completeness. The immensity of New Jerusalem dwarfs the greatest man-made cities of human history.

The number twelve figures prominently in John's description of the city. The walls have twelve gates. Twelve angels are at the gates. The names of the twelve tribes of Israel are inscribed on the gates. The city has twelve foundations, bearing the names of the twelve apostles. New Jerusalem measures 12,000 stadia in length, width, and height. The walls are 144 cubits thick – twelve by twelve cubits. And the gates consist of twelve massive pearls. So, what's the significance of the number twelve?

The number twelve appears 187 times in God's word, twenty-two times in the Book of Revelation.[25] It's considered a perfect number in that it symbolizes God's authority. The number twelve also depicts completeness, or the nation of Israel as a whole. For example, Jacob (Israel) has twelve sons who father the twelve tribes of the nation. This is important because if New Jerusalem in fact comprises the whole people of God under the Old and New Covenants, then we have in this heavenly city the *true Israel* to which the New Testament writers point.

It may help to note a few other places in Scripture where the number twelve is featured. In Leviticus 24, God specifies that twelve unleavened cakes of bread be placed every week in the temple. In the Gospels, Jesus selects twelve men as apostles; these men (with the apostles choosing Matthias to replace Judas Iscariot) carry on his authority after his ascension and bear witness of his finished work of redemption. In Revelation 7, we see 144,000 (12 x 12 x 1000) sealed servants of God, and in Revelation 14 these same servants appear on the heavenly Mount Zion with the Lamb.

Other examples could be listed, but the point is that the Lord uses this number throughout the Bible to indicate perfection, completeness, and authority. So, the extensive use of the number twelve in Revelation 21 seems to illustrate that New Jerusalem represents *true Israel*, or the redeemed people of God throughout human history. The redeemed form a massive holy of holies for God, whose radiance shines through them. This stands in contrast with the ancient tabernacle and temple, where the *Shekinah* glory, depicting the presence of God, is confined to the innermost sanctuary and rarely seen by his people.

Lastly, a few words about the city's ornamentation. John writes, "The building material of its wall was jasper, and the city was pure gold clear as glass" (Rev. 21:18). This image of transparent purity is echoed throughout Scripture to describe the refined character of God's sanctified people (e.g., Job 23:10; Zech. 13:9; Mal. 3:3; 1 Pet. 1:7; Rev. 3:18).

The twelve gems adorning the city's foundations (Rev. 21:19-20) call to mind the twelve precious stones the high priest wears on his breastplate, although the match is not identical (see Exod. 28:15-21). Steve Gregg writes, "Since these same stones bear the names of the twelve apostles, it could be understood as a statement about the leadership of the people of God having transferred from the high priesthood of the temple to the apostles of the church."[26]

Charles Swindoll notes four characteristics of the materials used to adorn the city.

First, "every kind of jewel" (Rev. 21:19) may symbolize the great diversity of people who dwell in the city. After all, Jesus' blood has purchased people from "every tribe and language and people and nation" (Rev. 5:9).

Second, the transparent nature of the city's walls contrast the solid and secret nature of physical barriers sinful and fallen people employ today to hide their sins and keep others at a distance.

Third, the gates leading into the city are each created from one giant pearl. The pearl is a gem formed within the oyster – the only organically produced precious stone John lists in this passage. Thus, the pearl symbolizes pain resulting in beauty – a perfect depiction of Christ, whose suffering had an eternal purpose and opened heaven for us (see John 10:9; 14:6).

Fourth, the gold streets of the city reveal an opulence that surpasses even the marble-paved streets of Ephesus, where John lived out his days. Swindoll writes, "Gold, for which countless criminals have killed, will be tread upon like asphalt. No vanity. No materialism.

No envy or greed. Best of all, no one will be poor in a place that paves its streets with gold."[27]

New Jerusalem lacks a temple, stellar lights, a closing time, and anything unclean (Rev. 21:22-27). After a detailed description of New Jerusalem's exterior, John turns his attention inside the city walls. He notes first of all the absence of a temple "because the Lord God the Almighty and the Lamb are its temple" (v. 22).

Historical Jerusalem is known as the city of God because his presence resides there in the temple (1 Kings 8:10-13). The people of God approach him through a mediator, a high priest who offers atoning sacrifices for the peoples' sins in the holy of holies on the Day of Atonement.

The atoning blood is carried through a thick veil and sprinkled on the mercy seat, above which the *Shekinah* glory blazes. There, the wrath of God is satisfied and his mercy is extended to sinful creatures. All of this activity inside the cube-shaped holy of holies bears forward-looking significance. The day is coming when God himself provides a sacrifice – the Lamb of God who takes away the sin of the world (John 1:29).

When Jesus dies on the cross, the veil of the temple tears in two, from top to bottom, signifying that Jesus has fulfilled the types and shadows of the Old Covenant and now makes way for the New Covenant in his blood. The redeemed now have direct access to the throne of God without the need for a human mediator. John captures the richness of this imagery as he gazes inside New Jerusalem. The Father and the Lamb *are* the temple.

The apostle further observes that the city does not need the sun or moon to shine on it "because the glory of God illuminates it, and its lamp is the Lamb" (Rev. 21:23). The light of God is distinct and divine, without earthly origins or natural explanation. We catch a glimpse at times: in the burning bush (Exod. 3), the pillar of cloud and fire (Exod. 13:21-22), the blazing heavenly chariot-throne (Ezek. 1:26-28), on the mount of transfiguration and the road to Damascus (Matt. 17:1-9; Acts 9:1-9), and in the fiery eyes of the glorified Christ (Rev. 1:14).

Joseph Seiss sees God's glory enveloping New Jerusalem:

... like an unclouded halo, permeates it, and radiates through it and from it so that there is not a dark or obscure place about it.... It is the uncreated light of Him who is light, dispensed by and through the Lamb as the everlasting Lamp, to the home, and hearts, and under-standings, of his glorified saints.[28]

There's no closing time in New Jerusalem. No curfew. No curtain call. The city's massive gates never close because daylight is contin-uous and darkness is dispelled. The kings of the nations walk the streets, bathed in divine light and leading their people to pay homage to the King of kings.

There remain national and ethnic distinctions in the new heavens and earth as a tribute to the one who redeemed people out of every tribe, language, people, and nation (Rev. 5:9). Their kings seek no personal gain nor political leverage. At the same time, the nations do not hunger for expanded boundaries or elite status. Instead, they are fully devoted to the one who calls them fellow heirs of the unfolding new creation.

While New Jerusalem is the capital city of the new heavens and earth, it is not the *only* city on the restored planet. The fact that nations and kings come and go demonstrates this fact. We should not presume to exclude those dwelling outside the city as lesser citizens of New Jerusalem. Perhaps the rewards Christ has granted them in judg-ment include ruling over cities and nations in other parts of the new world (see Luke 19:11-27). In any case, the city's gates are always open to them.

But the open gates don't beckon everyone. "Nothing unclean will enter it," John writes, "nor anyone who does what is detestable or false, but only those written in the Lamb's book of life" (Rev. 21:27). The people of God – joined under the Old and New Covenants – are safe in the presence of the Father and the Lamb. Those who have rejected the gracious revelation of God in creation, conscience, the canon of Scripture, and Christ have found themselves before a great white throne without excuse (Rom. 1:20; Rev. 20:11-15).

The lost have made it clear they do not want a relationship with their creator; instead, they prefer to live now and forevermore independently of God. They have crossed a line and passed a point of no return, known only to God but hinted at in the Scriptures as their limit of sins (see 1 Thess. 2:16). And now, because they have refused the gracious invitation to have their names written in the Lamb's book of life, they find themselves in outer darkness.

Like the rich man Jesus describes in Luke 16:19-31, they see a "great chasm" between themselves and those resting comfortably at Abraham's side. And like the insolent guest at the wedding banquet in Jesus' parable in Matthew 22:1-14, they find themselves bound, taken from the king's presence, and cast into the darkness of never-ending night.

The gates of New Jerusalem are open, and it is daylight there forever. But unbelievers remain separated in outer darkness. Like the bound and bounced guest in Jesus' parable of the wedding banquet, perhaps they see the light from a distance, which makes their darkness more intense. Perhaps they hear the music of heaven's choir but are forbidden from singing along. Perhaps they smell the aroma of heaven's banquet table but can never taste its delicacies. The nearness, yet inaccessibility, of New Jerusalem twists the gut and makes the consequences of divine rejection a perpetual nightmare.

New Jerusalem features a river, a broad street, a tree, and a throne (Rev. 22:1-5). The first five verses of the final chapter of Revelation describe four prominent objects in New Jerusalem.

First, the river of living water. John describes the water as "clear as crystal, flowing from the throne of God and of the Lamb down the middle of the city's main street" (vv. 1-2). Just a few verses earlier, the one seated on the throne says, "I will freely give to the thirsty from the spring of the water of life" (Rev. 21:6).

This promise draws deeply from the Old and New Testaments and speaks of eternal life received by God's grace through faith. The Greek word *potamos* is translated "river," "flood," or "stream" and is used metaphorically in John 7:38 to describe the blessing of eternal satisfaction found in Christ.

The river John sees in Revelation 22 calls to mind the river in Eden (Gen. 2:10), as well as prophetic references to water flowing from the temple in Ezekiel 47 (see also Joel 3:18; Zech. 14:8). John borrows from this prophetic imagery and applies it to the restored Eden in the new heavens and earth. Perhaps most significant is John's observation that the river flows from the throne, indicating both its source and its power to slake our spiritual thirst forever.

While these waters may be understood literally, a more fitting understanding is that this river signifies the third person of the Trinity – the Holy Spirit, who authors the words of life in Scripture; regenerates the dead spirits of unbelievers and grants them faith to trust in Jesus; indwells, seals, baptizes, and guides believers, ensuring that these children of God grow to full maturity and attain glorification at the resurrection of the just.

Joseph Seiss writes that the river "is the Holy Ghost for that celestial Tabernacle, as God and the Lamb are the Temple of it. It is the divine emanation from the Father and the Son which fills and cheers and forever rejoices the dwellers in that place."[29]

Robert Mounce says the central affirmation in this passage is that "in the eternal state the faithful will live at the source of the life-giving stream that proceeds from the very presence of God. In the hot and arid climate of Palestine this figure would hold special appeal."[30]

The second object of note in John's vision is "the broad street of the city" (Rev. 22:2 HCSB). Revelation 21:21 tells us the street is pure gold, transparent as glass. The term "broad street" also may be translated "public square," indicating a place of gathering, fellowship, and worship. Perhaps this square is what John describes earlier as resembling "a sea of glass, similar to crystal" (Rev. 4:6).

In any case, this broad street or public square accommodates a large number of people, who stand before the throne of God and enjoy the pure refreshment of the Holy Spirit as he moves among them.

Note that the street is broad, airy, and inviting – an especially welcome respite from the persecution so many believers suffer on earth. Its location before the throne and alongside life-giving waters makes it an integral part of the new city. Its appearance as pure gold reflects the idea of purity, accessibility, and immense value. And its wide expanse stands in contrast to the narrow way by which it is accessed. Jesus tells us we enter the kingdom only through "the narrow gate" (Matt. 7:13-14), and then he reveals himself as that exclusive way (John 14:6). Only those who entrust their lives to Christ stand on the broad streets of the heavenly city.

The third object is the tree of life. We first read of the tree in the Garden of Eden (Gen. 2:9). Adam and Eve eat freely from this tree until they fall into sin. Then, they are banished from the garden. The Lord stations cherubim and "the flaming, whirling sword east of the Garden of Eden to guard the way to the tree of life" (Gen. 3:24). Having lost immortality and innocence, the first humans are barred from partaking of the tree and thus locking themselves into a never-ending fallen state. This reflects the mercy of God as well as his divine wrath.

Now, however, we see in Revelation 22 that access to the tree is restored. Immortality and innocence are returned to God's imagers.

The tree of life represents eternal life or immortality in both Genesis and Revelation. Non-biblical Jewish portrayals of paradise feature the tree of life, the fruit of which enables partakers to live forever (e.g., 2 Enoch 8:3-4). In the garden, after Adam and Eve disobey God, they are denied access to the tree of life and thus experience spiritual death (immediately), death of the soul (slowly and continuously), and physical death (ultimately). The sacrificial system God introduces after the Fall enables sinful people to experience atonement for their sins and retain fellowship with their creator – although it's not the intimate, face-to-face fellowship enjoyed in the garden (see Gen. 3:21; 4:3-5).

All of this points to the promised Lamb of God who, being hanged on a tree and becoming a curse for us, takes away our sins and enables us to enjoy an unbreakable, intimate, and everlasting covenant relationship with God. In Revelation 2:7, the Spirit tells the church at

Ephesus, and in effect all redeemed people, "I will give the right to eat from the tree of life, which is in the paradise of God." Eating is a key component in establishing a covenant, and perhaps the fruit of the tree of life is a constant reminder of God's faithfulness to his covenant promises.

John tells us the leaves of the tree of life are for "healing the nations" (Rev. 22:2). Perhaps the best way to understand this is that the leaves are always present on the tree, a reminder of God's faithfulness, or eternal life, and an assurance that the fruit is produced continuously. Leaves tells us a lot about the health of a tree, in addition to adding beauty and form. Further, as leaves are used today as nutrients, health supplements, and even medicines, the leaves of the tree of life assure us of continued physical and spiritual health throughout eternity.

The fourth object John sees in his vision is the throne of God and of the Lamb. The Book of Revelation mentions a heavenly throne about forty times, leading some commentators to conclude that there are many different thrones in heaven. For example, we see the high and lofty throne Isaiah encounters (Isa. 6:1ff); the judgment seat of Christ to which Paul refers (2 Cor. 5:10); the dazzling rainbow-shrouded throne John sees in Revelation 4-5; the great white throne (Rev. 20:11-15); and the throne of God and of the Lamb (Rev. 22:1-3). Other commentators see a single throne from which God rules during different phases of human history. The manner in which these thrones appear and are experienced reflects the purpose for which God meets with people.

In Revelation 22:1-3, John sees servants of God around the throne. These servants behold God's face, serve him in the never-ending light of his glorious presence, and reign with him forever. John also notes that these servants bear God's name on their foreheads, just as the 144,000 bear the name of Jesus and of the Father on their foreheads (Rev. 14:1). This likely does not mean God has physically branded his people. Rather, it seems to signify two truths: (1) God knows his people and has marked them by his Spirit as his own; and (2) God's

people know him and joyfully keep him forever at the forefront of
their minds.

Long ago, Fanny Crosby wrote a hymn entitled *My Savior First of
All*. Included are the following words, which describe the blessedness
believers experience when they pass through the portals of heaven:

> When my lifework is ended, and I cross the swelling tide,
> When the bright and glorious morning I shall see;
> I shall know my Redeemer when I reach the other side,
> And His smile will be the first to welcome me.

> Through the gates to the city in a robe of spotless white,
> He will lead me where no tears shall ever fall;
> In the glad song of ages I shall mingle with delight,
> But I long to meet my Savior first of all.[31]

The lifting of the curse

In the midst of John's blissful vision of the new heavens and earth,
he records these simple but profound words: "and there will no longer
be any curse" (Rev. 22:3). What's the curse to which John refers? And
who or what causes the curse to end?

John's reference to the curse takes us back to Genesis 3 and the
Fall. There, Adam's sin plunges all creation into a morass of death and
decay. John also whisks us through the pages of the Old Testament,
where we see the parallel tracks of sin's destruction and God's
promise of a virgin-born redeemer. And he reminds us of the New
Testament truth that Jesus of Nazareth burst onto the scene two thousand years ago, divinely conceived, perfect in humanity, and sent into
a world sagging beneath the weight of sin. The Messiah's sinless life
and finished work on the cross conquer Satan, sin, and death, and his
promise to return enables us to rest in the certainty that the curse
cannot last forever.

Now, John's vision of the new heavens and earth shows us in stunning detail that Christ has ended the curse and reversed the effects of

the Fall. Satan, evil spirits, and rebellious humans are banished to the lake of fire. The created order, which for centuries has groaned beneath the weight of sin (Rom. 8:22), is finally liberated. Sin and its stain are purged from the earth, sky, and space. And, true to his promise, Jesus makes everything new (Rev. 21:5).

To better understand the curse, we should go back to the beginning. After declaring all creation "very good indeed" (Gen. 1:31), the Lord lays everything before Adam and invites him to enjoy it. But the creator places one restriction on the new administrator of the earth: "You are free to eat from any tree of the garden, but you must not eat from the tree of the knowledge of good and evil, for on the day you eat from it, you will certainly die" (Gen. 2:16-17). Put another way, the Lord warns Adam of severe consequences for disobeying the creator – a curse, if you will.

Adam rejects God's counsel; he takes matters into his own hands. And the curse materializes – though subtly at first. Adam isn't struck dead, but he comes to understand he's a condemned man who died spiritually on the day he disobeyed God. He's in the process of dying in his conscious being (his soul). And, in the future, he will die physically, although hundreds of years later. Adam and Eve realize they're naked, which they've always known. But now they're ashamed, and they cover themselves. Next, they hide from God among the trees and talk to him from what they perceive to be a safe distance.

When the Lord questions them about their actions, Adam blames his wife and implicates the Lord himself: "The woman *you* gave to be with me – she gave me some fruit from the tree, and I ate" (Gen. 3:12, emphasis added). In a similar manner, Eve points to the one who conned her: "The serpent deceived me, and I ate" (Gen. 3:13).

The Lord turns first to the serpent and curses him. No longer free to move between the unseen realm and the Garden of Eden, the anointed guardian cherub (Ezek. 28:14) is sent to the underworld, where he's associated with death. We later learn that a special future home is prepared for him: hell (Matt. 25:41). Further, the Lord declares there is to be hostility between the evil one's children and

Eve's children, and that a special "offspring" of Eve will strike the head of Satan, although at great personal cost (Gen. 3:15).

For Adam and Eve, this must be good news. A future redeemer is coming to rescue them. This is the *protoevangelium* – the first gospel, the beginning of roughly four hundred prophecies and foreshadows of the coming Messiah. But until Eve's special descendent comes and sets things right, the curse remains on human beings and the created order. There is pain in childbearing for women, rancor in the marriage bond, a cursed ground that grudgingly yields food, exhausting labor required to eke out a living, and, ultimately, a return to the dust from which God made Adam.

Further, Adam may no longer eat freely from the tree of life. This appears to be an act of mercy on God's part, for partaking of the tree now presumably would have made Adam live forever in his sinful state (Gen. 3:22).

From Eden, the curse spreads outward. The first couple is exiled from the garden. The first son, perhaps thought to be the promised redeemer, turns out to be a murderous rebel, and one of his descendants becomes the first polygamist. The first case of sexual misconduct involving fallen angels results in a violent race of giants that persists until the days of King David.

Human wickedness is so widespread, and the Lord is so grieved, God sends a global flood in judgment. The survivors descend quickly into mischief, building a tower to span the gap between earth and God's throne, and engaging in perverse behavior that calls down fire and brimstone on their communities.

The Lord calls out a special people for his own and miraculously delivers them from bondage in Egypt, but they bring divine wrath on themselves and discredit him before the pagan nations around them. The *Shekinah* glory leaves the temple, never to return – until a virgin-born son, the fulfillment of the *protoevangelium*, is born in a village outside Jerusalem.

In the Incarnation, Christ comes as the last Adam, to set us free from the law of sin and death (Rom. 8:2). He unravels the damage the first Adam wrought (Rom. 5:15-19; 1 Cor. 15:22, 45). Through his sinless life, Jesus succeeds where Adam fails. Then, by way of the cross and the resurrection, Christ makes a way to restore fallen people to a right relationship with God, and to restore the Eden in which God and the first humans walked side-by-side in the cool of the evening.

But this great reversal comes at a price. As Paul writes, "Christ redeemed us from the curse of the law by becoming a curse for us, because it is written, Cursed is everyone who is hung on a tree" (Gal. 3:13; cf. Deut. 21:23). It is precisely because Jesus bears our sins on a tree – the cross – that access to the tree of life is restored to mankind. God the Father lays our curse on the shoulders of his Son. Jesus becomes a curse in our place. And because of this, innocence and immortality, which the tree of life provides, are restored as the curse of sin is lifted forever.

And so, Revelation 22:3 tells us "there will no longer be any curse." When Christ returns to set things right, he not only casts Satan into hell (Rev. 20:10; cf. Gen. 3:15); he reverses the curse that resulted from the sinister partnership between the serpent and earth's first human beings.

Adam and Eve are the only humans to experience the earth as God created it – pristine, perfect, very good indeed. They watch the earth – and themselves – shrivel beneath the curse, and every human being who has followed them has dragged the ball and chain of the curse behind them.

But God does not leave us helpless or hopeless. Even fallen people are created in the image of God. Even the cursed heavens and earth we inhabit bear testimony of a divine designer. And the promise of restored humanity and a renewed heaven and earth have their seeds in the Garden of Eden after the Fall: God is sending an offspring of Eve to crush the head of Satan, banish the curse, and restore the universe to sinless perfection.

The restoration of Eden

Old Testament scholar Sandra Richter writes:

[E]verything that lies in between Eden's gate and the New Jerusalem, the bulk of our Bibles, is in essence a huge rescue plan. In fact, we could summarize the plot line of the Bible into one cosmic question: "How do we get Adam back into the garden?" In Genesis 3, humanity was driven out; in Revelation 21-22, they are welcomed home.[32]

The Garden of Eden is a temple where humans enjoy face-to-face friendship with their creator. The Fall results in human banishment from Eden and a divinely prescribed distance between holy God and sinful people. Even Moses, the great lawgiver, is forbidden to see the face of God because God has declared, "No one may see me and live" (Exod. 33:20 NIV). Moses is allowed only to see God's back as he passes by (v. 23). In the ancient world, criminals are banished from the presence of the king and not allowed to see his face, an apt picture of our separation from God (Esth. 7:8; cf. 2 Sam. 14:24).

John asserts that no person has seen God at any time. Even so, Jesus has declared God as deity veiled in human flesh (John 1:18). Jesus teaches that only the pure in heart will see God (Matt. 5:8). So, consider the transformation that takes place when the redeemed in eternity see God face-to-face and become like him (1 John 3:2).

After the Fall, God provides a tabernacle, and then a temple, where he meets behind a veil with representatives of sinful humans. Ultimately, God himself tabernacles with us in the person of Jesus (John 1:14). Finally, perfect fellowship is restored as the throne of God comes down out of heaven. The Lord resides once again with redeemed people in a restored Eden.

The answer to "How do we get Adam back into the garden?" is Jesus. From the Fall in Genesis 3 to the new heavens and earth in Revelation 21-22, we see God's rescue plan in action. That plan focuses on the eternal Son of God. He's in the garden as creator (John 1:1-3; Col. 1:15-17). He's the promised redeemer when mankind falls (Gen. 3:15). He appears numerous times in the Old Testament to inform, deliver, and judge as the angel of the Lord.

Further, he's the focus of some four hundred Old Testament messianic prophecies and foreshadows. He's the God-Man who pitches his tent with people (John 1:14). He's the Suffering Servant who bears our sins on the cross (Isa. 53:3-6; John 19:17-30). He's the resurrected and exalted king who holds the keys of death and *hades* (Rev. 1:18). He's the King of kings who returns in power and glory to set things right and make all things new (Rev. 19:11-16; 21:5).

Jesus is the bridge connecting fallen Eden and Eden restored. Notice how John captures this truth in Revelation 22.

Jesus restores the pure waters of Eden. "Then he showed me the river of the water of life, clear as crystal, flowing from the throne of God and of the Lamb" (Rev. 22:1). In the beginning, there's a river that waters Eden (Gen. 2:10-14). Adam and Eve may refresh themselves in it until they sin and are banned from it. But Jesus promises living water to those who come to him – a preview of the Holy Spirit and the guarantee of everlasting life (John 7:37-39).

Jesus restores human access to the tree of life. "The tree of life was on each side of the river, bearing twelve kinds of fruit, producing its fruit every month" (Rev. 22:2). Because Adam and Eve partake of the tree of the knowledge of good and evil, they are denied access to the tree of life (Gen. 2:9; 3:22-24). But Jesus dies on a tree, bearing humanity's sin debt. The innocent and immortal life Adam and Eve enjoy before the Fall is regained (John 11:25; 14:6; Gal. 3:13).

Jesus restores the perfect health of Eden. "The leaves of the tree are for healing the nations" (Rev. 22:2). There is no sickness in Eden, but banishment from the garden exposes Adam and Eve to every kind of physical, emotional, and societal malady. But Jesus comes as the great physician who provides wholeness in body, soul, and spirit (Luke 4:18-19; cf. Isa. 53:3-6; 61:1-2).

Jesus restores the throne room of Eden. "The throne of God and of the Lamb will be in the city, and his servants will worship him" (Rev. 22:3). Direct access to the triune Godhead is lost in the Fall. God's throne withdraws to the unseen realm. But Jesus leaves the throne room of heaven on a mission to restore our broken relationship with God. He wears a crown of thorns and a borrowed robe as he is mocked as a presumptuous king. But truly he is King of kings and Lord of lords, returning to the throne at his ascension and bringing the throne back to earth at his return (John 3:13; 19:2, 5; Rev. 19:16).

Jesus restores the intimacy of Eden between God and people made in his image. God's servants "will see his face, and his name will be on their foreheads" (Rev. 22:4). After the Fall, walking with God in the cool of the evening is a pleasure denied Adam and Eve. But Jesus comes to a fallen earth as God incarnate (John 1:1-18; 14:9). Eyewitnesses see him in his humanity – and Peter, James, and John see him in glorified humanity on the mount of transfiguration (Matt. 17:1-8; 1 John 1:1-3). One day, we will see him face-to-face, as Adam and Eve did in the garden (1 John 3:2).

Jesus restores the divine light of Eden. "Night will be no more; people will not need the light of a lamp or the light of the sun, because the Lord God will give them light, and they will reign forever and ever" (Rev. 22:5). Separation from God, bondage to sin, and the work of the evil one are associated with darkness throughout Scripture (e.g., Matt. 8:12; 22:13; 25:30; Acts 26:18; Eph. 5:8; Col. 1:13). But Jesus came as the light of the world – a light that shines in darkness (John 1:5; 8:12; 1 John 1:5).

Jesus restores mankind's dominion over the earth. God's servants "will reign forever and ever." Adam and Eve lose dominion over the earth when they rebel against God, seeking to become the masters of their own fates. But Jesus comes to serve, and to give his life as a ransom for us (Matt. 20:28). Because of this, redeemed people are more than bond-servants of Christ; we are adopted sons and daughters of the Father, and joint heirs with Jesus of the perfect world to come (John 13:1-17; Rom. 8:17).

Jesus restores Eden as God's dwelling place. "Look, God's dwelling is with humanity, and he will live with them" (Rev. 21:3). Sin results in banishment from God's presence for Adam and Eve – and for all human descendants. But the Son of God takes on human flesh and tabernacles with us so we might live forever with him (John 1:14; 14:1-13).

Jesus restores the proper balance of Eden between God and people. "They will be his peoples, and God himself will be with them and will be their God" (Rev. 21:3). God withdraws his presence from Adam and Eve after they sin. But Jesus leaves heaven in a mission from heaven's throne room to be with us, and he promises to prepare a place for us there (John 14:1-3). He takes us to heaven upon our physical death, and then returns with us to dwell in the newly minted heavens and earth (Rev. 19:11-16; 21-22).

Jesus destroys the bonds of sin and restores the sinless perfection humans once enjoyed in Eden. "He will wipe away every tear from their eyes. Death will be no more; grief, crying, and pain will be no more, because the previous things have passed away" (Rev. 21:4).

Outside Eden are a thousand sorrows. But Jesus identifies with us in our sin-wrecked world, becoming "a man of sorrows ... acquainted with grief" (Isa. 53:3 KJV). He weeps over the tomb of Lazarus and the city of Jerusalem. Sin and its consequences break his heart (Luke 19:41-44; John 11:35; 16:33). So, he dies that we might live; suffers so we might be secure; bears our shame so we might enjoy honor in his kingdom.

Jesus is the bridge between fallen Eden and Eden restored. He is the way, the truth, and the life (John 14:6). He is the door (John 10:7). He is the resurrection and the life (John 11:25). He is the good shepherd (John 10:11). He is our Passover lamb (1 Cor. 5:7). He is the Alpha and the Omega, the beginning and the end (Rev. 21:6). He is the firstfruits of those who have fallen asleep (1 Cor. 15:20). He is the Son of God and Son of Man (Matt. 3:17; 18:11 KJV). He is the Root and descendant of David, the bright morning star (Rev. 22:16). He is the one seated on the throne who declares, "Look, I am making everything new" (Rev. 21:5).

RESTORED, NOT REWOUND

Before closing this chapter, we should be clear that Eden restored is not Eden rewound. We do not erase thousands of years of human history and go back to an age before fire was discovered, the wheel was invented, and great cities were built. The new earth is not a "do-over" going back to Eden's original paradise. It's much better than that.

There's a historical link between the pre-fallen and post-fallen worlds. History won't start over with the new heavens and earth any more than history began again when Adam and Eve were banished from the garden. In the age to come, there is continuity between the present heavens and earth and the new heavens and earth. The former is purged of sin; the new retains the purified best of the old.

As Randy Alcorn writes:

> Culture won't regress to Eden, where musical instruments hadn't yet been invented or where metalworking and countless other skills hadn't yet been developed (Gen. 4:20-22). The fact that God mentions in Scripture these and other examples of technological progress suggests that he approved of the use of creativity and skills to develop society, even though people were hampered by the Curse.[33]

Life in the new heavens and earth is not a return to the way things were at the beginning. Rather, it's a restoration of God's "very good" creation, including the retention of all that is good and holy. Albert Wolters provides keen insight:

> Were the new creation to exclude the diversity of the nations and the glory of the kings of the earth, it would be impoverished rather than enriched, historically regressive and reactionary rather than progressive. To express the point in the form of a question: is it likely that the music of Bach and Mozart, the painting of Rembrandt, the writing of Shakespeare, the discoveries of science, etc., will be altogether lost upon life in the new creation?[34]

This by no means minimizes the value of Eden. In fact, it may be said that Eden *anticipates* the new earth. Consider just one example: the onyx stone. Pishon is the first of four rivers sourced from the river in Eden, and it flows through the land of Havilah, where there is pure gold, bdellium (an aromatic resin), and onyx. Onyx also is in Eden (Ezek. 28:13).

In the history of Israel's deliverance from Egypt and the giving of the law, God commands the high priest to wear two onyx stones with the names of the twelve tribes of Israel inscribed on them. The Lord refers to the onyx stones as "a reminder" (Exod. 28:9-12). But what do the stones memorialize? Eden.

The onyx stones borne by the high priest remind God's people of the perfect world that once existed, and spur the people to anticipate God's promise of Eden restored. In Eden, Adam and Eve lived in face-to-face communion with God. In the Eden to come, that special intimacy is revived.

The final biblical reference to onyx stones, and the only New Testament reference, tells us onyx stones grace the foundations of New Jerusalem (Rev. 21:19-20 KJV; "sardonyx" in CSB). "The onyx of Eden and on the high priest's shoulders – representing two places where God dwelled with his people – will be displayed in the Holy City, where God will live forever with his people."[35] The onyx adorning the high priest's garments and the foundations of New Jerusalem simultaneously point us to our past in Eden and our future in the new earth.

Though we live in a fallen world, it retains much of the beauty of God's original design. Majestic snow-capped mountains, thundering waterfalls, lush rain forests, and diverse creatures of all kinds take our breaths away. In the world to come, these stunning beauties are not lost; they are retained, redeemed, restored, and revived for our everlasting pleasure. Further, the advancements God has encouraged in human beings will serve as the launching pads for untethered exploration and discovery throughout all eternity.

Truly, in the new heavens and earth, we do not return to the good old days of Eden, but understand that the best is yet to come.

REVIEW

Key takeaways from this chapter

1. Heaven is not our final home. While we enjoy fellowship with Christ in the so-called intermediate state between physical death and future resurrection, our ultimate destiny is the new heavens and earth, which Peter and John describe as a place of righteousness and restored innocence (2 Pet. 3:10-13; Rev. 21-22).

2. The Bible generally uses the Hebrew *shamayim* and the Greek *ouranos* to describe three heavens:

- The atmospheric heaven, or the sky (Gen. 1:8); it's where the birds fly (Mark 4:32), the clouds carry storms (Luke 12:54, 56), and the rain falls (Jas. 5:18).
- The stellar heaven(s), where the moon and stars shine (Ps. 8:3; Heb. 11:12).
- The domain of God, or his dwelling place (1 Kings 22:19; Luke 20:4). Paul refers to it as "the third heaven" (2 Cor. 12:2).

3. While the third heaven is the joyous realm of all who trust in Jesus, the new heavens and earth are better by far. Satan, sin, and death – three enemies Christ conquered through his finished work on the cross – are banished to the lake of fire, along with all those who reject God's provision for eternal life. God wipes the tears from his children's cheeks and declares that the former things – death, grief, crying, and pain – have passed away.

4. Three New Testament passages enable us to better grasp the promise of our future home on a restored earth:

Matthew 19:28. Jesus refers to future earth as "the renewal of all things." Just as Christians look forward to receiving glorified bodies, we delight in knowing that the corrupted world in which we live is going to be redeemed one day as well.

2 Peter 3:10-13. Peter tells us the fires of judgment are intended to remove the dross from our fallen world and purify what remains. In a similar way, we should remember that salvation is holistic; it's intended for the full human being – body, soul, and spirit.

Revelation 21-22. Key components of the new heavens and earth that John sees in his visions from Patmos include: the descent of New Jerusalem; the lifting of the curse; and the restoration of Eden.

5. Some Bible commentators believe the fires of judgment annihilate the universe, but it appears more biblically faithful to understand the language of Scripture as describing a refining and restoration of the fallen earth. Consider:

(a) Jesus speaks of "the renewal of all things" (Matt. 19:28).

(b) Peter and John use the Greek word *kainos* to describe the new heavens and earth, meaning new in quality, not recreated *ex nihilo* (from nothing).

(c) Annihilation of the present heavens and earth would run contrary to God's promise to restore the cosmos.

(d) Annihilation would cast doubt on Christ's work of redemption.

(e) Annihilation implies that God's good, but fallen, creation is not fixable.

(f) For God to annihilate the present heavens and earth and start over from scratch would cede ground to Satan.

DISCUSS

Questions for personal or group study

1. Why is heaven not the ultimate destiny for Christians? Where, then, do we spend eternity?

2. Read 2 Corinthians 12:2. What does Paul mean by "the third heaven"? How does the third heaven compare with other references to "heaven" in the Bible?

3. What term does Jesus use in Matthew 19:28 to describe the new heavens and earth?

4. Read Revelation 21:27. Who and what are excluded from entrance into New Jerusalem? How do the following New Testament passages offer us a more detailed view?

- Matthew 25:41
- 1 Corinthians 6:9-10
- Galatians 5:19-21
- 2 Thessalonians 1:8-9
- Revelation 19:20
- Revelation 20:10, 14-15
- Revelation 21:8
- Revelation 22:15

5. What are the similarities and differences between the Garden of Eden before the Fall and the new heavens and earth John describes in Revelation 21-22?

* * *

SECTION IV: RECEIVE ME

THE PREPARATION FOR JESUS' RETURN

Christ gives us no timeline for his return, any more than a first-century Galilean Jew could tell his bride-to-be the day and hour he's coming to whisk her away to the marriage supper in his father's home. That precise moment is known only to the father, and kept close.

Jesus *does* promise to return, however. He offers signs of his coming. And he provides details about the nature of his return. But above all, he stresses preparation – his, and ours.

Likened to a bridegroom, Jesus tells his followers he's preparing a place for us in heaven. He urges us to be vigilant in light of his return. And he warns that his coming, like that of a bridegroom at midnight, is imminent. As the bride of Christ, we must make ourselves ready.

———————— A ————————

Just as a betrothed first-
century Jewish groom returns
to his father's house to prepare
a bridal chamber for his
beloved, Jesus secures a place
for us in heaven.

———————— Ω ————————

"I AM GOING TO PREPARE A PLACE"

JESUS IS COMING FOR HIS BRIDE

*F*ew events are more jubilant than a Jewish wedding. In Hebrew, it's described as a *simcha*, or "joyous occasion." As we think about the return of Jesus, it may help stir our passions to consider the details of an ancient Jewish wedding, which forms an apt parable of God's redemptive work.

Let's begin with John's report of hearing a thundering voice in heaven, a voice he describes as "the sound of cascading waters, and the rumbling of loud thunder" (Rev. 19:6):

Hallelujah, because our Lord God, the Almighty, reigns! Let us be glad, rejoice, and give him glory, because the marriage of the Lamb has come, and his bride has prepared herself. She was given fine linen to wear, bright and pure.... Blessed are those invited to the marriage feast of the Lamb! (Rev. 19:6-9).

A day is coming when Christ's bride – believers from every nation, tribe, people, and language – are gathered in heaven to consummate the marriage between Jesus and his followers. At that time, we enjoy the marriage supper of the Lamb. A look into ancient Jewish weddings reveals key truths about our covenant relationship with

Jesus, his promise to prepare a place in heaven for us, and the certainty of his return.

Jewish weddings, as known and practiced in first-century Israel, feature three distinct elements.

1. SHIDDUKHIN

First comes the *shiddukhin*, or marriage contract. It begins with the pairing of bride and groom – a careful process that fathers sometimes undertake on behalf of their sons and daughters while their children are quite young. It involves foresight, initiative, pursuit, and negotiation. The father of the groom often selects a bride for his son, as Abraham does for Isaac (Gen. 24:1-4). In these cases, marriage is viewed as a strategic alliance between two families for protection or enrichment.

There is a sense in which Yahweh presides over the very first *shiddukhin*. Observing Adam, the Lord says, "It is not good for the man to be alone. I will make a helper corresponding to him" (Gen. 2:18). The Lord then brings all the animals before Adam, who names them. While the diverse creatures of Eden are pleasing to the eyes and offer a form of companionship, Adam realizes that "no helper was found corresponding to him" (Gen. 2:20).

So, the Lord causes Adam to fall into a deep sleep. He removes a rib from Adam's side, and from it he forms the perfect mate – a woman, about whom Adam declares, "This one, at last, is bone of my bone and flesh of my flesh; this one will be called 'woman,' for she was taken from man" (Gen. 2:23).

Adam and Eve are a perfect match. This truly is a marriage made in heaven, and it sets the stage for the institution of marriage, in which one man and one woman unite in a covenant relationship for a lifetime. As the Lord says, "This is why a man leaves his father and mother and bonds with his wife, and they become one flesh" (Gen. 2:24).

Centuries later, when asked about proper grounds for divorce, Jesus directs the Pharisees back to Eden. "Haven't you read," he tells them, "that he who created them in the beginning **made them male and female** ... 'For this reason a man will leave his father and mother and be joined to his wife, and the two will become one flesh'?** So they are no longer two, but one flesh. Therefore, what God has joined together, let no one separate" (Matt. 19:4-6).

This always has been God's creative intent. And it pictures the covenant of salvation between God and fallen creatures made in his image. As we survey Scripture, we see the *shiddukhin* of redemption unfold – that is, the marriage contract between holy God and sinful humans. Immediately after the Fall, God reveals his plan of salvation, promising a redeemer who crushes the head of the evil one and sets things right (Gen. 3:15).

Later, the Lord graciously chooses Noah and his family to survive the flood in an ark that prefigures the finished work of Christ. Yahweh then selects Abraham as the father of his chosen people, who enter into a covenant with God by faith. The Lord refers to Israel as his wife, and he preserves a faithful remnant even when the people wander into spiritual adultery. God raises up priests as mediators, King David as a type of Messiah, and prophets to warn, guide, and encourage faithfulness to Israel's husband.

Ultimately, Yahweh sends his Son – the promised seed of woman – who depicts himself as the bridegroom. Jesus lives a sinless life for his bride, dies for her sins, and rises from the dead to defeat Satan, the ancient enemy that ruined the very first *shiddukhin*. The ransom Jesus pays on the cross is the dowry for his bride (Matt. 20:28; Mark 10:45).

Followers of Jesus may look back, not just into history, but into eternity past to see how God selects and pursues his Son's bride.

Consider that Scripture says we are *foreknown*, which means our omniscient God always has known us and loved us, reckoning us predestined, called, justified, and glorified (Rom. 8:29-30). Further, we are *elected*, which means God chose us in Christ before the foundation of the world (Eph. 1:4).[1]

And we are *predestined*, which describes God's plan from eternity past to complete the work of redemption in every saint, fully conforming us to the image of his Son (Phil. 1:6). Predestination cannot be separated from his other works of redemption before time, in time, or beyond time. From a human standpoint, God's predestination from the farthest reaches of eternity invades time, applies to us, and continues out into eternity future in glorification.

These three facets of salvation before time – foreknowledge, election, and predestination – cannot be divorced from human responsibility. God's sovereignty, and the endowed right of people to make decisions for which God holds us accountable, are seemingly parallel biblical truths. Where they intersect in the mind of God is a wondrous mystery to his creatures. Even angels scratch their heads as they plumb the depths of these remarkable works of God (1 Pet. 1:12).

Katubah

With this background in mind, let's return to an ancient Jewish *shiddukhin*. Whether the father selects his son's bride or involves him in the process, the father ultimately approaches the young maiden's father and seeks a mutual agreement. The parents of both the bridegroom and the bride sign a marriage contract, involving a dowry paid to the bride and her parents. The contract, called a *ketubah*, protects the rights of the bride by specifying the groom's responsibilities in caring for her, and the amount of support that's due her in the unlikely event of divorce.

None of this preparatory work overrides the freedom of the prospective bride, who must agree to terms of the marriage covenant, as well as agree to become the bride. This is an essential freedom in salvation, as it is in ancient Jewish marriage customs. You may recall that Rebecca is asked if she's willing to go back with Abraham's servant to marry his son, Isaac. Rebecca agrees to go; she is not forced (Gen. 24:57-59).

In a similar way, while the Lord extends an offer of covenant marriage between his Son and us, we must agree. Once we do, the Lord remains faithful, even if we engage in activity worthy of divorce. Our eternal life is secure – not because we're faithful, but because God has known us from eternity past and keeps his marriage covenant into eternity future, when we take part in the marriage supper of the Lamb.

Mikvah

One additional tie between the *shiddukhin* and God's work of redemption is the *mikvah*, or water ritual. *Mikvah* is a Hebrew word meaning "a gathering of waters." A *mikvah* often is a body of natural water such as a river, lake, or spring. But over time, it became common to construct special pools for water rituals. Traditionally, in preparation for the next phase of marriage, the bride and groom are separately immersed in water. This symbolizes their purity and acts as a token of spiritual cleansing.

Israelites practiced *mikvah* since the days of Moses. "For the observant Jew, the *mikvah* personifies both the womb and the grave and consequently, rebirth. It is regarded as a pure, unadulterated avenue of connection with God; and for that reason, it is a place where hope is reawakened and strengthened."[2]

Scripture commands entering the *mikvah* for a number of common life events. For example, a person who becomes ritually unclean through contact with a dead person must be immersed in water before re-entering the temple. A leper declared healed by a priest must enter the *mikvah* as well (see Lev. 14:1-4, 7, 9). And a woman who completes her menstrual cycle needs to be immersed before resuming sexual relations with her husband (Lev. 15:19-24).

Today, one of the most widely practiced uses of the *mikvah* is the pre-wedding preparation of the bride and groom.

The primary significance of the *mikvah* isn't for physical cleansing, but to symbolize a spiritual cleansing. That's how the *mikvah* in an ancient Jewish wedding ties into Christian baptism. As Peter writes, "Baptism, which corresponds to this, now saves you (not as the removal of dirt from the body, but the pledge of a good conscience toward God) through the resurrection of Jesus Christ" (1 Pet. 3:21).

A man who wants to become Jewish must undergo two rites: circumcision and immersion. A woman must be immersed. When

Gentile converts go down into the waters of the *mikvah*, they leave behind their pagan ways – symbolically dying to their old lives – and coming up out of the water as newborn children with new identities. The term "born again" actually originates in Judaism.[3]

When Jesus tells Nicodemus he must be "born again," Nicodemus may be thinking, not only of physical rebirth, but of converting to Judaism again. But Jesus explains that spiritual rebirth – not ethnic identity or religious ritual – is necessary to enter the kingdom of God (John 3:1-21).

Immersing oneself in a *mikvah* is an expression of rebirth. It's like re-entering the womb, a place of God's creative power, and being born again. In a similar manner, immersion represents death and resurrection. That's likely what Paul has in mind when he writes, "Therefore, if anyone is in Christ, he is a new creation; the old has passed away, and see, the new has come!" (2 Cor. 5:17).

Paul also understands the death and rebirth imagery of baptism and compares it with the death and resurrection of Jesus:

> Or are you unaware that all of us who were baptized into Christ Jesus were baptized into his death? Therefore we are buried with him by baptism into death, in order that, just as Christ was raised from the dead by the glory of the Father, so we too may walk in newness of life (Rom. 6:3-4).

In Matthew 3:13-17, Jesus submits to baptism in the Jordan River at the hands of John the Baptist.[4] Jesus has no need of spiritual cleansing; he's sinless. Yet, he's baptized, at least in part, as an open declaration that he's ready to enter into the next phase of his relationship with us: betrothal.

Further, his final instructions to his disciples show the important role baptism plays in making Jews and Gentiles disciples of the Messiah:

> Go, therefore, and make disciples of all nations, baptizing them in the name of the Father and of the Son and of the Holy Spirit, teaching

them to observe everything I have commanded you. And remember, I
am with you always, to the end of the age (Matt. 28:19-20).

So, in ancient times, having signed the marriage covenant, the
bride and groom separately enter the *mikvah*. In so doing, the bride
pledges herself to the groom and declares her desire to remain chaste.
The groom pledges fidelity to his chosen bride. It's a beautiful picture
of believer's baptism, in which followers of Jesus publicly declare their
devotion to the bridegroom and their confidence in his promised
return. Meanwhile, Jesus, in his baptism in the Jordan, proclaims his
love for his bride and his commitment to follow through as a faithful
bridegroom.

In summary, the *shiddukhin* is the formalization of a marriage
bond. It features the *ketubah*, or contract, by which the terms and
price are established, and to which both parties agree. It also involves
the *mikvah*, or ritual bath, which symbolizes the purity of the bride
and groom and acts as a token of spiritual cleansing.

In the Incarnation, Jesus comes to offer us an everlasting covenant
relationship with him. He pays the dowry – the bride price, our sin
debt – through his finished work on the cross, and submits to water
baptism to identify with us and to signal his readiness to enter the
next phase of the marriage covenant.

2. *ERUSIN*

After the *shiddukhim*, the second element of ancient Jewish weddings
is engagement, or betrothal, known as *erusin* in Hebrew. After their
immersion in the *mikvah*, the bride and groom enter a shelter known
as the *huppah*, or marriage canopy. This symbolizes the couple
entering into a contract to establish a new household.

Beneath the canopy, the groom offers the bride money or a valuable object such as a ring, and the couple shares a cup of wine to seal
their vows. This parallels the cup Jesus and the apostles share in the
last supper as a sign of the new covenant. As Matthew records:

Then he [Jesus] took a cup, and after giving thanks, he gave it to them and said, "Drink from it, all of you. For this is my blood of the covenant, which is poured out for many for the forgiveness of sins. But I tell you, I will not drink from this fruit of the vine from now on until that day when I drink it new with you in my Father's kingdom (Matt. 26:27-30).

Later, Paul writes that, in the Lord's Supper, we remember Christ's death until he comes again (1 Cor. 11:23-26).

In sharing the cup of wine, the groom assures his bride that, even though he's going away for a time, he will return for her. This may be what Jesus has in mind when he seeks to comfort his worried disciples in the face of his imminent crucifixion and departure for heaven:

Don't let your heart be troubled. Believe in God; believe also in me. In my Father's house are many rooms. If it were not so, would I have told you that I am going to prepare a place for you? If I go away and prepare a place for you, I will come again and take you to myself, so that where I am you may be also (John 14:1-3).

With similar words, the groom announces the beginning of an engagement period that typically lasts a year. Legally, the bride and groom are considered married, but they won't live together or engage in sexual relations until the groom returns for his bride. This contract is considered binding, and it may only be broken when the husband initiates a *get*, or religious divorce.

We find an example of this in the Gospels, when Joseph discovers that Mary, his espoused wife, is pregnant. Matthew writes:

The birth of Jesus Christ came about this way: After his mother Mary had been engaged to Joseph, it was discovered before they came together that she was pregnant from the Holy Spirit. So her husband, Joseph, being a righteous man, and not wanting to disgrace her publicly, decided to divorce her secretly.

But after he had considered these things, an angel of the Lord appeared to him in a dream, saying, "Joseph, son of David, don't be afraid to take Mary as your wife, because what has been conceived in her is from the Holy Spirit. She will give birth to a son, and you are to name him Jesus, because he will save his people from their sins."

Now all this took place to fulfill what was spoken by the Lord through the prophet:

See, the virgin will become pregnant and give birth to a son, and they will name him Immanuel, which is translated "God is with us."

When Joseph woke up, he did as the Lord's angel had commanded him. He married her but did not have sexual relations with her until she gave birth to a son. And he named him Jesus (Matt. 1:18-25).

We can see that living separately and chastely is the standard for *erusin*. Further, we may note that a bill of divorce is required to nullify the marriage, and that it could be a very public – and humiliating – step for both parties, but especially for the bride. Joseph, in his love for Mary, is determined to divorce her privately, until God sends an angel to Joseph in a dream. Joseph then embraces Mary's "shame" and takes it as his own, remaining faithful to her – as Mary does to him – despite the obvious conclusion others draw about their apparent lack of virtue.

During the year-long *erusin*, the groom returns to his father's house and prepares a wedding chamber for his bride. The father supervises the work, carefully observing every detail. That's because the day of the marriage feast is known only to the father, and it's announced only when the father declares everything is ready. Regarding his return, Jesus tells his followers: "Now concerning that day and hour no one knows – neither the angels of heaven nor the Son – except the Father alone" (Matt. 24:36).

Meanwhile, the bride returns to her home and prepares for the unknown day of the groom's arrival. This involves selecting wedding garments, securing oil lamps, and making other arrangements. Above all, the bride is to remain chaste, to cover herself in public as a symbol that she belongs to another, and to be ready at all times for the sound of the *shofar* (ram's horn) and the cry from the streets that the bridegroom is on his way.

Parable of the ten virgins: Matthew 25:1-13

In the parable of the ten virgins, Jesus compares the kingdom of heaven to this special time at the end of *erusin*, when the groom comes for his bride (Matt. 25:1-13). It's a riveting story, which begins with ten virgins (or bridesmaids, likely twelve to sixteen years of age) taking their lamps and going out to meet the groom.[5]

By most accounts, these lamps resemble torches, with oil-soaked cloth on the end of poles. Jars of olive oil are carried along as well, with bridesmaids dipping the fabric end of the poles in oil before lighting them. Five of the bridesmaids take extra oil along with their lamps, since the typical oil lamp would burn for only about fifteen minutes without additional fuel.[6] So, the bridesmaids bring their lamps, but only half of them are adequately prepared.

There is no shortage of opinions as to what the oil represents in this parable: good works, love, joy, grace, conscience, or the Holy Spirit. But no one can buy these items, and no true believer may possess the Holy Spirit only to run out of him. It's better to understand the oil in this parable simply as spiritual preparedness.

Next, we learn the groom is delayed. This may have been due to urgent matters such as finalizing a dowry, or it may have been intentional, heightening the element of surprise. In any case, all ten bridesmaids become drowsy and fall asleep. Suddenly, in the middle of the night, a cry in the streets awakens them all: "Here's the groom! Come out to meet him" (Matt. 25:6).

At his father's command, the son leads a procession from his house to the bride's house. The sound of the *shofar* and the shouts of the wedding party fill the streets. At last, the groom stands outside the bride's home and calls her out. She meets him, along with her bridesmaids, joins the wedding parade, and proceeds to the home where the marriage chamber awaits.

Hearing the distant cry, "Here's the groom! Come out to meet him," the virgins trim their lamps in order to join the procession, but the foolish virgins – unprepared, with no additional oil – find their lamps flickering. They implore the wise virgins, "Give us some of your oil, because our lamps are going out" (Matt. 25:8).

The wise virgins reply, "No, there won't be enough for us and for you. Go instead to those who sell oil, and buy some for yourselves" (Matt. 25:9).

Where the foolish virgins may find oil to purchase in the middle of the night is a mystery. Yet, after some period of time, they are successful. They rush through the streets to join the procession, but the entire wedding party has entered the house, and the door has been shut.

"Master, master, open for us!" they cry. But the haunting reply comes from behind the locked door, "Truly, I tell you, I don't know you!" (Matt. 25:11-12).

Jesus ends the parable with these words: "Therefore, be alert, because you don't know either the day or the hour" (Matt. 25:13).

While there are many details in this parable, we should not seek to allegorize it. That is, we should not impose meaning on every element. In most cases, parables are intended to convey one or more simple truths. In the case of this parable, three profound truths emerge.

First, Jesus is returning suddenly. We addressed this in detail in Chapter 7 ("I am coming like a thief"). While we don't know the exact time of the second coming, we are to eagerly anticipate the joyous surprise of seeing the Son of Man coming on the clouds of heaven (Matt. 24:30).

Second, Jesus' return is delayed, a truth Jesus shares in the parable of the talents (Matt. 25:14-30) and Peter addresses only a few decades after Jesus ascends into heaven:

Dear friends, don't overlook this one fact: With the Lord one day is like a thousand years, and a thousand years like one day. The Lord does not delay his promise, as some understand delay, but is patient with you, not wanting any to perish but all to come to repentance (2 Pet. 3:8-9).

It's now been nearly two thousand years since Jesus ascended into heaven from the Mount of Olives. Many people scoff, as unbelievers did in Peter's day (2 Pet. 3:3-4), arguing that our eagerness for the Lord's return is nothing more than false hope. But as it was in the days of Noah, when the wicked rejected Noah's preaching, so it is today (2 Pet. 3:5-7).

The Lord's delay in coming is two-fold. First, God doesn't reckon time the way we do. He is eternal; we're not. One day with him is like a thousand years, and a thousand years like one day. Second, the Lord's delay is an extension of his mercy, an opportunity for the wicked to repent and the redeemed to share the gospel.

Albert Mohler remarks, "Thus, the delay is for God's sovereign purpose, that the church be active in the world as the visible presence of the kingdom of Christ until such time that Christ returns in both judgment and glory."[7]

The third truth of this parable is that we are to be ready at all times, for indeed, like the bridegroom in an ancient Jewish wedding, "the day of the Lord will come like a thief" (2 Pet. 3:10). We are not to lose hope. Our bridegroom is busy preparing a place for us in his Father's house. And though he's delayed, he's not deterred. He will come again.

James Montgomery Boice describes the foolish virgins this way: "They are good church people. They would never think of speaking a word against Jesus. But they are not born again. They do not have that inward change which alone entitles them to enter heaven."[8]

Jesus often speaks prophetically to his followers, not just about the suddenness of his return, but of the condition of the church at the time of his *parousia*. In this regard, the parable of the ten virgins borrows a theme from the parables of the wheat and weeds (Matt. 13:24-29, 36-43), and from the parable of the dragnet (Matt. 13:47-50).

True believers and pretenders occupy the same congregations. In many respects, they look and act the same – the way wheat and darnel, a false and poisonous weed, do, or the way edible and nonedible fish do – but on the day of judgment, they are separated. These parables also come before the final parable in the Olivet Discourse, the parable of the sheep and goats. The sheep and goats graze together and even resemble one another, yet they're separated at the time of shearing (Matt. 25:31-46).

As Jesus makes clear in all his teachings, "Not everyone who says to me, 'Lord, Lord,' will enter the kingdom of heaven, but only the one who does the will of my Father in heaven" (Matt. 7:21).

Like the bride and her maidens, waiting for the groom to appear, we are to keep our lamps trimmed. That is, we are to be ready for the return of Christ. This is rooted in the confidence that we belong to Jesus. All who have trusted in him for salvation have that assurance – not based on emotions or human effort, but on the finished work of Christ.

Paul tells us the Lord's salvation spans from eternity past to eternity future. We are foreknown, predestined, called, justified, and (in the future) glorified (Rom. 8:29-30). God finishes the good work he has begun in us (Phil. 1:6). Jesus himself tells us he knows his sheep, calls us by name, and keeps us secure (John 10:27-29). And John tells us he has written to us about the finished work of Christ so that we may "know" we have eternal life (1 John 5:13).

We have no reason to fear that Christ might revoke his work of redemption, or that we may falter and thus cause our eternal life to come unraveled. Jesus has desired us, pursued us, betrothed us to him, and promised both to prepare a place for us and come for us. Jesus ascended into heaven two millennia ago. Today, he's still seated at the Father's right hand as our mediator and intercessor. And he's busy preparing a place for us in heaven.

But what, exactly, is this place?

The bridal chamber

Jesus returns to his Father's house in heaven following his finished work on the cross. He has paid the dowry for his bride. He has established the marriage contract – the New Covenant – in his blood. He has immersed himself in the *mikvah* of the Jordan River and in the baptism of his passion (Luke 12:50). And he has shared the cup of anticipation with us (Luke 22:17-18).

So, just as a groom returns to his father's house to prepare a bridal chamber for his beloved, Jesus prepares a place for us in heaven. This is not a mansion, as some English translations render the Greek word *mone*, unintentionally leading some to believe heaven is all about us and a future lavish lifestyle. Rather, *mone* means a dwelling place, abode, or room. In the context of John 14:2 – "In my Father's house are many rooms" – *mone* means an extension of the Father's house.

In Bible times, people didn't build houses with the idea that they would spend most of their time in them. Jewish families often preferred to be outside, and they considered their home more of a shelter, or resting place. The typical home of common people in the days of Jesus was a one-room dwelling, perhaps with an animal stall in the front and a guest room on the roof. Jews have always considered themselves sojourners on earth, so the idea was not to build elaborate mansions but workable living quarters.

A father's house in the ancient culture of Jesus' day was where the extended family lived. Rooms were added as the family grew through birth and marriage. So, what Jesus is telling us is that he's adding rooms onto his Father's house designed specifically for us. Exactly what this bridal chamber looks like, or what its dimensions are, is not revealed to us. But it's the most perfect dwelling place we'll ever experience.

Candice Lucey explains it this way: "Nothing can match the glory of this heavenly realm, and this is the home where Jesus went to prepare a room for us. No one who lives here will ever want to leave. To abide in Heaven is to fulfill one's purpose: living life in eternal devotion to and worship of Christ."[9]

But, as in ancient times, we won't stay in the bridal chamber forever. The bridegroom also is a king. And when he returns to earth with his bride and the holy angels, he sits on the throne of King David on a restored earth (see Chapter 13). And we rule with him (1 Cor. 6:1-3; 2 Tim. 2:12; Rev. 5:10; 20:4-6).

Jesus makes a comforting promise to his bride: "Where I am you may be also" (John 14:3). Today, Jesus is present in us by virtue of the indwelling Holy Spirit, whom Jesus and the Father sent. He has taken up residence in our human spirits. He is the down payment on our heavenly home (2 Cor. 1:22; Eph. 1:13-14). In the future, Jesus takes us to the bridal chamber he's preparing in heaven. After that, he returns to earth with us.

Our location – earth today, heaven tomorrow, and a renewed earth in the future – is not nearly as important as the one who shares it with us. Christ, living in us, proves to be a magnificent reality we can barely comprehend. Our bridal chamber in heaven is beyond our wildest dreams. And our future home in an earthly paradise purged of sin can only be compared to what little we read of Eden in the Book of Genesis before the Fall. But in every instance, the focal point is the eternal Son of God, our bridegroom, prophet, priest, and king.

If you're blessed with a husband or wife, think back to the first days of your married life. Likely, you didn't live in a mansion. Perhaps you stayed in your parents' home, or a guest house, for a while. Perhaps your home was a small apartment, married student housing on a university or seminary campus, or a barely functional starter home in a sketchy neighborhood. But you and your spouse were together, and that was enough.

Our place in heaven is beautiful beyond imagination, yet it's not our focus. Our focus is – and forever will be – on the bridegroom, who reminds us that we will live with him and be with him wherever he is. Forever. Heaven is not our final home; it's the intermediate state between physical death and future glorification, which is pictured in the third and final act of ancient Jewish wedding ceremonies.

3. NISSUIN

We've examined the *shiddukhin*, or marriage contract, and the *erusin*, or engagement. Now, we come to the *nissuin*, or marriage. This

Hebrew word is derived from *naso*, which means to lift up.[10] At this time, there's great fanfare as the groom fetches his bride and escorts her to his father's house. The couple again enters the *huppah*, recites a blessing over a cup of wine – a symbol of joy – and finalizes their vows.

At last, after a year of separation, the husband and wife enter the bridal chamber and consummate their marriage. A friend of the groom waits outside until he's informed that the new couple has engaged in marital relations for the first time. The friend announces this to the guests and, with resounding joy, the marriage feast begins. Often, the celebration lasts for days, as we see in the wedding at Cana, where Jesus performs his first miracle (John 2:1-11).

We don't have intricate details of the earthly *nissuin*, but John captures a view of the marriage supper of the Lamb in heaven and invites us to look with him:

> Then I heard something like the voice of a vast multitude, like the sound of cascading waters, and like the rumbling of loud thunder, saying, Hallelujah, because our Lord God, the Almighty, reigns! Let us be glad, rejoice, and give him glory, because the marriage of the Lamb has come, and his bride has prepared herself. She was given fine linen to wear, bright and pure. For the linen represents the righteous acts of the saints. Then he said to me, "Write: Blessed are those invited to the marriage feast of the Lamb!" He also said to me, "These words of God are true" (Rev. 19:6-9).

John hears the voices of the redeemed in heaven, a vast multitude whose praise sounds like Niagara Falls or peals of thunder. They echo the cry of the twenty-four elders in Revelation 11:17: "We give you thanks, Lord God, the Almighty, who is and who was, because you have taken your great power and have begun to reign." Babylon has fallen, and all who have profited from its corruption lament their loss. But God's people rejoice at the inauguration of Christ's kingdom.

John notes that "the bride has prepared herself." This is the true church, which has kept herself pure and ready for the Lord's coming.

"She was given fine linen to wear, bright and pure. For the linen represents the righteous acts of the saints." It's probably best to understand these linens as something God provides for the bride, clothing us in his righteousness rather than our own merit (although his righteousness proves itself in believers' good works).[11] Consider the white robes of Revelation 7:9 and 14, which are washed in the blood of the Lamb. It must always be the righteousness of Christ that merits salvation, not our own good works.

Isaiah foresees God's provision of clothing for his bride: "I rejoice greatly in the LORD, I exult in my God; for he has clothed me with the garments of salvation and wrapped me in a robe of righteousness, as a groom wears a turban and as a bride adorns herself with her jewels" (Isa. 61:10).

It makes the most sense to see the wedding of the Lamb as a reference to the resurrection and glorification of the saints. The bride has made herself ready in that she has taken seriously her vows of chastity and has waited eagerly for the coming of the groom. As a result, the Lord has given his bride garments of fine linen to wear – the imputed righteousness of Christ. Now, glorified and perfected in body, soul, and spirit, the bride is united with the groom and they begin a new and joyous phase of their relationship for all eternity. Paul describes the bride of Christ as "a radiant church, without stain or wrinkle or any other blemish" (Eph. 5:27 NIV).

But why don't we actually see the bride in the parable of the ten virgins (Matt. 25:1-13)? Why don't we actually see the bride and groom in the parable of the wedding banquet (Matt. 22:1-14)? And why does John say, "Blessed are those invited to the marriage feast of the Lamb" (Rev. 19:9)? Why not, "Blessed are the bride and groom"?

It seems the symbolism is flexible throughout the New Testament. Just as the people of God are symbolized both as the sun-clothed woman (Israel) and as her children in Revelation 12, so the church is both the bride of Christ and the individual Christians invited to the wedding feast of the Lamb.

Note a further curiosity: the bride is identified as "the New Jerusalem" in Revelation 21:2, 9. John notes in Revelation 21:1-2:

> Then I saw a new heaven and a new earth; for the first heaven and the
> first earth had passed away, and the sea was no more. I also saw the
> holy city, the new Jerusalem, coming down out of heaven from God,
> prepared like a bride adorned for her husband.

The bride of Christ is best understood as the church (see 2 Cor.
11:2; Eph. 5:25-27, 32; cf. Isa. 54:5-7). The New Testament also likens
followers of Jesus to the temple of God – individual temples of the
Holy Spirit (1 Cor. 3:16; 6:19), and living stones being built to create a
corporate habitation for the Lord (1 Pet. 2:5). So, it shouldn't seem
strange for the people of God to be compared with a city.

God's presence often manifests in natural and man-made structures – a burning bush, a pillar of cloud and fire, a tabernacle, a
temple, and so on. Consequently, as the Spirit inhabits each of us as
temples of the Holy Spirit, New Jerusalem may be seen as the corporate dwelling place of God. It needs no formal temple, because the
Father and Son are its temple (Rev. 21:22).

Put another way, the New Jerusalem that comes down out of God
from heaven may be seen as the redeemed of all ages collectively
forming a dwelling place for the Lord, who descends to the earth in
the second coming, sits on the throne of King David, drives out his
enemies, and provides security for his people.

As Eckhard Schnabel writes:

> The "holy city Jerusalem" is God's true people, the followers of Jesus
> who had remained faithful to the Lamb (rather than joining the Great
> Harlot of Babylon), described in Rev. 20:9 as "the camp of the saints
> and the beloved city." The New Jerusalem is the community of the
> redeemed, the faithful who have refused to commit immorality
> through idolatry, the believers in Jesus who have persevered even in
> the midst of suffering and martyrdom. The people are themselves the
> city and also the temple in which God's presence resides (21:2-3,
> 12-14).[12]

Next, we should ask: In what way, specifically, has the bride made herself ready (Rev. 19:7)? She has appeared before the judgment seat of Christ as a resurrected, glorified, and rewarded community of saints. At the judgment seat, her works are evaluated and all her spots and blemishes are removed (see 1 Cor. 3:11-15; 2 Cor. 5:10). With this completed, the bride is ready to return to earth with the bridegroom.

In ancient times, the wedding feast after the *nissuin* might have included seven full days of food, music, dancing, and celebration (see Judg. 14:1-12). This happens before the bride and groom settle into their new life together.

Some interpreters see this as support for a pre-tribulation rapture in which the church (the bride) and Jesus (the bridegroom) celebrate in heaven while seven years of judgments are poured out on the earth. Others believe the marriage supper of the Lamb takes place on earth after the return of Jesus with his saints. Still others see it taking place in heaven just after resurrection and glorification but without a seven-year delay before Christ's return. In any case, the marriage supper of the Lamb is a time of celebration associated with our future glorification and the return of Christ to earth.

Whether the marriage supper of the Lamb takes place in heaven during an earthly tribulation, or at some other point, it's important to keep in mind that it's the fulfillment of God's promise to the redeemed. And in our glorified bodies, now fully adorned for the wedding, we consummate the marriage and return with Jesus to live forever in new heavens and a new earth.

There's little doubt that the marriage supper of the Lamb involves the redeemed of every tribe, language, people, and nation (Rev. 5:9). Jesus makes this clear when he tells those observing a Roman centurion's faith, "I tell you that many will come from east and west to share the banquet with Abraham, Isaac, and Jacob in the kingdom of heaven. But the sons of the kingdom will be thrown into the outer darkness where there will be weeping and gnashing of teeth" (Matt. 8:11-12).

The banquet hall is filled. The marriage of the Lamb and his bride is upon us. And the feast is about to begin. This scene in heaven harkens back, not only to the parable of the ten virgins, but to Jesus' parable of the wedding banquet (Matt. 22:1-14).

Parable of the wedding banquet: Matthew 22:1-14

Once more Jesus spoke to them in parables:

"The kingdom of heaven is like a king who gave a wedding banquet for his son. He sent his servants to summon those invited to the banquet, but they didn't want to come. Again, he sent out other servants and said, 'Tell those who are invited: See, I've prepared my dinner; my oxen and fattened cattle have been slaughtered, and every-thing is ready. Come to the wedding banquet.'

"But they paid no attention and went away, one to his own farm, another to his business, while the rest seized his servants, mistreated them, and killed them. The king was enraged, and he sent out his troops, killed those murderers, and burned down their city.

"Then he told his servants, 'The banquet is ready, but those who were invited were not worthy. Go then to where the roads exit the city and invite everyone you find to the banquet.' So those servants went out on the roads and gathered everyone they found, both evil and good. The wedding banquet was filled with guests. When the king came in to see the guests, he saw a man there who was not dressed for a wedding. So he said to him, 'Friend, how did you get in here without wedding clothes?' The man was speechless.

"Then the king told the attendants, 'Tie him up hand and foot, and throw him into the outer darkness, where there will be weeping and gnashing of teeth.'

"For many are invited, but few are chosen" (Matt. 22:1-14).

In the previous chapter (Matt. 21), we learn that Jesus has made his triumphant entry into Jerusalem and cleansed the temple complex, driving out those who were buying and selling. He has received the praise of children and cursed the barren fig tree. He has answered the Pharisees' challenges to his authority and provided parables of the two sons and the vineyard owner to expose the Jewish leaders' hardened hearts. Stung by Jesus' rebuke, they look for a way to arrest him.

Now, as Matthew 22 begins and Jesus' crucifixion draws near, he remains in the temple in the presence of the Pharisees and tells the parable of the wedding banquet.

The central theme of this parable is that Israel will be judged for its rejection of the Messiah. The kingdom of heaven has been opened to the Gentiles – a joyous event the Jews should have celebrated as friends of the king and his son, the bridegroom. Yet, because the generation of Israelites witnessing Messiah's appearance have rejected him, God's wrath will fall upon them.

The wedding banquet is likely an evening meal. For an event of this type, two invitations are sent. The first one invites chosen guests to attend – and who would refuse such an honor from the king? The second announces that all is ready. It provides further details, including the time at which guests are expected to arrive. In this parable, the king offers a third invitation – quite exceptional, revealing the king's graciousness – but the invited guests respond by treating the king's slaves cruelly, even killing them.

The banquet is a picture of the covenant fellowship between Christ (the king's son) and the church (his bride). The Jews under the Old Covenant are the invited guests who disregard the Father's invitation, treat his slaves (the prophets) viciously, and despise his Son. There's also a sense in which this refers not only to Jews, but to all people and cultures that close their eyes to the light of the promised Messiah.

The king responds with rage to the mistreatment of his servants and the disregard for his son. So he marshals an army, destroys the murderous rebels, and burns down their city. This is Jesus' prophecy of the judgment that befalls Israel in A.D. 70, when the Roman armies under Titus sack Jerusalem, completely destroy the temple, kill more than one million Jews, and scatter the rest of the Jewish nation. Jesus also speaks of this terrible day in Matthew 24:1-2.

Now, the king directs his servants to go where the roads exit the city and invite everyone they find to the banquet. In Luke's account of this parable (Luke 14:16-24), he adds the word "hedges" or "lanes" (v. 23) to indicate the people to whom the apostles are sent – the poor, the outcast, and others outside the elite circle of the privileged and powerful. This verse points out the Jews' final rejection of Christ and the calling of the Gentiles.

So, the servants fill the banquet hall with "everyone they found, both good and evil" (Matt. 22:10), a picture of the visible, or professing church. Scripture is abundantly clear that not everyone who claims the name of Jesus truly knows him, despite appearances to the contrary (see Matt. 7:21-23). In the same way, the church throughout the present evil age consists of professors and possessors – those who profess to know Christ, and those who truly have his Spirit within them as the distinguishing mark of true believers (Rom. 8:9).

Next, we come to the guest who is not dressed for a wedding (Matt. 22:11). In ancient times, kings and princes provided fresh clothing to their guests. Normally, these were long white robes. To refuse such gifts, or to appear at the banquet without them, was an expression of highest contempt for the host and his guests.

It's a perfect picture of hypocrites. They are in the church, enjoying its fellowship and benefitting from its ministries. They may speak the Son's name, but they don't know him, nor are they known by the Son. They bask in the glow of the redeemed, share a covenant meal with them, and rub shoulders with their leaders. They are offered the robe of Christ's righteousness but prefer the filthy rags of their own deeds. They have no true regard for Jesus, except for how employing his name may advance their status among others. When pressed for a defense of their faith, they have none.

The king confronts the guest in verse 12: "Friend [companion is a better term], how did you get in here without wedding clothes?" he asks. The man is speechless – "muzzled" or "gagged" in some translations. Just as the guest is silenced by his own conscience, the unbeliever stands before God one day "without excuse" (Rom. 1:20). As a result, the king orders his guest to be bound hand and foot and thrown into "the outer darkness," away from the fellowship of the wedding party, perhaps even into a dungeon. In a similar way, Christ casts unbelievers out of his kingdom into everlasting punishment on the day they are summoned before the great white throne (Rev. 20:11-15; cf. Matt. 7:21-23; 8:12; 25:30).

Finally, we come to the phrase Jesus uses often in the Gospels, "For many are invited [called], but few are chosen" (Matt. 22:14). This is an allusion to the Roman method of raising an army. All men are mustered, but only those fit for duty are chosen to serve. Many are invited to the wedding feast, but most ignore the invitation, make light of it, find themselves otherwise engaged in worldly matters, abuse the king's messengers, or show up in the filthy rags of their own righteousness; a comparatively small number enter the kingdom through the narrow gate (Matt. 7:13-14).

To enter the fellowship of the king, we must make sure we are clothed in the righteousness of Christ – true possessors of the Holy Spirit and not merely professors of the faith.

In both parables – the parable of the ten virgins and the parable of the wedding feast – there is great celebration. There is ample food, drink, music, and fellowship. At the same time, there is despair outside the banquet hall. In Jesus' parable of the ten virgins, the foolish virgins are unprepared, revealing they are uncommitted. The door is shut. The groom tells them he does not know them. They are barred from the festivities.

In the parable of the wedding banquet, the emphasis is not so much on preparation as it is on rejection. The invited guests refuse to come. And through their violent actions against the king's servants, they demonstrate their hatred of the king and his family. These are the Jews under the Old Covenant, who initially say they're all in (Exod. 19:8; 24:3) but consistently illustrate they have their own agenda.

They are like the wicked in the days of Noah, who hear a message of repentance but reject it out of contempt for God. The one improperly dressed for the wedding feast comes for convenience and comfort, much like the crowds that follow Jesus – as long as he's feeding them and wowing them with miracles (see John 6). But the poorly clothed man is utterly self-righteous and thus cast out of the banquet hall, and he joins the invited guests who never wanted to be there in the first place.

The marriage supper of the Lamb is a time of great rejoicing. It's also a time of great disappointment and despair. Those who enter the banquet hall and feast with the groom are those who are both humble and ready – humble, in that they know their invitation is offered in grace and the wedding garment donned in faith; ready, in that they are truly committed to the groom and seek nothing so much as the joy of hearing the *shofar* sound and the call, "Behold, the bridegroom comes!"

COMING FOR HIS BRIDE

Jesus is indeed coming for his bride. And while the precise order of events is unclear, the unmistakable truths of these parables are not. Jesus is the bridegroom who has entered into a New Covenant with his bride. He has paid the dowry and secured our eternal lives. He has promised to return, and today he's in heaven preparing a place for us. We don't know when he's coming for us. Further, the bridegroom is delayed – and for good reason (2 Pet. 3:8-9).

We are to be ready for his return at all times, demonstrating our devotion to him through faithful lives and the authentic endurance of hardship. When he comes, he's coming suddenly and surprisingly, at which time there's a separation between those who claim to know him and those who truly do know him. He takes his bride into heaven, and there we feast at the marriage supper of the Lamb.

Meanwhile, many who pretend to be followers of Christ are barred from admission, despite their protests. They have no one to blame but themselves, and their absence from the banquet hall in no way diminishes the joy of the Lamb, his bride, and his guests.

While the marriage supper of the Lamb is a joyous time of celebration for the church and her bridegroom, the second coming provides a different kind of supper for those who have rejected the bridegroom, as well as those who are unprepared for his coming – a funeral supper of dead flesh for the fowls of the earth:

> Then I saw an angel standing in the sun, and he called out in a loud voice, saying to all the birds flying high overhead, "Come, gather together for the great supper of God, so that you may eat the flesh of kings, the flesh of military commanders, the flesh of the mighty, the flesh of horses and of their riders, and the flesh of everyone, both free and slave, small and great....
>
> The rest were killed with the sword that came from the mouth of the rider on the horse [Jesus], and all the birds ate their fill of their flesh (Rev. 19:17-18, 21).[13]

REVIEW

Key takeaways from this chapter

1. Jewish weddings in ancient Israel featured three distinct elements: the *shiddukhim*, or marriage contract; the *erusin*, or betrothal; and the *nissuin*, or marriage ceremony. These events reveal key truths about our covenant relationship with Jesus, his promise to prepare a place in heaven for us, and the certainty of his return.

2. The *mikvah*, or water ritual involving both the bride and groom, portrays Christian baptism in that it symbolizes purity and acts as a token of spiritual cleansing. Further, baptism signifies death to an old way of life and the embrace of a new life with a new identity. Though he is sinless, Jesus submits to the *mikvah* as an open declaration that he's ready to move from the marriage contract into the next phase of his relationship with us: betrothal.

3. As a bride and groom enter the second phase of their wedding – the *erusin*, or betrothal – they enter a shelter known as the *huppah*. Here, the couple shares a cup of wine to seal their vows. This is much like the Lord's Supper, in which we remember Christ's death – his dowry – until he returns for us.

4. The parable of the ten virgins (Matt. 25:1-13) reminds us that Jesus has gone to prepare a place in heaven for us, and that he's

returning unexpectedly, just as a first-century Jewish bridegroom comes for his bride. Though the day and hour are unknown to us, we are to keep our lamps trimmed and be ready at all times for his glorious appearing. Those who delay getting ready – who focus on themselves rather than on the returning Christ – find themselves locked out when the bride and groom initiate the marriage supper.

5. The parable of the wedding banquet (Matt. 22:1-14) foretells the judgment of Israel for her rejection of Jesus as Messiah. It also warns us that today's church is populated both with true followers of Jesus and false professors of the faith. Those who desire to enjoy the trappings of Christian life while refusing to wear the robe of Christ's righteousness are cast out on judgment day.

DISCUSS

Questions for personal or group study

1. What are the distinct roles of the groom and bride in a Jewish wedding? How do these roles picture the work of Christ (the groom) and the appropriate response of Christians (the bride)?

2. How does the *mikvah*, or water ceremony, of a Jewish wedding symbolize Christian baptism?

3. In a first-century Jewish setting, what are some reasons a bridegroom may be delayed in coming for his bride? Read 2 Peter 3:8-9. What are two reasons the Lord has delayed his return to earth?

4. Read Matthew 25:1-13. How are the wise and foolish virgins similar to one another? What are the key differences between them? Why do you think the bridegroom refuses entrance to the foolish virgins, even after they acquire oil and light their lamps?

5. Read Matthew 22:1-14. How does this parable apply to first-century Israelites? When and how is this parable fulfilled? What does this parable also say to professing Christians in the church today?

* * *

"I AM COMING SOON"

JESUS' RETURN IS IMMINENT

*T*hroughout history, the element of surprise has birthed many dramatic victories. In 1184 B.C., a massive wooden horse is left at the gates of Troy, ostensibly as an offering to the goddess Athena. The horse, however, conceals soldiers who, once wheeled into the city, open the gates for an invading Greek army.

A detachment of 2,400 troops crossing the icy Delaware River on Christmas night of 1776 uses the cover of darkness and the drunken stupor of defending German troops (whom the British hired as mercenaries) to secure a surprise victory for General George Washington's beleaguered Continental Army.

And in the early hours of June 5, 1967, the Israeli Air Force launches Operation Mivtza Moked with two hundred aircraft. The pilots catch their Egyptian counterparts napping. By the end of the day, five hundred Egyptian aircraft are destroyed, and their military airstrips are rendered inoperable. Jordanian and Syrian aircraft are similarly targeted. As a result, the Six-Day War radically alters the geopolitics of the Middle East.[1]

Unlike these historic upsets, the return of Christ doesn't hinge on stealth. Jesus is not returning in disguise. He's not scheming with Mother Nature. Nor is he descending from heaven under the radar.

Quite the contrary. Jesus openly tells us he's coming back. He offers signs as obvious as a red sky at dawn. He urges us to be ready at all times. Scripture foretells his return as personal, physical, visible, and powerful. John declares that "every eye will see him" (Rev. 1:7).

And yet, it's clear from Scripture that Christ's return will catch many people off-guard. There's no excuse for this, any more than the Trojans, British, or Egyptians should have been surprised when invading armies breached their defenses. We have a particular advantage in that Jesus states plainly he's coming back – and he doesn't hide the particulars of his return, only the day and hour.

And yet, that proves to be the catch for many people. We simply don't know *when* Jesus is returning, only *that* he's coming back – and coming back *soon*.

Consider these passages from the Book of Revelation, with emphasis added:

> **Revelation 1:1-3** - The revelation of Jesus Christ that God gave him to show his servants *what must soon take place*. He made it known by sending his angel to his servant John, who testified to the word of God and to the testimony of Jesus Christ, whatever he saw. Blessed is the one who reads aloud the words of this prophecy, and blessed are those who hear the words of this prophecy and keep what is written in it, because *the time is near*.

> **Revelation 22:6** - Then he said to me, "These words are faithful and true. The Lord, the God of the spirits of the prophets, has sent his angel to show his servants *what must soon take place*."

> **Revelation 22:7** - "Look, *I am coming soon* ...."

> **Revelation 22:12** - "Look, *I am coming soon*, and my reward is with me to repay each person according to his work."

> **Revelation 22:20** - He who testifies about these things says, "Yes, *I am coming soon*." Amen! Come, Lord Jesus!

"Near" and "soon" are relative terms. An asteroid passing within 1.2 million miles of Earth in January 2022 got NASA's attention, as do all so-called *near-earth objects* that breach a thirty-million-mile perimeter around our planet.[2] And anyone stuck on hold during a phone call with an internet provider takes little comfort in hearing the recurring message, "We look forward to serving you *soon*."

So, we shouldn't be too hard on Jesus and the apostles when they speak and write about the nearness of the Lord's return. Yes, it's been nearly two thousand years since Jesus ascended into heaven and angels told the gawking apostles to watch for his reappearance. But, perhaps, we may take comfort in knowing that the apostles seem to believe they'll be alive to witness the second coming.

IMMINENCE AND UNCERTAINTY

There are a number of New Testament passages that reflect the early church's belief in the imminent return of Jesus, but an uncertainty as to *when* he returns.

Paul commends the Corinthians because they "eagerly wait for the revelation of our Lord Jesus Christ" (1 Cor. 1:7). He further encourages them: "So don't judge anything prematurely, before the Lord comes, who will both bring to light what is hidden in darkness and reveal the intentions of the hearts" (1 Cor. 4:5).

Paul advises the unmarried in Corinth:

> The time is limited, so from now on those who have wives should be as though they had none, those who weep as though they did not weep, those who rejoice as though they did not rejoice, those who buy as though they did not own anything, and those who use the world as though they did not make full use of it. For this world in its current form is passing away (1 Cor. 7:29-31).

He further urges all Corinthian believers to be holy, warning that they're living in "the ends of the ages" (1 Cor. 10:11).

Paul reminds the Philippians, "Our citizenship is in heaven, and

we eagerly wait for a Savior from there, the Lord Jesus Christ"
(Phil. 3:20).

The writer of Hebrews reminds us that God has spoken to us by
his Son in "these last days" (Heb. 1:2). James encourages his readers to
"be patient until the Lord's coming.... Strengthen your hearts, because
the Lord's coming is near.... Look, the judge stands at the door!"
(Jas. 5:7-9). And Peter writes that Jesus was "foreknown before the
foundation of the world but was revealed in these last times for you"
(1 Pet. 1:20).

Christians of nearly every era expect to witness the second
coming. Curiously, that expectation mirrors the anticipation of every
generation of Israelites that Messiah is about to be revealed. While
observant Jews await Messiah's first appearance on Earth, faithful
Christians look for his glorious return. "Near" and "soon" are watch-
words for both groups.

As we studied in Chapter 7, Jesus says he's coming back "like a
thief" (Rev. 16:15), meaning his return is both carefully planned and
dramatically executed. The Lord also tells us he's coming at an hour
we don't expect (Matt. 24:44). Many of his parables illustrate the
suddenness of his *parousia*. He's coming on a day that surprises
wicked servants (Matt. 24:45-51), unsuspecting bridesmaids
(Matt. 25:1-13), distracted doorkeepers (Mark 13:32-37), and careless
homeowners (Luke 12:39-40). In every instance, the wise listener
focuses, not on the day or hour of Christ's return, but on being ready
for his return whenever it comes.

The delay, which we discussed in some detail in Chapter 14, is
purposeful. It shows that God, not humans or angelic beings, is in
sovereign command of human history. It shows that he reckons time
differently than we do, and that his delay is a merciful opportunity for
sinners to receive him before it's too late (2 Pet. 3:8-9).

And it's an act of grace that enables Christians to live in the
tension between God's present and future kingdoms. How would we
behave if we knew the exact day of our Lord's return? Because we're
not omniscient, it's highly unlikely we could handle the stress of
knowing the future, especially a future beyond our control.

SOON, SHORTLY, SPEEDILY

It may help to look more closely at the Greek word often translated "soon," or "quickly," in the New Testament. The adverb *tachys* means shortly, speedily, or without delay. It usually refers to a brief period of time, focusing on the speed of an activity or event. It does not necessarily mean immediately, nor does it specify a precise moment, although it may describe a relatively brief time subsequent to another point in time.

Tachys is found numerous times in the New Testament. For example, an angel at the empty tomb of Jesus instructs two women to go "quickly" (*tachy*) and tell Jesus' disciples the good news. As they depart hastily with fear and great joy, they encounter the resurrected Christ (Matt. 28:7-9).

Paul expresses his desire to send Timothy to the Philippians "soon" (*tacheos*; Phil. 2:19). And in his final instructions to Timothy, an abandoned Paul urges the young pastor to come to him "soon" (*tacheos*; 2 Tim. 4:9).

In Jesus' parable of the lost son, the father wants the celebration – featuring robe, ring, sandals, and a fattened calf – to begin without delay, for he addresses his servants with the command, "Quick!" (*tachys*; Luke 15:22).

James reminds us that we should be "quick (*tachys*) to listen, slow to speak, and slow to anger" (Jas. 1:19).

These examples express the idea of relative speed without specifying an exact frame of time. So, what do we make of Jesus' use of *tachys* in Revelation 22, when he promises to come "soon," or "quickly"? And how should we understand John's warning of events that "must soon take place" because "the time is near"? (Rev. 1:1-3).

As one writer notes, "The meaning [of *tachys*] seems to be that events have been set in motion that will usher in His arrival without any unnecessary delay. Everything is moving along according to God's timetable."[3]

As we discussed in Chapter 14, the delay between Jesus' first and second comings is for two reasons. First, God isn't bound by time the way we are. Because he's eternal – and we're not – he reckons one day like a thousand years and a thousand years like one day (2 Pet. 3:8). Second, he's patiently waiting for people to come to him (2 Pet. 3:9). Jesus is coming soon in that God's plan of redemption is advancing. He foreknows all who come to him in belief and repentance, and he necessarily postpones his return until these have passed from death into life (John 5:24).

Jesus wants every generation to live expectantly, knowing we will joyously welcome his *parousia* on the clouds of heaven, and aware that we must all stand before the judgment seat of Christ (2 Cor. 5:10). Yes, he's coming soon. That is, he's returning without unnecessary delay. Just as Christ came the first time at just the right time (Gal. 4:4), he's coming again at just the right time – when the last sons and daughters are adopted, and the last one taken captive by Satan is set free.

TACHYS IN REVELATION

John and Jesus employ *tachys* several times in the Book of Revelation. Let's explore the use of this term more closely, and in context.

Revelation 1:1-3

> The revelation of Jesus Christ that God gave him to show his servants *what must soon take place*. He made it known by sending his angel to his servant John, who testified to the word of God and to the testimony of Jesus Christ, whatever he saw. Blessed is the one who reads aloud the words of this prophecy, and blessed are those who hear the words of this prophecy and keep what is written in it, because *the time is near* (emphasis added).

Since John has been instructed to write to seven contemporary churches in Asia Minor, we should seek to understand his words in a first-century context. John braces his readers for "what must soon take place." As G. K. Beale writes, "John probably views the death and resurrection of Christ as inaugurating the long-awaited kingdom of the end times, which the OT (e.g., Daniel) had predicted and which will continue to exist throughout the church age."[4]

This embraces an extended period of tribulation. Believers continue to suffer for their faith while wickedness expands and darkens. And it implies the many comings of Christ to comfort the suffering saints and to judge evil. Ultimately, it casts our view forward to the personal, glorious return of Christ with his holy angels to vindicate and reward the righteous and to condemn the wicked.

John's promised blessings on the ones who read aloud, hear, and keep what is about to be revealed are available now "because the time is near." This echoes the already-but-not-yet quality of the kingdom of God (see Chapter 8), which Jesus proclaims early in his earthly ministry: "The time is fulfilled, and the kingdom of God has come near. Repent and believe the good news!" (Mark 1:15).

The kingdom is present wherever Jesus appears. His sinless life, miracles, and parables offer first-century eyewitnesses a foretaste of the kingdom, which comes in fullness at his return. In a similar manner, Christ's blessings and judgments visited on people in the present day cast a long shadow leading to his *parousia*.

Statements throughout Revelation about Christ's coming quickly, soon, or like a thief – for example, Revelation 2:16; 3:11; 16:15 – likely don't allude primarily to his glorious return at the end of the age, but "to all his unseen comings in judgment throughout the age and climaxing with the final Parousia."[5] So, when we read in Revelation that Christ is "coming quickly" and "the time is near," we should embrace the same principles of the kingdom of God and see that they simultaneously hold already-but-not-yet promises. This takes the pressure off followers of Jesus to explain why everything prophesied hasn't happened by the end of the first century. It also prevents us from holding to a strict linear timeline for the unfolding of events in the Apocalypse of John.

When we jump from the first chapter of Revelation to the last chapter, we see how the formal conclusion of the whole book (Rev. 22:6-21) is linked with the introduction in Revelation 1:1-3. The key difference is that the introduction promises a blessing on all who obey the revelation; the conclusion issues a curse on those who disobey it. The common thread running through Revelation is that we're reading a communication from God, who holds human history – past and future – in his hands.

Revelation 2:16; 3:11

In his letter to the church at Pergamum, Jesus implores his followers to repent. "Otherwise," he says, "I will come to you *quickly* and fight against them [the Nicolaitans] with the sword of my mouth" (Rev. 2:16, emphasis added). Here, Jesus announces a coming judgment, not at the end of human history, but more immediately in the future.

In his letter to the church at Philadelphia, Jesus encourages believers to remain faithful. He promises to deliver them from an hour of testing that is coming on the whole world. "I am coming *soon*," he promises. "Hold on to what you have, so that no one takes your crown" (Rev. 3:11, emphasis added). This reference seems aimed at the second coming, and runs more consistently with Christ's words in Revelation 22 about his imminent return.

Revelation 22:6

Jesus' words in Revelation 22 are eschatological. They point to the day when he judges the world in righteousness and creates new heavens and a new earth.

In this verse, either an angel or Jesus speaks: "Then he said to me, 'These words are faithful and true. The Lord, the God of the spirits of the prophets, has sent his angel to show his servants what must *soon* take place [emphasis added].'"

These words follow God's revelation of new heavens and a new earth. Just as tribulation, suffering, and judgment are coming as markers of the church age (Rev. 1 ff.), final victory over Satan, sin, and death is equally assured in the return of Christ.

Yes, there is tribulation now. Followers of Jesus have been persecuted since before his crucifixion; today, millions of faithful Christians have lost their lives for the cause of Jesus. But suffering gives way to triumph in the glorious return of Christ, the Suffering Servant who is seated at the Father's right hand and comes back to earth to establish his kingdom in fullness. The already-but-not-yet quality of God's kingdom resounds through the pages of Revelation, and it's punctuated here.

Revelation 22:7

Here, Jesus clearly is the speaker. He says, "Look! I am coming *soon*. Blessed is the one who keeps the words of the prophecy of this book [emphasis added]." Included in the events that "must soon take place" (v. 6) is Christ's glorious return to earth. This refers to his final and climactic coming with his angels (Matt. 25:31), but it doesn't prevent numerous interim visitations by the omnipresent Son of God.

For example, Jesus promises to send his followers another advocate like himself, who is going to reside in his followers (John 14:16). This, of course, is the Holy Spirit, or Spirit of Christ (Rom. 8:9). In his high priestly prayer, Jesus tells the Father, "I am in them and you are in me, so that they may be made completely one" (John 17:23).

So, there's a sense in which Jesus is on earth today, dwelling in the spirits of his people. We also may understand that Jesus is present with us in the waters of baptism, as we identify with him in his death, burial, and resurrection. And he's with us in the ordinance of the Lord's Supper, where the bread and cup symbolize his body and blood offered for our salvation on the cross.

Jesus appears to many people after his resurrection over a period of forty days. And even after he ascends to the Father's right hand, he comes in blessing and judgment. New Testament writers record that these visits come in dreams and visions. When he finally returns physically, every eye will see him (Rev. 1:7).

Jesus appears from heaven to Saul on the road to Damascus and dramatically transforms the Pharisee into an apostle (see Acts 9:1-31). He comes in judgment against the nation of Israel for its rejection of him as Messiah (see Mark 14:62). All of this happens while it's quite apparent he remains in heaven until his triumphant return (cf. John 14:2-3; Acts 1:10-11; 2:33; 3:20-21; 7:55-56; Rom. 8:34; Phil. 3:20; Col. 3:1; 1 Thess. 1:10; Heb. 8:1; 10:12-13; 12:2; 1 Pet. 3:22; Rev. 14:1).

In addition, Jesus tells us he will not visit Earth physically again until his return:

> The days are coming when you will long to see one of the days of the Son of Man, but you won't see it. They will say to you, "See, there!" or "See here!" Don't follow or run after them. For as the lightning flashes from horizon to horizon and lights up the sky, so the Son of Man will be in his day (Luke 17:22-24).

Those in the New Testament who witness an appearance of Jesus after his ascension always see him in heaven, never on Earth. When Jesus confronts Saul on the road to Damascus around A.D. 34, he appears physically from the heavens (Acts 9:3; 22:6). Some twenty years later, Paul insists that he is the last one to see the resurrected Christ (1 Cor. 15:8; cf. Acts 22:14-15).

Yet, Jesus orchestrates events from heaven, such as the judgment on Israel in A.D. 70 for the nation's rejection of him as Messiah (Mark 14:62). And he warns the churches in Pergamum and Philadelphia that he may come soon to render judgment (Rev. 2:16; 3:11). He no doubt has a hand in the deaths of Ananias and Sapphira (Acts 5:1-11), as well as a mighty spiritual presence among the faithful being persecuted in Jerusalem (Acts 4:23-31).

Still, the only way Jesus is seen after his ascension is in dreams and visions (Acts 9:10; 18:8-10; 22:17-21; 23:11). Even his appearance to Paul in Acts 23:11 most likely is a vision, similar to what we encounter in Acts 18:9-10 (Paul's night vision in Corinth). And when Stephen is being stoned and captures a vision of Jesus, the Lord is in heaven (Acts 7:55-56).

Jesus' departure into heaven is a necessary precondition for the ministry of the Holy Spirit (John 16:7). Peter makes this clear in his sermon on the Day of Pentecost: "Therefore, since he has been exalted to the right hand of God and has received from the Father the promised Holy Spirit, he has poured out what you both see and hear" (Acts 2:33).

No member of the Trinity works independently. The Father, Son, and Spirit together create the universe (Gen. 1:2; John 1:1-3; Col. 1:15; Heb. 1:3). The three persons of the Godhead play distinct roles in our salvation (e.g., Rom. 5:1-6; 8:14-17; 2 Cor. 1:21-22; Eph. 1:3-14; 2:18; Tit. 3:4-7; Heb. 10:29-30; 1 Pet. 1:1-2). All three are credited with raising Jesus from the dead (John 2:18-19; 10:18; Acts 2:32-33; Rom. 8:11; Gal. 1:1; 1 Pet. 3:18). And all three work collaboratively to create new heavens and a new earth.

So, we may rightly say that "Christ's coming is a series of comings in blessing and judgment and will be consummated by a climactic coming in final blessing and condemnation. Nevertheless, the greater focus here [Rev. 22:7] at the end of the book is likely on the consummate coming."[6]

Grant Osborne makes these helpful observations:

> God in his sovereignty has already determined the time of the end (see Rev. 6:11), and we can only hold on to the certainty of his promises and wait for his predestined time. The church in every age is to await Christ's "soon" return, but the actual timing is up to him.[7]

So, in salvation history, the next eschatological event after Christ's death, resurrection, ascension, and Pentecost is the second coming. Whether his return is two years after John writes Revelation or two thousand years later, it's still "near" in salvation history.

Revelation 22:12

Jesus declares, "Look, I am coming *soon*, and my reward is with me to repay each person according to his work [emphasis added]."

This echoes Isaiah 40:10, "See, the Lord GOD comes with strength, and his power establishes his rule. His wages are with him, and his reward accompanies him." Here, the promise is that God would deliver his people from destruction and exile, and his reward is a return to the land. In Revelation 22:12, the "reward" is eschatological and relates to the eternal compensation promised believers for their faithfulness to Christ.

This verse addresses Christ's future coming for all the world to see. At that time, he rewards the faithful and condemns the wicked. This is the time to which Jesus refers in John 5:28-29:

> ... a time is coming when all who are in the graves will hear his voice and come out – those who have done good things, to the resurrection of life, but those who have done wicked things, to the resurrection of condemnation.

Christ's reference to "good things" and "wicked things" is not the establishment of works as the basis of salvation, for just a few verses earlier he sets the requirements for redemption: "Truly I tell you, anyone who hears my word and believes him who sent me has eternal life and will not come under judgment but has passed from death to life" (John 5:24).

So, the works to which Jesus alludes are evidences of one's faith in or rebellion against Christ. Rewards, or loss of rewards, are granted to believers based on their stewardship of all that Christ has entrusted to them. Degrees of punishment in hell await those who reject the Lord (see Chapters 9-11).

The New Testament often repeats the theme of judgment based on works. For example, Jesus declares, "For the Son of Man is going to come with his angels in the glory of his Father, and then he will reward each according to what he has done" (Matt. 16:27). The parable of the sheep and goats expresses a separation of the righteous and the wicked based on how their works reveal their character (Matt. 25:31-46).

Paul writes to the Romans:

> Because of your hardened and unrepentant heart you are storing up wrath for yourself in the day of wrath, when God's righteous judg-

ment is revealed. He will repay each one according to his works: eternal life to those who by persistence in doing good seek glory, honor, and immortality; but wrath and anger to those who are self-seeking and disobey the truth while obeying unrighteousness (Rom. 2:5-8).

The believer, indwelled and empowered by the Holy Spirit, lives a life of conformity to the image of God. The unbeliever, driven by the flesh, produces works worthy of eternal separation from God. Peter writes, "And if you address as Father the One who judges impartially based on each one's work, you are to conduct yourselves in fear during the time of your temporary residence" (1 Pet. 1:17 HCSB).

This does not even begin to suggest that forgiveness of sins and eternal life are earned through good behavior. As Jesus and the New Testament writers make clear, salvation is by the grace of God alone, through faith in Christ alone (see, for example, John 3:16; 5:24; Rom. 4:4-5; 6:23; Eph. 2:8-9; Tit. 3:5-7). Jesus left the portals of heaven and came to earth for the express purpose of paying our sin debt. To advocate a works-based path to eternal life – even a faith-plus-works salvation – is to trample on the blood of the crucified, buried, and risen Lord.

So then, why does Jesus say in Revelation 22:12 that his reward is with him to "repay each person according to what he has done?" We should keep in mind that the Greek *misthos* ("reward") does not automatically carry a positive connotation. More literally, it means "payment for work done," and as such it may refer to punishment as well as reward.[8]

Misthos appears twenty-nine times in the New Testament, often as "reward," but also as "wages," "pay," "payment," or "profit." The Greek noun means "pay for service" and can be used to describe compensation for good or bad service. Jesus is the one to whom all judgment has been given (John 5:22) and the one before whom all people stand one day. The focus of final judgment is not *where* people spend eternity, but *how*.

A person's eternal destiny is based on how he or she answers the question Jesus asks in Matthew 16:15, "who do you say that I am?" Those who respond, "You are the Christ, the Son of the living God," and who entrust their lives to Jesus, are granted eternal life; they have applied the finished work of Christ to their lives and thus are declared in right standing with God.

The ones who reject Christ have chosen to spend this life, as well as the life to come, apart from Christ and thus spend eternity in hell, to which Satan and demons are consigned (Matt. 25:41). So, the "reward" for what each person has done is God's way of setting things right in a world where people make a wide variety of choices for which they must give an answer.

One of the oldest prayers of the Christian church is *Maranatha* – our Lord, come! Paul shares this heartfelt petition in 1 Corinthians 16:22, and it's combined with a blessing for believers and a curse for unbelievers: "If anyone does not love the Lord, a curse be on him. Our Lord, come!"

Revelation 22:20

> He who testifies about these things says, "Yes, I am coming *quickly* [emphasis added]" (HCSB; "soon" in CSB).

Jesus reminds us one final time that his return is both certain and imminent. Although it has been nearly two thousand years since our Lord uttered these words, we know his promise is true. As the eternal Son of God, he is our Savior, and his work on our behalf is not completed until he resurrects us, judges and rewards us, purges the created order of sin and its stain, and creates new heavens and a new earth.

As God, Jesus cannot lie; it goes against his very nature. As a gracious and merciful sovereign who transcends time, his promise to come "quickly" needs to be taken in the context of the one to whom one day is as a thousand years and a thousand years as one day, and to whom this seeming delay is for the benefit of all who call upon him while there is yet time (2 Pet. 3:8-9).

Lastly, Jesus' promise assures us that his return is personal. "I am coming quickly," he says. Not an angel, or an exalted human, or an invisible force, but the same Jesus who ascended physically into heaven after showing himself alive for forty days (Acts 1:10-11).

Three times in the closing paragraphs of Revelation, Christ promises to come soon. Eternity may seem far off to us. Yet, there is an immediacy in the events foretold in John's apocalypse. As Lawrence Richards writes, "Soon may be tomorrow! There is nothing that must happen before the events we have read of in Revelation may begin. These paragraphs also make it clear that we are to learn to live with this sense of immediacy."[9]

To the promises of Jesus, John rapturously responds, "Amen! Come, Lord Jesus!" (Rev. 22:20). We, too, may share in the apostle's enthusiastic reply.

As we read God's word, meditate on it, and draw fresh illumination from the Holy Spirit, we say, "Amen! Come, Lord Jesus!"

As we worship with fellow believers in the community of the local body of Christ, we proclaim, "Amen! Come, Lord Jesus!"

As we pray, seeking the heart of God and allowing him to conform us to his image – even in our deepest despair and most bruising divine discipline – we sigh, "Amen! Come, Lord Jesus!"

As we share the gospel with lost friends, defend the faith against those who sully it, give back to God our time and treasure, and walk through this sinful and fallen world as if in a foreign land, we cry, "Amen! Come, Lord Jesus!"

CAN CHRISTIANS HASTEN THE RETURN OF JESUS?

Is it possible for followers of Jesus to hasten his return? In seeking to answer this question, let's examine two seemingly paradoxical New Testament passages regarding the coming Day of the Lord.

First, Paul ends his address on Mars Hill with these words:

Therefore, having overlooked the times of ignorance, God now commands all people everywhere to repent, because *he has set a day*

when he is going to judge the world in righteousness by the man he
has appointed. He has provided proof of this to everyone by raising
him from the dead (Acts 17:30-31, emphasis added).

Not long before his death, in seeming contrast to Paul, Peter
writes:

But the day of the Lord will come like a thief; on that day the heavens
will pass away with a loud noise, the elements will burn and be
dissolved, and the earth and the works on it will be disclosed. Since all
these things are to be dissolved in this way, it is clear what sort of
people you should be in holy conduct and godliness as you wait for
the day of God and *hasten its coming*. Because of that day, the heavens
will be dissolved with fire and the elements will melt with heat. But
based on his promise, we wait for new heavens and a new earth, where
righteousness dwells (2 Pet. 3:10-13, emphasis added).

So, Paul tells us God has set a day for the judgment of all people,
while Peter seems to imply that Christians may "hasten" that day. Are
Paul and Peter at odds in their understanding of God's revealed plan
for the ages? Both apostles claim divine inspiration for their writing.
So, why do they seem to take different approaches to the Day of the
Lord?

To begin, we should acknowledge that the Bible is replete with
warnings about a future, final judgment of all people. There are
dozens of Old and New Testament passages that tell us all people
must stand before God one day and give an account of our lives.

For example, the writer of Ecclesiastes closes his book with these
words, "For God will bring every act to judgment, including every
hidden thing, whether good or evil" (Eccles. 12:14). Paul writes to the
Corinthians, "So don't judge anything prematurely, before the Lord
comes, who will both bring to light what is hidden in darkness and
reveal the intentions of the hearts" (1 Cor. 4:5). The writer of Hebrews
notes, "it is appointed for people to die once – and after this, judgment" (Heb. 9:27). And Jesus reminds us, "Look, I am coming soon,

and my reward is with me to repay each person according to his work" (Rev. 22:12).

We could cite other Scriptures, including those that focus specifically on believers, unbelievers, Satan, and evil spirits. But there's a palpable thread running through the Bible that indicates God has fixed a time when he judges all people and all angels.

Even so, do Peter's words in 2 Peter 3 indicate that followers of Jesus may move up the day of judgment on God's calendar? If so, how? And why would we want to do that?

Peter acknowledges that the Lord has delayed his coming – a message consistent with Jesus' teachings and parables. Peter reminds us that God reckons time differently than we do because he is neither bound by time nor obligated to its machinations. More important, however, according to Peter, the Lord's delay is a byproduct of his mercy, enabling all those who will trust in Jesus to do so – and to give Christ's followers more time to share the gospel.

This beneficial delay is not open-ended to God. One day, Jesus steps from the portals of heaven and returns to earth with his holy angels and the redeemed to resurrect and judge all people. Believers should not abuse Christ's delay to drift into slothfulness or complacency. Unbelievers should not wrongly think the delay means ultimately God changes his mind about their appointment with him at the great white throne.

God is omniscient. He has always known all things, including the names of those who receive his Son and those who reject him, as well as the precise moment of his Son's return to earth in glory. That means God is decisive as well. He's not tentatively gazing upon the earth and wondering how much longer he should wait to draw an end to human rebellion. He has always known exactly what he's doing, and what he's going to do. Even so, he is a compassionate God who takes no pleasure in the death of the wicked (Ezek. 18:23; 33:11). He desires all people to repent and turn to him (2 Pet. 3:9).

So, how do we rectify the seeming contradiction between a definite day of judgment and the possibility that humans may alter it? Peter appears to be saying that God's slowness to anger and his desire that all come to repentance do not – in fact, cannot – nullify the certainty of the Day of the Lord. The Lord eventually decides that the delay is over and the opportunity for sinful humans to repent is at an end. This occurs without prior announcement to people on earth, and thus it happens as quickly as the coming of a thief in the night.

Some commentators, like Peter Davids, read 2 Peter 3 as teaching that Christians, through their conduct, may hasten or slow the day of Christ's return. Davids argues that Peter's phrase, "hasten its coming," means the Day of the Lord is not a fixed date; rather, it's something believers can change by holy living. This idea is based on Isaiah 60:22, in which the Lord hastens a day of bringing his glory to Zion: "I am the LORD; I will accomplish it quickly in its time."

Second-Temple Jewish authors, and some early Christian writers, embraced the idea that God hastens or delays judgment due to Israel's repentance, or lack thereof. Davids notes, "in the first couple of centuries after Jesus such sentiments are attributed to more than one rabbi."[10]

Davids further points to Acts 3:19-20, which ties repentance to the return of Christ: "Therefore repent and turn back, so that your sins may be wiped out, that seasons of refreshing may come from the presence of the Lord, and that he may send Jesus, who has been appointed for you as the Messiah." The same idea is found in the extra-biblical book of 2 Clement 12:6: "When you do these things [good deeds, forsaking hypocrisy, sexual purity], the kingdom of my Father will come" (12:6).[11]

Davids summarizes:

> Thus we see that our author [Peter] is following a solid Jewish tradition, including one found in the early Jesus movement, in declaring that the coming (Greek *parousia*) of the Day of God is not a fixed date, but that under the sovereignty of God and due to his mercy ... it can be sped up (or, conversely, slowed down) by the behavior of the followers of Jesus. Thus an exhortation to hasten the day was appropriate then (and continues to be appropriate now).[12]

Thomas Schreiner, in his commentary on 2 Peter, holds much the same view. "Peter clearly taught that believers can advance or hasten the arrival of God's day by living godly lives," he writes. "We think here of the prayer, 'Your kingdom come' (Matt. 6:10). Surely the idea is that our prayer has some impact on when the kingdom arrives."[13]

Schreiner goes on to offer this insight: After two thousand years of history, how could we ever be sure Christians could live righteously enough to usher in the Day of the Lord? God's sovereignty isn't challenged. He foreknows – even foreordains – what we do (see Prov. 16:33; Isa. 46:9-11; Lam. 3:37-38; Eph. 1:11). Even so, this doesn't cancel out the call to live godly lives, knowing it may hasten the return of the Lord.

"We must not fall prey to rationalism that either squeezes out divine sovereignty or ignores human responsibility," Schreiner says. "Both of these must be held in tension, and here the accent falls on what human beings can do to hasten the day of God."[14]

If this tension between God's sovereignty and human responsibility proves troubling to us, we should take heart first of all in the steadfastness of God's attributes: eternality, omniscience, omnipotence, omnipresence, immutability, and so on. Nothing undermines the qualities of God's divine being. "Because I, the LORD, have not changed" (Mal. 3:6).

Next, be encouraged that while we struggle with scriptural paradoxes – seeming contradictions that, when fully investigated, prove true – God does not. One day, when we see Jesus as he is (1 John 3:2), we understand more clearly what we view as dim reflections today (1 Cor. 13:12).

Finally, consider the paradox of a fixed vs. fluid judgment day in light of other biblical enigmas. For example, Jesus teaches the already-but-not-yet qualities of the kingdom of God; it's here now, yet it's coming in the future. Or, ponder the doctrine of divine election, which embraces God's sovereign choice of individuals to salvation, and the freedom he endows on all people to make choices for which he holds us accountable. Many other challenging biblical teachings confront us: Are we to judge or not to judge (Matt. 7:1; John 7:24)? Do we answer a fool or not (Prov. 26:4-5)? And should we test God or not (Mal. 3:10; Luke 4:12)?

It's okay to embrace the mysteries of the Bible, and to wrestle with difficult passages of God's word. The Lord has spoken clearly in so many ways. And for reasons beyond our grasp, he has chosen to leave some biblical doctrines more obscure – at least for now. Among these ambiguities, of course, is the question at hand: Can we hasten the day of the Lord's return?

It's best to rest in the knowledge that God has, indeed, set a day when he judges the world (Acts 17:31). This day is fixed according to God's divine will and in keeping with his foreknowledge of all human activities. At the same time, we should live as if we may hasten that day through spiritual purity and godly living, for one day we all stand before the judgment seat of Christ to give an account of our lives (2 Cor. 5:10; 2 Pet. 3:12). Whether we can truly hasten the Day of the Lord or not, it has no bearing on the certainty of Christ's return and the inevitability of our day of judgment.

There is a point at which divine sovereignty and human freedom intersect. We can't override God's authority, yet we have real choices for which God holds us accountable. That much is biblically clear. When divine sovereignty and human freedom meet at Christ's judgment seat, we'll understand in real time what it means to experience the Day of the Lord.

REVIEW

Key takeaways from this chapter

1. Jesus states plainly that he's coming back – and he doesn't hide the particulars of his return, only the day and hour. And yet, that proves to be a catch for many people. We simply don't know *when* Jesus is returning, only *that* he's coming back – and coming back *soon*. The imminence of the second coming should be a concern for all people.

2. A number of New Testament passages reflect the early church's belief in the imminent return of Jesus, as well as an uncertainty as to

when he actually will return. For example, James encourages his readers to "be patient until the Lord's coming.... Strengthen your hearts, because the Lord's coming is near.... Look, the judge stands at the door!" (Jas. 5:7-9).

3. Many of Jesus' parables illustrate the suddenness of his *parousia*. He's coming on a day that surprises wicked servants (Matt. 24:45-51), unsuspecting bridesmaids (Matt. 25:1-13), distracted doorkeepers (Mark 13:32-37), and careless homeowners (Luke 12:39-40). In every instance, the wise listener focuses, not on the day or hour of Christ's return, but on being ready for his return whenever it comes.

4. John and Jesus employ the Greek *tachys* – "soon," "quickly," "speedily," "without delay" – several times in the Book of Revelation. These statements likely don't allude primarily to his glorious return at the end of the age, but to all his unseen comings in judgment throughout the age and climaxing with his glorious *parousia*. At the same time, the words of Jesus in Revelation 22 clearly warn us to be ready for his second coming.

5. Paul tells us God has set a day for the judgment of all people (Acts 17:30-31), while Peter seems to imply that Christians may "hasten" that day (2 Pet. 3:10-13). How do we rectify the seeming contradiction between a definite day of judgment and the possibility that humans may alter it? Peter seems to be saying that God's slowness to anger and his desire that all come to repentance do not – in fact, cannot – nullify the certainty of the Day of the Lord. The Lord eventually decides that the delay is over and the opportunity for sinful humans to repent is at an end. This occurs without prior announcement to people on earth, and thus it happens as quickly as the coming of a thief in the night.

DISCUSS

Questions for personal or group study

1. If you knew the day and hour of Christ's return, how would that knowledge change the way you live? Do you think it's better that we don't know this date with destiny? Why or why not?

2. Jesus tells us three times in Revelation 22, "I am coming soon."
In which verses are these statements found? And is Jesus speaking of
his second coming, or of some other visitation in judgment?

3. Several New Testament writers seem to think Christ is returning, or at least might return, in their lifetimes (see 1 Cor. 1:7; 7:29-31;
Heb. 1:3; Jas. 5:7-9; 1 Pet. 1:20). Were they foolish to think so? How
does their view of the last days set an example for us in the 21st
century?

4. When was the last time Jesus was seen physically, and to whom
did he appear (see 1 Cor. 15:8)? In what ways do Stephen (Acts 7:55-
56), John (Rev. 1:9-20), and others in the New Testament see Christ
after his ascension (physically, or otherwise)? When is the next time
Jesus will appear physically on earth? How does this realization help
us discern the claims of some people today that Jesus has appeared to
them?

5. Peter writes that Christians should be holy in conduct and
godliness as we wait for the day of God and *hasten* its coming (see
2 Pet. 3:10-13). Do you believe we can actually accelerate the day the
Lord returns?

* * *

"THEREFORE, BE ALERT"

JESUS WARNS US TO BE READY

*F*amous last words. William Brahms catalogued the final sayings of 3,500 prominent figures in his work, *Last Words of Notable People*. Other researchers also have captured the pithy statements of people on their deathbeds. A sampling:

While slipping towards the end of his life, Irish wit Oscar Wilde expressed disdain for the surroundings in his Paris hotel room. "Either that wallpaper goes, or I do," he blurted. Wilde went first, but hotel management noted his grievance and later refurbished the suite.

Standing before a firing squad, convicted murderer James W. Rodgers was asked if he had a final request. His reply: "Bring me a bullet-proof vest."

With death drawing near, television announcer Charles Gussman quietly removed his oxygen mask and whispered, "And now for a final word from our sponsor ...."

Leonardo da Vinci, who gave us such masterpieces as the Mona

Lisa, was awkwardly modest as he faced death, saying only, "I have offended God and mankind because my work did not reach the quality it should have."

Drummer Buddy Rich, being prepped for a major surgical procedure he wouldn't survive, was asked by his nurse, "Is there anything you can't take?" His response: "Yeah, country music."

Finally, Karl Marx reputedly offered these last words: "Get out of here and leave me alone. Last words are for fools who haven't said enough already."[1]

Last words may be pithy or droll – Winston Churchill is noted to have said, "I'm bored with it all," before slipping into a coma – yet they often reveal a perspective on the lives we have lived and, perhaps, our readiness to step through the portal of death. This is true, not only of noted authors, artists, and statesmen, but biblical characters as well.

In Chapter 7, we focused on the suddenness of Christ's return. We looked at numerous parables of Jesus, and we surveyed other New Testament texts that urge us to be prepared for the second coming. Indeed, Christ's parables of the last days shed no light on the exact timing of his return. However, they place a strong emphasis on our need to be faithful, expectant, and busy about kingdom business, for the *parousia* is as certain as it is sudden.

At the core of Jesus' teaching about his return is a clear warning: be on guard. Nowhere is this spoken with more clarity than in the Olivet Discourse. Here, Jesus combines prophecies of the pending destruction of the temple – fulfilled in A.D. 70 – with details about his return. Often, it's difficult to discern which event he's addressing, but watchfulness certainly applies to both. Not long after telling his disciples even he doesn't know the day and hour of his return, he states plainly:

Therefore *be alert*, since you don't know what day your Lord is coming. But know this: If the homeowner had known what time the thief was coming, he would have *stayed alert* and not let his house be broken into. This is why you are also to *be ready*, because the Son of Man is coming at an hour you do not expect (Matt. 24:42-44, emphasis added).

What will Jesus find us doing when he returns? What might be our last words? More importantly, when we stand before the judgment seat of Christ, will our footprints be found on the path of good works God laid out for us in eternity past (Eph. 2:10)?

As we come to grips with our own mortality and the certainty of judgment to follow, it may help to see how two biblical characters face their impending deaths, and how their final words express both a readiness to die and an eagerness for the life to come. We begin with Joseph, then move on to Jesus. We also look briefly at several New Testament figures: Stephen, Paul, Peter, and John.

JOSEPH

The story of Joseph (Gen. 37-50) is both heartbreaking and heart-warming. It's a tale of tragedy and triumph, punishment and pardon, incarceration and exaltation, abandonment and reunion, fear and power, famine and plenty, deep sadness and unrestrained joy. We are introduced to Joseph as the favorite son of Jacob, a preference that spurs jealousy and betrayal in the hearts of Joseph's brothers, who opportunistically sell Joseph into slavery and then soak his robe in animal blood in a ruse to fake their brother's death.

Joseph ends up in Egypt in the home of Potiphar, an officer of Pharaoh and captain of the guards. Potiphar sees that the Lord is making Joseph successful. So, the Egyptian officer makes Joseph his personal attendant and places everything in his household under the young servant's authority.

Joseph captures the eye of Potiphar's wife, who makes repeated sexual advances towards the strapping young man. When Joseph rebuffs her siren calls, she falsely accuses him of attempted rape, which lands him in jail with Pharaoh's prisoners. Again, the Lord grants Joseph favor, this time with the warden, who puts Joseph in charge of all other captives. This includes Pharoah's imprisoned cupbearer, who later secures Joseph's release by telling Pharaoh of Joseph's ability to interpret dreams.

Pharaoh has suffered two troubling dreams that his magicians are unable to decode. He looks to Joseph, who humbly confesses, "It is God who will give Pharaoh a favorable answer" (Gen. 41:16).

The two dreams mean the same thing: Egypt is about to enjoy seven prosperous years, followed by seven lean years. Joseph urges Pharoah to appoint a wise man to oversee the nation's affairs, storing up excess food during the good years so people may survive the famine to come.

Pharoah places his signet ring in Joseph's hand, dresses him in fine linen, and places a gold chain around his neck. In a matter of moments, Joseph goes from forgotten inmate to prime minister of Egypt. His godly wisdom and tactical skills enable Egypt not only to survive the famine, but to serve as the world's breadbasket during that time, enriching Pharaoh and indebting the people to him.

All of this leads to a reunion between Joseph and his family. First, Jacob sends ten of his sons to Egypt, where they buy grain from the prime minister but fail to recognize him as Joseph. After accusing his brothers of spying, Joseph holds them in prison for three days. Then, he keeps only Simeon in custody and sends the others back home with a strict command not to return unless they bring their youngest brother, Benjamin.

The famine continues unabated, and the grain runs out. Jacob sends his sons back to Egypt, grudgingly agreeing to allow Benjamin to accompany them. Joseph hosts a dinner for the brothers, including Simeon, and asks about their father. He shows favor to Benjamin and then sends his brothers back to Israel with full sacks of grain. Only, he orders his servants to place his cup in Benjamin's sack. On their way home, the brothers are overtaken by Joseph's servants, who reveal that

Benjamin is in possession of the prime minister's cup. Terrified, the brothers are brought back to Egypt.

Joseph tells the brothers they may return home, but Benjamin must remain in Egypt as his slave. That's when Judah steps forward to plead for his younger brother's life, offering to be Joseph's slave in Benjamin's place. Joseph has tested his brothers harshly, but he finds them kinder and more mature than the petulant gang of conspirators that tossed him into a cistern more than a decade earlier.

In a most touching scene, Joseph tells his brothers, "I am Joseph, your brother ... the one you sold into Egypt" (Gen. 45:4). He continues:

> And now don't be grieved or angry with yourselves for selling me here, because God sent me ahead of you to preserve life.... God sent me ahead of you to establish you as a remnant within the land to keep you alive by a great deliverance. Therefore it was not you who sent me here, but God. He has made me a father to Pharaoh, lord of his entire household, and ruler over all the land of Egypt (Gen. 45:5, 7-8).

With Pharaoh's blessing, Joseph sends for his father and the rest of his family. They travel to Egypt and settle in the best part of the land, per Pharaoh's orders. Pharaoh welcomes Jacob, who in turn blesses the king. Joseph provides for his father, his brothers, and all their dependents. Together, they acquire land, become prosperous, and multiply.

Years later, when Jacob dies, his sons fear Joseph will finally take vengeance on them for their past misdeeds. They send a message to Joseph:

> "Before he died your father gave a command: 'Say this to Joseph: Please forgive your brothers' transgression and their sin – the suffering they caused you.' Therefore, please forgive the transgression of the servants of the God of your father" (Gen. 50:16-17).

His brothers also prostrate themselves before Joseph and confess, "We are your slaves!" (v. 18).

But there isn't a hint of vengeance in Joseph. He weeps upon receiving their message. And when they come into his presence, he tells them, "Don't be afraid. Am I in the place of God? You planned evil against me; God planned it for good to bring about the present result – the survival of many people" (Gen. 50:19-21).

This is a recap of Joseph's words to his brothers in Egypt many years earlier (Gen. 45:5-8), only Joseph didn't identify his brothers' evil intent the first time. He does so now in order that everything is in the open. Sin is confessed, acknowledged, repented of, and completely forgiven.

All that's happened to Joseph – betrayal, imprisonment, false accusations, neglect, deliverance, and rise to prominence – are under God's providential care.

"Therefore don't be afraid," Joseph says again. "I will take care of you and your children" (Gen. 50:21).

Joseph wants his brothers and their children to know his kindness will outlive him. His brothers have nothing to fear. Joseph's care for them in Egypt will continue long after his death.

Finally, Joseph's last words are meant to assure his brothers: "I am about to die, but God will certainly come to your aid and bring you up from this land to the land he swore to give to Abraham, Isaac, and Jacob" (Gen. 50:24). Joseph then urges his brothers to take an oath: "When God comes to your aid, you are to carry my bones up from here" (v. 25).[2]

Joseph's last words carry no hint of remorse, doubt, or anger. While his life experiences span from being a favored child to becoming prime minister of Egypt, and from knowing the terror of abandonment, the isolation of prison, and the burden of false accusation to experiencing the comforts of Pharaoh's courts, Joseph rests confidently in the providence of God. He breathes his last in sublime peacefulness.

His final instructions about his bones reveal more than an ancient custom. Joseph would have little use for his bones after death. But commanding the return of his remains to the Promised Land shows confidence in God's promise to Abram to give his descendants a permanent homeland. Just as Joseph's bones would be buried in the land of his ancestors, his descendants ultimately would rest in a home where God promised to place his name.

As the writer of Hebrews puts it, "By faith Joseph, as he was nearing the end of his life, mentioned the exodus of the Israelites and gave instructions concerning his bones" (Heb. 11:22).

In many ways, Joseph's life foreshadows the life of Christ. Joseph is despised, rejected, betrayed, falsely accused, and abandoned. Yet, he emerges from prison as the voice of God – a wise counselor, a prince, a deliverer of his people. Jesus, too, is strongly opposed, disbelieved, reviled, betrayed, abused, and neglected. Yet, he rises from the grave as the exalted Son of God, our Savior and deliverer.

Joseph's request for his bones to rest in Canaan shows his confidence in the Lord's promise. Though Joseph is prime minister, Egypt is not his home. It's a nation that symbolizes slavery, foreshadowing the New Testament concept of bondage to sin. While Joseph dies in Egypt, his home is in Canaan and his hope is in God. And while Jesus dies outside the city walls of Jerusalem, his home is in heaven and his hope is in the Father.

Eric Watkins shares this observation:

> Canaan was the earthly antithesis of Egypt and was the much-hoped-for destination of the people of Israel. Though time might dim the memory and hope of Israel, the promise did not dim in the mind of God, and as surely as He pledged, He would also fulfill. Joseph's hope, then, was in the sure and steadfast promises of God.[3]

The God of Israel is faithful. He rescues his people from bondage in Egypt after more than four hundred years. Similarly, Christ is faithful. As the incarnate Son of God, and through his sinless life, death, burial, and resurrection, he rescues us from bondage to sin and death. Joseph sees this in types and shadows. Christ reveals it in his incarnation and finished work on the cross.

Joseph's last words echo through the corridors of time, fulfilled in freedom from Egyptian slavery, and ultimately realized in freedom from bondage to sin. His final words also offer an example of the way we are to live our lives and prepare for our deaths. Famous last words don't define a life – or redefine it. They reflect a life lived and a view toward the life to come.[4]

JESUS

No one is better prepared to die than Jesus. As the Lamb of God slain from the foundation of the world (Rev. 13:8), the eternal Son of God collaborates with the Father and the Holy Spirit before creation to plan their joint redemptive work. The incarnate Christ declares that he has come to seek and save the lost, a mission requiring his death (Matt. 16:21; Luke 19:10). After Peter's remarkable declaration of Jesus as Messiah, Son of the living God, Jesus tells his disciples he must go to Jerusalem, where he is to suffer, die, and rise again – over Peter's objection, which Christ condemns as Satanic (Matt. 16:16-23).

Jesus' willingness to lay down his life reveals a divine sense of purpose, humility, submission to the Father's will, and keen insight into what his death is accomplishing. There's even a sense of anticipatory mirth. As the writer of Hebrews notes, "For the joy that lay before him, he endured the cross, despising the shame, and sat down at the right hand of the throne of God" (Heb. 12:2).

Despite his followers' best efforts to keep Jesus out of harm's way, the Lamb of God walks deliberately into the slaughterhouse. In the Garden of Gethsemane, a mob with swords and clubs sets upon Jesus. Peter rushes to Jesus' defense, lopping off the ear of the high priest's servant with a sword.

Rather than thank Peter, Jesus rebukes him: "Put your sword back in its place …. Do you think that I cannot call on my Father, and he will provide me here and now with more than twelve legions of angels? How, then, would the Scriptures be fulfilled that say it must happen this way?" (Matt. 26:52-54).

The rapid-fire events that follow showcase Jesus' economy of words and laser-sharp focus. To the observer, Jesus is at the mercy of his captors. Yet, he's completely in control, as he signaled the questioning crowds earlier: "I lay down my life so that I may take it up again. No one takes it from me, but I lay it down on my own. I have the right to lay it down, and I have the right to take it up again. I have received this command from my Father" (John 10:17-18).

Jesus allows himself to be arrested, bound, and led to Annas, the father-in-law of Caiaphas the high priest. He allows himself to be sent to Caiaphas, questioned by Pilate, shuttled to Herod, mocked by Roman soldiers, summoned before the Sanhedrin, brutally beaten, stripped naked, led to Golgotha, and hoisted on a cross between two criminals.

He allows the soldiers tending his death to cast lots for his clothing. He allows the Jewish religious leaders gathered around his quivering body to taunt him to rescue himself, if he can. He allows the skies to darken and the rocks to rend as he bears the sins of humanity on his bloody back. He tends to business while struggling against asphyxiation – caring for his grieving mother, crying out in abandonment, declaring his work finished, and surrendering his spirit.

It all seems perfectly calculated. And it is. Caiaphas and the religious leaders get what they want: the death of Jesus. Pilate gets what he wants: an escape from a Jewish insurrection. Herod gets what he wants: a few moments of entertainment at Jesus' expense. Satan gets what he wants: a humiliating end to his creator.

But they all figured wrongly. Yes, Pilate killed Jesus. The Sanhedrin killed Jesus. Satan killed Jesus. Sinful people killed Jesus. But ultimately, God the Father killed Jesus. And Jesus died willingly. And just three days later – on a quiet Sunday morning in spring – there is a stunning reversal of fortune. The stone of Jesus' tomb is rolled away, and the Son of Man emerges victoriously to conquer Satan, sin, and death.

It is the perfect plan. It requires the death of Jesus. And no one is better prepared for his own death than the Son of Man. Consider just a few of Jesus' actions and statements in the hours leading up to his death.

First, Jesus teaches openly. Jesus never turns anyone away who has an interest in his message – not tax collectors, prostitutes, Pharisees, Roman autocrats, or would-be disciples. "I have spoken openly to the world," Jesus tells Annas. "I have always taught in the synagogue and in the temple, where all the Jews gather, and I haven't spoken anything in secret" (John 18:20-21).

If ever there was a time to soften his message or change his tune in order to save his skin, Jesus could have seized the opportunity now, standing before the religious leaders who are seeking his head. But, as always, he rejects the path of least resistance.

Not long before this scene, Jesus confronts a mob armed with swords and clubs in the darkness of Gethsemane: "Have you come out with swords and clubs, as if I were a criminal, to capture me?" he asks. "Every day I used to sit, teaching in the temple, and you didn't arrest me. But all this has happened so that the writings of the prophets would be fulfilled" (Matt. 26:55-56).

Second, Jesus offers a kingdom perspective. The events surrounding Jesus' crucifixion are more than religious chicanery or political theater. Jesus knows it and isn't afraid to school Pilate on the particulars. "My kingdom is not of this world," he tells the Roman governor. "If my kingdom were of this world, my servants would fight, so I wouldn't be handed over to the Jews. But as it is, my kingdom is not from here" (John 18:36).

"You are a king then?" Pilate asks.

"You say that I'm a king," Jesus replies. "I was born for this, and I have come into the world for this: to testify to the truth. Everyone who is of the truth listens to my voice" (v. 37).

Jesus is no threat to Pilate, the Romans, or the Jews. Quite the contrary, he is King of kings, the Savior of the world. Pilate doesn't get the big picture, but he's convinced Jesus does not deserve death. Yet, being a politician in an earthly kingdom, he understands the value of preventing a Jewish uprising and holding his office a little while longer.

Third, Jesus is silent when words do nothing to advance his mission. When the men holding Jesus start mocking and beating him, he says nothing. When they blindfold him and demand of him, "Prophesy! Who was it that hit you?" he says nothing (Luke 22:63-65). When Pilate sends Jesus to Herod, who makes sport of the Jewish prophet, Jesus says nothing (Luke 23:6-12). When Caiaphas receives false accusations against Jesus, he presses the Messiah: "Don't you have an answer to what these men are testifying about you?" Jesus says nothing (Mark 14:55-61). When the chief priests and elders bellow accusations before Pilate, Jesus says nothing in his own defense, leading Pilate to marvel: "Don't you hear how much they are testifying against you?" The governor is "quite amazed" (Matt. 27:12-14).

When Roman soldiers strip Jesus, dress him in a scarlet robe, press a crown of thorns on his head, place a staff in his right hand, kneel down and mock Jesus – "Hail, king of the Jews!" – he says nothing in his own defense (Matt. 27:27-31). It is as Isaiah prophesied, "He was oppressed and afflicted, yet he did not open his mouth. Like a lamb led to the slaughter and like a sheep silent before her shearers, he did not open his mouth" (Isa. 53:7).

Fourth, Jesus speaks truth to power to make his mission clear. Caiaphas puts the matter plainly to Jesus: "Are you the Messiah, the Son of the Blessed One?" (Mark 14:61). Here is a chance for Jesus to recant, to plead for mercy, to save his skin. But without skipping a beat, Jesus replies, "I am ... and you will see **the Son of Man seated at the right hand** of Power and **coming with the clouds of heaven**" (v. 62).

This is more than a claim to being the Messiah, which is not necessarily blasphemous. But claiming to be the Son of Man who will sit at the right hand of Yahweh is a self-condemning statement – unless it's true. Jesus ties himself to the Son of Man who approaches the Ancient of Days in Daniel 7:13. This is an unambiguous claim of deity – a claim so ostentatious that Caiaphas nearly strokes out when he hears it.

The high priest tears his robes and shouts, "Why do we still need witnesses? You have heard the blasphemy. What is your decision?" Then, they all condemn him as deserving of death (Mark 14:63-64).

Before Pilate, Jesus barely speaks – until the right moment. Pilate presses Jesus, "Do you refuse to speak to me?" he asks. "Don't you know that I have the authority to release you and the authority to crucify you?" (John 19:10).

Jesus replies, "You would have no authority over me at all if it hadn't been given you from above" (v. 11).

While Jesus' claims of deity and divine power enrage the chief priest and Sanhedrin, they frighten Pilate, who seeks vainly to release Jesus (v. 12).

Fifth, Jesus focuses on the people for whom he is about to die. On the way to Golgotha, in such wretched physical condition that the Romans compel a bystander to carry his cross, Jesus musters enough breath to speak to women lamenting his verdict:

> "Daughters of Jerusalem, do not weep for me, but weep for yourselves and your children. Look, the days are coming when they will say, 'Blessed are the women without children, the wombs that never bore, and the breasts that never nursed!' Then they will begin to say to the mountains, 'Fall on us!' and to the hills, 'Cover us!' For if they do these things when the wood is green, what will happen when it is dry?" (Luke 23:28-30).

Jesus warns these women of dark days ahead, when the nation is punished for its rejection of Messiah. This occurs in A.D. 70 at the hands of Roman commander Titus, and it is utter ruin. A siege of Jerusalem leads to infighting, starvation, and suffering long before Titus breaches the city walls. The massive invasion seeks to extinguish any and all forms of resistance. The Romans are thorough and ruthless. The temple is destroyed. The city is conquered. More than one million Jews lose their lives. If the mocking religious leaders staring up at Jesus on the cross think the Father has abandoned him, they will see true abandonment forty years later.

But Jesus' focus now is not to drink in the women's pity, but to warn them as his followers to prepare for the days when Israel's wickedness comes home to roost. It is a stern warning, and a compassionate one.

At Golgotha,[5] Jesus is crucified between two criminals. As he surveys the scene – the spikes being driven through his wrists, the hoisting of three condemned people into the air, the crowds pressing in around him – Jesus prays simply, "Father, forgive them, because they do not know what they are doing" (Luke 23:34). His attention is outward, toward those who have beaten him severely, or petitioned the governor for his death, or scuttled to the hill to witness a gruesome scene. Jesus asks the Father to forgive them, and pleads their ignorance as a just reason.

Matthew records that those who pass by hurl insults at Jesus, shaking their heads and saying, "You who would destroy the temple and rebuild it in three days, save yourself! If you are the Son of God, come down from the cross" (Matt. 27:40).

The chief priest, along with the scribes and elders, mock Jesus as well, saying, "He saved others, but he cannot save himself! He is the King of Israel! Let him come down now from the cross, and we will believe in him. He trusts in God; let God rescue him now – if he takes pleasure in him! For he said, 'I am the Son of God'" (Matt. 27:41-43).

Even the two criminals who share Jesus' fate join the jeering crowd. "Aren't you the Messiah?" asks one. "Save yourself and us!" (Luke 23:39).

But Luke records that one of the thieves has a change of heart. Seeing the manner in which Jesus suffers, forgives, and cares for others while in excruciating pain, he rebukes his fellow criminal: "Don't you even fear God, since you are undergoing the same punishment? We are punished justly, because we're getting back what we deserve for the things we did, but this man has done nothing wrong" (Luke 23:40-41). Then, he turns to Jesus, straining against gravity to fill his lungs for one more statement, and says, "Jesus, remember me when you come into your kingdom" (v. 42).

Jesus tells the believing criminal, "Truly I tell you, today you will be with me in paradise" (v. 43).

That simple statement communicates much. Jesus acknowledges the criminal's faith and rewards him with everlasting life. Jesus has the power to forgive sin (see Mark 2:1-12). His pending death would pay the criminal's debt owed to God. His resurrection would secure everlasting life. His death would not be the end of Jesus – or the criminal. Jesus would be in paradise[6] – heaven – that very day, and so would be the spirit of the dying criminal. Finally, all the work necessary for life eternal is accomplished in the sinless life of the Son of Man, who seeks and saves a lost man dying next to him.

This brings up a key point: On the cross, Jesus doesn't have to say anything in order to accomplish redemption. In profound physical pain, and deeper inner anguish as he who knew no sin became sin for us (2 Cor. 5:21), Jesus could have turned inward, enduring the pain until he breathed his last. But, instead, he speaks in brief lines that illustrate the truth that no one takes his life from him; he lays it down and will take it up again (John 10:17-18).

What remarkable self-control and sense of purpose. Jesus could come down from the cross. He could call legions of angels to rescue him and destroy those who raise their hands against him. He could vindicate himself through a miracle of self-deliverance. But instead, he perseveres, knowing his death is required to pay our sin debt.

Standing by the cross is Jesus' mother, accompanied by John, the beloved disciple. Jesus tells Mary, "Woman, here is your son." And to John, "Here is your mother." In immediate and enduring obedience, John takes Mary into his home (John 19:25-27).

Sixth, Jesus bears our sins. Having cared tenderly for those around him – even those seething with hatred and demanding his death – Jesus turns his attention toward heaven. Near the time of his death – Matthew says about three in the afternoon – Jesus exposes the utter horror of bearing humanity's sin debt. Exhausted and bleeding out, he spends much of what little strength remains to loudly repeat a cry that fulfills David's words in Psalm 22:1: "My God, my God, why have you abandoned me?" (Matt. 27:46).

A reading of Psalm 22 reveals David offering an agonized prayer. He feels God has abandoned him to his enemies and to his own infirmities. In a sense, he echoes the voices of countless faithful servants who face times of terrible hardship, wondering how a loving heavenly Father can stand aloof to our distress.

David provides a litany of complaints. He cries out day and night but receives no response (Ps. 22:2). People scorn, despise, and mock him for his trust in God (vv. 6-8). Distress engulfs him, with no one to offer relief (v. 11). Bulls of Bashan surround him – perhaps a reference to demons, or at least human agents of the evil one who reject Yahweh – roaring like lions (vv. 12-13). He is poured out like water, his bones are disjointed, and his heart melts like wax (v. 14). His strength is evaporating, and he suffers thirst (v. 15). Dogs surround him; evil-doers close in, piercing his hands and feet (v. 16). People stare at him in disdain and divide his clothing without a whiff of remorse (vv. 17-18).

Even so, David refuses to forsake hope. His first words, "My God, my God," draw a picture of one who knows Yahweh is still his God. He remembers God's faithfulness: "Our ancestors trusted in you; they trusted, and you rescued them. They cried to you and were set free; they trusted in you and were not disgraced" (vv. 4-5). Then, he recalls God's past care in his life: "It was you who brought me out of the womb, making me secure at my mother's breast. I was given over to you at birth; you have been my God from my mother's womb" (vv. 9-10).

Finally, in the first half of the psalm, David appeals to God as his ultimate hope: "But you, LORD, don't be far away…. Rescue my life from the sword, my only life from the power of these dogs. Save me from the lion's mouth, from the horns of wild oxen" (vv. 19-21).

The second half of David's prayer rises to a crescendo of praise. "You answered me!" he exults. "I will proclaim your name to my brothers and sisters. I will praise you in the assembly" (vv. 21-22). He calls on his fellow countrymen to praise and revere the Lord, for the Lord listens and answers (vv. 23-24). And he reminds them that one day the whole world will remember and turn to the Lord, "for king-ship belongs to the LORD; he rules the nations" (vv. 27-28). This is a promise for current and future generations (v. 31).

As Robert Godfrey notes:

This ardent praise is for the success of the cause of God. The failure that at the beginning of the psalm seemed certain is now swallowed up in victory. This success will not just be personal or individual but will be worldwide.... After suffering comes the glory of a worldwide kingdom.[7]

But this is not the end of the psalm's intended message. David not only expresses his anguish, hope, and ultimate victory. And he not only echoes the voices of the faithful as they suffer, pray, and finally enter God's kingdom. David projects his cries forward many centuries into the mouth of the Son of God as he hangs on the cross, for the psalmist's hope is in the Lord who himself becomes the Suffering Servant and Savior of the world.

In remarkable fulfillment of David's prayer, Jesus, in his humanity, suffers the same torment. He's in physical agony – the pain of scourging, beating, and being nailed to a cross. He's in emotional distress – ridiculed, insulted, and mocked for his seemingly futile cries to his heavenly Father. He's in spiritual flux – surrounded in the unseen realm by a demonic horde and in the physical landscape by sneering Romans and Jews. And he's in cosmic grief – the one who knew no sin becoming sin for mankind (2 Cor. 5:21).

But, like the psalmist, Jesus holds to his intimate relationship with the Father as he cries out, "My God, my God." He never loses sight of the purpose for which he suffers. And he knows his death on behalf of others satisfies the wrath of God, while his victorious emergence from the grave three days later will crush the serpent's head and devour the evil one's kingdom.

As the writer of Hebrews notes:

Now since the children have flesh and blood in common, Jesus also shared in these, so that through his death he might destroy the one holding the power of death – that is, the devil – and free those who were held in slavery all their lives by the fear of death (Heb. 2:14-15).

As we see shortly, Jesus moves from agony to ecstasy as he declares his work finished, and as he surrenders his spirit into the Father's loving hands.

I'm thirsty

Seventh, Jesus moves from anguish to elation. We see this transition in Jesus' simple declaration, "I'm thirsty." John records this in the context of Jesus knowing "that everything was now finished that the Scripture might be fulfilled" (John 19:28). John continues, "A jar of sour wine was sitting there; so they fixed a sponge full of sour wine on a hyssop branch and held it up to his mouth" (v. 29).

The significance of this event might be lost to us if we move on too quickly. Of course Jesus is thirsty. He's lost a lot of blood and has suffered extreme physical trauma. But we must not overlook the instrument by which a Roman soldier offers Jesus some relief: a hyssop branch.

Hyssop is a small, bushy plant that generally grows in arid, rocky places. Its key feature is the sponge-like shoots that gather moisture and transfer it to other objects, especially when shaken. As Michael Barrett notes, "Its simple ability to collect and disperse liquids is what made it suitable for its most significant function in the ceremonial rituals of the Old Testament, all of which were picture prophecies pointing to the sacrificial work of Christ."[8]

Passover offers us the first ceremonial glimpse of hyssop, as faithful Israelites obey God's instructions to sacrifice a lamb, dip hyssop in the blood, and sprinkle the blood on the posts and upper part of their doors (Exod. 12:22). Wherever the blood is applied, there is deliverance from the angel of death.

This points to Jesus, our Passover, who is sacrificed for us (1 Cor. 5:7). It also reinforces the consistent teaching of Scripture that the sacrificial blood must not only be shed, but *applied* in order to secure deliverance. Many people may believe as a matter of history that Jesus actually died – and even died as a sacrifice – but if his blood is not personally received by faith as God's payment for our sins, we are still dead in those sins.

Cleansing from leprosy is the next ceremonial use of hyssop in the Old Testament (Lev. 14). A leper who is quarantined and then healed must present himself to the priest, who kills one bird and mingles its blood with water. The priest then takes a second bird, dips it in the bloody water, and releases it. Finally, the priest dips hyssop into the bloody water and sprinkles it on the leper, declaring him clean. The healed leper is restored to the covenant community and may freely enter the tabernacle to worship.

This prefigures the work of Jesus, whose blood cleanses us from all sin (1 John 1:7). We are restored to a right relationship with God and declared free by the blood of Jesus. The bird released is, in some respects, similar to the scapegoat driven into the wilderness on the Day of Atonement. He symbolizes the separation from sins accomplished through the death of another goat, who is sacrificed (Lev. 16). In a similar way, the shed blood of Jesus cleanses us – separates us – from our sins and restores us to fellowship with God.

The curse of death takes us to the next application of hyssop under the Old Covenant. Numbers 19 records a procedure for dealing with the consequences of coming into contact with a dead body. A red heifer is taken outside the camp, slain, and burned completely. Its ashes are kept in reserve so that when an Israelite comes into contact with a corpse, a "clean" Israelite may mix the ashes with water and use hyssop to sprinkle the mixture on whoever and whatever has come into contact with the dead body.

Just as this ritual involving hyssop provides temporary purification from the curse of physical death, the blood of Jesus delivers us completely from sin's curse of death of body, soul, and spirit, as Jesus becomes a curse for us (Gal. 3:13; Heb. 9:11-14).

David's prayer of confession in Psalm 51 brings theological focus to the Old Testament use of hyssop. Having committed adultery and murder, David finds himself deeply convicted of his sin and longing for restored fellowship with Yahweh. He cries out, "Purify me with hyssop, and I will be clean; wash me, and I will be whiter than snow" (Ps. 51:7). David expresses his faith in the cleansing power of sacrificial blood and asks that it be applied to his sin, resulting in deliverance, healing, purification, and restored fellowship.

As Barrett summarizes, "So it is that we must appeal to the blood of Jesus in order to experience the forgiveness of sins and the enjoyment of restored fellowship with Him (1 John 1:7, 9). There's more to hyssop than meets the eye."[9]

All of which brings us back to the cross, and to Jesus' simple declaration, "I'm thirsty." As the sponge soaked in sour wine is hoisted on the end of a hyssop branch and offered to Jesus, he receives the wine and then cries out, "It is finished" (John 19:30).

Agony gives way to ecstasy. Bondage gives way to deliverance. The leprosy of sin gives way to healing. The curse of sin gives way to restoration with our offended God. Just as hyssop is the means by which the purifying blood is applied to the one in need, faith is the way Christ's sacrificial blood – fulfilling the types and shadows of the Old Covenant – is applied to believing sinners, rendering us forgiven, delivered, healed, purified, and restored.

Jesus receives the sour wine offered on a hyssop branch, and in so doing he fulfills the prophetic significance of this otherwise common desert plant. With David, we may cry out in our sin, "Purify us with hyssop, and we will be clean. Wash us, and we will be whiter than snow."

It is finished

Now, let's turn our attention to a brief statement by Jesus that drips with redemptive significance. John records, "When Jesus had received the sour wine, he said, 'It is finished.' Then bowing his head, he gave up his spirit" (John 19:30). These three words of our Savior – "It is finished" – appear only here in the Gospels.

As we explored in Chapter 8, the Greek word translated "It is finished" is *tetelestai* and offers many applications. For example, merchants use *tetelestai* as an accounting term that means "paid in full." So, with Jesus' simple statement, "It is finished" – possibly the "loud cry" of Mark 15:37 – he declares that the debt of mankind's sin, owed to his Father in heaven, has been wiped away.

But those around the cross may understand Jesus' words differently. To the Roman soldier, *tetelestai* is a declaration of military conquest. To the Jew, *tetelestai* is the statement from the high priest on the Day of Atonement, when the final sacrifice of the day has been offered. In every case, *tetelestai* signals victory – a paid-in-full debt, a battlefield rout, and a covering of sin.

We may find even deeper significance here. The verb *teleo*, from which *tetelestai* is derived, denotes the completion of a task. In religious contexts, it bears the overtone of fulfilling one's obligations. Perhaps that's why John says of Jesus, "Having loved his own who were in the world, he loved them *to the end*" (*eis telos*, John 13:1). Later, Jesus tells his Father, "I have glorified you on the earth by *completing* (*teleiosas*) the work you gave me to do" (John 17:4). So now, on the brink of death, the Son of Man declares that he has finished the redemptive work for which he was sent.[10]

Paul and the writer of Hebrews echo this truth as they write that Jesus' death took place once for all time; that is, it's a finished work (Rom. 6:10; Heb. 7:27; 9:12; 10:10). Further, John twice records the expression "It is done" from the lips of Jesus in heaven as our Savior prepares to banish sin forever from the created order. The first time is revealed as a "loud voice" out of the temple as an angel pours out the seventh bowl, signaling the last in a series of judgments (Rev. 16:17).

The second time appears as John sees a vision of the new heavens and new earth. Seated on the throne, Jesus declares, "Look, I am making everything new.... It is done! I am the Alpha and the Omega, the beginning and the end. I will freely give to the thirsty from the spring of the water of life" (Rev. 21:5-6). Christ's own thirst on the cross, as he finishes his redemptive work, results in streams of living waters for future generations (cf. John 7:37-38).

We can't know what Satan is thinking when he hears the words of Jesus. Perhaps the evil one considers *tetelestai* the ravings of a delirious man who's lost too much blood. Maybe the words are a vicious sarcasm offered to Jesus' heavenly Father. Maybe they're nothing more than relief that death, and the removal of pain, is near.

But Jesus' declaration before he bows his head in death is a cry of victory. Satan gets the message on Sunday morning, when this same Jesus, whose body has lain wrapped in burial clothes and anointed with spices, emerges victoriously from a borrowed tomb.

The resurrection of Jesus assures us not only that our sin debt is paid in full, but the consequences of sin are being rolled back. Spiritual death gives way to regeneration. Alienation from God surrenders to the Spirit's indwelling. Guilt fades as justification takes its place before the heavenly bar. Abandonment is removed and adoption is conferred. Hell is poorer and heaven rejoices.

Through his finished work, Jesus conquers Satan, sin, and death for us. We are more than conquerors through the one who loved us (Rom. 8:37). The Resurrection is a great victory for Jesus and his followers; a stunning defeat for the evil one, evil spirits, and rebellious humans. The victory is full and final, but not finally realized. Satan still roams the earth like a lion, seeking whom he may devour (1 Pet. 5:8). Evil runs rampant through the streets of our cities and in the hearts of people. Sorrow, pain, aging, and death continue to claim every human life – eventually, if not suddenly.

But at the return of Jesus, the victory is fully implemented. Satan, evil spirits, and wicked people are cast into hell. The righteous are rewarded and granted access to the New Jerusalem. The creation, which groans beneath the weight of sin, is purged of sin and its stain and gives way to new heavens and a new earth, where righteousness dwells (Rom. 8:22; 2 Pet. 3:10-13).

Tetelestai. It is finished. The work of redemption is complete. The effects carry forward into eternity future.

Into your hands

Luke alone records this epilogue in Jesus' work on the cross: "And Jesus called out with a loud voice, 'Father, **into your hands I entrust my spirit**.' Saying this, he breathed his last" (Luke 23:46).

Moments earlier, Jesus cries out, "My God, my God," echoing David's despair of abandonment while clinging to his trust in God's faithfulness (Matt. 27:46; cf. Ps. 22). Now, having declared his work on the cross finished (John 19:30), Jesus exults in his pending return to the Father. Yes, his body is destined for the grave, where it rests until Sunday morning. But his divine spirit lives on, departing the earthly tabernacle of his body to visit the heavenly temple, where his Father resides.

Jesus' final words from the cross draw from Psalm 31:5 – "Into your hand I entrust my spirit: you have redeemed me, LORD, God of truth." Israelites often quote this psalm of David in their evening prayers, commending themselves to God's care during the night's sleep. In a similar manner, Jesus' final words "expressed his faith, his relationship to God, and his insistence that death and the cross did not represent the last word. Death led only to paradise, to protection in God's hands, to the kingdom."[11]

A victorious reunion is about to take place – one that eclipses the Israelites' homecoming after seventy years in Babylonian captivity, and one far more joyful than the return of the prodigal son. This is an arrival of cosmic proportions as Jesus returns to the throne room of heaven and resumes his place at the Father's right hand – a faithful and obedient son, and an exalted king. This is more fully realized, of course, in the bodily resurrection and ascension of Christ, just as our salvation is completed in glorification, our future resurrection in which we are fully conformed to the image of Christ.

What's more, Jesus does not return to heaven empty-handed. He brings with him the thief on the cross, to whom he promised, "Today you will be with me in paradise" (Luke 23:43). He also brings – in a figurative sense – his shed blood into the holy of holies of the heavenly temple in payment for humanity's sins. As the writer of Hebrews notes: "In the greater and more perfect tabernacle not made with hands (that is, not of this creation), he entered the most holy place once for all time, not by the blood of goats and calves, but *by his own blood*, having obtained eternal redemption" (Heb. 9:11-12, emphasis added).

Theories abound as to what the writer of Hebrews means by the phrase, "by his own blood." Does Jesus actually take blood from his corpse into heaven? If so, when: after his death on the cross, his resurrection, or his ascension? Is it actually Jesus' human blood, or a new type of blood infused into his resurrected body? Scripture is silent on these matters, and we should be careful not to impose too literal a meaning on the text.

It seems best to understand "by his own blood" as the basis on which Christ enters heaven. He does not literally sprinkle his blood on the heavenly mercy seat, as the high priest does in the temple in Jerusalem. Rather, as Albert Barnes notes:

> ... that blood, having been shed for sin, is now the ground of his pleading and intercession for the pardon of sin – as the sprinkled blood of the Jewish sacrifices was the ground of the pleading of the Jewish high priest for the pardon of himself and the people.[12]

Put simply, Christ's blood, shed on the cross, is applied to heaven on our behalf on the basis of his sacrifice alone. We might say that Jesus not only escorts the repentant thief on the cross into paradise, but, by means of his finished work on the cross, he takes *us* there as well. As Zane Hodges writes, "It was by the blood shed at the cross that he entered heaven. All of Jesus' work for our salvation occurred at the cross, not subsequent to it."[13]

Veils and rocks

As we complete our examination of the words of Jesus just prior to his death on the cross, we should note several unusual events that transpire. First, there is *extraordinary darkness*, as Luke records: "It was now about noon, and darkness came over the whole land until three, because the sun's light failed" (Luke 23:44-45; cf. Matt. 27:45; Mark 15:33).

This marks a great, if temporary, reversal of God's declaration, "Let there be light." This command in Genesis 1:3 is the first time in recorded history that God speaks, and it results in a rending of the impenetrable darkness even before the sun, moon, and stars are created. The source of this light likely is the same we see in the Book of Revelation, where we learn that in the new heavens and earth people don't need the light of a lamp or the sun, "because the Lord God will give them light" (Rev. 22:5).

But in Luke 23:44-45, we witness the opposite. At noon, when the sun is near its peak, God speaks and the world is plunged into darkness. This is not natural darkness – an eclipse, or mere overcast skies. It's darkness by divine fiat, and it's connected to God's judgment. Like the ninth plague on Egypt, which brought "a darkness that can be felt" (Exod. 10:21); like the pillar of cloud and fire that turns its dark side toward the Israelites' Egyptian pursuers; and like Jesus' parables of those cast far from God's presence into outer darkness, we see in the darkness that envelopes the Son of God a divine wrath on humanity's sin. It is darkness to the full. Darkness like the chaotic and impenetrable darkness of the days before God speaks and the light appears.

Sent outside the city walls to be crucified, and becoming a curse, Jesus not only is the sacrificial Lamb who bears the weight of another's sins; he's the scapegoat who separates our sin as far as the east is from the west (Ps. 103:12). The darkness covers Christ, but not only him. It descends on the eyewitnesses, chills them, and threatens them. It seeps into the homes of those who care nothing about what's happening outside the city walls. It mirrors the blackness of the hearts of those who cry out for Jesus' crucifixion.

We should note that while darkness often is a sign of judgment in Scripture, it could also indicate the overwhelming closeness of God. Just as he descends in dark clouds on Mount Sinai, and hovers over the tabernacle and the temple in thick shadows, it's possible he may be assuring his Son he has not abandoned him during a crucial time when the one who knew no sin becomes sin for us (2 Cor. 5:21).

And then, *the veil separating the holy place from the holy of holies in the temple is torn in two*, from top to bottom. Matthew, Mark, and Luke record this event (Matt. 27:51; Mark 15:38; Luke 23:45). This is significant, not only because of its physical improbability, but because of its symbolic stature.

The veil is large and thick – thirty feet high, forty-five feet wide, and serving as a wall of partition between the holy place and the holy of holies in the temple. It's designed to separate sinful human beings from the place where God's presence dwells as the *Shekinah* glory, above the ark of the covenant, over the mercy seat, and between the wings of golden cherubim. Only the high priest may enter the holy of holies, and only on the Day of Atonement. Even then, he may enter only after he has brought blood atoning for his sins (see Lev. 16).

The stunning fashion in which the veil is ripped – from top to bottom – demonstrates that God is the one performing this feat. Satisfied with the blood of Jesus, the atoning blood of bulls and goats is no longer necessary. Christ's own body, depicted in the Book of Hebrews as the veil, is torn for us, and it opens the way for sinful people to come directly into the presence of God. As the writer of Hebrews puts it, "Therefore, brothers and sisters, since we have boldness to enter the sanctuary through the blood of Jesus – he has inaugurated for us a new and living way through the curtain (that is, through his flesh) ...." (Heb. 10:19-20).

In essence, the Father tears down the sign between holy God and sinful people that warns, "No Admittance." As R. C. Sproul notes, "The sentinel that stood at the gates of Paradise [Gen. 3:24] had his sword extinguished and put back in his scabbard as he was dismissed from service, as for the first time since the fall we could go home without shame and without fear to the presence of God."[14]

Then, there is *a mass resurrection*. Matthew is the only Gospel writer to record this event, and the details are sparse: "The tombs were also opened and many bodies of the saints who had fallen asleep were raised. And they came out of the tombs after his resurrection, entered the holy city, and appeared to many" (Matt. 27:52-53).

Matthew places this incident at the time of Christ's death, the rending of the veil, and an earthquake. Since it is customary for Jews to bury their dead in graves carved into rock, it's possible the earthquake, which "split" the rocks (Matt. 27:51), exposed many tombs in the vicinity of Golgotha. This is natural. But what happens next is supernatural. Many bodies of the saints – Old Testament saints buried outside Jerusalem – are brought back to life *after* the resurrection of Christ. They enter the city and show themselves – physically brought back to life – to many eyewitnesses.

What are we to make of this? Which saints are revived? How many are brought back to life? What do they say to the eyewitnesses? How long do they testify? Are they given glorified bodies that ascend with Jesus into heaven forty days later? Or, like Lazarus and others Jesus raised from the dead, do they die physically again?

There's no further mention of this miracle in the New Testament, so we must be careful not to venture too far into speculation. However, we may say with certainty that Christ's finished work on the cross defeated the last enemy: death (1 Cor. 15:21, 26; 2 Tim. 1:10; Heb. 2:14). In his death, Jesus removed the sting of the grave, so that death no longer is a consequence of sin but a point of departure into a far better life.

We know that followers of Jesus enter directly into his presence in heaven upon physical death (2 Cor. 5:8). Even better, we await the day when we're physically resurrected and fully conformed to the image of Christ in glorification (1 Cor. 15:51-56; Phil. 3:20-21; 1 John 3:2). So, whether the saints who rise from the dead immediately after Jesus' resurrection have glorified bodies or not, they bear witness of Christ's victory over the grave. And just as followers of Jesus are given the Holy Spirit as a down payment on our future inheritance (2 Cor. 1:22; 5:5; Eph. 1:13-14), perhaps the resurrected saints who enter Jerusalem offer a foretaste of the glorious life to come.

One final event deserves our attention: *a declaration of belief.* A Roman centurion, and other soldiers watching over Jesus, witness the darkness and the earthquake, and they're *terrified.* The Greek word used here is *phobeo.* It means to be put to flight, struck with fear, or seized with alarm. Surely, the events surrounding Jesus' crucifixion shock the centurion and his fellow soldiers. This is no ordinary crucifixion, like the many they have carried out in the past. This one challenges their duty as Roman soldiers with an urge to flee for their own safety.

However, *phobeo* often carries another meaning: to revere, venerate, or treat with reverential obedience. This seems to be more in keeping with the context of the Gospel accounts. Matthew writes that the soldiers cry out, "Truly, this man was the Son of God!"

(Matt. 27:54). Mark places greater emphasis on the centurion, who perhaps speaks for the other soldiers: "When the centurion, who was standing opposite him, saw the way he breathed his last, he said, 'Truly this man was the Son of God!'" (Mark 15:39). Luke writes that the centurion "began to glorify God, saying, 'This man really was righteous!'" (Luke 23:47).

So, it's not just the remarkable events in nature – the darkness, the earthquake – that spur the soldiers' awe. Mark specifically notes the words of Jesus, and the victorious manner in which he dies, as deeply impacting the centurion. His declaration of Jesus as the Son of God echoes Peter's words in Matthew 16:16, "You are the Messiah, the Son of the living God." Further, it stands in opposition to the reaction of Caiaphas when he hears Jesus acknowledge this truth. The high priest tears his robes and accuses Jesus of blasphemy, a charge resulting in crucifixion (Matt. 26:65-66).

As Charles Spurgeon observes of the Roman soldiers:

> It was strange that those men should confess what the chief priests and scribes and elders denied; yet since their day it has often happened that the most abandoned and profane have acknowledged Jesus as the Son of God while their religious rulers have denied his divinity.[15]

A date with destiny

Jesus keeps a date with destiny. He comes into this world to die, and nothing deters him – not the lure of a comfortable kingship that Satan offers, or the attempts of some Jews to make him king, or the campaigns of others to snuff out his life prematurely. He sometimes informs listeners that his hour has not yet come (John 2:4; 7:6). John notes the same (John 7:30; 8:20).

Jesus knows just the right time to come into the world (Gal. 4:4), perform his first miracle (John 2:1-11), ride in peace on the back of a donkey as Israel's humble king (Matt. 21:1-10), set in motion the events of his passion (John 12:23-24), be betrayed and taken captive

(John 18:1-11), declare himself the Son of Man (Mark 14:61-62; cf. Dan. 7:13-14), and breathe his last (Matt. 27:50).

There is nothing short of death Jesus can do to accomplish his rescue mission to earth. The matter is settled from eternity in the counsel of the Trinity. It is first announced to a fallen Adam and Eve in the wake of their rebellion. It is foretold in hundreds of Old Testament prophecies, and foreshadowed in the sacrificial system under the Old Covenant. It is realized in the virgin birth, verified in Christ's defeat over temptation in the wilderness, explained in parables, and confirmed in miracles. It is carried out through the betrayal, arrest, illegal court proceedings, mocking, beating, and crucifixion of the Lord of glory. It is fulfilled in Christ's victory over the grave and displayed in his ascension to the Father's right hand. And it will be completely fulfilled in the return of "this same Jesus" (Acts 1:11).

No one is more ready to die than Jesus. And his death secures eternal life for all who trust in him.

CHRISTIAN MARTYRS

We have explored the last words of Joseph and Jesus, both of whom express a readiness to die. As we close this final chapter in our study, let's look briefly at the final words of a few first-century Christian martyrs, beginning with Stephen.

Stephen: the first Christian martyr

Stephen is a man full of faith and the Holy Spirit (Acts 6:5). He is the first among seven deacons listed. Luke also describes Stephen as a man "full of grace and power," who performs "great wonders and signs among the people" (Acts 6:8). When members of the Freedmen's Synagogue oppose him, they are unable to stand against his Spirit-empowered wisdom (Acts 6:9-10).[16]

These freed slaves, who either are Jews or converts to Judaism, present false witness against Stephen. They stir up the people, elders, and scribes. Ultimately, they seize Stephen and take him to the

Sanhedrin, the supreme court of Israel consisting of seventy men plus the high priest. As Stephen stands before them, the members look intently at him and see that his face is "like the face of an angel" (Acts 6:15).

The high priest asks Stephen if the accusations against him are true. Stephen launches into a lengthy message that begins with God's appearance to Abram in Mesopotamia. It continues with the patriarchs in Egypt, Moses as a rejected savior who returns to Egypt as God's appointed deliverer, and the Israelites' abandonment of Yahweh for worship of the stars in heaven.

Stephen further recounts the building of the tabernacle and then the temple as the places where God's presence dwells. No doubt, the second temple, still being completed in the days of the apostles, is a matter of great national and religious pride. But Stephen reminds them that "the Most High does not dwell in sanctuaries made with hands" (Acts 7:48).

Finally, after recounting the Israelites' unbroken cycles of rebellion against God across the centuries, Stephen declares, "You stiff-necked people with uncircumcised hearts and ears! You are always resisting the Holy Spirit. As your ancestors did, you do also" (Acts 7:51).

Enraged, the religious leaders gnash their teeth. Note Stephen's preparation for what comes next: "Stephen, full of the Holy Spirit, gazed into heaven. He saw the glory of God, and Jesus standing at the right hand of God. He said, 'Look, I see the heavens opened and the Son of Man standing at the right hand of God!'" (Acts 7:55-56).

Stephen testifies to the three persons of the Godhead. As the Spirit fills him, he sees Jesus standing at the Father's right hand, and he shares this vision with bystanders who seethe with anger. The whole point of his sermon becomes clear: Israel is guilty of rejecting God's chosen leaders throughout history. Moses, Joseph, and the prophets either are types of the Messiah, or they point to him, and now Israel's religious elites have killed the one they should have embraced.

But Stephen's listeners want no part of his message. They yell, cover their ears, and rush Stephen. They drag him outside the city and begin to stone him. The witnesses lay their garments at the feet of a young man named Saul, leading some commentators to believe Saul – later known as Paul – is a member of the Freedmen's Synagogue.

Luke's account of the stoning is curious. First, it's doubtful the Sanhedrin has the legal authority to carry out capital punishment during the Roman era (cf. John 18:31). Either they deliberately violate Roman law, or they incite others to pick up stones.

Second, Stephen's stoning doesn't fit what's known of the Jewish method for carrying out this form of death penalty. According to the Mishna, the first major written collection of Jewish oral traditions, stoning takes place outside the city. There, those who have testified against the condemned persons are to perform the activity (Sanhedrin 6:1-6). So far, so good. There's nothing too out-of-the-ordinary here.

However, the condemned person is supposed to be stripped and then pushed over a cliff ten to twelve feet in height. Then, he is to be rolled onto his chest while the first witness pushes a boulder off the cliff above, designed to land on the victim and crush him. If by some chance the victim survives both the fall and the first boulder, a second large stone is rolled off the cliff.

But Luke's account in Acts depicts an angry mob pelting Stephen with stones. It seems unlikely Stephen would be able to kneel or offer prayers if he has just been crushed with a boulder. Further, his death seems to come more slowly – and likely, more painfully as he absorbs a shower of smaller rocks.

In the midst of this frenzy, Stephen calls out, "Lord Jesus, receive my spirit!" (Acts 7:59). This echoes the words of Jesus on the cross, "Father, **into your hands I entrust my spirit**" (Luke 23:46; cf. Ps. 31:5). Then, kneeling down, Stephen cries with a loud voice, "Lord, do not hold this sin against them!" (Acts 7:60). This is another echo of Jesus' words from the cross, "Father forgive them, for they do not know what they are doing" (Luke 23:34).

Stephen's life exemplifies Spirit-fueled wisdom, truthfulness, and boldness to speak truth to power. He does not appear to resist when seized. When speaking, he defends the faith, not himself. While being stoned, he directs his gaze heavenward, and he bears no animosity toward those violently taking his life.

Luke ends his report with these simple words: "And after saying this, he fell asleep" (Acts 7:60). *Sleep* is a euphemism for physical death (see 1 Cor. 11; 15). It also seems to communicate a peaceful surrender to the will of God – Stephen's request of God that he suffer as the fledging church's first martyr.

Paul: the worst of sinners

Look how Paul describes himself to Timothy in his first letter to the young pastor: formerly a blasphemer, a persecutor, an arrogant man, and the worst of sinners (1 Tim. 1:13, 15). This is the once-infamous Saul of Tarsus, who held the coats of witnesses so they could more easily fling stones at Stephen, and the Jewish fanatic who wreaked havoc in the early church as he zealously hounded followers of Jesus.

Paul writes, "But I received mercy for this reason, so that in me, the worst of them, Christ Jesus might demonstrate his extraordinary patience as an example to those who would believe in him for eternal life" (1 Tim. 1:16).

No longer the Jewish extremist, but a devoted follower of the same Jesus he once persecuted, Paul suffers greatly for the cause of his Savior. Judaizers, pagans, intellectuals, and merchants alike shout him down, beat him, imprison him, drive him from their cities, stone him, and leave him for dead. At last, he finds himself a prisoner in Rome, awaiting beheading under the Roman Emperor Nero.[17]

Paul writes a second letter to his beloved Timothy. In some respects, Paul reveals feelings of abandonment and loneliness. But he looks past his circumstances to express a shepherd's care for Timothy and the Christian church. He uses his last words to encourage Timothy and his fellow believers to persevere in faith and proclaim the gospel (2 Tim. 3:14; 4:2).

The apostle to the Gentiles then confirms he is about to die. "For I am already being poured out as a drink offering," he writes, "and the time for my departure is close. I have fought the good fight, I have finished the race, I have kept the faith" (2 Tim. 4:6-7). He looks forward to what lies beyond the vale of a martyr's death: "There is reserved for me the crown of righteousness, which the Lord, the righteous Judge, will give me on that day, and not only me, but to all who have loved his appearing" (v. 8).

Before closing his letter, Paul wraps up some loose ends. He expresses a longing to see Timothy once more because Demas has deserted him and others have moved on. He asks for Mark, a restored brother with whom he had a serious falling out earlier in his ministry (Acts 15:36-40). He asks for a cloak to keep him warm, and for scrolls and parchments to keep him company. He warns Timothy of Alexander the coppersmith, who has done much harm.

Finally, Paul testifies that while others have deserted him, the Lord has been his steadfast companion. And for whatever time remains for Paul, he declares confidently, "The Lord will rescue me from every evil work and will bring me safely into his heavenly kingdom" (2 Tim. 4:18).

Shortly – perhaps a few months later – Paul is added to the growing list of Christian martyrs. But his last written words express a readiness to die and see his Savior. Clement I, bishop of Rome late in the first century A.D., describes Paul as suffering tremendously for his faith and then being "set free from this world and transported up to the holy place, having become the greatest example of patience" (1 Clement 5:5-7).

Peter: the brash martyr

Peter is well-known for his bravado, displayed for us in glorious affirmations and humiliating gaffes. In a single day, he declares Jesus the Messiah, Son of the living God, only to become Satan's pawn as he seeks to prevent Jesus from carrying out his mission on the cross (Matt. 16:13-23). He walks briefly on the storm-tossed Sea of Galilee, only to lose heart and cry out to Jesus for rescue (Matt. 14:22-33). He rebuffs Jesus' ministry of foot-washing, only to ask the Lord to cleanse his entire body (John 13:1-9). He boldly proclaims a willingness to die with Jesus, only to deny him three times (Luke 22:31-34,

54-62). He slices off Malchus' ear in defense of Jesus, only to abandon the Lord with the other disciples (John 18:10-11; Mark 14:50).

On the Day of Pentecost, Peter preaches the resurrected Christ to Jews from around the world gathered in Jerusalem, resulting in the conversion of three thousand. He witnesses the deaths of Ananias and Sapphira, explaining to the early church the seriousness of sin (Acts 5:1-11). Later, an angel delivers him from prison, and Peter tells the high priest who seeks to silence him, "We must obey God rather than people" (Acts 5:29). He receives a vision from God that confronts his Jewish pride, then defends the right of Gentiles to receive the Holy Spirit (Acts 10-11). He is revered for his message and miracles, but receives a strong rebuke from Paul for promoting division between Jews and Gentiles in the church (Gal. 2:11-14).

What a remarkable life of ups and downs. And in his second epistle, as Peter faces imminent death, he writes a final, sobering message that urges his readers to holiness, cautions them about the damage false teachers can do, and encourages them to look expectantly for new heavens and a new earth.

Peter doesn't lament past mistakes or boast of his accomplishments. He doesn't submit his own obituary for consideration. He simply seeks to make it clear that he's ready to exchange this life for a far better life to come. He writes, "I know that I will soon lay aside my tent, as our Lord Jesus Christ has indeed made clear to me. And I will also make every effort so that you are able to recall these things at any time after my departure" (2 Pet. 1:14-15).

"These things" are Peter's true legacy: the gospel of Jesus Christ, obedience, humility, love of the truth, and a strong doctrinal spine. Peter has devoted his life to these teachings, always remembering the words of Jesus that Peter would suffer a martyr's death. Perhaps Peter thinks back to that time when the Lord told him, "Truly I tell you, when you were younger, you would tie your belt and walk wherever you wanted. But when you grow old, you will stretch out your hands and someone else will tie you and carry you where you don't want to go." John then records, "He said this to indicate by what kind of death Peter would glorify God" (John 21:18-19).

The Bible doesn't tell us when, or how, Peter dies. The most commonly accepted church tradition is that Peter is crucified in Rome in the mid-60s A.D. According to that tradition, Peter asks to be put to death on an inverted cross. Because he had once denied his Lord, Peter does not feel worthy to die in the same manner Jesus did.

Sean McDowell, in *The Fate of the Apostles*, offers this perspective:

> … his upside-down state symbolizes that fallen humanity has now been restored through the cross. The world has been turned upside down by sin, and so Peter can see the upside-down nature of the world clearly while hanging with his head downward on the cross. His speech [according to *The Acts of Peter*] makes clear that Adam, the "first man," fell head-downwards and turned the cosmos upside down but only through Christ can the world be seen "upright." Thus, the crucifixions of Jesus and Peter restore the creation, through the New Adam, to its intended functioning.[18]

Whatever the significance of Peter's crucifixion, it seems the apostle shares with Jesus "the joy that lay before him" (Heb. 12:2). As another writer puts it, "For Peter to die a martyr's death clinging to the hope of heaven testifies to the courage, faith, patience, and perseverance of this great man of God who rejoiced to be counted worthy to die for the name of Jesus."[19]

John: the beloved apostle

Jesus grants John detailed views of heaven, the unseen realm, and the events of the last days. The Book of Revelation propels us from John's exile on Patmos to the churches of Asia Minor, into Israel, Rome, and Babylon, across the seas, up through the heavenlies and to the very throne of God. Through a visionary telescope that compresses time, we see the events of the church age hurtling toward history's climax with the personal, glorious, triumphant return of the Lord Jesus, who sits on the throne of David and sets everything right.

The Book of Revelation is a stunning voyage through time and space. It's also well-grounded in history. John borrows heavily from prophetic literature, along with the worship language of the Psalms.[20] While he never offers a direct, word-for-word quotation from the Old Testament, he weaves prophetic words and phrases into his writing to exhort readers to godly living, and to prepare them for the return of their King.[21] John draws pieces of the prophetic puzzle together and helps us understand how the Messiah's first coming and return are parts of a unified work of redemption that results in the defeat of Satan, the cancelling of the curse, and the restoration of Eden.

All through Revelation, John rides an emotional roller coaster as he captures breathtaking visions of heavenly glory, Satanic deception, and human depravity. The sights and sounds buckle his knees. But nothing compares to the sight of a white horse and its rider, called "Faithful and True," who judges rightly and wages a just war. His eyes are like a fiery flame. He wears many crowns on his head. He bears a name no one knows except himself. He wears a robe dipped in blood. His name is the Word of God. Armies of angels and redeemed people follow him from heaven; they, too, ride white horses and wear white linen. A sharp sword protrudes from the rider's mouth, symbolizing the divine authority by which Christ created all things and by which he now judges them. He tramples the winepress of the fierce anger of God, the Almighty. And he bears a special name on his robe and on his thigh: KING OF KINGS AND LORD OF LORDS (19:11-16).

John sees the beast from the sea and the beast from the earth thrown alive into the lake of fire (19:20). He witnesses an unnamed angel confine Satan to the abyss for a thousand years (20:1-3), only to be released for a short time and then cast into hell to be tormented night and day forever (20:7-10). He watches the world's unbelievers stand before a great white throne and be cast into outer darkness with Satan; their names are not written in the Lamb's book of life (20:11-15).

Finally, John sees new heavens and a new earth, purged of sin and its stain (Rev. 21-22). Eden is restored, complete with the tree of life, living waters, and New Jerusalem as its capital. As in the beginning, so it is in John's vision of the future. Redeemed people enjoy intimate face-to-face fellowship with God and walk with him in the cool of the day. Satan is banished; so are demons and wicked humans. There is no more curse; no more sorrow, suffering, pain, aging, disease, or death. These are the former things that have passed away. John stands exhausted and exulting as the story ends, turning the last page to a new and never-ending chapter in human history.

The Book of Revelation ends with messages from Jesus and the angel who is sent to unveil the truths John is to record. "Look, I am coming soon!" Jesus tells John twice (22:7, 12). "I am the Alpha and the Omega, the first and the last, the beginning and the end. Blessed are those who wash their robes, so that they may have the right to the tree of life and may enter the city by the gates" (22:13-14).

While there are frightening visions of the last days, true followers of Jesus welcome his return in glory to set things right. "Both the Spirit and the bride say, 'Come!' Let anyone who hears, say, 'Come!' Let the one who is thirsty come. Let the one who desires take the water of life freely" (22:17). John ends with a warning to anyone who adds to or takes away from the prophecy in this book. God will take away their share of the tree of life and the holy city, both of which are written about in this book (22:18-19).

John reminds us, "He who testifies about these things says, 'Yes, I am coming soon,'" to which an exhausted but exuberant John replies, "Amen! Come, Lord Jesus!" (22:20). This is not the end of John's life. He survives his exile on Patmos, although little is known of his life afterward. It is believed he is freed, possibly due to old age, returning to Asia Minor and dying peacefully as an old man.

Other theories say a band of Jewish men kill John, or that he ascends into heaven as Enoch and Elijah did. At the end of the day, it's less important to know how John died than to marvel at how he lived – a long and faithful ministry in which some of his last recorded words bear testimony to the life he lived and his readiness to face death: "Come, Lord Jesus!"

REVIEW

Key takeaways from this chapter

1. At the core of Jesus' parables and teachings about his return is a clear warning: *be on guard*. Nowhere is this spoken with more clarity than in the Olivet Discourse, where Jesus tells his disciples, "Therefore be alert, since you don't know what day your Lord is coming.... This is why you are also to be ready, because the Son of Man is coming at an hour you do not expect" (Matt. 24:42, 44).

2. Joseph's last words, recorded in Genesis 50:24-25, carry no hint of remorse, doubt, or anger. Even with all the peaks and valleys he has experienced over 110 years of life, Joseph rests confidently in the providence of God. He breathes his last in sublime peacefulness. Further, his request to be buried in Canaan displays confidence in God's promise to Abram to give his descendants a permanent homeland.

3. No one is better prepared to die than Jesus. His willingness to lay down his life reveals a divine sense of purpose, humility, submission to the Father's will, and keen insight into what his death is accomplishing. Consider just a few of Jesus' actions and statements in the hours leading up to his death:

- He teaches openly.
- He offers a kingdom perspective.
- He is silent when words do nothing to advance his mission.
- He speaks truth to power to make his mission clear.
- He focuses on the people for whom he is about to die.
- He bears our sins.
- He moves from anguish to elation.

4. There is nothing short of death that Jesus can experience to accomplish his rescue mission to earth. The matter is settled in eternity past in the counsel of the Trinity. It is first announced to Adam and Eve in the wake of their rebellion. It is foretold by the prophets. It is realized in the virgin birth, sinless life, and sacrificial and substitu-

tionary death of the Messiah. It is confirmed in his victory over the grave, displayed in his ascension to the Father's right hand, and fulfilled one day in the return of "this same Jesus" (Acts 1:11).

5. The last recorded words in Scripture of Stephen, Paul, Peter, and John reveal their willingness to die for the sake of the gospel. Stephen is the first Christian martyr, and his final words echo the cries of Jesus on the cross. Peter and Paul are killed in Rome – one by beheading and the other by crucifixion. John is exiled to Patmos, where he receives visions recorded in the Book of Revelation. As they suffer independently, their common goal is the glory of the cross.

DISCUSS

Questions for personal or group study

1. Read Matthew 24:36-44. What do you hope to be found doing when Jesus returns suddenly and unexpectedly? What do you most fear Jesus will find you doing when he comes back?

2. What does the life of Joseph teach us about trusting in God, despite our circumstances? What's significant about Joseph's last request to be buried in Canaan? And how does God's faithfulness to establish the Promised Land connect with Christ's promise to return?

3. Read Revelation 13:8. In what way is Jesus, the Lamb of God, slaughtered from the foundation of the world? What are some statements of Jesus in the Gospels that tell us he has come into the world to die? Start with Matthew 16:21; 26:52-54; Luke 19:10; John 10:17-18. How is the death of Jesus a prerequisite to his return?

4. How do the last recorded words of Stephen, Paul, Peter, and John anticipate the return of Jesus? Who are some biblical figures that clearly are not ready to face death and what lies beyond?

5. What do you want to be your last words? Put another way, what would you like inscribed on your gravestone?

* * *

CLOSING THOUGHTS

*I*n the Olivet Discourse (Matt. 24-25; cf. Mark 13; Luke 21), Jesus shares a parable about faithful service to Christ. He has just confessed that he doesn't know the day and hour of his return (Matt. 24:36). He has likened the setting of his return to the days of Noah, when the flood came suddenly on those who were unprepared (Matt. 24:37-39). And he has called his disciples to be alert, like a homeowner on constant vigil against thieves (Matt. 24:43). "This is why you are also to be ready," he says, "because the Son of Man is coming at an hour you do not expect" (Matt. 24:44).

Now, Jesus compares the vigilant Christian to a trustworthy servant:

> Who then is a faithful and wise servant, whom his master has put in charge of his household, to give them food at the proper time? Blessed is that servant whom the master finds doing his job when he comes. Truly I tell you, he will put him in charge of all his possessions. But if that wicked servant says in his heart, "My master is delayed," and starts to beat his fellow servants, and eats and drinks with drunkards, that servant's master will come on a day he does not expect him and at an hour he does not know. He will cut him to pieces and assign him a

place with the hypocrites, where there will be weeping and gnashing of teeth (Matt. 24:45-51).

Our purpose in this study has been to focus on what the Bible teaches about the Day of the Lord. Try as we might, we can't pinpoint the exact time when the Lion of Judah splits the skies and attends to unfinished business on earth. Nor should we speak with prideful certainty about the precise order of events surrounding that great day. But as followers of Jesus, we can – and should – understand the non-negotiable truths of the Lord's return, and be ready.

We should trust Jesus. He promises to return. He affirms what the Old Testament prophets envisioned about the Messiah's two-stage rescue mission to earth. And he empowers the eyewitnesses of his passion to write confidently of his return for his glory and our glorification.

We should behold Jesus. The Word who became flesh pitched his tent with people who saw him with their own eyes. Equally important, he gave them – and us – an understanding of the nature of his future return. He is coming back personally – not sending a proxy. He's coming back physically, visibly, powerfully, victoriously, and suddenly.

We should hear Jesus. He has plenty to say about the reasons he's coming back. He's returning to establish his kingdom in fullness; to resurrect and judge all people; to glorify the saints and condemn the wicked; to cast Satan and demons into hell; and to restore Eden as the intersection between heaven's throne room and mankind's paradise.

Finally, we should receive Jesus. This begins with surrendering our lives to him as Savior and Lord. It continues with proclaiming to all people the good news of salvation by grace alone, through faith alone, in Christ alone. It involves understanding that Jesus has returned to the Father to prepare a place for us. And like a bridegroom in a first-century Galilean wedding, he's coming for us soon, meaning we should prepare ourselves for the sound of the shofar and the shouts from the wedding party, "Here's the groom! Come out to meet him" (Matt. 25:6).

All of this is tethered to the parable at hand. The faithful and wise servant may be distinguished from the wicked servant based on his or her regard for the master. The master finds the true servant "doing his job when he comes" and rewards him lavishly (Matt. 24:46-47). In contrast, the master catches the wicked servant off-guard, living rebelliously and self-indulgently. That servant is punished severely and sent away, "where there will be weeping and gnashing of teeth," an image drawn from Jesus' depiction of hell (v. 51).

The actions of both servants reveal their loyalties – one to the master, and the other to himself. Salvation – that is, forgiveness of sins and eternal life – is a matter of faith, not works. Even so, the way we live reveals what we believe, in whom we believe, and where our citizenship lies.

True followers of Jesus will find ourselves busy, employing the time, talents, opportunities, resources, and spiritual gifts God has entrusted to us, when Christ returns. We embrace the certainty of our master's return and live in the light of eternity. We understand Christ could return at any moment, so we live accordingly, and expectantly.

Unbelievers have rejected the master and care little about his return, if they believe in it at all. They may draw a paycheck, enjoying the creator's common graces for a while. But by their wicked and self-centered lives, they prove themselves pretenders. The master comes by surprise and casts them out. And while they may plead their case as those who proclaimed the name of Christ and performed righteous deeds in his name, the master tells them, "I never knew you. Depart from me …." (Matt. 7:23).

If you're reading these lines, you know Jesus has not yet returned. And you may, with brutal honesty, ask yourself whether you care. The master *is* coming. How you respond to that truth reveals whether you're a faithful and wise servant, or a wicked one. It's not too late to decide.

* * *

_____ A _____

"O LORD, I live here as a fish in a vessel of water, only enough to keep me alive, but in heaven I shall swim in the ocean."

- Puritan Prayer

_____ Ω _____

APPENDIX I

FOUR VIEWS OF THE END TIMES

Eschatology is the field of Christian theology concerned with the end times, which encompass Christ's future return, the resurrection and judgment of all people, the final casting of Satan and other rebellious angels into hell, the purging of sin from the cosmos, and the creation of new heavens and a new earth. The term *eschatology* is derived from two Greek words: *escha*, meaning "last" or "farthest," as in the last point on a spectrum, and *ology*, meaning "the study of." So, when we place these two terms together, we find that eschatology is the study of last things.

While this book has been devoted to the study of Christ's return, and its surrounding events, we have deliberately avoided laying out a chronological sequence for the last days. That's so we could focus on the facets of the second coming clearly stated in Scripture without forcing them into detailed timelines. Even so, these events *are* important, as is their chronology. That means coming to grips with one of the most debated passages in the Book of Revelation. And it means wrestling with a number of views of the millennium.

WHAT IS THE MILLENNIUM?

The word *millennium* means "one thousand years." For our purposes, this word comes from Revelation 20, where it's used six times in the first seven verses:

> Then I saw an angel coming down from heaven holding the key to the abyss and a great chain in his hand. He seized the dragon, that ancient serpent who is the devil and Satan, and bound him for a *thousand years*. He threw him into the abyss, closed it, and put a seal on it so that he would no longer deceive the nations until the *thousand years* were completed. After that, he must be released for a short time.
>
> Then I saw thrones, and people seated on them who were given authority to judge. I also saw the souls of those who had been beheaded because of their testimony about Jesus and because of the word of God, who had not worshiped the beast or his image, and who had not accepted the mark on their foreheads or their hands. They came to life and reigned with Christ for a *thousand years*. The rest of the dead did not come to life until the *thousand years* were completed.
>
> This is the first resurrection. Blessed and holy is the one who shares in the first resurrection! The second death has no power over them, but they will be priests of God and of Christ, and they will reign with him for a *thousand years*.
>
> When the *thousand years* are completed, Satan will be released from his prison .... (Rev. 20:1-7, emphasis added).

When do these one thousand years take place? Have they already occurred? Are they happening now, or are they in the future? Do these events unfold in heaven or on earth? Are we to take references to the millennium literally or figuratively?

Christians have answered these and related questions differently throughout the church age, and some have argued heatedly for their particular points of view. This appendix highlights four major views of the millennium: postmillennialism, amillennialism, historic premillennialism, and dispensational premillennialism.

Generally speaking, the millennium describes a period in which Christ and his followers reign; when Satan is bound; when righteousness overshadows (but does not yet eradicate) wickedness; and when, according to some views, there are significant (but not yet perfect) improvements in nature and the animal kingdom. Whether one understands the millennium literally or figuratively has a lot to do with his or her view as to when and where these events take place.

All of these views call us to look for a future physical return of Christ and to anticipate the time when he creates new heavens and a new earth. The primary differences center around whether Jesus returns before or after the millennium; whether the events described take place in heaven or on earth; whether the one thousand years should be understood literally or figuratively; whether Christ's return is a singular event or a two-stage event (the rapture and the glorious appearing); and whether Christians endure some or all of the tribulation – a time of intense persecution prior to the second coming.

As we look at different scenarios of the end times, it's important to note the biblical truths affirmed by proponents of all four views: 1) Jesus will return personally, powerfully, victoriously, and suddenly in the future; 2) Jesus will resurrect and judge all people, assigning each to heaven or hell; and 3) Jesus will create new heavens and a new earth where righteousness dwells and in which Satan, demons, and unbelievers have no part.

Please keep in mind that each view of the millennium addressed below is somewhat flexible. That is, champions of a particular view don't necessarily agree on every detail. In this appendix, we attempt to share the majority view while acknowledging some differences.

Finally, regardless of your perspective on the order of events surrounding the Day of the Lord, embrace its joyous certainty, as does the writer of this Puritan prayer:

O LORD,
I live here as a fish in a vessel of water,

only enough to keep me alive,
but in heaven I shall swim in the ocean.

Here I have a little air in me to keep me breathing,
but there I shall have sweet and fresh gales;

Here I have a beam of sun to lighten my darkness,
a warm ray to keep me from freezing;
yonder I shall live in light and warmth forever….

Give me to know that heaven is all love,
where the eye affects the heart,
and the continual viewing of thy beauty
keeps the soul in continual transports of delight.

Give me to know that heaven is all peace,
where error, pride, rebellion, passion raise no head.

Give me to know that heaven is all joy,
the end of believing, fasting, praying,
mourning, humbling, watching, fearing, repining;

And lead me to it soon.[1]

THE POSTMILLENNIAL VIEW

The prefix *post* means "after." According to this view, Jesus returns after the millennium, a lengthy era of peace and righteousness not necessarily one thousand years in length. Basically, postmillennialists believe that as the gospel spreads and the church grows, a larger proportion of the world's people become Christians. This generates a positive impact on society at all levels – government, commerce, social interaction, etc. – resulting in a world that functions more in accordance with God's standards.

Loraine Boettner defines postmillennialism this way:

> Postmillennialism is that view of the last things which holds that the Kingdom of God is now being extended in the world through the preaching of the Gospel and the saving work of the Holy Spirit in the hearts of individuals, that the world eventually is to be Christianized, and that the return of Christ is to occur at the close of a long period of righteousness and peace commonly called the "Millennium."[2]

The postmillennial view is optimistic about the power of the gospel to change lives and permeate society in positive ways. Satan currently is bound, and the good news of the kingdom is advancing. For example, ninety-eight percent of the world's people have the Bible in their own language. Christian radio and television, not to mention web and social media platforms, take the gospel into countless homes around the world. Bible institutes, universities, and seminaries are training more people than ever before, and Christian organizations are sending vast numbers of career missionaries and volunteers into remote places unreachable a century ago.[3]

The postmillennial view is most popular when the church is experiencing revival and when there is a general absence of war, international conflict, and suffering. This view was particularly popular in the 19th century, and it was the view embraced by major theologians of the late 19th and early 20th centuries. World Wars I and II, along with the proliferation of nuclear weapons, put a damper on postmillennialism. However, it's enjoying a modest resurgence today.

Arguments in favor of postmillennialism

(a) The Great Commission leads us to expect a Christianized world. Jesus said all authority in heaven and on earth has been given to him, and he has promised to be with us as we take the gospel to the ends of the earth. Therefore, we have every reason to believe the gospel will triumph in the hearts of individuals and around the world.

(b) Jesus' parables of the kingdom indicate that the gospel will permeate the whole world. The parables of the mustard seed (Matt. 13:31-32) and leaven (Matt. 13:33) are specifically cited.

(c) The world is becoming more Christianized. Christianity, for example, is the largest religion on earth, outpacing Islam, Hinduism, and other major world religions.

Arguments against postmillennialism

(a) Although Christ does indeed have all authority in heaven and on earth, and while people from every tribe, nation, and language will be in heaven (Rev. 5:9), this does not mean a majority of the world's people become Christians or that the world dramatically improves prior to Christ's return.

(b) While the parables of Jesus indicate that the kingdom of heaven begins humbly and then grows dramatically, they do not tell us the extent to which this growth takes place. In fact, other parables of Jesus indicate there is to be much wickedness leading up to the days of Christ's return (e.g., the parables of the wheat and tares (Matt. 13:24-30), dragnet (Matt. 13:47-50), and sheep and goats (Matt. 25:31-46).

(c) While Christianity is indeed the world's largest religion, evil is both rampant and pervasive.

(d) We might further note that it's unknown how many people who claim to be Christians actually are redeemed – likely a considerably smaller number than those who check the box marked "Christianity."

Leading proponents of postmillennialism include: B. B. Warfield; Charles Hodge; Jonathan Edwards; John Owen; W. G. T. Shedd; A. H. Armstrong; and, more recently, James White.

(See graphic on page 460.)

THE AMILLENNIAL VIEW

The *a-* in *amillennialism* negates the term. Therefore, amillennialism means there is no literal, future millennium believers should anticipate.

Amillennialists say Revelation 20:1-6 describes the present church age, not some future era of one thousand years. Specifically, they believe this passage refers to the present reign of the souls of deceased believers with Christ in heaven. Meanwhile, the kingdom of God is present on earth as Christ rules his people by his Word and Spirit. Amillennialists affirm the future return of Jesus, but they reject a literal thousand-year reign of Christ on earth.

According to amillennialism, the kingdom of God *is* the present church age. Satan is bound, so his ability to influence mankind is restricted while the gospel message reaches the ends of the earth. At the consummation of the age, Christ returns to inaugurate the eternal state without any intervening millennium. For this reason, some amillennialists prefer the term *realized millennialism* to illustrate they don't deny a millennium but believe it is fulfilled entirely in the present age.[4]

Christ's reign in the millennium is not his physical presence on earth. Rather, it's his authority being exercised in heaven as he sits at the Father's right hand, having received all authority in heaven and on earth (Matt. 28:18). The exact duration of the millennium / church age cannot be known, and the phrase "thousand years" in Revelation 20 is simply a figure of speech to indicate a long period of time during which Christ accomplishes his will on earth.

Amillennialists speak of an already-but-not-yet tension in which present-day Christians live. That is, while we enjoy the inaugurated kingdom, with Christ reigning from heaven, the day is coming when his kingdom is fully realized. Until then, Christians endure tribulation and suffering, but also victory as Christ's kingdom expands. At the return of Jesus, he creates new heavens and a new earth, and all resurrected and glorified saints enjoy eternal rest.

Arguments in favor of amillennialism

(a) In all of Scripture, only one passage (Rev. 20:1-7) mentions a thousand-year earthly reign of Jesus, and this passage is obscure. It's best not to base a major doctrine on a single passage in the Bible. Instead, Revelation 20:1-7 is better understood as describing the present church age.

(b) The Scriptures teach only one resurrection, not two (or more) separated by a thousand years. Regarding the "first resurrection" of Revelation 20:6, amillennialists say this is a *spiritual* resurrection that takes place throughout the church age.[5]

(c) Daniel 12:2, John 5:28-29, and Acts 24:15 indicate a single, or general, resurrection of all people.

(d) It seems unreasonable to think glorified believers, unglorified believers, and lost sinners would live on earth at the same time, even if only for a thousand years.

(e) If Jesus is literally ruling the earth from the throne of David during the millennium, it seems unreasonable that people would continue to reject him and persist in sin.

(f) There seems to be no ultimate purpose for a literal thousand-year reign of Christ on earth. Once Jesus has returned, what's the point of delaying the eternal state?

(g) Scripture seems to indicate that all major events of the end times occur at once, not spread out over a thousand years or more.

Arguments against amillennialism

(a) In response to the statement that only one passage (Rev. 20:1-7) mentions a thousand-year earthly reign of Jesus, it may be said that, even if this were true, the Bible only needs to say something once for it to be true and to command our attention. Further, premillennialists do not find this passage obscure by any means, and they see numerous Old and New Testament passages indicating a long period of time in the future, yet before the final state, during which Messiah reigns.

(b) Revelation 20 speaks of the "first resurrection," implying there will be a second one. It also addresses those who have no part in the first resurrection; they will come to life *after* the thousand years and experience the "second death." A straightforward (not figurative) understanding of this chapter seems best.

(c) The idea of glorified believers, unglorified believers, and unbelievers inhabiting the earth at the same time may be difficult to comprehend, but it's not impossible. The resurrected and glorified Christ walked among believers and unbelievers in their natural state after his resurrection.

(d) Jesus' physical presence on earth following his return does not rule out the possibility that many will reject him. Many people rejected Christ during his earthly ministry as the Suffering Servant. Even Judas, who shared in Jesus' ministry for three years, ultimately betrayed him. We should not underestimate the ability of sinful and fallen people to resort to great evil.

(e) An earthly millennial reign of Christ would show "the outworking of God's good purposes in the structures of society, especially the structures of the family and civil government."[6]

(f) Critics contend that the amillennial view lacks a meaningful purpose for Revelation 20.

Leading proponents of amillennialism include: Augustine; Martin Luther; John Calvin; J. I. Packer; John Murray; and G. K. Beale.

(See graphic on page 461.)

THE HISTORIC / CLASSICAL PREMILLENNIAL VIEW

The prefix *pre-* means "before," and therefore premillennialists believe Christ returns before the millennium. Historic, or classical, premillennialism has a long history dating back to the early centuries of the church. It's called "historic" because it resembles an ancient view of the end times known as *chiliasm*.

According to historic premillennialism, the present church age continues until followers of Jesus experience a time of intense persecution known as the tribulation. At the end of the tribulation, Christ returns to earth to establish the millennial kingdom, which some premillennialists understand as a literal one thousand years, while others simply take to mean a long period of time. It should be noted that Jesus has reigned as messianic king since his resurrection and ascension; the millennium introduces a change in venue for his throne from heaven to earth.

At the return of Jesus, deceased Old and New Testament saints are resurrected and given glorified bodies. Living believers on earth at this time also receive glorified bodies, and all believers then reign with Christ throughout the millennium. Satan is bound and cast into the abyss, where he has no influence over mankind until the millennium ends. As a result of Christ's rule and believers' service to their king, many unbelievers on earth trust in Jesus as Savior.

At the end of the millennium, Satan is loosed and joins forces with wicked people on earth, many of whom have submitted outwardly to Christ's reign but inwardly are rebellious. Together, they wage war against the Messiah, who decisively defeats them. Satan and demons are cast into the lake of fire. All unbelievers are then resurrected, stand in final judgment, and are separated eternally from God in hell. All believers then enter the eternal state in the new heavens and new earth.

This interpretation assumes that the events described in Revelation 19 and 20 are chronologically successive, in contrast to the postmillennial and amillennial positions. Further, while historic premillennialists generally believe the church has replaced Israel as God's covenant people, they also recognize a literal future for national Israel.

Arguments for historic premillennialism

(a) Revelation 20 is best understood as referring to a future earthly reign of Christ prior to the eternal state.

(b) Several Old Testament passages seem to fit neither the present age nor the eternal state and therefore suggest a millennial reign of righteousness (e.g., Ps. 72:8-14; Isa. 11:6-9; 65:20; Zech. 14:5-17).

(c) There are New Testament passages other than Revelation 20 that suggest a future millennium (1 Cor. 15:23-24; Rev. 2:26-27).

(d) The New Testament suggests that persecution/tribulation affects all believers, who should not expect to be spared a time of trial (2 Tim. 3:12).

Arguments against historic premillennialism

(a) Only Revelation 20:1-7 mentions a thousand-year earthly reign of Jesus, and this passage is obscure. It is best not to base a major doctrine on a single passage in the Bible.

(b) The Scriptures teach only one resurrection, not two (or more) separated by a thousand years. Daniel 12:2, John 5:28-29, and Acts 24:15 indicate a single, or general, resurrection of all people.

(c) There seems to be no ultimate purpose for a literal thousand-year reign of Christ on earth. Once Jesus has returned, what's the point of delaying the eternal state?

(d) Scripture indicates that all the major events of the end times occur at once; they are not spread out over a thousand years or more.

Leading proponents of historic / classical premillennialism include: Irenaeus; Justin Martyr; John Warwick Montgomery; George Eldon Ladd; and Henry Alford.

(See graphic on page 462.)

THE DISPENSATIONAL / PRETRIBULATIONAL PREMILLENNIAL VIEW

This view is similar to historic premillennialism with one major exception and two distinctions. As for the major exception, dispensational premillennialists hold that the present church age ends suddenly with the *rapture* – the physical removal of believers, dead and living, from the earth – prior to a seven-year tribulation, after which Christ returns. Put another way, the rapture is the first stage (albeit a secret one) in Christ's two-stage return – the second stage being his "glorious appearing" or physical descent to earth (Tit. 2:13 KJV). Roughly seven years separate these two events.

Some interpreters hold to a mid-tribulation rapture, meaning the church must endure the first half of the tribulation before being caught up into heaven. Others promote different versions of a post-tribulation rapture, more closely connecting believers' future resurrection with the return of Christ.

As for two distinctions between the historic and dispensational models: (1) dispensationalists hold to a more literal interpretation of prophetic passages, understanding words and statements in their customary way rather than reading them figuratively; and (2) dispensationalists draw a sharp line between Israel and the church. In their view, the term *Israel* always refers to Jacob's descendants, never to the church.

Jesus rewards the raptured church in heaven at the judgment seat of Christ (Rom. 14:10; 1 Cor. 3:9-15; 2 Cor. 5:10). Later, before returning to earth with the saints, Jesus and his bride (the church) enjoy the marriage feast of the Lamb (Rev. 19:7-9).

Meanwhile, on earth, many of the signs predicted to appear before Christ's return are fulfilled – for example, the redemption of many Jews as they receive Jesus as Messiah, and effective worldwide evangelism led largely by Jewish Christians. In addition, God uses a series of judgments during the tribulation – the seal, trumpet, and bowl judgments – to punish unbelieving Gentiles and disobedient Israel.

At the end of the seven years, Jesus returns to earth with the saints to inaugurate the millennium and reign for a thousand years from King David's throne in Jerusalem. Satan is bound in the abyss. The earth's environment is greatly improved. Its inhabitants enjoy peace, joy, comfort, financial soundness, and good health. This is a time of righteousness, obedience, truth, and fullness of the Holy Spirit. It's nearly perfect – but not quite and not yet.

Following the millennium, Satan is released from the abyss. Immediately, he rallies unbelievers on earth – those born during the millennium who have rejected Jesus, despite his perfect rule – and engages in a frontal assault on God's people. Jesus quashes the rebellion and casts Satan into the lake of fire (Rev. 20:7-10).

Finally, wicked people of all ages are resurrected and stand before the great white throne, where Christ judges their evil deeds, resulting in varying degrees of torment in hell (Rev. 20:11-15). Jesus then purges the cosmos of sin and its stain and creates new heavens and a new earth, ushering in the eternal state (2 Pet. 3:10-13; Rev. 21-22).

While historic premillennialism is rooted in ancient Christianity, dispensationalism is far more recent, marking its beginning in the mid-1800s with John Nelson Darby, an Anglican priest in Ireland and an influential leader among the Plymouth Brethren. Dispensationalism became especially popular in the United States and the United Kingdom in the late 19th and 20th centuries, advanced by the popularity of the Scofield Reference Bible. Christian authors Hal Lindsey (*The Late Great Planet Earth*), along with Tim LaHaye and Jerry B. Jenkins (*Left Behind* series), propelled this view to global popularity as their novels tied current events to end-times prophecies.

Arguments for and against dispensational premillennialism are much the same as those for and against historic premillennialism.

Leading proponents of dispensational premillennialism include: C. I. Scofield; Gleason Archer; Hal Lindsey; John MacArthur; Tim LaHaye; and Charles Stanley.

(See graphic on page 463.)

Postmillennialism

Christ comes after the millennium; not necessarily 1,000 years

Christ

Church Age - Millennium   Judgment   Eternal State

All People

Resurrection of believers and unbelievers at the same time, followed by judgment leading to heaven and hell; establishment of eternal state with new heavens and a new earth.

Amillennialism

No future millennium; no literal 1,000 years; Rev. 20:1-6 describes the church age

Christ

Church Age   Judgment   Eternal State

All People

Resurrection of believers and unbelievers at the same time, followed by judgment leading to heaven and hell; establishment of eternal state with new heavens and a new earth.

Historic/Classical Premillennialism

Christ comes before the millennium; tribulation is part of the church age

Christ

"Catching up" of believers to be
with Christ, followed by return
with Him.

Church Age - Tribulation   Millennium   Eternal State

Judgment

Believers   The Lost

Resurrection and judgment of believers and unbelievers separated by millennium.
Historic premillennialists differ as to whether the new heavens and earth begin
with the millennium or the eternal state.

Dispensational/Pretribulational Premillennialism

Christ raptures the church before the tribulation and returns 7 years later to usher in the millennium

Christ

Christ
and
Believers

"Catching up" of believers to be
with Christ, followed by return
with him after the tribulation.

Church Age | Tribulation | Millennium | Eternal State

Judgment

Believers

The Lost

Resurrection and judgment of believers and unbelievers separated by millennium.
Some dispensational premillennialists teach numerous believers' resurrections
between the "Rapture / catching up" and the resurrection of the lost.

	Postmillennial	Amillennial	Historic Premillennial	Dispensational Premillennial
Are the 1,000 years literal?	No	No	Yes (some say no)	Yes (some say no)
Will Jesus return physically?	Yes	Yes	Yes	Yes
When will Jesus return?	After the millennium	Any time	After the tribulation, before the millennium	Rapture before, or during, the tribulation; 2nd coming after the tribulation, before the millennium
Do the rapture and 2nd coming occur at the same time?	Yes	Yes	Yes	No. They are separated by 7 years (pretrib) or 3.5 years (midtrib)

	Postmillennial	Amillennial	Historic Premillennial	Dispensational Premillennial
Will there be a great tribulation?	The tribulation is happening now; it is the conflict between good and evil since Jesus' death and resurrection	The tribulation is happening now; it occurs when Christians are persecuted, or when wars or disasters break out	Yes; it will occur in the days just prior to Jesus' return	Yes; it will take place during the last 3.5 years of the 7-year tribulation
How long is the tribulation?	As long as the church age	As long as the church age	7 years (or more)	7 years
How do Christians suffer during the tribulation?	Christians suffer as the gospel is opposed	Christians endure persecution, which increases as the church age draws to a close	Christians go through the tribulation and suffer persecution for the cause of Christ	Christians are either raptured before the tribulation (pretrib) or in the middle of it (midtrib)
How is Israel viewed?	Not relevant to the prophecies in Revelation	Most references to Israel in Revelation symbolize the people of God on earth	The church has replaced Israel as God's covenant people; but there's a future for national Israel	Important. All references to Israel in Revelation refer to the nation of Israel

	Postmillennial	Amillennial	Historic Premillennial	Dispensational Premillennial
What are key Scriptures supporting this view?	Dan. 12:2-3; Matt. 24:14; Mark 13:10; John 5:28-29	Dan. 12:2-3; John 5:28-29; Bible uses "1,000" figuratively (Ps. 50:10; 90:4; 105:8; 2 Pet. 3:8); saints on earth during tribulation (Rev. 13:7)	2 Thess. 2:3-4; Rev. 2:22-23, 13:7; NT uses "Israel" and "twelve tribes" to refer to Christians (Matt. 19:28-29); Rom. 9:6-8	Gen. 15:7-21 (Israel); 1 Thess. 5:9; Rev. 3:10; church not mentioned in Rev. 4-19
When was this view most popular?	May have been held as early as A.D. 300; popular before world wars of 20th century; enjoying a resurgence now	Popularized around A.D. 400; still popular today, especially among Reformed Christians	Emerged at end of 1st century A.D.; still popular today	Became popular about 1860; has increased in popularity
Who are key supporters of this view?	Jonathan Edwards, B.B. Warfield, Augustus H. Strong, Charles Hodge	Augustine, Martin Luther, John Calvin, J.I. Packer	Irenaeus, Justin Martyr, John Warwick Montgomery, George E. Ladd	C.I. Scofield, Gleason Archer, Hal Lindsey, John MacArthur, Charles Stanley, Tim LaHaye

APPENDIX II

KEY SCRIPTURES ON HELL

Scripture	Author/ Speaker	What It's Called	How It's Experienced
Ps. 21:8-9	David	Not named	The wicked will "burn like a fiery furnace;" be "engulfed in wrath;" and "fire will devour them"
Ps. 145:20	David	Not named	God "destroys all the wicked"
Isa. 66:15-16	The Lord	Flames of fire	When the Lord comes on the last day, he will come "with fire … to execute his anger with fury and his rebuke with flames of fire." He will "execute judgment … with his fiery sword"

Scripture	Author/ Speaker	What It's Called	How It's Experienced
Isa. 66:24	The Lord	Not named	Those who rebel against the Lord will be expelled from his kingdom; "their worm will never die, their fire will never go out ...."
Dan. 12:2	An angel (to Daniel)	Not named	"... disgrace and eternal contempt"
Matt. 3:12	John the Baptist	Fire that never goes out	The "chaff" will burn in a fire of God's judgment
Matt. 5:22	Jesus	Hellfire (lit. "the gehenna of fire")	Whoever says, "You fool!" will be subject to hellfire
Matt. 5:29-30	Jesus	Hell	"... it is better that you lose one of the parts of your body than for your whole body to go into hell"
Matt. 7:13	Jesus	Destruction	The gate is wide and the road is broad that lead to destruction, contrasted with the narrow gate and difficult road that lead to life

Scripture	Author/ Speaker	What It's Called	How It's Experienced
Matt. 7:21-23	Jesus	Not named	On the day of judgment, Jesus will say to false prophets, "Depart from me, you lawbreakers!"
Matt. 8:12	Jesus	Outer darkness	There will be weeping and gnashing of teeth for the unbelieving "sons of the kingdom"
Matt. 10:28	Jesus	Hell	Soul and body are destroyed
Matt. 13:41-42	Jesus	Blazing furnace	The Son of Man will send out his angels to cast all who "cause sin and those guilty of lawlessness" into the blazing furnace, where there will be "weeping and gnashing of teeth"
Matt. 13:50	Jesus	Blazing furnace	Evil people will be thrown there; there will be "weeping and gnashing of teeth"

Scripture	Author/ Speaker	What It's Called	How It's Experienced
Matt. 18:8	Jesus	Eternal fire	"It is better for you to enter life maimed or lame than to have two hands or two feet and be thrown into the eternal fire"
Matt. 18:9	Jesus	Hellfire	"It is better for you to enter life with one eye than to have two eyes and be thrown into hellfire"
Matt. 23:15	Jesus	Hell	Christ pronounces a woe on scribes and Pharisees for making converts "twice as much a child of hell as you are!"
Matt. 23:33, 35	Jesus	Hell (lit. "the judgment of gehenna")	Jesus calls the scribes, Pharisees, and hypocrites "Snakes! Brood of vipers!" The righteous blood shed on earth will be charged to them.

Scripture	Author/ Speaker	What It's Called	How It's Experienced
Matt. 24:51	Jesus	A place with the hypocrites	The wicked servant will be cut to pieces and assigned a place with the hypocrites, where there will be "weeping and gnashing of teeth"
Matt. 25:41	Jesus	Eternal fire	The cursed (wicked) are ordered to depart from Jesus into eternal fire prepared for the devil and his angels
Matt. 25:46	Jesus	Not named	"… eternal punishment"
Mark 9:43-48	Jesus	Hell; the unquenchable fire	It's better to enter life maimed, lame, or one-eyed than to be cast into hell, where "their worm does not die, and the fire is not quenched"
Luke 3:17	John the Baptist	Fire that never goes out	Jesus will burn "the chaff" with "fire that never goes out"

Scripture	Author/Speaker	What It's Called	How It's Experienced
Luke 12:5	Jesus	Hell	Jesus has the authority to throw people into hell after death; thus, he should be feared.
Luke 13:24-28	Jesus	Not named	One day, Jesus says to evildoers, "Get away from me ... There will be weeping and gnashing of teeth in that place" when you are "thrown out" of the kingdom.
John 3:16-19	Jesus	Not named	Those who reject Jesus will "perish;" they are "condemned already" because they love darkness
John 5:28-29	Jesus	Condemnation	The wicked face "the resurrection of condemnation"

Scripture	Author/ Speaker	What It's Called	How It's Experienced
Rom. 1:20	Paul	Not named	The wicked who suffer in hell are "without excuse" (without a defense) because they rejected God, who revealed himself in creation
Rom. 2:5-9	Paul	Wrath; anger	Those with hardened and unrepentant hearts face "the day of wrath, when God's righteous judgment is revealed." They experience "wrath and anger … affliction and distress …."
Rom. 5:9	Paul	Wrath	Those justified through the blood of Jesus will "be saved through him from wrath"

Scripture	Author/ Speaker	What It's Called	How It's Experienced
2 Thess. 1:8-9	Paul	Not named	Jesus will take "vengeance with flaming fire" on those who don't know God and those who don't obey the gospel of Jesus. They will "pay the penalty of eternal destruction...."
Heb. 10:27	Writer of Hebrews	A fire	Those who trample on the Son of God, regard as profane his blood, and insult the Spirit of grace face "a terrifying expectation of judgment and the fury of a fire about to consume the adversaries"
Heb. 12:29	Writer of Hebrews	Consuming fire	"...our God is a consuming fire" (his holiness will consume the wicked)
Jas. 3:6	James	Hell	The tongue is "set on fire by hell"

Scripture	Author/ Speaker	What It's Called	How It's Experienced
2 Pet. 2:17	Peter	The gloom of darkness	This is "reserved" for false teachers
2 Pet. 3:9	Peter	Not named	The Lord is patient, not wanting any to perish but all to come to repentance
Jude 7	Jude	Not named	"…the punishment of eternal fire"
Jude 13	Jude	The blackness of darkness	This is "reserved forever" for false teachers
Rev. 2:11	Jesus (to the church at Smyrna)	The second death	Those faithful until death – the conquerors – will never be harmed by the second death

Scripture	Author/Speaker	What It's Called	How It's Experienced
Rev. 14:9-11	John	God's wrath; the cup of his anger; fire and sulfur	Those who worship the beast will "drink the wine of God's wrath;" be "tormented with fire and sulfur in the sight of the holy angels and in the sight of the Lamb;" "the smoke of their torment will go up forever and ever;" they have no rest day or night
Rev. 19:20	John	The lake of fire that burns with sulfur	The beast and false prophet are cast alive into the lake
Rev. 20:6	John	The second death	The second death has no power over those who share in the first resurrection
Rev. 20:10	John	The lake of fire and sulfur	The devil is thrown there, where the beast and false prophet are, and they are "tormented day and night forever and ever."

Scripture	Author/ Speaker	What It's Called	How It's Experienced
Rev. 20:14	John	The lake of fire; the second death	Death and Hades are thrown there
Rev. 20:15	John	The lake of fire	Those whose names are not found written in the book of life are thrown there
Rev. 21:8	"the one seated on the throne" (Jesus)	The lake that burns with fire and sulfur; the second death	"... the cowards, faithless, detestable, murderers, sexually immoral, sorcerers, idolaters, and all liars" have "their share" there
Rev. 22:18-19	John	Not named	Those who add to or take away from the words of prophecy in the Book of Revelation ... God will "add to him the plagues" written in this book, and God will "take away his share of the tree of life and the holy city...."

NOTES

Chapter 1: *"I will come again"*

1. "General MacArthur leaves Corregidor," https://www.history.com/this-day-in-history/macarthur-leaves-corregidor.
2. Kendell H. Easley, *Revelation*, Vol. 12, Holman New Testament Commentary (Nashville, TN: Broadman & Holman Publishers, 1998), 289–290.
3. The seven beatitudes of Revelation may be found at Rev. 1:3; 14:13; 16:15; 19:9; 20:6; 22:7, 14.
4. Joseph A. Seiss, *The Apocalypse: An Exposition of the Book of Revelation* (Grand Rapids, MI: Kregel Publications, 1987; originally published by C.C. Cook, 1900), 23.

Chapter 2: *"We eagerly wait for a Savior"*

1. Craig S. Keener, *The IVP Bible Background Commentary: New Testament*, Second Edition (Downers Grove, IL: IVP Academic, 2014), 378.
2. Keener, 583.
3. Keener, 589.
4. Keener, 629.

5. Keener, 654.

6. Jared V. Ingle, "Today in Hebrews: an opportunity to enter his rest," https://www.patheos.com/blogs/jaredingle/2019/09/today-in-hebrews-an-opportunity-to-enter-his-rest/.

7. Donald Guthrie, *Hebrews: An Introduction and Commentary*, Vol. 15, Tyndale New Testament Commentaries (Downers Grove, IL: Inter-Varsity Press, 1983), 226.

8. For more on believers' crowns, see Rob Phillips, *What Every Christian Should Know About Salvation* (Jefferson City, MO: High Street Press, 2018), 268-271.

9. Colin G. Kruse, *The Letters of John*, The Pillar New Testament Commentary (Grand Rapids, MI; Leicester, England: W.B. Eerdmans Pub.; Apollos, 2000), 112–116.

10. David H. Stern, *Jewish New Testament Commentary* (Clarksville, MD: Jewish New Testament Publications, Inc., 1989), 789.

11. Some commentators contend that Revelation 19:11-16 describes the victory of the Word of God on earth between Christ's first and second comings. Certainly, the Bible – the Word of God – is accomplishing much on earth today (Heb. 4:11-12). At the same time, the Word of God – Jesus – is active on earth as well. His finished work on the cross is proclaimed to the nations and results in the plundering of Satan's goods as people are rescued from the kingdom of darkness and brought into the kingdom of light. Yet it appears Revelation 19 describes a more final judgment of the earth's wicked, leading to the great white throne and the lake of fire (Rev. 20:11-15), and to the creation of new heavens and a new earth (Rev. 21-22).

12. "Why Did Jesus Ride a Donkey into Jerusalem? The Triumphal Entry," https://www.christianity.com/wiki/jesus-christ/why-did-jesus-ride-a-donkey-into-jerusalem.html.

13. J. F. Walvoord, R. B. Zuck, *The Bible Knowledge Commentary: An Exposition of the Scriptures*, Rev. 19:11-13, Logos Bible Software.

14. Matthew Henry, *Matthew Henry's Commentary on the Whole Bible: Complete and Unabridged in One Volume*, Rev. 19:11-21, Logos Bible Software.

15. Warren W. Wiersbe, *The Bible Exposition Commentary*, Vol. 2 (Wheaton, IL: Victor Books, 1996), 618.

16. For example, see Deut. 33:2; Job 5:1; 15:15; Isa. 66:15-16; Jer. 25:30-32; Dan. 4; 7:10; Zech. 14:5.

17. Consider a few of the many Scriptures relating to the return of Christ, and the supporting role of angels and redeemed people: Dan. 7:9-27; Zech. 14:5; Matt. 13:39-41, 49-50; 16:27; 24:30-31; 25:31; Mark 8:38; 1 Cor. 6:2-3; 1 Thess. 3:13; 2 Thess. 1:7-10; Rev. 2:26; 3:21; 19:14; 22:1-5.

18. It should be noted that some commentators see these messengers as human. They are, it is said, pastors, just like the angels/messengers of the seven churches (Rev. 1:20). The reasoning goes like this: True angelic beings are ministering spirits who desire to look into the mysteries of the gospel, but nowhere else in Scripture are they charged with proclaiming the message of salvation.

Chapter 3: *"He will judge the nations"*

1. Wayne A. Grudem, *1 Peter: An Introduction and Commentary*, Vol. 17, Tyndale New Testament Commentaries (Downers Grove, IL: InterVarsity Press, 1988), 72-78.

2. Marvin Richardson Vincent, *Word Studies in the New Testament*, Vol. 1 (New York: Charles Scribner's Sons, 1887), 635.

3. Leon Morris, *Luke: An Introduction and Commentary*, Vol. 3, Tyndale New Testament Commentaries (Downers Grove, IL: InterVarsity Press, 1988), 125-127.

4. Darrell L. Bock, *Luke*: The IVP New Testament Commentary Series (Downers Grove, IL: InterVarsity Press, 1994), Luke 4:16-30.

5. "Second Coming," Encyclopedia of the Bible, https://www.biblegate way.com/resources/encyclopedia-of-the-bible/Second-Coming.

6. Psalm 110:1 is referred to in one way or another no fewer than twenty-seven times in the New Testament, according to Roger Ellsworth, *Opening Up Psalms*, Opening Up Commentary (Leominster: Day One Publications, 2006), 185-192.

7. Robert Jamieson, A. R. Fausset, and David Brown, *Commentary Crit-*

ical and Explanatory on the Whole Bible, Vol. 1 (Oak Harbor, WA: Logos Research Systems, Inc., 1997), 380.

8. Ellsworth, 185-192.

Chapter 4: *"This same Jesus"*

1. For an exploration of the preincarnate Christ, see Rob Phillips, *Jesus Before Bethlehem: What Every Christian Should Know About the Angel of the LORD* (Jefferson City, MO: High Street Press, 2020).

2. For an in-depth study of the doctrine of the Trinity, see Rob Phillips, *What Every Christian Should Know About the Trinity* (Jefferson City, MO: High Street Press, 2019).

3. *The Baptist Faith & Message* (Nashville, TN: LifeWay Press, 2000), 7.

4. The word "nature" refers to essence or substance, and these two natures of Jesus – divine and human – are inseparable, unmixed, and unchanged.

5. Bruce Ware, *The Man Christ Jesus: Theological Reflections on the Humanity of Christ* (Wheaton, IL: Crossway, 2012), 26.

6. Fred Zaspel, "Jesus Christ, the Son of Man," https://www.thegospel coalition.org/essay/jesus-christ-son-man/.

7. *Ibid.*

8. *Ibid.*

9. For more on this subject, see *Jesus Before Bethlehem: What Every Christian Should Know About the Angel of the LORD.*

10. T. D. Alexander, "Jesus as Messiah," The Gospel Coalition, https://www.thegospelcoalition.org/essay/jesus-as-messiah/.

11. *Ibid.*

12. *Ibid.*

13. *Ibid.*

14. Eugene E. Carpenter and Philip W. Comfort, *Holman Treasury of Key Bible Words: 200 Greek and Hebrew Words Defined and Explained* (Nashville, TN: Broadman & Holman Publishers, 2000), 378.

15. "What happened on the Mount of Olives?" https://www.gotques tions.org/Mount-of-Olives.html.

16. For a detailed examination of this view, see Joel Richardson's *Sinai*

to Zion: The Untold Story of the Triumphant Return of Jesus (Leawood, KS: Winepress Media, 2020).

17. John R. W. Stott, *The Message of Acts: The Spirit, the Church & the World,* The Bible Speaks Today (Leicester, England; Downers Grove, IL: InterVarsity Press, 1994), 49-51.

Chapter 5: *"Coming on the clouds"*

1. John M. Frame, "The Omnipotence, Omniscience, and Omnipresence of God," https://www.thegospelcoalition.org/essay/omnipotence-omniscience-omnipresence-god.

2. *Theological Dictionary of the New Testament*, Vol. II, Gerhard Kittel, ed. (Grand Rapids, MI: Wm. B. Eerdmans Publishing Company, 1964-1976), 306.

3. Leon Morris, *1 Corinthians: An Introduction and Commentary*, Vol. 7, Tyndale New Testament Commentaries (Downers Grove, IL: Inter-Varsity Press, 1985), 52.

4. Regarding Luke 10:1, some manuscripts say "seventy."

5. *Theological Dictionary of the New Testament*, Vol. II, 302.

6. R. C. Sproul, *Mark*, St. Andrew's Expositional Commentary (Sanford, FL: Reformation Trust Publishing, 2011), 208-209.

7. Stuart K. Weber, *Matthew*, Vol. 1, Holman New Testament Commentary (Nashville, TN: Broadman & Holman Publishers, 2000), 403-404.

Chapter 6: *"King of Kings and Lord of Lords"*

1. Warren W. Wiersbe, *The Bible Exposition Commentary*, Vol. 1 (Wheaton, IL: Victor Books, 1996), 384.

2. See D. A. Carson, *The Gospel According to John*, The Pillar New Testament Commentary (Leicester, England; Grand Rapids, MI: InterVarsity Press; W. B. Eerdmans, 1991), 618-622.

3. *Matthew Henry's Commentary on the Whole Bible: Complete and Unabridged in One Volume* (Peabody, MA, 1994), 2048.

4. For more on Satan as "the serpent," see Rob Phillips, *What Every*

Christian Should Know About Satan (Jefferson City, MO: High Street Press, 2021), 23-69.

5. Lois Tverberg, "Eve's Error," En-Gedi Resource Center, https://engediresourcecenter.com/2015/07/03/eves-error/.

6. *Ibid.*

7. According to Alfred Edersheim, a teacher of languages and Warbutonian Lecturer at Lincoln's Inn (Oxford), there are at least 465 messianic references in the Old Testament. See John Ankerberg, John Weldon, and Walter C. Kaiser Jr., *The Case for Jesus the Messiah: Incredible Prophecies That Prove God Exists* (Chattanooga, TN: The John Ankerberg Evangelistic Association, 1989), 12.

8. Leon Morris, *Revelation: An Introduction and Commentary*, Vol. 20, Tyndale New Testament Commentaries (Downers Grove, IL: Inter-Varsity Press, 1987), 218-221.

9. Easley, 352-355.

10. John F. Walvoord, "Revelation," in *The Bible Knowledge Commentary: An Exposition of the Scriptures*, ed. J. F. Walvoord and R. B. Zuck, Vol. 2 (Wheaton, IL: Victor Books, 1985), 976.

11. Henry, 2482.

12. James M. Freeman and Harold J. Chadwick, *Manners & Customs of the Bible* (North Brunswick, NJ: Bridge-Logos Publishers, 1998), 552.

13. Easley, 352-355.

14. Morris, *Revelation*, 218-221.

15. Ramsey Michaels, *Revelation*, Vol. 20, The IVP New Testament Commentary Series (Downers Grove, IL: InterVarsity Press, 1997), Rev. 19:11-16.

16. Wiersbe, *The Bible Exposition Commentary*, Vol. 2, 618.

17. Jamieson, Fausset, and Brown, *Commentary Critical and Explanatory on the Whole Bible*, Vol. 2, 596-597.

18. Easley, 352-355.

Chapter 7: *"I am coming like a thief"*

1. "Boston thieves pull off historic Brink's robbery," https://www.

history.com/this-day-in-history/brinks-armored-car-depot-robbery-boston-1950.

2. Greg Daugherty, "Butch Cassidy and the Sundance Kid: Their Biggest Heists," https://www.history.com/news/butch-cassidy-sundance-kid-robberies-death, Oct. 28, 2020.

3. D. B. Cooper, https://en.wikipedia.org/wiki/D._B._Cooper.

4. Leon Morris, *The Gospel according to Matthew*, The Pillar New Testament Commentary (Grand Rapids, MI; Leicester, England: W.B. Eerdmans; InterVarsity Press, 1992), 614.

5. *Ibid.*

6. The first parable recorded in the Bible is that of the trees choosing for themselves a king (Judg. 9:7-15).

7. Trent C. Butler, *Luke*, Vol. 3, Holman New Testament Commentary (Nashville, TN: Broadman & Holman Publishers, 2000), 208.

8. In Jesus' parable in Matthew 25:1-13, nothing should be made of the fact that there are ten virgins, other than that Jews would not hold synagogue, a wedding, or another ceremony without at least ten witnesses. The fact that five of the virgins are wise and five are foolish should not be taken to mean that half of all professing Christians are lost. There's folly in reading too much into the details of any parable.

9. The summary of this parable is taken from Rob Phillips, *The Kingdom According to Jesus: A Study of Jesus' Parables on the Kingdom of Heaven* (Bloomington, IN: CrossBooks, 2009), 77-82.

10. James R. Edwards, *The Gospel According to Mark*, The Pillar New Testament Commentary (Grand Rapids, MI; Leicester, England: Eerdmans; Apollos, 2002), 408-410.

11. Bock, Luke 12:35–48.

12. Henry, 1677.

13. Thomas D. Lea and Hayne P. Griffin, *1, 2 Timothy, Titus*, Vol. 34, The New American Commentary (Nashville: Broadman & Holman Publishers, 1992), 310.

14. Douglas J. Moo, *The Letter of James*, The Pillar New Testament Commentary (Grand Rapids, MI; Leicester, England: Eerdmans; Apollos, 2000), 224.

15. Thomas R. Schreiner, *1, 2 Peter, Jude*, Vol. 37, The New American
Commentary (Nashville: Broadman & Holman Publishers, 2003), 211.
16. *Ibid.*
17. Wayne Grudem, *Systematic Theology: An Introduction to Biblical
Doctrine* (Leicester, England: InterVarsity Press; Grand Rapids, MI:
Zondervan, 1994), 1097-1099.
18. Grudem, *Systematic Theology*, 1094.

Chapter 8: *"Your kingdom come"*

1. Jesus' coronation as king takes place in heaven after his ascension.
When he returns to earth, he brings his throne with him and sits on it
to judge people and nations.
2. George Eldon Ladd, *The Gospel of the Kingdom: Scriptural Studies in
the Kingdom of God* (Grand Rapids, MI: William B. Eerdmans
Publishing Company, 1959), 19.
3. Burk Parsons, "What Is the Kingdom of God?", *Tabletalk*, November
2021, 2.
4. Charles S. Kelley Jr., Richard Land, and R. Albert Mohler Jr., *The
Baptist Faith & Message*, 6-part Bible Study (Nashville, TN: LifeWay
Press, 2007), 63.
5. Tim Mackie, "Isaiah and the Messianic King: A Hope for the
Distant Future," https://bibleproject.com/blog/isaiah-messianic-
king/.
6. "Kainos," Blue Letter Bible, https://www.blueletterbible.org/lexi
con/g2537/csb/mgnt/0-1/.

Chapter 9: *"All who are in the graves"*

1. "Death & Taxes Quote Origin + Who Said It (Ben Franklin?),"
https://blackalliance.org/death-taxes-quote/.
2. *Expository Dictionary of Bible Words: Word Studies for Key English Bible
Words Based on the Hebrew and Greek Texts*, Stephen D. Renn, ed.
(Peabody, MA: Hendrickson Publishers, 2005), 388.
3. G. K. Beale, *The Book of Revelation: A Commentary on the Greek Text*,

NIGTC (Grand Rapids, MI: Eerdmans, 1999), 191; quoted in *The New American Commentary: An Exegetical and Theological Exposition of Holy Scripture, Vol. 39: Revelation* (Nashville, TN: B&H Publishing Group, 2012), 60.

4. The fact that Jesus retains the marks of his crucifixion in his glorified body does not mean you and I keep our scars, deformities, and disfigurations after our resurrection. Our physical imperfections result *from* sin; Christ's wounds are borne *for* our sins. Further, Jesus' marks are everlasting evidence of his redemptive work on our behalf, and help us positively identify him in the company of false Messiahs.

5. Some Bible commentators argue that the judgment seat of Christ and the great white throne are two different perspectives of the same final judgment of all people, with Paul focusing on believers and John focusing on unbelievers.

6. J. Daniel Hays, J. Scott Duvall, and C. Marvin Pate, *Dictionary of Biblical Prophecy and End Times* (Grand Rapids, MI: Zondervan, 2007), 236.

7. Seiss, 479.

8. *Ibid.*

9. Charles R. Swindoll, *Insights on Revelation* (Grand Rapids, MI: Zondervan, 2011), 266-67.

Chapter 10: *"So that mortality may be swallowed up by life"*

1. Barrie Barber, "Memphis Belle to go on display at Air Force Museum in 2018," Dayton Daily News, March 9, 2017, http://www. daytondailynews.com/news/local/memphis-belle-display-air-force-museum-2018/xkJg6sCmeIi4qYR4Nk96WI/.

2. Grudem, *Systematic Theology*, 828.

3. Francis Brown, S. R. Driver, and Charles A. Briggs, *Hebrew and English Concordance of the Old Testament* (New York: Oxford University Press, 1955), 458-459.

4. William D. Mounce, *Mounce's Complete Expository Dictionary of Old & New Testament Words* (Grand Rapids, MI: Zondervan, 2006), 290.

5. *Ibid.* See also Rom. 11:33-36; 1 Cor. 10:31; 2 Cor. 4:15; Gal. 1:5;

Eph. 3:21; 2 Peter 3:18; Rev. 5:12-13.

6. ESV Study Bible (Wheaton, IL: Crossway Bibles, 2008), 2418.

7. While Evangelicals are united in their belief in future resurrection and glorification of the saints, they view the order of events surrounding Christ's return in various ways. Stanley J. Grentz offers a historical, biblical, and theological perspective on the four major positions held by Evangelicals – postmillennialism, dispensational premillennialism, historic premillennialism, and amillennialism – in *The Millennial Maze* (Downers Grove, IL: InterVarsity Press, 1992).

8. CSB Study Bible (Nashville, TN: Holman Bible Publishers, 2017), 1888.

9. ESV Study Bible, 2229.

10. Kenneth E. Bailey, *Paul Through Mediterranean Eyes: Cultural Studies in 1 Corinthians* (Downers Grove, IL: IVP Academic, 2011), 464.

11. Bailey, 458.

12. Bailey, 467.

13. Mounce, 558.

14. Wiersbe, *The Bible Exposition Commentary*, Vol. 1, 540–541.

15. William D. Mounce, *Interlinear For The Rest of Us* (Grand Rapids, MI: Zondervan, 2006), 817.

16. John A. Witmer, "Romans," in *The Bible Knowledge Commentary: An Exposition of the Scriptures, Vol. 2*, ed. J. F. Walvoord and R. B. Zuck (Wheaton, IL: Victor Books, 1985), 474.

17. Vincent, *Word Studies in the New Testament*, Vol. 3, 285-286.

18. Mounce, *Interlinear For The Rest of Us*, 859.

19. Mounce, *Complete Expository Dictionary*, 28.

Chapter 11: *"Thrown into the lake of fire"*

1. Robert A. Morey, *Death and the Afterlife* (Minneapolis, MN: Bethany House Publishers, 1984), 74-75.

2. Alan W. Gomes, *40 Questions About Heaven and Hell* (Grand Rapids, MI: Kregel Academic, 2018), 277.

3. John MacArthur, *The MacArthur New Testament Commentary: Revelation 12-22* (Chicago: Moody Publishers, 2000), 256.

4. Timothy R. Phillips, "Hell," *Evangelical Dictionary of Biblical Theology*, Walter A. Elwell, ed. (Grand Rapids, MI: Baker Books, 1996), 339.

5. Ralph E. Powell, "Hell," *Baker Encyclopedia of the Bible* (Grand Rapids, MI: Baker Book House, 1988), 952-955.

6. Steve Gregg, *All You Want to Know About Hell: Three Christian Views of God's Final Solution to the Problem of Sin* (Nashville, TN: Thomas Nelson, 2013), 86-98.

7. Powell, 952-955.

8. C. H. Spurgeon, "The Resurrection of the Dead," *Spurgeon's Sermons*, Vol. 2, No. 66, Feb. 17, 1856.

9. Gomes, 283.

10. William Crockett, *Four Views on Hell* (Grand Rapids, MI: Zondervan, 1996), 44.

11. Charles Hodge, *Systematic Theology*, Vol. 3 (Grand Rapids, MI: William B. Eerdmans Publishing Company, 1975), 868.

12. Joseph Henry Thayer, *A Greek-English Lexicon of the New Testament* (New York: Harper, 1887), 96.

13. Walter Bauer, Frederick W. Danker, William F. Arndt, and F. Wilbur Gingrich, *A Greek-English Lexicon of the New Testament and Other Early Christian Literature*, 3rd ed. (Chicago: University of Chicago Press, 2000), 168.

14. Gomes, 287.

15. Morey, 90.

16. *Ibid.*

17. Augustine, *City of God* 21:26.

18. For a rebuttal of the doctrine of purgatory, see Rob Phillips, *What Everyone Should Know About the Afterlife: A Biblical View of What Lies Beyond the Grave* (Jefferson City, MO: High Street Press, 2017), 27-34; Gomes, *40 Questions About Heaven and Hell*, 119-136.

19. C. S. Lewis, *The Problem of Pain*, cited in "Banished from Humanity: C. S. Lewis and the Doctrine of Hell" by Randy Alcorn, March 18, 2015, http://desiringgod.org/articles/banished-from-humanity.

20. Lewis, cited in "Seeing Hell through the Reason and Imagination of C. S. Lewis" by Douglas Beyer, Jan. 1, 1998, http://discovery.org/a/507.

21. "Our Need of Satisfaction," *Tabletalk*, April 2022, 59.

22. *"Aionios,"* Strong's G166, *Thayer's Greek Lexicon*, Blueletter-bible.com.

23. R. T. France, *Matthew: An Introduction and Commentary*, Vol. 1, Tyndale New Testament Commentaries (Downers Grove, IL: Inter-Varsity Press, 1985), 357-362.

24. Moses Stuart, *Exegetical Essays on Several Words Relating to Future Punishment* (Andover, MA: Perkins & Marvin, 1830), 56.

Chapter 12: *"The eternal fire prepared for the devil"*

1. Quinn Myers, "5 Most Inescapable Prisons in the World," https://www.maxim.com/maxim-man/5-most-inescapable-prisons-world.

2. In Rom. 10:7, Paul freely adapts Deut. 30:12-13, in which Moses contrasts going "up to heaven" with traveling "across the sea." The Israelites need to do neither, for the Lord's command is "certainly not too difficult or beyond your reach."

3. Grant R. Osborne, *Revelation: Baker Exegetical Commentary on the New Testament* (Grand Rapids, MI: Baker Academic, 2002), 699.

4. Jamieson, Fausset, and Brown, *Commentary Critical and Explanatory on the Whole Bible*, Vol. 2, 598.

5. Osborne, 700.

6. Mounce, *Mounce's Complete Expository Dictionary of Old & New Testament Words*, 465.

7. Walter A. Elwell and Barry J. Beitzel, "Bottomless Pit," *Baker Encyclopedia of the Bible* (Grand Rapids, MI: Baker Book House, 1988), 375.

8. Easley, 369-371.

9. *On First Principles* 1.6.1. Origen felt he had scriptural support of *apocatastasis* in such New Testament passages as Acts 3:21; Rom. 5:17; 11:36; 1 Cor. 15:26-28; Phil. 2:10; and 1 John 4:8.

10. Graham A. Cole, *Against the Darkness: the Doctrine of Angels, Satan, and Demons* (Wheaton, IL: Crossway, 2019), 220.

11. Cole, 223.

12. Easley, 369-371.

Chapter 13: *"The renewal of all things"*

1. Rute Ferreria, "Maggie Simpson, is that you?" *DailyArt Magazine*, Feb. 11, 2022, https://www.dailyartmagazine.com/worst-artworks-restorations/.

2. Randy Alcorn, *Heaven* (Wheaton, IL: Tyndale House Publishers, 2004), 42.

3. *Theological Dictionary of the New Testament*, Gerhard Kittel and Gerhard Friedrich, eds. (Grand Rapids, MI: William B. Eerdmans Publishing Company, 1985), 388.

4. Franz Delitzsch, *Biblical Commentary on the Prophecies of Isaiah*, 3rd edition (London: 1890-1892), Vol. II, n.p.; cited in Wilbur W. Smith, *The Biblical Doctrine of Heaven* (Chicago: Moody Press, 1968), 224.

5. J. I. Packer, quoted in Hank Hanegraaff, *AfterLife: What You Need to Know About Heaven, the Hereafter & Near-death Experiences* (Brentwood, TN: Worthy Publishing, 2013), 16.

6. Millard J. Erickson, *Christian Theology*, Third Edition (Grand Rapids, MI: Baker Academic, 2013), 928.

7. R. C. Sproul, *Matthew: An Expositional Commentary* (Sanford, FL: Reformation Trust Publishing, 2019), 532.

8. *Theological Dictionary of the New Testament*, Gerhard Kittel and Gerhard Friedrich, eds.; Geoffrey W. Bromiley, trans. and ed., (Grand Rapids, MI: Eerdmans, 1964-1976), 1:686.

9. Renn, *Expository Dictionary of Bible Words*, 797.

10. Alcorn, *Heaven*, 94.

11. MacArthur, 249.

12. Donald Grey Barnhouse, *Revelation: An Expository Commentary* (Grand Rapids, MI: Zondervan, 1971), 391.

13. Scholars favoring the renewal position include Richard Bauckham, *Jude, 2 Peter*, WBC 50 (Nashville, TN: Thomas Nelson, 2003), 326; G. K. Beale, *The Book of Revelation*, 1040; and Peter H. Davids, *The Letters of 2 Peter and Jude*, The Pillar New Testament Commentary (Grand Rapids, MI: Eerdmans, 2006), 284-287.

14. Alcorn, *Heaven*, 88-89.

15. Albert M. Wolters, *Creation Regained: Biblical Basis for a Reformational Worldview* (Grand Rapids, MI: Eerdmans, 1985), 62.

16. Strong's G3928: *Parerchomai*, https://www.blueletterbible.org/lexicon/g3928/csb/mgnt/0-1/.

17. Vincent, *Word Studies in the New Testament*, Vol. 1, 705-707.

18. John MacArthur, *The MacArthur New Testament Commentary: 2 Peter & Jude* (Chicago: Moody Publishers, 2005), 124.

19. Strong's G3098: *lyo*, https://www.blueletterbible.org/lexicon/g3089/csb/mgnt/0-1/.

20. Davids, 282-293.

21. Vic Mizzy, songwriter, *Green Acres* lyrics, Orion Music Publishing Inc.

22. Some commentators believe New Jerusalem is laid out in a pyramid, not a cube.

23. Gomes, 216.

24. Swindoll, 282.

25. BibleStudy.org.

26. Steve Gregg, *Revelation: Four Views, A Parallel Commentary* (Nashville, TN: Thomas Nelson Publishers, 1997), 496.

27. Swindoll, 284-285.

28. Seiss, 499.

29. Seiss, 504-505.

30. Robert H. Mounce, *The Book of Revelation, Revised*, The New International Commentary on the New Testament (Grand Rapids, MI / Cambridge, U.K.: William B. Eerdmans Publishing Company, 1997), 398.

31. Fanny J. Crosby, "My Savior First of All," 1891, public domain.

32. Sandra L. Richter, *The Epic of Eden: A Christian Entry into the Old Testament* (Downers Grove, IL: InterVarsity Press, 2010), 128.

33. Alcorn, *Heaven*, 234.

34. Wolters, 37.

35. Alcorn, *Heaven*, 236.

Chapter 14: *"I am going to prepare a place"*

1. The Reformed (Calvinist) position on election is that it is unconditional; that is, God selected specific persons for everlasting life based solely on his divine will and good pleasure, not on foreseen faith. The non-Reformed (Arminian) view is that election is conditional; in other words, God selected specific persons for salvation based on foreseeing they would respond in belief and repentance to the gospel message. In either case, God endows all people with an ability to make choices for which he holds us responsible, and he calls on all people everywhere to repent (Acts 17:30).

2. "Mikvah (Baptism): The Connection Between Immersion, Conversion and Being Born Again," https://free.messianicbible.com/feature/mikvah-baptism-the-connection-between-immersion-conversion-and-being-born-again/.

3. Talmud: Yevamot 47b; Rabbi Yose, 48b.

4. John the Baptist serves as the "friend of the groom," or *shadkhan*, a matchmaker of sorts who seeks a bride for his friend.

5. The lamps in the parable of the ten virgins (Matt. 25:1-13) are different from the household lamps mentioned earlier in Matthew (see Matt. 5:15; 6:22), which are made of pottery and shaped like circular, covered bowls. A loop-like handle is affixed to one side. In another place is a small opening where the wick is inserted. And finally, there's another opening on top into which oil is poured. These are small lamps that hold limited amounts of oil, so it's necessary to bring oil in reserve if light is needed for an extended period of time. Neil R. Lightfoot, *Lessons from the Parables* (Grand Rapids, MI: Baker Book House, 1965), 166.

6. R. Albert Mohler, *Tell Me the Stories of Jesus: The Explosive Power of Jesus' Parables* (Nashville, TN: Nelson Books, 2022), 209.

7. Mohler, 210.

8. James Montgomery Boice, *The Parables of Jesus* (Chicago: Moody Publishers, 1983), 114.

9. Candice Lucey, "Did Christ Really 'Go to Prepare a Place' for Me?",

https://crosswalk.com/faith/spiritual-life/did-christ-really-go-to-prepare-a-place-for-me.html.

10. "Ancient Jewish Wedding Customs and Yeshua's Second Coming," https://free.messianicbible.com/feature/ancient-jewish-wedding-customs-and-yeshuas-second-coming/.

11. G. K. Beale argues that the white robes given the saints are rewards for their faithful perseverance. He paraphrases the final clause of Revelation 19:8, "the fine linen is *the reward for (or result of)* the righteous deeds of the saints." He further explains: "The white robes, then, might represent two inextricably related realities: (1) human faithfulness and good works (as necessary evidence of right standing with God) and (2) vindication or acquittal accomplished by God's judgments against the enemy on behalf of his people." G. K. Beale, *The Book of Revelation*, 936.

12. Schnabel, 280.

13. According to some commentators, there is another marriage supper, with a different bride and a different groom. This occurs during the millennium, and it involves the marriage of God (specifically, the Father) and the nation of Israel. Briefly, here's the background:

> The Old Testament teaches that God betrothed Israel – that is, bound Israel to himself – through the Mosaic Covenant at Mount Sinai (Jer. 2:2; Ezek. 16:8), but Israel repeatedly broke the covenant through spiritual adultery (Jer. 3:1-3, 6-9, 20; Ezek. 16:32, 59; Hos. 1:2; 2:2, 5; 3:1; 4:12, 18; 5:3-4; 6:7, 10; 7:4; 8:1; 9:1). God divorced Israel, but not permanently (Isa. 50:1; 54:7-8; Jer. 3:12). He does not regard the divorce as a termination of his marriage with the nation (Jer. 3:14).

> God is currently judging Israel for its spiritual adultery (Ezek. 16:38). Through this judgment, he's putting an end to Israel's unfaithfulness (Ezek. 16:41-42). When Israel repents at the return of Jesus (Hos. 3:5; 5:15 – 6:1; Zech. 12:10-14), God cleanses the nation (Zech. 13:1), loves it freely (Hos. 14:1-4),

and betroths Israel to himself forever (Hos. 2:19-20) through the establishment of an everlasting covenant (Isa. 55:3; 61:8; Jer. 32:40; 50:4-5; Ezek. 16:60-62; 37:21-28). Israel is then adorned like a bride (Isa. 61:10), and God rejoices over Jerusalem as a groom rejoices over his bride, and the land of Israel is married to God (Isa. 62:1-5).

Thus, at the second coming, God (the Father) and Israel go through betrothal and marriage a second time, and then their marriage supper will take place during the millennium. The future marriage of God and the marriage of the Lamb have two different brides. The marriage of God has the nation of Israel as its bride. The marriage of the Lamb has the church as its bride. The marriages have different grooms, as well, with Christ the groom of the marriage of the Lamb and the Father as the groom of the marriage of God. Nowhere in the Old Testament is the Messiah depicted as a bridegroom, so the marriage references there are to God (the Father) and Israel.

"The Marriage And Marriage Supper of the Lamb: Revelation 19:7-9," https://israelmyglory.org/article/the-marriage-and-marriage-supper-of-the-lamb-revelation-197-9/.

Chapter 15: *"I am coming soon"*

1. Alan Green, "The 9 Most Memorable Attacks That Caught the Enemy Off Guard," https://www.historynet.com/the-9-most-memorable-surprise-attacks-that-caught-the-enemy-off-guard/.
2. Katie Hunt, CNN, "An asteroid more than a half a mile wide will make its closest pass by Earth next week," https://www.wpbf.com/article/an-asteroid-more-than-half-a-mile-wide-will-make-its-closest-pass-by-earth-next-week/38737207#, Jan. 11, 2022.
3. "Is Jesus coming soon?" https://gotquestions.org/Jesus-coming-soon.html.
4. Beale, 185.

5. *Ibid.*

6. Beale, 1127.

7. Osborne, 782-783.

8. Osborne, 788.

9. Lawrence O. Richards, *The Teacher's Commentary* (Colorado Springs, CO: Cook Communications Ministries / Scripture Press Publications, 1987), 1089.

10. See *Sir.* 36:10 (36:7 LXX); *2 Apoc. Bar.* 20:1-2; 54:1; 83:1; *Pseudo-Philo, Bib. Ant.* 19:13; *Barn.* 4:3. Cited in Davids, 282–293.

11. It's doubtful that Clement, the first bishop of Rome, actually wrote 2 Clement, although 1 Clement, a letter to the church in Corinth, is attributed to him. As such, 2 Clement is of historical interest but is not of much spiritual value.

12. Davids, 282-293.

13. Schreiner, 388–392.

14. *Ibid.*

Chapter 16: *"Therefore, be alert"*

1. William B. Brahms, *Last Words of Notable People: Final Words of More than 3500 Noteworthy People Throughout History*, Kindle Edition; Rochelle Rietow, "The 19 Most Memorable Last Words Of All Time," https://blog.funeralone.com/grief-and-healing/memorable-last-words/; https://www.forbes.com/quotes/5787/; Chris Higgins, "64 People and Their Famous Last Words," https://www.mentalfloss.com/article/58534/64-people-and-their-famous-last-words.

2. Joseph dies at the age of 110. He is embalmed and placed in a coffin in Egypt. Moses takes the bones of Joseph with him when the Israelites leave Egypt (Exod. 13:19). Finally, his bones are buried in Shechem, on a parcel of land Jacob bought from the sons of Hamor (Josh. 24:32).

3. Eric Watkins, "Joseph's Dying Request About His Bones," *Tabletalk*, Feb. 13, 2019, https://tabletalkmagazine.com/posts/josephs-dying-request-about-his-bones/.

4. Many figures in the Old Testament face death *without* proper preparation, in stark contrast to Joseph. To cite a few examples: The earth swallows up the rebellious sons of Korah (Num. 16); fire consumes Nadab and Abihu (Lev. 10:1-3); the prophet Samuel, called from *Sheol* to testify against Saul, tells the king he will join his sons in the realm of the dead the next day (1 Sam. 28); Babylon's King Belshazzar dies at the hands of invading Medes and Persians after seeing a terrifying message written on the wall of his banquet hall (Dan. 5). And on it goes. Not one of these figures seems prepared for death or the judgment that lies beyond it.

5. It's likely Jesus and the two criminals are crucified, not at the crest of the place called "The Skull," but at the hill's base, where a public road offers passersby easy access. There, Rome may showcase the price to be paid for rebellion. The Jewish religious leaders may escort a throng of faithful devotees. Merchants, travelers, and the curious may gather quickly and easily to watch three men struggle to take their next breaths.

6. The Greek word translated "paradise" appears three times in the New Testament (Luke 23:43; 2 Cor. 12:4; Rev. 2:7). *Paradeisos* carries a range of meanings: a shady and well-watered hunting ground; a garden or park; the part of *hades* thought to be the abode of pious souls between death and resurrection; the place where Adam and Eve lived before the Fall; and heaven. Paul seems to equate paradise with the "third heaven," or the throne of God (2 Cor. 12:2, 4). It may be best to understand "paradise" in connection with Eden before the Fall *and* with New Jerusalem, where God now resides, and which he brings down to the restored earth as his dwelling place with redeemed people.

7. W. Robert Godfrey, "The Suffering and the Glory of Psalm 22," *Tabletalk*, June 5, 2019, https://www.ligonier.org/learn/articles/suffering-and-glory-psalm-22.

8. Michael P. V. Barrett, "Hyssop," *Tabletalk*, August 2022, 11.

9. Barrett, 13.

10. See Carson, 618-622.

11. Butler, 397.

12. Albert Barnes, *Notes, Explanatory and Practical, on the Epistle to the Hebrews* (Harper & Brothers Publishers, 1859), 203.

13. Zane C. Hodges, "Hebrews," in *The Bible Knowledge Commentary: An Exposition of the Scriptures*, ed. J. F. Walvoord and R. B. Zuck, Vol. 2 (Wheaton, IL: Victor Books, 1985), 801.

14. R. C. Sproul, *Luke: An Expositional Commentary* (Sanford, Fla.: Reformation Trust Publishing, 2020), 566.

15. C. H. Spurgeon, *Commentary on Matthew: The Gospel of the Kingdom* (Edinburgh, UK; Carlisle, PA: The Banner of Truth Trust, 1893/2013), 432.

16. Some scholars believe members of the Freedmen's Synagogue are Roman slaves who have been set free, become proselytes of the Jewish religion, and operate a synagogue in Jerusalem. The New Living Translation calls this group the Synagogue of Freed Slaves. Other scholars contend that these freedmen are not Jewish proselytes. Rather, they are Jews by birth who have been taken into captivity by the Romans, set free, and subsequently called *liberti* or *libertini*. There were many such Jews. Some have speculated that among these zealous members of the Synagogue of the Freedmen was Saul of Tarsus, who would have been more than capable of sparring with Stephen in matters of religion.

17. Sean McDowell, "Was Paul Beheaded in Rome?" https://seanmc dowell.org/blog/was-paul-beheaded-in-rome.

18. McDowell, "Was Peter Crucified Upside Down?" https://seanmc dowell.org/blog/was-peter-crucified-upside-down.

19. "How did the apostle Peter die?" https://www.gotquestions.org/apostle-Peter-die.html.

20. In the Book of Revelation, John draws from the Pentateuch eighty-two times; the Psalms ninety-seven times; Isaiah 122 times; Jeremiah forty-eight times; Ezekiel eighty-three times; Daniel seventy-four times; and the minor prophets seventy-three times, according to S. Moyise, *The Old Testament in the Book of Revelation*, ed. Stanley E. Porter, Vol. 115, Journal for the Student of the New Testament Supplement Series (Sheffield: Sheffield Academic Press, 1995), 15.

21. For a detailed study of John's use of prophetic literature in Revelation, see Michael S. Heiser, *The Old Testament in Revelation: Notes from the Naked Bible Podcast* (Naked Bible Press, 2021).

Appendix I

1. "Earth and Heaven," *The Valley of Vision: A Collection of Puritan Prayers & Devotions*, ed. Arthur Bennett (Edinburgh, UK; Carlisle, PA: The Banner of Truth Trust, 1975), 370-371.
2. Loraine Boettner, *The Millennium* (Philadelphia: Presbyterian & Reformed, 1966), 14.
3. Paul Enns, *The Moody Handbook of Theology* (Chicago: Moody Publishers, 1989, 2008, 2014), 414.
4. Jay E. Adams, *The Time Is at Hand* (Philadelphia: Presbyterian & Reformed, 1970), 7-11.
5. "More specifically," writes Matt Waymeyer, "amillennialists interpret the 'first resurrection' in one of two ways. According to some, it refers to the regeneration of believers at the point of conversion, a spiritual resurrection that occurs throughout the present age as those who were previously dead in their sins are made alive in Christ and live to reign with Him during the millennium. According to others, it refers to the believer's entrance into the intermediate state at the point of death. As one amillennialist explains: 'The first resurrection occurs when [the believer] departs this life and is immediately ushered into the presence of Christ to reign with him.'" Excerpted from "Amillennialism, Revelation 20, and the Importance of Grammatical Precision," https://thecripplegate.com/amillennialism-revelation-20-and-the-importance-of-grammatical-precision/.
6. Grudem, *Systematic Theology*, 1121.

OTHER BOOKS FROM ROB PHILLIPS AND HIGH STREET PRESS

The Apologist's Tool Kit: Resources to Help You Defend the Christian Faith

Understanding The Baptist Faith & Message: A Simple Study for Southern Baptists

What Every Christian Should Know About Satan: Biblical Names and Titles that Reveal His Nature, Activities, and Destiny

Jesus Before Bethlehem: What Every Christian Should Know About the Angel of the LORD

What Every Christian Should Know About the Trinity: How the Bible Reveals One God in Three Persons

What Every Christian Should Know About Salvation: Twelve Bible Terms That Describe God's Work of Redemption

The Last Apologist: A Commentary on Jude for Defenders of the Christian Faith

What Everyone Should Know About the Afterlife: A Biblical View of What Lies Beyond the Grave

What Every Christian Should Know About Islam: A Primer on the Muslim Faith from a Biblical Perspective

What Every Christian Should Know About Same-sex Attraction: A Biblical Primer for the Local Church

Print and Kindle editions are available from Amazon.

Print editions also are available from other book sellers.

Audio-book editions of *Jesus Before Bethlehem*, *What Everyone Should Know About the Afterlife*, and *What Every Christian Should Know About Satan* are available at Audible.com.